In Search of Authority

In Search of Authority

Anglican Theological Method from the Reformation to the Enlightenment

Paul Avis

BLOOMSBURY

LONDON • NEW DELHI • NEW YORK • SYDNEY

Bloomsbury T&T Clark

An imprint of Bloomsbury Publishing Plc

50 Bedford Square
London
WC1B 3DP
UK

1385 Broadway
New York
NY 10018
USA

www.bloomsbury.com

Bloomsbury is a registered trade mark of Bloomsbury Publishing Plc

First published 2014

© Paul Avis, 2014

British Library Cataloguing-in-Publication Data
A catalogue record for this book is available from the British Library.

ISBN: HB: 978-0-5673-2846-5
PB: 978-0-5670-2648-4
ePDF: 978-0-5672-7751-0
ePub: 978-0-5675-6718-5

Library of Congress Cataloging-in-Publication Data
A catalog record for this book is available from the Library of Congress.

Typeset by Deanta Global Publishing Services, Chennai, India
Printed and bound in Great Britain

CONTENTS

PREFACE

Authority plays a key role in Christian churches. There is probably no aspect of church life where authority is not an issue and it is always controversial. Questions of authority are at the heart of ecclesiology. So there is a need in all churches for both a sound theology and a salutary practice of authority. Authority in Anglicanism is no exception. The question of authority has been at the heart of the debate about Anglican identity as that has been fashioned, in conflict or dialogue, internal and external, over time. The identity of Anglicanism has been forged on the anvil of contested authority during the past five centuries.

Questions of authority became particularly acute for Anglicans at the beginning of the twenty-first century and continue to be urgent. The issues that have recently been generating serious tensions within the Anglican Communion are ostensibly concerned with various aspects of human sexuality. But the deeper divisions and uncertainties that these debates reveal are related to issues of authority – the authority of Scripture and how it should be interpreted and applied in different cultural contexts with regard to issues of human sexuality; the authority of tradition with regard to the admission of women to holy orders; and the authority of reason, experience and conscience and what weight should be accorded to insights from the human sciences with regard to sexuality and gender, together with questions related to the authority of the Lambeth Conference vis-á-vis the synods of the member churches of the Communion, and the role of the Archbishop of Canterbury.

In a broader cultural perspective, the very credibility of the Christian faith, currently under attack in the West by secularists and atheists, depends on a defensible understanding of authority in theology: how we understand and interpret the Bible, what claim tradition in all its diversity has on our thinking, whether received teachings and practices are open to revision in the light of new knowledge, and whether that comes from biblical research or from the findings of other relevant academic disciplines. The impact of scientific methods and discoveries, from Bacon to Newton, is given due weight in this book, and three great apologists of their time are included: Butler, who is treated substantially, and Berkeley and Paley, who receive brief attention.

The theological discussion of authority falls into three main divisions: (a) the *sources* of authority: Scripture, tradition, reason, conscience, what experience teaches us, and the role of non-theological knowledge and insight; (b) the *structures* of authority – personal, collegial and communal – and how they function in the institutional life of the Church: its forms of consultation, decision-making and reception; and (c) the *dynamics* of authority: how authority works, how it is experienced, how it plays out in relation to leadership, example, vision, strategy, obedience, consent and conflict.

Much of my work over the years has been located in this terrain. I explored the *dynamics* of authority – how it works in practice, good and bad, and how salutary models of authority can be applied – in *Authority, Leadership and Conflict in the Church* (Mowbray 1992) and I have covered some of the same ground recently in *Becoming a Bishop: Theological Handbook of Episcopal Ministry* (Bloomsbury T&T Clark, Forthcoming). I tackled *structures* of authority – how the church is governed, the scope and limits of power, the play off between monarchical and conciliar or synodical structures – in the medieval, Reformation and modern periods in *Beyond the Reformation? Authority, Primacy and Unity in the Conciliar Tradition* (T&T Clark 2006).

The present study is almost entirely concerned with the *sources* of authority. Where do we look for guidance and inspiration, for norms and parameters, and for models and precedents when facing new questions and challenges in our faith and in church teaching? The present volume is a successor to *Anglicanism and the Christian Church: Theological Resources in Historical Perspective* (2nd edition, T&T Clark 2002) and *The Identity of Anglicanism: Essentials of Anglican Ecclesiology* (T&T Clark 2008) and will, I trust, match, if not exceed, these earlier studies in appeal and usefulness.

The debate over the sources of authority in Anglican theology focuses on the role of the familiar trio of Scripture, tradition and reason – to which I add conscience, and some would add experience. The pages that follow demonstrate that the common but usually unexamined idea that Anglicanism appeals to Scripture, tradition and reason, as separate, discrete sources of doctrine and in that order, is naïve. It is the ecclesiastical version of an 'urban myth', and is ripe for deconstruction. Modern biblical scholarship and historical research, influenced by ideological critique (sociology of knowledge and critical theory), call for a much more sophisticated and nuanced approach to the sources of authority. The issue is fundamentally hermeneutical, concerned with the interpretation and application of the raw material of Scripture and the Christian tradition in all their amazing diversity. What do we – what do the churches – really appeal to when attempting to decide matters of doctrine, worship, ministry or ethics? How do we – how do the churches – actually use the Bible in working out questions of right belief and behaviour? What authority, if any, does tradition have in contested matters and how do we rightly interpret and appropriate it? How do the Scriptures and the Church's tradition form and define us in subtle ways? How does the culture we inhabit as we live our lives in society shape us, in subtle or not so subtle ways? What claims do the insights of 'non-theological' disciplines, especially the social and human sciences, have on theological argument? What is the role of reason in theological reflection and what do we mean by 'reason' anyway? What of the ethical dimension of theological reflection and how does conscience guide us? Can we be sure of our convictions? Is certainty available? What does it mean to 'walk by faith', and what about the place of prayer and worship, individual and corporate, in all our considerations?

Anglican theology has been a hotbed of debate about these issues since the Reformation. Not only Reformation theology itself, but the Renaissance, the Enlightenment, the rise of the scientific method, and the social and human sciences, have inevitably impacted on Anglican theology. The debate is very much alive today between Evangelical, Liberal and Catholic Anglicans around the world and centres mainly on issues of human sexuality, the ordination of women as priests and bishops, and questions of ministry and the sacraments (including lay presidency at the Eucharist). Beyond these mainly internal and domestic debates, that are opaque and baffling to most people outside the Church, there is the larger question of how the Christian faith can be defended and commended to thoughtful, open-minded individuals in society and how the Christian stance can hold its own in the face of the crude attacks of militant atheists such as Richard Dawkins and Sam Harris. The Bible is mocked, the Church's tradition is pilloried, and Christian belief is held up as absurd, fanatical and irrational. On what grounds do we as Christian apologists base our defence? The question of authority is crucial, though not always recognized, in the context of apologetics and evangelization.

So this book focuses on Anglican theological sources, norms and methods, rather than on structures of governance or on the way that the dynamics of authority impact on individuals and church communities. I look at the way that Anglican theologians have developed their theories of authority with regard to the Bible, tradition, reason, experience, conscience and the question of certainty or probability of belief. These theories were articulated in relation to the burning issues of the time, whether they were the attacks on the integrity of the Church of England by Roman Catholic controversialists and Puritan reformists, or the corrosive effect of the philosophical scepticism that was revived from ancient sources at the Renaissance, or the supposedly more rational alternative to orthodox, credal, sacramental Christianity that was put forward by the deists in the late seventeenth and early eighteenth centuries.

Of course, I do not think that Scripture, tradition and reason are the only sources of theology, but they are undoubtedly the principal formal sources of Church doctrine and that is why they enjoy their position of pre-eminence. But the work of theological reflection and endeavour is profoundly stimulated and enriched by the creative arts. I don't think that theology would be worth our trouble if it had nothing to do with poetry, novels, drama, painting, sculpture and music. On some interpretations, the worlds of the arts and sciences would be embraced by the term 'reason' and that is the approach I would favour myself, but it is not what scholars usually meant by reason once it became a major criterion in our period: it referred to assessing the evidence of Scripture and tradition (Church doctrine and practice), weighing probabilities of truth in a rather common-sense way. Nevertheless, this book engages somewhat with the world of literature, and painting and music are not completely absent. Taking the broader cultural context seriously has implications for the decisions that have to be taken about who is to be included in the ranks of Anglican thinkers. So, as well as forcing a reassessment and reconstruction of the classical 'threefold cord, not quickly broken' of Scripture, tradition and reason, the present study challenges other stereotypes.

In particular, there are the daring thinkers and scholars, who appeared to go to the edge of orthodoxy and beyond and who have been classed by some (we note them in the proper place) as hostile to Christianity, as subversive of faith and theology: Bacon, Descartes, Montaigne, Charron, Hobbes, Swift, Bayle, Vico, Hume and Gibbon. I look at them in what is probably an unfamiliar light to some readers and show their true relation to Christianity, as far as this can be discerned. In their different ways and in varying degrees, these were all men to whom God was important, and in most cases the Church. It is often ignorance of the range and diversity of Christian theology, as well as secular bias, on the part of interpreters, that accounts for the false stereotyping of such figures as merely sceptical unbelievers whose churchmanship (in the case of clergy like Charron, Swift and Bayle) was a smoke screen to gain a living and/or to avoid prosecution. But surely the Christian faith – and the Christian Church – is hospitable enough to include those who wrestled with doubt, like Montaigne, Charron and Bayle, and those who grappled with radical or extreme ideas, like Bacon, Hobbes, Vico and Swift – all of whom professed a genuine faith, whether Anglican, Protestant or Roman Catholic.

In that connection, I offer a different interpretation of the Enlightenment to the one that is usually found in contemporary Christian writers. I distinguish between the *philosophes* – secular, anticlerical, and either deistic or atheistic – and the Christian Enlightenment that took not only Anglican but Roman Catholic, Lutheran and Reformed expressions. I treat John Wesley as an Anglican theologian (though not simply as that) and an Enlightenment intellectual. As these names suggest, the scope is not restricted to pure exponents of Anglican theological method, but includes the wider theological, philosophical and cultural context. Room is found in this book for Erasmus, Luther, Melanchthon, Calvin, Cranmer, Field, Locke, Newton, Johnson, Addison, Sir Thomas Browne, William Law, Hume and Burke – in addition to Hooker and Butler, the greatest names in Anglican theology. (How many Anglican ordinands, around the world, I wonder, now read any Hooker as part of their training? How many have even heard of Butler, who was probably the most effective and widely read apologist for Christian faith before C. S. Lewis?)

I am conscious, particularly with regard to the eighteenth century, that I have only scratched the surface and that I have simplified much more than I would wish. My school history teacher, Ian Shaw, once said, 'There were approximately 197 causes of the French Revolution, but for your benefit, Avis, I have reduced them to five.' I also regret that I ran out of space before I could attempt some evaluation of the legacy of the Enlightenment and try to come to terms with it from a theological point of view. For some modern theologians, the Enlightenment has been their *bête noire*; they have tended to lay all our troubles as modern thinkers at its door. I think I have indicated clearly enough that I do not share that prejudice; and anyway I am temperamentally averse to scapegoating.

This volume, which covers the period from the Reformation to the Enlightenment, is the first instalment of a major project with the overall title *In Search of Authority*. The next volume will probably bring the story up to the present, covering the nineteenth, twentieth and early twenty-first centuries. It will show Anglican theological method evolving in dialogue with modern European theology, philosophy and biblical criticism. That volume, the immediate sequel to this, will begin with the influence of the Romantic movement and go on to consider in depth the contributions, among others, of Coleridge, Newman and his fellow Tractarians, Maurice, *Essays and Reviews*, Westcott, *Lux Mundi* and Charles Gore, followed by William Temple, the Anglican Modernists, Edwyn Hoskyns and Michael Ramsey (who memorably said that Anglicanism was not a body of doctrinal divinity, but 'a method, a use and a direction'). This sequel will need to conclude with an analysis of contemporary Anglican theological method – which, needless to say, cannot be confined to the Church of England. Finally, if the reader, the publisher, and I can stay the course, I will be looking for the opportunity to lay out a constructive account of Anglican theological method, focusing on what, in crude shorthand, it is still convenient to call Scripture, tradition and reason, but not overlooking the ethical dimension, and coming to terms with the Enlightenment, modernity and postmodernity. All subject to this once familiar rubric: *DV*.

The overall title of the project, *In Search of Authority*, could be perhaps be taken by some cynical commentators to mean that

I think Anglicans are always searching and never finding or that I subscribe uncritically to the proverb, 'The journey, not the arrival matters'. *Au contraire*, I think that in this connection that saying is a half-truth and that the destination is as important as the journey, fascinating though that is. My title could also, I suppose, be taken to support the contention of the Roman Catholic Church historically that the English Church and consequently Anglicanism as a whole took the wrong path at the Reformation and will therefore always go astray, always remain incoherent, never able to resolve its issues of authority. Aidan Nichols' *The Panther and the Hind: A Theological History of Anglicanism*[1] and Jean-Louis Quantin, *The Church of England and Christian Antiquity: The Construction of a Confessional Identity in the 17th Century*[2] are notable recent examples of that contention. Needless to say, it is not my intention to suggest that Anglican theology is always searching and never finding or that the search for authority has been a wild goose chase, leading nowhere. Why that is so has to do with the meaning of method and the nature of theology.

Christian theology is an unceasing exploration into 'the unsearchable riches of Christ' (Eph. 3.8 KJB). As Michael Polanyi's philosophy of knowledge shows, when we seek purposefully for truth and knowledge in a particular area, we are being led on by tacit clues in the relevant environment that we pick up as we proceed. We seek what is almost within our grasp.[3] 'You would not seek me if you had not found me', says Christ to the seeking heart of Pascal.[4] Method is a venture from the known to the unknown, a journey into mystery, 'to fresh fields and pastures new', towards a distant horizon. Nietzsche said that 'the most valuable insights are *methods*'.[5] A method is a principle of continuous progression. That progression or process is a dialectical one, containing controversy, conflict, even contradictions. As MacIntyre has reminded us, healthy traditions are narratives of internal argument, embodying 'continuities of conflict'. 'A living tradition', he points out, 'is an historically extended, socially embodied argument, and an argument

---

[1]Edinburgh: T&T Clark, 1993.
[2]Oxford: Oxford University Press, 2009.
[3]Polanyi, *Personal Knowledge*; id., *The Tacit Dimension*.
[4]Pascal, *Pensées*, p. 314 ('The Mystery of Jesus').
[5]Nietzsche, *The Antichrist*, p. 123 (emphasis original).

precisely in part about the goods which constitute that tradition'.[6]
Progression in method is not smooth, but jagged and often violent.
Blake suggests that enquiry cannot get on without oppositions:
'Without Contraries is no progression'.[7] The turbulent theological
debate that characterizes the period from the Reformation, through
the Civil War and its aftermath, to the Anglican Enlightenment,
begins to look fairly healthy.

The Church of England holds – as do the other Anglican
Churches of the worldwide Anglican Communion, each in its own
way – that 'the Church is called upon to proclaim afresh in each
generation' the historic faith of the Church, 'uniquely revealed
in the holy Scriptures and set forth in the catholic creeds'.[8] The
search for appropriate, salutary understandings of authority must
be undertaken anew in the face of the questions that every new
challenge brings with it: they may not have been asked in quite the
same way before. Theology is still an adventure.

Paul Avis
August 2013

---

[6]MacIntyre, *After Virtue*, p. 222.
[7]Blake, *Complete Poems*, p. 181 ('The Marriage of Heaven and Hell').
[8]Preface to the Declaration of Assent, Canon C 15.

ABBREVIATIONS USED IN THE FOOTNOTES AND BIBLIOGRAPHY

Details, where appropriate, are in the Bibliography

AL	Francis Bacon, *The Advancement of Learning*
BCP	The Book of Common Prayer, 1662 (unless an earlier version is specified)
CH	*Church History*
Conciliorum	Alberigo, et al. (eds.), *Conciliorum Oecumenicorum Decreta*
DS	Denzinger and Schönmetzer (eds.), *Enchiridion Symbolorum* (references are to the entry number)
EP	Hooker, *Of the Lawes of Ecclesiastical Polity* (see Folger)
EW	Hobbes's *English Works*
Flannery	Flannery (ed.), *Vatican Council II: The Conciliar and Post Conciliar Documents*
Folger	*The Folger Library Edition of the Works of Richard Hooker* (references to Hooker's *Lawes* (*EP*) in my footnotes are to book, chapter and section, with references to the Folger edition by volume and page.
Institutes	Calvin, *Institutes of the Christian Religion*
JAS	*Journal of Anglican Studies*

JEH	*Journal of Ecclesiastical History*
JHI	*Journal of the History of Ideas*
JTS	*Journal of Theological Studies*
KJB	King James Bible (Authorized Version), 1611
LACT	*Library of Anglo-Catholic Theology*
LCC	*Library of Christian Classics* (London: SCM Press; Philadelphia, PA: Westminster Press)
Lev.	Hobbes, *Leviathan*
LW	*Luther's Works*
ODNB	*Oxford Dictionary of National Biography*
PFB	Bacon, *The Philosophy of Francis Bacon*
PS	Parker Society Edition of the Works of the English Reformers
PW	Bacon, *Philosophical Works*
SJT	*Scottish Journal of Theology*
ST	Thomas Aquinas, *Summa Theologiae*
SVEC	*Studies on Voltaire and the Eighteenth Century*
WA	*D. Martin Luthers Werke*

1

Authority in the theology of the Reformation: I. Polemics and the Bible

Few questions come closer to the heart of the Reformation and the identity of those traditions, including Anglicanism, that have been shaped by it, than the question of authority. Authority issues in theology and the Church fall into three categories: dynamics, structures and sources. The Reformation was concerned with all three. (1) The Reformers challenged the way that authority was exercised in the Church (*dynamics*): they believed – even if they did not always practise what they preached – that it should be pastoral and fraternal, not dictatorial and oppressive. Therefore, bishops should be teachers of true doctrine and dispensers of the sacraments, not princely, imperial prelates.[1] (2) The Reformers also made changes (not always intended) to the *structures* that mediated authority in the Church. Notably they rejected the jurisdiction of the pope, at least until the papacy should be reformed, and in some cases they conceded oversight of the Church to civil rulers (the Prince or Magistrate), at least temporarily, as in Luther's concept of the *Notbischof* (emergency bishop).[2] Although the Reformers generally took episcopal oversight for granted (and sometimes – in England and Sweden especially – the Reformers *were* bishops), they regarded episcopacy as dispensable if that was the only way of preserving the gospel. (3) More far-reachingly, the Reformers reconstructed

---

[1] *Augsburg Confession* XXVIII: Tappert, *Book of Concord*, p. 81.
[2] Spitz, 'Luther's Ecclesiology'.

the *sources* of authority – Scripture, tradition, learning, reason –
in order to give uncompromising doctrinal priority to Scripture,
to critique traditions in the light of Scripture, and to bring the
new scholarly methods of Renaissance humanism to bear on both
Scripture and traditions.[3]

Our concern in this chapter and the following one is with
Reformation attitudes to the *sources* of authority in theological
teaching, and Church policy and our focus is on the so-called
Magisterial Reformers (i.e. those who accepted the intimate
connection between church and state, and the role of the 'godly
prince' in the governance of the Church and the work of reform)
on the Continent of Europe and in England. In this period, it is
historically and theologically correct to include Anglican theology
within the category of Protestantism without qualification.

To acknowledge that the English Church of the second half of
the sixteenth century belonged firmly within the Protestant family
of churches with its centre of gravity in continental Europe does
not, of course, imply that the faith and order, theology and practice,
of the Anglican Reformers and their continental predecessors and
counterparts was not also catholic in many important respects – and
moreover, was authentically catholic or at least aspired to be so. For
a position to be regarded as catholic, I suggest it must demonstrably
be consonant with the essential faith and practice of the early Church
and of the universal Church through the ages and continuous in
certain respects (though perhaps discontinuous in others) with the
mainstream of Christian theology, internally variegated though that
theological tradition undoubtedly is. It also goes without saying that
to claim catholicity for one's tradition is to make an ideological and
polemical claim and, with regard to the Reformation, it is not one
that we have the space to fully evaluate here.[4]

In the centuries following the Reformation, questions concerning
the authority of the Bible, of tradition, of the teaching Church,

---

[3]Evans, *Problems of Authority*, Intro. and Part 1 unusually deals with tools, skills
and texts for issues of authority in the Reformation period. Chapman, *Anglican
Theology*, usefully brings out the contested nature of Anglican theological identity
throughout the period covered in this volume and in particular conflicting
retrospective interpretations.

[4]See further *The Catholicity of Protestantism*; Aulén, *Reformation and Catholicity*;
Pelikan, *Obedient Rebels*; Oberman, *Dawn of the Reformation*; Strehle, *Catholic
Roots*.

of reason, and of conscience continued to be the major issues at stake in both Roman Catholic–Protestant and intra-Protestant controversy. All the sixteenth-century Reformers were fighting on two fronts: first against the claims of the Roman Church that sought to prohibit their initiatives for reform and to re-impose papal authority, and secondly against more radical forms of Protestantism that wanted to push the Reformation further, in the direction of 'the best reformed churches', particularly the Geneva of Calvin and Beza. Against Rome, the Reformers appealed to Scripture and the primitive Church; against incipient Puritanism, they added an appeal to reason and to the practice established by the magistrate (the civil ruler) to their prior appeal to Scripture and primitive tradition.

The Protestant conscience

Authority was the key issue at stake in Martin Luther's bid for reform of medieval abuses and doctrinal errors. Summoned to the Diet of Worms in 1521, Luther protested that he would not recant, unless convinced by Scripture and sound argument; the mere assertion of the authority of the Church hierarchy, with the weight of medieval tradition behind it, was not enough. His conscience was his guide. 'Unless I am convinced by the testimony of the Scriptures or by clear reason (for I do not trust either in the pope or in councils alone, since it is well known that they have often erred and contradicted themselves)', Luther testified, 'I am bound by the Scriptures I have quoted and my conscience is captive to the Word of God. I cannot and will not retract anything, since it is neither safe nor right to go against conscience.'[5] Whether he added the famous words, 'Here I stand; I can do no other; so help me God,' is somewhat doubtful. But what is clear is that at this crucial juncture in the unfolding of Luther's witness to the gospel, he stated crisply the issues that would be endlessly debated in the sixteenth and the following centuries, right up to the present day: the binding authority of Scripture, the claims of reason, the authority of the teaching Church, the weight of tradition (and therefore how we understand and value history),

---

[5] LW, vol. 32, p. 112 (both friendly and hostile accounts are included, pp. 101–31); cf. Bainton, *Here I Stand*, p. 144.

the dictates of conscience, and the scope of assurance of the truth. The same issues of authority – albeit overshadowed by the supreme political authority of the sovereign – lay behind the English Reformation through all its ups and downs, twists and turns for well over a century – England's long Reformation, as it has been called by some.[6] In his *Apologia Ecclesiae Anglicanae,* John Jewel insisted that the reformed English Church had taken upon itself 'to profess the Gospel of Christ' and therefore had 'returned to the apostles and old catholic fathers'.[7] Here we have in a nutshell the crucial Reformation appeal to authority: it was to the authentic gospel, inscribed in the Scriptures and expounded in the primitive Church.

As Luther's stand at Worms suggests, the conscience of 'reforming' Christians was a pivotal factor in the Reformation; it underpins the whole sixteenth-century debate about the authority of Scripture over ecclesiastical traditions and pervades Protestant polemic against oppressive ceremonies and obligations imposed by the medieval Western Church. Luther went well beyond the medieval schoolmen generally, Thomas Aquinas, the Council of Trent and Robert Bellarmine, in holding that the conscience could testify to assurance of forgiveness and acceptance (justification) before God, that doubts about our standing with God are not our inevitable portion in this life, part of our probation or testing, but are to be wrestled with and overcome. Such assurance, however, rests not in our perception of our state of grace (or not), which was the issue at stake in medieval debates, but in dependent obedience to God's word of promise, spoken personally to the believer.[8] (The question of assurance of salvation is not exactly the same as the question of certainty about the truth of Christian theology, which will become a major theme, in terms of probability, later in our account; it is to some extent the difference between subjective and objective forms of certainty and the grounds for it.) So I dwell on the role

---

[6]Tyacke, 'Introduction: Rethinking the "English Reformation"'. Tyacke (ed.), *England's Long Reformation,* stretches the 'Reformation' over two and a half centuries!
[7]Jewel, *Apology,* pp. 10, 17.
[8]Zachman, *Assurance of Faith;* Strehle, *Catholic Roots,* ch. 1; Althaus, *Theology of Luther,* pp. 43–55. For clarification of the difference between Luther's position and that condemned by the Council of Trent, see Pannenberg, *Systematic Theology,* vol. 3, pp. 162–3; and for an account of medieval and modern Roman Catholic teachings on conscience, Hogan, *Confronting the Truth.*

of conscience in the Reformation for a moment before moving on to consider the sources of theological authority in Scripture, tradition and reason. Luther's stance at the Diet of Worms provides a natural link.

At that historic confrontation, John Eck retorted to Luther: 'Lay aside your conscience, Martin . . . it is in error.'[9] But that was one thing that Luther could not do; not then, not ever. It is certainly too much to claim, as one scholar did, that Luther was 'the discoverer of conscience'; the clergy and the religious in the late Middle Ages dealt with the troubled conscience of their penitents with great skill. But conscience was the sensitive nerve at the heart of Luther's theology. Karl Holl was right to say that Luther's was a 'religion of conscience'. For Luther, the conscience was the seat of the strongest human emotions and struggles. It was in the forum of conscience that one felt the condemnation of the law, and in the forum of conscience that one experienced the liberating power of the gospel. What Luther says about conscience is an aspect of his *theologia crucis*, where God's word, act and grace are veiled under their opposite. The word of God speaks to the conscience. The conscience is receptive of the word in faith. It relies wholly on grace and cannot be assured by good works. Assurance of faith is testified in the conscience. Faith and conscience are correlative. God wants to be present in the conscience and to inform it by his word. But in Luther, the conscience is not autonomous – it is not the Kantian conscience with its impersonal categorical imperative – but relational and interpersonal; it stands before God, *coram Deo*, seeking acceptance, and before one's neighbour, seeking to serve, to minister. 'The conscience is that which either puts us to shame or honors us before God,' as Luther puts it in the final paragraphs of his 1515 *Lectures on Romans*. He adds that there is no one whose conscience does not sometimes accuse him/her – otherwise Christ would have died in vain – but one should cherish a clear conscience, not violate or injure it; then 'what is left over' is covered and forgiven through Christ.[10] Neither was Luther's conscience politically motivated; it was not driven by rebellion against authority as he experienced it. It was only eventually that Luther's obedience to an ethical imperative led him to challenge the ecclesiastical authority that underpinned

---

[9]*LW*, vol. 32, p. 130.
[10]*LW*, vol. 25, pp. 522–3.

church practices that he believed were harming the conscience of Christian folk. Ironically, later in his career, Luther was not prepared to concede the liberty of conscience that he had claimed for himself to the 'fanatics' and Anabaptists: their conscience was not rightly informed by the word.[11]

One of the Luther's most moving accounts of conscience occurs in his late *Lectures on Genesis*.[12] Speaking autobiographically, Luther remarks that those with a suffering, oppressed conscience believe that God is angry with them. Luther felt the force of the Psalmist's words, 'My flesh trembleth for fear of thee; and I am afraid of thy judgements' (Ps. 119.120, KJB). But a Brother of his monastery (presumably Staupitz, Luther's confessor and mentor at that time) used to say, 'God is not angry with you, but rather you are angry with God.'[13] Only the word of the gospel, spoken to the soul, can salve this bruised conscience. '[W]hen it finally lies prostrate, the whole world does not suffice to raise it up. For it is the death of the soul, and to raise up and arouse conscience is nothing else than raising the dead.' Conscience is 'greater than heaven and earth'. It is killed by sin and quickened by the word of God. Then a joyful, untroubled conscience triumphs over sin, death and the devil.

Similarly, when we turn to John Calvin, we find that the authority of Scripture, interpreted with the help of the early Fathers and the skills of Renaissance learning and informed by a conscience sensitive (or hypersensitive, we might say) to divine judgement, was the crucial factor in his monumental theological achievement, both in his *Institutes of the Christian Religion* and in his biblical commentaries. In his *apologia* for the Reformation, the *Reply to Cardinal Sadoleto*, Calvin professes: 'Ours is the Church, whose

---

[11]Lohse, 'Conscience and Authority in Luther'.

[12]*LW*, vol. 7, pp. 332–3. See also: Luther, *Bondage of the Will*, pp. 313–14: 'If I lived and worked to all eternity, my conscience would never reach comfortable certainty . . . ,' etc.; *LW*, vol. 44, pp. 223–9, 'An Instruction to Penitents' (those who were troubled by the banning of his books; Luther insists that priests hearing confessions should not require penitents to enumerate their sins, presumably including admitting having read his books); pp. 235–42, 'A Sermon on the Three Kinds of Good Life for the Instruction of Consciences,' in which Luther uses the image of churchyard, nave and sanctuary to stand respectively for external ceremonies, the Christian virtues and Christ present to justify.

[13]Cf. Steinmetz, *Misericordia dei*.

supreme care it is humbly and religiously to venerate the word of God, and submit to its authority.'[14] Just as for Luther conscience stands *coram Deo*, before the face of God, so for Calvin, 'conscience bears reference to God'. It exists, says Calvin, in the space between God and humankind. Conscience drags us unwillingly before God's judgement seat and convicts us of sin in the light of God's righteousness. However, through Christ's saving death and the indwelling of the Spirit, Christians are set free from the accusations of conscience and enjoy assurance of salvation through the promises of God's word. Their conscience testifies to them of their salvation and their works of charity confirm this to them, though these should themselves be seen as gifts of God and are so swamped by remaining sins that they produce more fear and alarm than assurance. The conscience of Christians, Calvin boldly proclaims, is 'exempted from all human authority'. No ecclesiastical regulations regarding ceremonies, ways of worship, self-denial, etc., can be imposed on the conscience, as though they were in themselves necessary to salvation, rather than *adiaphora*, things that make no difference to salvation. We must distinguish between the external forum of civil and ecclesiastical obligation to obey constituted authority, on the one hand, and the internal forum of conscience which appeals to God's verdict, on the other. So Christians are no less subject than others to human laws, even though their consciences are 'unbound before God', says Calvin.[15] Though there is some difference in emphasis, Luther and Calvin are agreed that God's word is the sole foundation of Christian assurance and that assurance is confirmed to the conscience by the reality of grace in the life of the believer.

The irony of the debate on assurance is that the polemics of the Reformation eroded the foundations of assured belief and fostered scepticism about whether we can really know the truth, as each side – Roman Catholic against Protestant and Protestant against Protestant – demolished the claims of the other. As they sank beneath the weight of controversy, they dragged their adversaries down with them. In both the sixteenth and the seventeenth centuries, internecine Christian conflict reduced the credibility of Christianity in many deeply reflective minds.[16]

---

[14]Calvin, *Tracts and Treatises*, vol. 1, p. 50.
[15]*Institutes*, III, xix, 14–20; IV, x, 2. Niesel, *Theology of Calvin*, pp. 169–81.
[16]Popkin, *History of Scepticism*, ch. I: 'The Intellectual Crisis of the Reformation'.

John Jewel

Pioneer of Anglican theological method

In England, the lines of the debate with Rome were well established before Elizabeth came to the throne in 1558, but soon after her accession, John Jewel (1522–71) transformed the state of polemical theology by turning what had been a largely defensive – albeit aggressive – stance against Roman Catholic claims of authority into an offensive campaign, grounded in an appeal to the primitive Church. Jewel figures at this stage in our discussion as a model of the polemical deployment of Scripture and early tradition. In a series of sermons of which the first and last were preached at St Paul's Cross (1559–60), Jewel carried the attack into the enemy camp. Listing 27 significant Roman Catholic beliefs and practices, mostly relating to the Mass, he offered to convert to Rome 'if any learned man of all our adversaries or if all the learned men that be alive, be able to bring any one sufficient sentence out of any old catholic doctor or father, or out of any old general council, or out of the holy scriptures of God, or any one example of the primitive church' to prove that such had been held or done during the first six centuries of the Christian Church.[17] Jewel's political backers held their breath, fearing that he had gone too far, but their fears were unfounded. Jewel was sure of his ground; his challenge could not be refuted. This appeal to the primitive Church would provide the pattern of Anglican argument against Rome for the next two or three centuries – until defenders of Roman Catholicism, following John Henry Newman, introduced the notion of development of doctrine and so changed the ground rules of the debate. No longer would it be necessary to establish that controverted aspects of Roman Catholicism were apostolic and primitive to the letter: catholicity implied development and change.[18]

Jewel followed his triumph at St Paul's Cross with his *Apologia Ecclesiae Anglicanae* (1562).[19] The *Apology* and its successive prolix

---

[17]Jewel, PS, vol. 1, p. 20; Southgate, *John Jewel*, p. 50. For the whole controversy see Morrissey, *Politics and the Paul's Cross Sermons*, pp. 62–77.
[18]For the ecclesiological aspects of the dispute with the Roman Church and for the English Reformers' view of Rome see Avis, *Anglicanism and the Christian Church*, ch. 1.
[19]Jewel, *Apology*.

vindications, it has been said, comprise 'one of the most complete pieces of controversy in the world'.[20] Jewel's writings, it has also been claimed, 'constitute the first thoroughgoing attempt to prove to the world the catholicity of English doctrine, to demonstrate that the teachings of the English church at no point departed from the church of the apostles and the fathers'.[21] Jewel's appeal was to the Scriptures as containing all things necessary to salvation and to the consensus of antiquity in disputed points. His tactics were effective: with huge learning, vast labour and enormous polemical skill 'he succeeded time and again in placing his opponent in the position of having directly contravened patristic authority'.[22] No wonder Archbishop Parker wanted the *Apology* appended to the Articles of Religion! It is one of the classical documents of Anglican self-definition.

'The worthiest divine'

The 'judicious' Richard Hooker described Jewel as 'the worthiest Divine that Christendome hath bred for the space of some hundreds of yeers'.[23] Hooker did not claim that Jewel was the most learnt, or the most eloquent, or the most profound, or the most courageous of all the divines who had flourished in the late medieval period and during the Reformation, but that he was the 'worthiest'. Although Hooker was praising his patron and mentor, he was not entirely leaving his celebrated good judgement to one side when he implied that Jewel was 'worthier' than, say, the great Conciliarists (Pierre d'Ailly, Jean Gerson or Nicholas of Cusa) or the great Reformers (Martin Luther, John Calvin or Thomas Cranmer). Even if we allow for some rhetorical exaggeration, Hooker's words imply that, at the least, he found real spiritual, moral and intellectual integrity in Bishop Jewel.

Indeed, John Jewel was acclaimed in his day, and esteemed long afterward by a succession of Anglican divines, as the formidable controversialist of St Paul's Cross, as the author of the elegant *Apologia Ecclesia Anglicanae* and of the exhaustive *Defence of the*

---

[20]Dixon, *History*, vol. 5, p. 320.
[21]Southgate, *Jewel*, p. 120.
[22]Ibid., p. 87.
[23]*EP*, II, vi, 4: vol. 1, p. 171.

Apology, and as the admirably dutiful Bishop of Salisbury. Worn out by the time of his death at the age of 49, he had spent himself in the cause of the reformed English Church, both by his pen and by his pastoral labours. The *Apologia* was considered by Archbishop Matthew Parker to be worthy to go in parish churches, to refute any parish-pump anti-Reformation polemics, and was translated into English by Lady Bacon, the mother of Sir Francis Bacon.

The qualities of spiritual, moral and intellectual integrity that Hooker and many other Anglican divines saw in Jewel are precisely those that the author of a recent study attempts to strip away in a swinging attack.[24] Questions of authority and integrity are at stake. If Jewel was basically a fraud, as seems to be claimed, no *apologia* will really suffice!

Jewel under attack

Gary Jenkins attempts to prove that Jewel was 'illogical' in argument, 'duplicitous' in controversy, slapdash with his sources, and unpatristic and uncatholic in his theology. He takes issue with the pioneering twentieth-century Jewel scholars, W. M. Southgate and John Booty, who saw Jewel as one the founders and fashioners of what eventually became Anglicanism.[25] As far as Jenkins is concerned, Jewel could not have been a founder of Anglicanism, or of anything else, because he had no positive or coherent contribution of his own to make. Jewel, insists Jenkins, was without a coherent or distinctive theology, and derived whatever theology he did possess from Peter Martyr Vermigli, his acknowledged spiritual father. Though how anyone could ever be said to have founded, or even not founded, an entity as 'protean', 'nebulous', and 'malleable', as Jenkins finds Anglicanism to be, is a paradox. Citing Cox's and Jewel's affirmation at Frankfurt that the exiles there 'would have the face off [of] an English churche', Jenkins gratuitously glosses this as 'a Church independent of an intangible entity called the universal Church' (p. 164) – as though the English Reformers did not explicitly acknowledge the universal or Catholic Church and

---

[24]Jenkins, *John Jewel*; page references to Jenkins are embedded in my text. Here I have drawn on my Article Review of Jenkins: Avis, 'John Jewel'.

[25]Southgate, *Jewel*; Booty, *Jewel as Apologist*.

moreover insist that it was wider than the Church of Rome and that the Church of England remained a part of it, while asserting that each particular church had authority to decide human rites and ceremonies for itself.[26]

Jewel's characteristic method in controversy, first publicly deployed at St Paul's Cross, aimed, as we have seen, to show that many medieval practices, mainly connected with the Eucharist, were innovations that could not be substantiated from the first six centuries of the Church's history. (In the St Paul's Cross sermon in its final form he catalogued 27 such practices or beliefs.) Not only were they, in Jewel's view, not patristic and not Catholic, and therefore without authority, but they were actually corruptions and abuses that obscured the truth of the gospel and the integrity of the Lord's Supper. Jenkins takes Jewel to task for his negative argumentation, portraying it as hollow and cynical. But he does not refer to Richard Hooker's explicit vindication of Jewel's method and of Jewel himself, where Hooker concludes that Jewel's approach was justified, though limited in what it set out to achieve.[27]

What the author fails to grasp is that, for Jewel and the Reformers generally, reform of the Church (inevitably an ideological construct) meant precisely the stripping away of superfluous and corrupt medieval accretions in order to reveal the purity of the doctrine and practice of the primitive Church. They were men of their time in postulating a golden age in the past, which could come again. The Reformers did not share our modern assumptions that you cannot put the clock back, that development is inevitable and healthy, and that nothing can ever be the same again. They believed that the reformed churches were as close in principle, though not in attainment of holiness, as one could get to the Church of the Apostles and early Fathers. The idea of development began to emerge only in the

---

[26]Cf. Article XXXIV of the Thirty-nine Articles: 'It is not necessary that Traditions and Ceremonies be in all places one, or utterly like; for at all times they have been divers, and may be changed according to the diversities of countries, times and men's manners, so that nothing be ordained against God's Word. . . . Every particular or national Church hath authority to ordain, change, and abolish, ceremonies or rites of the Church ordained only by man's authority, so that all things be done to edifying.'

[27]*EP*, II, vi, 4: vol. 2, pp. 314–18.

seventeenth century and was not fully articulated until Newman's famous essay on the development of doctrine in 1845.[28]

Jewel, like Chillingworth after him, revelled in exposing the differences and even contradictions among the Fathers: there were Fathers against Fathers, popes against popes and councils against councils, as Chillingworth put it.[29] Jewel used this tactic against those who appealed to tradition as the ultimate arbiter. For Jewel himself, only Scripture could be the final authority: tradition, in the form of the teaching of the Fathers and even the decrees of councils, was secondary – valuable as a guide to interpretation on matters that did not impinge on the way of salvation (which was revealed with unambiguous clarity in Scripture), or as a negative test against accretions of tradition. However, the fact that contradictions abounded in the patristic period was not Jewel's last word on the Fathers. His use of this weapon does not mean, as Jenkins supposes, that Jewel set out to cut patristic authority down to size and that he rubbished the idea of a *consensus patrorum* ('the whole goal of his enterprise was to rid the Fathers of any normative, authoritative consensus', p. 74), with the result, it is alleged, that he lost touch with the faith of the early Church (p. 58). On the contrary: Jewel and all the Reformers believed that their faith was grounded on the teaching of the Fathers and early Councils, but that such teaching had to be substantiated from Scripture. In Jewel's day, this principle was expressed in the Thirty-nine Articles (especially, VI, VIII and XX) and is now enshrined in Canon A 5 of the Church of England: 'The doctrine of the Church of England is grounded in the Holy Scriptures, and in such teachings of the ancient Fathers and Councils of the Church as are agreeable to the said Scriptures.' The Reformers' quarrel was not with the Fathers – quite the reverse, for they appealed to them and claimed that Rome had departed from them – but with the medieval additions and corruptions, that obscured and distorted the patristic foundation, and with a Roman magisterium that defended those corruptions and inhibited those who wanted to get back to primitive purity.

Related to what Jenkins sees as Jewel's 'negative' method (using the Fathers to refute but not to construct) and (as Jenkins claims) the lack of a coherent, positive position, is what he dubs the

---

[28]Chadwick, *From Bossuet to Newman*; Newman, *Essay on Development*.
[29]Chillingworth, *Religion of Protestants*.

'minimalist' or 'lowest common denominator approach' (pp. 58, 112). Jenkins asserts that the cutting away effect of the Reformation, combined with the negative appeal to primitive tradition, left the Church of England without a theological foundation: 'a doctrinally bereft church' (p. 113). In keeping with this supposed theological penury of the reformed Church of England, Jewel himself had what Jenkins calls a 'reductionist approach to dogma' (p. 249), reducing it to a bare minimum, in place of the fullness of the Catholic faith.

Jenkins links what he believes to be Jewel's cavalier disregard for the authority of the Fathers and Councils and his 'minimalist' approach to doctrine (though if anything is cavalier it is this) to his subject's view of Church unity. According to Jenkins, Jewel 'attacked the notion of the unity of the Catholic Faith' (p. 79) and 'obliterated – at least to his own mind – unity as a prerequisite of true religion' (p. 92). This will hardly do. The English Reformers insisted on both the political unity (indeed uniformity) of the realm, the godly commonwealth and – related to this – the harmony of Protestant doctrinal confession. So what sort of theological unity was important to the Reformers?

Theological integrity

Jewel was not impressed with a naked outward show of unity and was suspicious of consensus when it was not a consensus in biblical truth. Here he was at one with all the Reformers, who had to counter Roman Catholic arguments that appealed to the size, numerical strength and historical continuity, and alleged worldwide extent of that church's authority. How could one friar (Martin Luther) be right against the consensus of Christendom? The Reformers could not permit size to matter when it came to truth. Jewel excelled himself in his rhetorical response to the argument from majority. Consensus was enjoyed by the crowd that worshipped the Golden Calf and the mob that cried with one accord, 'Crucify him!.'[30] As Archbishop Sandys put it, Adam and Eve and the serpent in the Garden of Eden were all of one mind.[31] Both catholicity and apostolicity were

---

[30]Jewel, PS, vol. 3, p. 69.
[31]Sandys, PS, p. 94.

qualitative, not quantitative ideas for the Reformers. They were grounded in the truth of the gospel and rested on the authority of Scripture. As they so often said: unity must be in verity. At their heart, catholicity and apostolicity were doctrinal matters. So the English Reformers pitted an apostolic succession of true doctrine against an apostolic succession of unworthy prelates. As William Whitaker put it: 'we regard not the external succession of places or persons, but the internal one of faith and doctrine'.[32]

In Jenkin's opinion, Jewel is not only not catholic, but also not patristic, because he and the English Reformers generally were, he believes, seriously unsound on the theology of the Eucharist. Jenkins' first indictment is that Jewel's eucharistic theology at the time of the St Paul's Cross Sermon was 'an almost bald Zwinglian interpretation' (p. 29), because Jewel challenged his Roman opponents to deny that the doctrine of the Eucharist taught in the first six centuries did not include the belief that 'Christ's body is really, substantially, corporally, carnally or naturally in the sacrament' (Jewel's fifth article). Although Jewel, in the rough and tumble of public controversy, is not refining his terms as carefully as he should, it seems entirely possible that what he is denying is the physical or material location of Christ's body and blood in the sacrament, which as it happens was also rejected by St Thomas Aquinas when he taught that Christ's body is not in the sacrament as in a place.[33] Jewel is not denying that there is a true, real, actual participation in Christ and union with him in the sacrament.

The second charge is that Cranmer's Second Prayer Book of Edward VI's reign (1552), was 'quasi-Zwinglian' (p. 31), that is to say merely memorialist, without a real participation in the body and blood of Christ. It is true that the aspect of memorial is to the fore, but 'quasi-Zwinglian' is a misnomer for the highly realist language with which the feeding on the body and blood of Christ is evoked in that Prayer Book. If Jenkins is making a first-hand judgement on that Prayer Book, he may have been misled by the repeated word 'spiritually' in the third Exhortation in the service of Holy Communion. In the context of broadly Calvinist theology, it does not mean 'notionally' but 'in or through the Holy Spirit'. The real

---

[32]Whitaker, PS, *Disputation of Holy Scripture*, p. 510; cf. Jewel, PS, vol. 3, p. 348; Philpott, PS, p. 139.
[33]*ST*, 3a. 76, 5.

communion with Christ is abundantly clear: 'then we spirituallye eate the fleshe of Christ, and drynke hys bloode, then we dwel in Christ and Christ in us, we be one with Christ and Christ with us'. The union of the communicant with the divine manhood of Jesus Christ is unambiguously explicit in the Prayer of Humble Access: 'graunt us therefore (gracious Lord) so to eate the fleshe of thy daere sonne Jesus Christe, and to drinke his bloud, that our synfulle bodyes maye be made cleane by his body, and our soules wasched through his most precious bloud, and that we may euermore dwel in him and he in us'.[34]

The third count is that Jewel and Cranmer are accused of 'eucharistic receptionism' (p. 139). The Second Prayer Book (1552) insists that, in order to receive Christ's body and blood and to indwell him and to become one with him, 'a truly penitent heart and liuely fayth' are needed.[35] If Jenkins' charge of 'receptionism' means that Cranmer and Jewel believed that receptive faith is the proper context of Holy Communion and necessary to a true communion with Christ in the sacrament, it is perfectly sound and catholic. If it means that they taught that the presence of Christ in the Lord's Supper was entirely dependent on the faith of the communicant and not on divine action at work in the sacrament, it is a distortion.

Finally, what is particularly outrageous is the claim that for Jewel, Holy Communion was 'not a union with Christ', but merely an expression of fellowship one with another, 'an act of the people' (p. 132; cf. p. 139). Of course, the Eucharist certainly is a communion of love between the faithful and binds them together, but the idea that it is merely that is expressly condemned by the Thirty-nine Articles, XXVIII: 'The Supper of the Lord is not only a sign of the love that Christians ought to have among themselves one to another, but rather it is a sacrament of our redemption by Christ's death: insomuch that to such as rightly, worthily, and with faith, receive the same, the Bread which we break is a partaking [Latin: *communicatio*] of the Body of Christ; and likewise the Cup of Blessing is a partaking [*communicatio*] of the Blood of Christ.'

---

[34]*The First and Second Prayer Books*, pp. 385, 389. On this issue see Richardson, *Zwingli and Cranmer* and Avis, *Identity of Anglicanism*, ch. 5: 'Anglicanism and Eucharistic Ecclesiology'.
[35]*The First and Second Prayer Books*, p. 385.

Here, of course, the Article is quoting St Paul in 1 Corinthians 10.16 where the Greek equivalent of 'partaking' or *communicatio* is *koinonia*. Jewel would have known this Article in the form of the Forty-two Articles of 1553 (where it is Article XXIX and *communicatio* is translated 'communion'). It is absurd to suggest that he would have advocated a doctrine that was condemned by the formularies of his Church.

Although Jenkins lists C. W. Dugmore's *The Mass and the English Reformers*[36] in his bibliography, he does not refer in the text to Dugmore's thesis that the English Reformers subscribed to the Augustinian realist–symbolist tradition of eucharistic presence. Although Dugmore's interpretation has been attacked (notably by T. M. Parker),[37] it is not so easily dismissed. While admittedly Jewel insisted that, after the Consecration, the bread remained bread, this did not prevent him expounding an elevated view of the communicant's union with Christ through the sacrament. He asserted that 'Christ's body and blood indeed and verily is given unto us; that we verily eat it; that we verily drink it; that we verily be relieved and live by it; that we are bones of his bones, and flesh of his flesh; that Christ dwelleth in us and we in him . . .'[38] If, as is thought, Jewel himself was the author of the homily 'Of the Worthy Receiving of the Sacraments' in *The Seconde Tome of Homelyes* (1563), we have there Jewel speaking of the 'marueilous incorporation' of the communicant into the body of Christ.[39] If this is to be interpreted, with Jenkins, as 'not a union with Christ', then words have become meaningless. What Dugmore understood and Jenkins does not is that, in the Calvinist doctrine of the Lord's Supper, the union with Christ that is effected by the Holy Spirit, in uniting believers with Christ in the heavenly places, is just as real and strong as a traditional Catholic doctrine of Real Presence, such as is expressed in the theory of Transubstantiation or is reflected in modern Anglican eucharistic liturgies and theologies.[40]

---

[36]Dugmore, *Mass and English Reformers*. An encyclopedic survey of Anglican eucharistic thought is provided in Douglas, *Companion to Anglican Eucharistic Theology*, though the short chapter on Jewel is not the best example of Douglas' approach. See also Null, *Cranmer's Doctrine of Repentance*.

[37]T. M. Parker, review of Dugmore, *Mass*.

[38]Jewel, PS, vol. 1, pp. 448–9, cited Dugmore, *Mass*, p. 229.

[39]Dugmore, *Mass*, p. 232.

[40]See, for example, the Church of England's *Common Worship* and the statement of the Church of England's House of Bishops, *The Eucharist*.

Jenkins is adamant that Jewel was completely in thrall to the theology of Peter Martyr Vermigli and had no mind of his own. But there is little in Martyr's writings to support a reductionist theology of the Eucharist. Union with Christ is the pivot of Martyr's theology, a union *realiter*. Though Christ is not corporeally present in the sacrament and the role of faith is played up, 'the communion with the Lord [Martyr insists] is not less than if it were given as the transubstantiators imagine: nay rather it is more excellent'. As we lift up our hearts in adoration at the Lord's Supper (*sursum corda*), we feed upon Christ's risen body in heaven. Faith and the Holy Spirit annihilate cosmic distance. So the body and blood of Christ 'are truly given and offered unto us'.[41]

Against the background of those caveats, we can bring forward what Jewel himself says in the *Apology*. Far from there being no doctrinal substance to Jewel's position, he sets out at length the belief of the reformed Church of England. As far as the Lord's Supper is concerned (or *eucharistia*, as Jewel calls it),[42] he affirms that 'there is truly given unto the believing the body and blood of the Lord, the flesh of the Son of God, which quickeneth our souls, the meat that cometh from above, the food of immortality, grace, truth, and life . . . the communion of the body and blood of Christ, by the partaking thereof we be revived, we be strengthened, and be fed unto immortality; and whereby we are joined, united, and incorporate into Christ, that we may abide in him and he in us' (p. 62). Again: 'For Christ himself altogether is so offered and given us in these mysteries, that we may certainly know we be flesh of his flesh, and bone of his bones' (p. 64).

Jewel's Conciliarism

However, one merit of Jenkins' book on Jewel is that, comparatively rarely among studies of the Reformation, it recognizes that the Reformers were heirs of the Conciliar Movement and does justice to Jewel's use of Conciliarist texts (such as Nicholas Cusanus' *De Concordantia Catholica*). Jenkins shows how Jewel drew on Conciliarist arguments to defend the English Church's non-participation in the Council of Trent: it was not the kind of free

---

[41]McLelland, *Visible Words*, pp. 142–3, 145, 163, 165, 168.
[42]Jewel, PS, vol. 3, p. 62.

and fair council that the Conciliarists had advocated. Jenkins brings out the Conciliarist appeal to the twin principles of *epieikeia* (moderation, flexibility) and *aequitas* (equity), and understands the pivotal role of the dictum *quod omnes tangit ab omnibus approbare debet*, pointing out that Jewel imbibed the principle that what concerns all must be approved by all, while not quoting the words (p. 101).

Jenkins cites Calvin's view that a council is the proper body to decide on disputed interpretations of Scripture (p. 98). But he could hardly be more wrong in implying that Luther had little interest in councils and that this was because he taught a 'doctrine of the right of private judgment' and 'the priesthood of all believers' (p. 99) and therefore had no regard to the mind of the Church. I doubt whether Luther ever used the German or Latin equivalents of either of those expressions. He taught the universal priesthood of the baptized, which is a thoroughly biblical, catholic and ecumenical doctrine, which was articulated by the Second Vatican Council.[43] Luther consistently appealed to a Council, from as early as 1518 until his death. He prepared carefully for Trent, even though he could not be present in person, writing a substantial treatise *On the Councils and the Church* (1539). All the Reformers worked in the shadow of the Conciliar Movement and its eventual defeat by a resurgent papacy.[44]

A further strength of Jenkins' work is the attention paid (in the whole of Chapter 3) to Roman Catholic responses to Jewel's *Apology* and *Defence*. The Roman riposte was pretty massive: 13 writers produced at least 34 volumes (*ODNB* says 41), none slender, and some running to over 800 pages. They attacked Jewel for being carried away by rhetoric without substance, for mangling logic in his arguments, and for unpatristic and uncatholic views on the Eucharist and – potentially most devastating of all – for an ecclesiology that had departed from catholicity. Some of their charges struck home at the time, though Jenkins seems to have been unduly swayed by them centuries later. Controversy was not cool or moderate on either side in the sixteenth century and Jewel was far from immune from polemic excess and was capable of both overstating his case and

---

[43]See further on the universal or royal priesthood of the baptized Avis, *Ministry Shaped by Mission*. Cf. Vatican 2: LG 10–12.
[44]See further on this theme Avis, *Beyond the Reformation?*.

misrepresenting his opponents. For the explicit appeal to reason as an instrument of theological method, we have to wait for Jewel's protégé Richard Hooker, but the appeal is implicit in Jewel himself: 'Let reason lead thee,' he urges, 'let authority move thee; let truth enforce thee.'[45] Jewel's approach both presupposed and significantly developed the earlier English Reformers' established method of appealing to Scripture and antiquity.

Doctrinal orthodoxy

Crucial issues of authority are at stake in these opposed interpretations of Jewel, Jenkins and mine. The Reformers, English or Continental, had no need or wish to erect a superstructure of dogma or to elaborate doctrinal formulae for the reformed churches. They presupposed the catholic faith: the trinitarian and christological teaching of the early Councils and the expositions of these by the Fathers. They repudiated the claim that they were manufacturing novel doctrines. They had no need to do so. In the sphere of fundamental dogma, the teaching of the Creeds, the Church of England needed no particular doctrines of its own. Where the Reformers, including the English Reformers such as Jewel, had to assert doctrinal claims was not with respect to trinitarian and christological doctrine, but in the areas of soteriology and ecclesiology – the reception, appropriation and outworking of salvation, including the consummation of this process after death. They had sharply distinctive things to say about justification, sanctification, authority in the Church, the tasks of the ministry, the sacraments of Christian initiation and the Lord's Supper, the destiny of the soul *post-mortem*. But, even here, they believed that they were harking back to the early Church, before papal corruptions set in.

It was central to the ideological platform of the Anglican Reformers, articulated in seminal form by Jewel, to insist that they did not set out to make changes to the substance of Christian truth. Their aim was to recover and preserve 'the faith once for all delivered to the saints' (Jude 3). Christian doctrine was unchanging; it was what had been, is and always would be.[46] In this

---

[45]Jewel, PS, vol. 3, pp. 122–3.
[46]Philpott, PS, p. 37.

insistence, the Anglican Reformers were appealing to the famous canon of Vincent of Lérins in the fifth century: *semper, ubique et ab omnibus*. The legislation of the 1530s to secure the independence of the English Church from Roman jurisdiction took pains to claim that no change of doctrine was involved. The Dispensations Act of 1534 included the caveat that nothing in it should be interpreted to mean that the English Church, under her earthly governor and protector, King Henry VIII, intended 'to decline or vary from the congregation of Christ's Church in any things concerning the very articles of the Catholic Faith or Christendom; or in any other things declared by Holy Scripture and the word of God' as necessary for salvation.[47]

With regard to the accusation of forsaking the Church, Jewel in his *Apology* had echoed the words of Peter Martyr who wrote: 'We have not departed from the Church, but have rather returned to it. . . . Wherefore in going from the Romanists we have not forsaken the Church, but have fled an intolerable yoke, and a conspiracy against the evangelical doctrine. . . . We go unto the Catholic and Apostolic Church, because the Church from which we separate ourselves lacks both.'[48] As Jewel elaborated the point: we have not forsaken the communion of the universal Church, but only the oppressive jurisdiction of the Church of Rome.[49]

For the Anglican Reformers, the true doctrine of Christianity is to be found only in the Scriptures. They contain everything necessary to be believed for salvation. The Roman Church therefore has no power to insist on any conditions as necessary to salvation (such as absolution by a priest; the performing of satisfactions as part of penance for sin committed; being in communion with the pope; and so on) that are not found clearly taught in Scripture. The message of salvation, the Christian gospel, is clearly revealed on the page of Scripture and needs no interpretation by ecclesiastical authority. But there are other teachings that can be inferred or deduced from Scripture that it is incumbent on the Church to follow, such as the christological and trinitarian dogmas of the early General Councils and aspects of the ministry and the sacraments, that are not clear

---

[47]Elton, *Tudor Constitution*, p. 354.
[48]McLelland, *Visible Words*, p. 125 (from Peter Martyr, *De Schismate*).
[49]Cf. Jewel PS, vol. 3, p. 79.

without assistance. Here, the English Church appealed to the guidance of the consent of antiquity and the General Councils of the undivided Church. Thus the Elizabethan Act of Supremacy (1559) laid it down that any charge of heresy must be proven by Scripture or the first four General Councils or any one of them, or any other General Council where such views were expressly condemned by the words of Scripture.[50]

The centrality of Scripture

It has been claimed that 'The Bible is the centrepiece of the Protestant faith.'[51] This was undoubtedly true for the continental Reformers and their followers in the sixteenth century and remains the case today, for all that modern historical–critical methods of biblical study (for those who are aware of them) have significantly changed the way that we read the Bible. The Anglican Reformers shared the bibliocentrism of their continental counterparts or mentors, and evangelical Anglicans today retain the Bible as the centrepiece of their faith. But a moment's reflection tells us that the Bible cannot and must not take sole centre stage in our faith, for it cannot and must not replace Jesus Christ in that position. Of course, the Reformers did not for a moment intend that it should. Their passionate commitment and devotion was to the Word made flesh, the incarnate, crucified and risen Christ. They applied themselves assiduously to the biblical text, using the best texts, tools and techniques of Renaissance humanism, in order to hear the word of God for the Church. In this pursuit the Bible came to have a sacramental quality – as an outward, visible sign of an inward, invisible grace – for the faith of the first Protestants and their successors through the centuries to the present day.[52]

The Second Vatican Council of the early 1960s encouraged the reading and study of Scripture in the Roman Catholic Church by

---

[50]Elton, *Tudor Constitution*, p. 368.
[51]Carrigan 'Bible', p. 222.
[52]For a survey of this theme see Greer, *Anglican Approaches*; and for the broader context, Reventlow, *Authority of the Bible*.

both clergy and the lay faithful.[53] Nevertheless, it would not, I think, be true of most Roman Catholics – though perhaps it would be true of some – that the Bible is the undisputed centrepiece of their faith. That position would be held by the Blessed Sacrament of the Eucharist, the Mass, and the same would be true of many Anglicans, those of a more catholic spirituality. However, any polarization of word and sacrament, whether by Protestants or Roman Catholics, would be retrograde. There is no sacrament without the word and no word without its visible sacramental expression. Vatican II sought to overcome any such opposition: *Dei Verbum* 21 puts it beautifully when it affirms that there is 'one table of the Word of God and the Body of Christ'.[54] Karl Rahner seems to go further when he argues that the word is the primary and the dominant factor, constituting the essence of the sacrament. I would probably not agree with Rahner that you can have a sacrament without a visible sign (as he seems to suggest with regard to marriage and penance, two of the seven sacraments recognized by the Roman Catholic Church): if there is no sign, surely there is no sacrament, since a sacrament, from Augustine through Peter Lombard to the Reformers (including the Church of England Catechism), is an outward, visible sign of an inward invisible grace, instituted by our Lord in the Gospels. In marriage the joining of hands and the giving of the ring(s) contribute to the sacramental sign. If penance has no visible sign, it probably is not a sacrament (though penance was certainly recognized as a sacrament by Luther at one time). The formal act of absolution, following confession, is the 'form' in penance and therefore part of the sign, though it remains somewhat problematic to say what the 'matter', the physical element, is: the *quasi materia* are the actions of the penitent: contrition, confession and satisfaction.[55] Be that as it may, Rahner's essential point stands: sacraments are not a substitute for the word; they are manifestations

---

[53]DV 25: Flannery, p. 764: '. . . all clerics . . . who . . . are officially engaged in the ministry of the Word, should immerse themselves in the Scriptures by constant sacred reading and diligent study. . . . Likewise, the sacred Synod forcefully and specifically exhorts all the Christian faithful, especially those who live the religious life, to learn "the surpassing knowledge of Jesus Christ" (Phil. 3:8) by frequent reading of the divine Scriptures.'
[54]DV 21: Flannery, p. 762.
[55]DS 1323; *Conciliorum*, p. 524.

of the word and that is precisely why they effect what they signify, for the word of God is powerful and effective.[56]

This is to adopt the emphasis of the Reformation, particularly in its Lutheran form, which was on the complementarity and reciprocity of word and sacrament: they are mutually constitutive, one cannot exist without the other. For Luther, God speaks to the world in a threefold way, through oral, written and sacramental forms of his word.[57] The sacraments are 'visible words' – though not merely exemplifying what they signify, but effectual in their action through the power of God – and the word received in faith also unites us to Christ and has transforming power. Without using the scholastic terminology of form and matter (words and elements), Luther defines baptism as 'water with the Word of God'.[58] We join the water to the word, according to Christ's command, and his word makes it a baptism. And with regard to the Supper: 'According to his command we join bread and wine to the word of Christ; however, not this action of ours, but Christ's word and ordinance effect the change.'[59] Again Luther asks, How would we know what the sacraments meant if it were not for the words? 'The words are the first thing, for without the words the cup and the bread would be nothing . . . the words first connect the bread and the cup to the sacrament.'[60] As Dietrich Bonhoeffer, a Lutheran theologian, says, the sacrament 'fully mediates the presence of the Word. . . . The sacrament is the Word of God, for it is the proclamation of the gospel . . . an action consecrated and interpreted through the Word.'[61]

Bible translation and commentary

The combination of the rise of nation states in the later medieval period, each operating economically and politically in its own language, the revival of ancient literature in Renaissance humanism,

---

[56]Rahner, *Theological Investigations*, vol. 14, pp. 137–9 ('What is a Sacrament?').
[57]This perspective is brought out in Kolb, *Martin Luther*, ch. 8.
[58]*WA*, vol. 37.262.18–19.
[59]*LW*, vol. 38, p. 202.
[60]*LW*, vol. 37, p. 338.
[61]Bonhoeffer, *Christology*, p. 53.

and the ideological turn to origins (*ad fontes*), together with the advent of printing on a mass scale gave enormous impetus to the diffusion of biblical knowledge throughout Europe. The explosion of passionate interest in the Bible was both cause and effect of the rash of vernacular translations, of which Luther's German Bible (1534) was the first in the Reformation period, though there had been numerous translations of the Scriptures in whole or part into German before Luther. William Tyndale's New Testament of 1525 and Old Testament of 1534, for which he gave his life, was the first English Bible since the work of the Wycliffites or Lollards two centuries before. The Geneva Bible of 1560, with its annotations of Reformed theology, was probably the most widely used translation in private homes for a century.[62] The 'Bishops' Bible' of 1571 was a new official English translation of the Bible for the reformed English Church. Queen Elizabeth I's Archbishop of Canterbury, Matthew Parker, ordered churchwardens to place a copy of the Bishops' Bible in every parish church. The Bishops' Bible was based on the 'Great Bible' of 1538 which Miles Coverdale, later Bishop of Exeter, had produced, drawing on the translation work of Martin Luther and the martyred William Tyndale. Notwithstanding popular crude uses of the Scriptures and their use as a polemical football in controversy, a crucial factor in the rapid spread of the reform was that, as people read or heard their Bibles in their own tongue, one thing that stood out starkly was the contrast between the Roman Church as they knew it and the picture of early Christian faith and life in the New Testament.

But we can go further. The crucial catalyst of the Reformation was not primarily economic or political factors, nor the legacy of the Conciliar Movement, nor the pastoral needs of the late-medieval Western Church – all these prepared the ground – but Martin Luther's prolonged wrestling with Scripture in the face of his personal spiritual struggles. The Bible was the dominant factor in sparking off the sixteenth-century reform with all its repercussions and consequences for good and ill down to the present day. And the Scriptures had that role not because the Reformers were the first to assert the primacy of Scripture or because they were unique in privileging the literal or natural sense of the text, but because they

---

[62]See Hall, 'The Geneva Version of the English Bible'.

insisted that ecclesiastical authority, whether of popes, councils or theologians, must give way to the teaching of Scripture where truths touching salvation were concerned.[63]

The intellectual dimension of the Reformation can be seen, without special pleading, as a prolonged prayerful meditation on Scripture, though of course a good deal of biblical interpretation on the part of the Reformers was evoked by controversy. The early Protestants were utterly enthralled by Scripture, as we all should be. 'How sweet are thy words unto my taste! yea, sweeter than honey to my mouth' (Ps. 119.103, KJB). It could also be said that the dominant genre of the Reformers was the biblical commentary, but this should not be separated from biblical translation, to which Luther and Calvin devoted a significant proportion of their lives. Luther was first and foremost a biblical theologian, *doctor biblia*; his German Bible proved to be formative for the language and – though revised from time to time – is still in use today. Luther and Calvin were not the only Reformers to engage in biblical commentary in a massive way: Martin Bucer and Philip Melanchthon also commented extensively and even repeatedly on the Bible, especially on Paul's Epistle to the Romans and Melanchthon's commentaries on that epistle exerted a seminal influence, considering that Luther's lectures on Romans were not published until the twentieth century. But Luther and Calvin hold the palm. For example, Luther spent a decade commentating on Genesis; his commentary in the American edition of his works occupies eight volumes.[64] Calvin produced commentaries on every book of the Bible except Revelation and some of the Wisdom literature, translating as he went along into Latin or French. His exegetical insights are still referred to with respect by modern commentators and his approach retains a remarkable freshness.[65] The Reformers were thrilled by the word of God, devoted themselves to its scholarly study and sought to submit themselves to it, even when it became a polemical weapon in their hands.

---

[63]For example, *LW*, vol. 36, pp. 136–7. See also Pelikan, *Luther the Expositor*.
[64]*LW*, vols. 1–8.
[65]Calvin, *Commentaries*. For Calvin as a biblical commentator see T. H. L. Parker, *Calvin's Old Testament Commentaries*; idem., *Calvin's New Testament Commentaries*; McKim (ed.), *Calvin and the Bible* (ch. 11, Steinmetz, 'John Calvin as an interpreter of the Bible' is an accessible introduction).

Luther said that while he and his colleagues Philip Melanchthon and Nicholas Amsdorf simply sat and drank beer, the word of God swept through the Church.[66]

Sola scriptura: What does it mean?

The Reformers' view of the authority of Scripture is often said to be encapsulated in the phrase *sola scriptura* ('by Scripture alone'). A recent study – otherwise helpful – claims that, together with *sola gratia* and *sola fide, sola scriptura* was 'the battle cry of the Reformers'.[67] Perhaps, but not in so many words! This slogan, it seems, does not go back to the Reformation itself. I regard *sola scriptura* as singularly unhelpful as a pointer to the Reformation doctrine of the authority of Scripture. It comes as something of a relief when two recent writers manage to describe the views of Luther and Melanchthon, respectively, on biblical authority without mentioning *sola scriptura*![68]

For Luther, the Word was not primarily a text, but a dynamic reality, spoken more than written. Luther's grasp of the significance of the Hebrew *dābār*, which means both word and thing, led him to think of natural phenomena and historic events as also God's word to us, though not to be understood without Christ the incarnate Word and only in the light of Christ, for they were also 'masks of God' *(larva Dei)*, concealing divine action.[69] Luther did not believe that the Scriptures were given to prescribe every aspect of worship or even Christian morals; he would have thought that demeaning to the Word of God, when we have human wisdom and natural law to guide us. He was relaxed about many aspects of church order

---

[66]*LW*, vol. 51, p. 77: 'I simply taught, preached, and wrote God's Word; otherwise I did nothing. And while I slept, or drank Wittenberg beer with my friends Philip and Amsdorf, the Word so greatly weakened the papacy that no prince or emperor ever inflicted such losses upon it. I did nothing; the Word did everything.'

[67]Holder, 'Revelation and Scripture', at p. 32.

[68]Thompson, 'Biblical Interpretation in the Works of Martin Luther' and Wengert, 'Biblical Interpretation in the Works of Philip Melanchthon'.

[69]Pelikan, *Luther the Expositor*, ch. 3: 'The concrete things of the created world were all words of God, because each of them owed its existence to God's creating deed. The concrete events of human history were all words of God, because, in the mystery of divine providence, each of them was a deed of God.' (p. 54)

(images, vestments, etc.), provided that they were not imposed on the conscience. Scripture was the sole test of saving belief.

For Calvin, it was the unity of Scripture that was uppermost: 'The truth of God is one' (*Una est Dei veritas*). Calvin's powerful mind was captivated by a sense of the totality and unity of the truth of God (*una et tota scriptura*), but that did not mean that every part of the Bible was equally applicable to the Church today; it meant that Scripture should be taken as a whole and interpretation should have integrity. 'Sound doctrine' derives from 'a pure and natural handling of God's Word'.[70]

Clearly the rule 'Scripture alone' cannot exclude a role for tradition as a guide to interpretation, for we cannot extricate ourselves from the tradition that has nurtured us, or a place for the teaching authority of the Church, which is part of its essential tasks, or for the use of scholarly resources in understanding the Bible, for they shed light on the meaning of the text which is held to be all-important. To exclude these helps would amount to an impossible, indeed suicidal, kind of theological solipsism. Right interpretation became all the more vital in the light of the Reformation's 'Scripture principle' – tradition or the magisterium did not provide a safety net – and gave impetus to the development of the discipline of hermeneutics.[71] So what have modern Protestant theologians made of *sola scriptura*? Interestingly, what we find is that they are sometimes not very complimentary about their own tradition.

Emil Brunner discusses this theme under the rubric of the 'Scriptural principle': Christian doctrine can be regarded as in accord with divine revelation and as the truth of God when it agrees with the teaching of the Bible. But how are we to understand the character of the Bible as divine revelation? While Luther himself did not identify the word of God (divine revelation) with the text of Scripture, a doctrine of biblical inerrancy and infallibility soon came to hold sway in Protestant theology and this distorted the Scripture principle. The basis of Protestant theology remained unclear until the work of Kähler, Schlatter, Barth and, though he does not say so, Brunner himself. The literalistic view of biblical

---

[70]Calvin on 1 Tim. 1.3 and 2 Tim. 4.3: *Calvin's Commentaries: The Second Epistle of Paul to the Corinthians; The Epistles of Paul to Timothy, Titus and Philemon* (1964), pp. 189, 334; D'Assonville, 'Exegesis and *Doctrina*', p. 380.
[71]Ebeling, *Word and Faith*, pp. 305–7.

revelation was prevalent in the early and medieval Church, though weakened by the dominant allegorical method of interpretation. The struggle of the Reformers for the supremacy of Scripture as the norm of doctrine became significant because it was combined with the literal–historical method. The Scriptures are normative for doctrine because they are the primary witness to the revelation of God in Jesus Christ. That revelation is mediated to us through the testimony of the Apostles, Jesus Christ himself being the absolute authority, transcending the biblical witness, though present in it. The interpretation of Scripture, as we seek that authority, remains a venture of faith.[72]

Karl Barth discusses the Scripture principle in a long excursus in *Church Dogmatics* 1.2. While the Council of Trent set out to identify Scripture, Church and divine revelation, the Reformers aimed at 'a clear and critical confrontation of Scripture and tradition'. However, Barth recognizes that there was a tradition of witness which is older than Scripture and which in fact produced Scripture – but it also produced the Church. That witness was reasserted in the Reformation, but it became discredited by the excessive deference paid to the names of Luther and Calvin and to the confessional documents of the Reformation during the protracted period of Protestant orthodoxy. The successors of the Reformers had treated their own tradition with 'equal reverence' with Scripture – precisely what they rejected in Trent. The Protestant Churches were, therefore, in no position to criticize Tridentine Roman Catholicism: they had fallen into the same error, the reification, almost the deification, of tradition.[73]

Gerhard Ebeling believes that the concept of *sola scriptura* cannot be simply carried into modern critical theology, but needs reinterpreting and restating in the light of the historical revolution, particularly in view of the historical reconstruction of the emergence of the canon of Scripture. Ebeling points out that the Reformers accepted the reality of tradition when they appealed to the primitive Church and when they codified their own teachings in confessions. But historical science, which brings out the contingency and diversity of tradition, has the effect of relativizing its authority. The Roman Catholic position, set out by Trent

---

[72]Brunner, *The Christian Doctrine of God*, pp. 43–9, 107–13.
[73]Barth, *Church Dogmatics*, I.2, pp. 544–72; words quoted p. 549.

and Vatican I, that Scripture needs tradition (i.e. what the Church decides are the relevant traditions) to interpret it, is especially vulnerable: it is incapable of meeting the historical research criteria of modern theology. But the received Protestant stance is also susceptible because it has to reckon with the fact that the gospel has come to us in the form of a history. However, what *sola scriptura* essentially stands for – and this remains valid – is Luther's fundamental principle that Scripture is its own interpreter: *sui ipsius interpres.* Scripture contains within itself its own hermeneutic and needs no outside authority to tell us what it should mean. Luther was very conscious of the scriptural and canonical rule that no biblical text is of private interpretation (*non esse sanctas proprio spiritu interpretandas*). He did not advocate self-reliant private judgement, but cast himself on the guidance of the Holy Spirit, the author of Scripture, in the conviction that one is never as close to the Spirit as when dwelling on the biblical text.[74]

While praising Luther's instinct for the biblical idiom and noting that exegesis was Luther's preferred mode of theological operation, Ebeling exposes the fallacy that the substance of theology could ever be based on Scripture alone. Of course, Luther never suggested that it could be and such was not his practice: he drew on history, on the Fathers, on medieval theologians and mystics, on the work of humanists such as Erasmus, and on German proverbial wisdom; but it is one possible interpretation of *sola scriptura*. Because Luther did not develop a methodology for theology overall, he left the door open for the return of Aristotle to the heart of theology – something he abominated – and the emergence of Lutheran scholastic, confessional orthodoxy. What was needed, Ebeling argues, was the integration of exegetical and systematic or dogmatic theology. Lutheran theology was left unprepared to face the implications of the historical–critical method as it revealed the diversity within the biblical literature. The challenge of eliciting 'the inner unity of the manifold testimony of the Bible' can only be met, Ebeling believes, by all the theological disciplines working together.[75]

In conclusion, *sola scriptura* can reasonably only mean, and rightly should mean, the primacy or supremacy or paramount authority of Scripture – that the Bible is the final authority or critical

---

[74]Ebeling, '"Sola Scriptura" and Tradition', in *The Word of God and Tradition*, ch. 6.
[75]Ebeling, 'The Meaning of "Biblical Theology",' in *Word and Faith*, quotation p. 97.

norm for Christian belief, for the *credo*. And what is that *credo* if it is not the account given by the faith of the Church concerning God's saving acts in Jesus Christ, the way of salvation that God has revealed and accomplished in him and in the Church that is his body? It is in this christological sense, I venture to say, that *sola scriptura* – a principle that was not invented by the Reformers but was familiar to medieval theology in the sense of the material sufficiency of Scripture for the truths necessary to salvation – was and remains the pivotal principle of the Reformation. Nevertheless, I do not find the slogan helpful.[76]

In upholding the supremacy of Scripture in the Church as the sole source of saving truth, the Reformers were taking sides in a long-standing, complex debate among medieval theologians. The Council of Trent, reacting against the reform movement, came down on the opposite side: there were saving truths that had been conveyed by unwritten traditions. Although it avoided the extreme formula *partim . . . partim*, that appeared to distribute divinely revealed truth roughly equally between the Scriptures and unwritten apostolic tradition, that was the sense (as some modern Roman Catholic scholars acknowledge) in which the Council's teaching was defended and expounded subsequently, right up to the Second Vatican Council in the early 1960s.[77]

Medieval biblical interpretation

Despite the general assumption that the Bible had been dictated word for word by the Holy Spirit, medieval scholars were occupied in their own way with the same sort of questions that concern modern biblical scholarship: seeking by means of analysis, comparison and

---

[76]Lane, '*Sola Scriptura*: Making Sense of a Post-Reformation Slogan'. See also McGrath, *Intellectual Origins*, pp. 148–51. For a general orientation to the views of the Continental Reformers see Bainton, 'The Bible in the Reformation', in Greenslade (ed.), *Cambridge History of the Bible: The West*. See also Gerrish, 'The Word of God and the Words of Scripture: Luther and Calvin on Biblical Authority', in *Old Protestantism and the New*; Norman Sykes, 'Scripture and Tradition at the Reformation and since', in *Man as Churchman*. On the hermeneutical principles and methods of the Reformers see Thiselton, *New Horizons*, pp. 179–203.

[77]Tavard, *Holy Writ*; Congar, *Tradition and Traditions*; O'Malley, *Trent*, pp. 89–98; for the late medieval background in nominalism, see Oberman, *Harvest*, pp. 361–411.

attention to context to arrive at what the text 'intends' to say. They were not always taking off on flights of allegorical fancy. In the twelfth century, as Gillian Evans points out, scholars 'helped to shift the earlier preoccupation with figurative interpretations to a serious concern with making the literal sense make sense'.[78] The medievals were quite capable of critiquing legends, superstitions and apocryphal material. Their approach was marked to a significant extent by what today we call narrative realism; as Beryl Smalley puts it, they had 'a driving desire to understand exactly how things happened'.[79]

Thomas Aquinas gave impetus to prioritizing the literal–historical sense, but this embraces metaphorical and symbolic language because, according to Thomas, by nature we attain to the world of intelligence by penetrating through the world of sense to intelligible meaning.[80] The literal–historical sense equated to 'the full meaning of the author', as Beryl Smalley puts it.[81] But for Thomas, the true author of Scripture is God, so in reading the Bible we are listening for the word that God intends to speak to the world and to the soul.[82] The literal–historical sense is our primary concern and doctrine can be derived only from that, but because God is able to make the text bear several meanings, the figurative (allegorical, moral and anagogical) senses point to spiritual realities ('things') beyond the words and to the bearing of those realities on the life of faith.[83] As medieval scholars conversed with the rabbis, they were brought sharply down to earth by the Jewish interpretation of Hebrew prophecy: it was a different frame of reference.[84] These developments in favour of the plain meaning of the text provide a precedent and something of a foundation for the concern of Renaissance humanists and Protestant Reformers to establish scriptural meaning on the basis of the literal-historical sense. Although the principle of the centrality of Scripture

---

[78]Evans, *Language and Logic of the Bible: The Earlier Middle Ages*, p. 166; cf. p. 168. For the later Middle Ages see id., *Language and Logic of the Bible: Road to Reformation*; and, as far as the Old Testament is concerned, see Saebø (ed.), *Hebrew Bible/Old Testament*.

[79]Smalley, *Study*, pp. 363, 371.

[80]*ST*, Ia, I, 9, *Responsio*. See also Torrance, 'Scientific Hermeneutics'.

[81]Smalley, *Study*, p. 368.

[82]*ST*, Ia, I, 10, *Responsio*.

[83]Ibid.

[84]Smalley, *Study*, p. 364.

for theology was strongly affirmed by the medievals, they lacked the appropriate hermeneutical skills and methods to apply it rigorously and consistently.[85]

Nevertheless, the medieval scholar attempted to indwell the text of Scripture spiritually and to engage with it actively in a way that promoted subjective interpretations. As Beryl Smalley says, 'he put his own meaning into it'.[86] Of course, every interpreter does that to some extent – it is a vital element in hermeneutics – but there is a difference between the medieval experience of Scripture and that of the Reformers. The greater objectivity and respect for the givenness of the text that we see particularly in Calvin represents a development towards a more critical and disciplined approach. Karl Barth pinpoints this quality in Calvin's exegesis: 'its extraordinary objectivity'. We can learn from Calvin, Barth continues, 'what it means to stay close to the text, to focus with tense attention on what is actually *there*. Everything else *derives* from this. But it has to derive from *this*. If it does not, then the expounding is not real questioning and readiness to listen.'[87] However, we should not infer from all this that the Reformers valued the Bible more than the medievals did: in the monasteries and the schools, the study of the sacred page was the highest branch of learning.[88]

Neither should we imagine that the Reformers were propounding a revolutionary new method when they insisted that all doctrine should be grounded in Scripture: Aquinas says the same. As T. F. Torrance puts it:

> St Thomas unquestionably bases the doctrines of theology upon sacred scripture. Theologial science receives its *principia* immediately from God through the divine revelation given to the prophets and apostles. The authoritative pronouncements of the canonical books have supreme place – sacred doctrine can only make use of other authorities or teachers as extrinsic or probable arguments. And so again and again in St Thomas' systematic works *sacra scriptura* and *sacra doctrina* are taken as equivalents.[89]

---

[85]McGrath, *Intellectual Origins*, p. 151.
[86]Smalley, *Study*, p. vii.
[87]Barth, *Theology of Calvin*, p. 389; see Barth's full discussion, pp. 388–93. Torrance drives home the same point, the objectivity of Calvin's method, in *Hermeneutics of Calvin*.
[88]Smalley, *Study*, p. xxvii.
[89]Torrance, 'Scientific Hermeneutics', pp. 286–7.

However, Torrance goes on to argue that the doctrinal supremacy of Scripture is not consistently carried through in Aquinas, claiming that he does not provide in his method for Scripture to critique Church teachings; that he deploys scriptural texts to support the idea of unwritten apostolic truths; and that he allows his Aristotelian philosophical framework to dominate unduly his exegesis.[90] Making allowance for Torrance's well-known particular theological interests, it remains clear that what was innovatory and radical in the Reformers' use of Scripture was its deployment in critique of Church traditions, however prestigious they might be.

There is difference, though, in the respective attention given by medieval scholars to the two Testaments. For many medievals, the Old Testament was favoured above the New: after all, the history of their world began with Genesis 1 and to learn Greek entailed long and dangerous journeys for some, while instruction in Hebrew could conveniently be acquired from local rabbis. Even within the New Testament, the Epistles were the domain of theologians rather than exegetes; dialectic was the method applied to St Paul's writings. The *Glossa Ordinaria*, the anthology of comment put together by Anselm of Laon, Peter Lombard and others, survived the battle of the books at the Reformation and remained a standard reference work for both Roman Catholic and Anglican scholars into the seventeenth century.[91] The young Luther used the gloss as a method of commentary in his *Lectures on Romans* of 1515.[92]

Patristic and early medieval thought had assumed a co-inherence, a harmony, of Bible and Church, to the extent that the concept of canonicity was weak and the boundary between biblical books and other sacred writings, especially those of the Fathers, the popes and the later commentators on the Bible, was somewhat blurred, though the canonical books held pride of place among the *divina pagina*.[93] Medieval thinkers were not good at distinguishing between primitive or apostolic tradition and the accumulated traditions of the Church. In the thirteenth century, it was Thomas Aquinas once again who sought to reserve the concept of revelation for the canonical Scriptures and, among the various later schools of thought, the Thomistic tradition tended to give the highest place to Scripture.

---

[90]Ibid., pp. 288–9.
[91]Ibid., p. 367.
[92]*LW*, vol. 25.
[93]Congar, *Tradition*, pp. 92–3.

In the later medieval period, canon lawyers began to inflate the authority of the papacy, expanding the pope's teaching and ruling power effectively without limit.[94] In response to this development, certain writers, notably Marsilius of Padua (?1275–1342) and William of Ockham (1285–1347), began to set the Bible and General Councils against the expanding executive power of the pope. Marsilius invoked the authority of Augustine for the view that the canonical Scriptures were those only that were in the Bible, 'not the decretals or decrees of the Roman Pontiffs or the College of their clergy'.[95] 'It is not necessary to our eternal salvation,' Marsilius averred, 'that we believe or recognize as irrevocably true any scripture excepting those that are called canonical, or those that necessarily follow upon these, or the interpretations or determinations of what is obscure in the Sacred Scriptures, when they are taught by a general Council of the faithful or Catholics.'[96] And William of Ockham maintained: 'The rule of our faith is the Sacred Scripture and the doctrine of the universal Church, which cannot err. To it one must always have recourse in all questions concerning faith. To it, and not to the Supreme Pontiff if he opposes it, one must give the most firm faith.'[97]

Biblical scholarship in Renaissance humanism[98]

It is ironic that the word 'humanist' now stands for a nonreligious view of life – secular, agnostic, if not atheistic. The humanists of the Renaissance were Christian believers. Even when, as in the Italian Renaissance, the focus was on the attainments, the potential and

---

[94]Ullmann, *Medieval Papalism*; id., *Growth of Papal Government*. Congar is bold to say that curial canonists and theologians were 'exalting the papal power to an extreme where the expressions used are almost blasphemous' (p. 94).
[95]Tavard, *Holy Writ*, p. 30.
[96]Ibid., p. 29.
[97]Ibid., pp. 30–1 (Ockham, *Tractatus contra Joannem XXII*).
[98]Bentley, *Humanists and Holy Writ*; Gilmore, 'Italian Reactions to Erasmian Humanism'; Bousma, 'Renaissance and Reformation'; Streuver, *Language of History*; McGrath, *Intellectual Origins*, ch. 2; Kristeller, *Renaissance Thought*; Saebø (ed.), *Hebrew Bible/Old Testament*.

the glory of humankind, the framework was biblical and patristic, as well as Neo-Platonic. Pico della Mirandola's celebrated oration on *The Dignity of Man* sets out what is still a Christian theological anthropology. Enthused as he is by Platonic and apocryphal writings (particularly IV Esd.), Pico finds in them all the central Christian mysteries – the Trinity, the Incarnation, the deity of Christ, the atonement, heaven and hell, angels and devils.[99] The religious character of autobiographical writings influenced by humanism from the twelfth century onward reinforces the point. Let me take some perhaps counter-intuitive examples from across our period. The *Secretum* of Petrarch, who is regarded as the founder of the Italian Renaissance, is essentially a dialogue with his, as it were, mentor and confessor St Augustine, whose *Confessions* had been his companion and study for many years.[100] The brash and violent narrative of Benvenuto Cellini receives what structure its rambling method can sustain from his vision of Christ and conversion to a new life in which he devotes his enhanced creative powers as a goldsmith and sculptor to God.[101] Montaigne turns out (as we shall see) to be a man of prayer and Catholic devotion. The semi-autobiographical writings of Descartes revolve around the central reality of God, the postulate of a rational universe. Even the autobiography of Lord Herbert of Cherbury, the father of English deism, is pious in its way, as will become clear. In the early eighteenth century, the autobiography of Giambattista Vico, claimed by some as a subversively secular thinker, reflects his sustaining sense of the providential guidance of his labours on the *Scienza Nuova*.[102] As Gilmore has pointed out, 'it is difficult, if not impossible, to find a humanist of the fifteenth or sixteenth centuries who was not a Christian'.[103] Kristeller also refutes the notion, prevalent at one time, that the Renaissance was essentially pagan and anti-Christian. He includes among the Christian humanists not only Erasmus, Vives, Budé, More and Hooker, but also Calvin, Melanchthon and certain early Jesuits.[104]

---

[99]Pico, *Dignity of Man*, p. 32. See also Reventlow, *Authority of the Bible*, pp. 16–21. IV Esdras contains some Christian material.
[100]Petrarch, *Petrarch's Secret*; Augustine, *Confessions*.
[101]Cellini, *Autobiography*.
[102]Vico, *Autobiography*.
[103]Gilmore, 'Italian Reactions', p. 61.
[104]Kristeller, *Renaissance Thought*, ch. 4: 'Paganism and Christianity'.

A strong case can be made that Luther should also be enrolled among the humanists. Trained in humanist principles and methods at the University of Erfurt, Luther deployed humanist tactics and skills in many ways: in promoting education; in his writing style (when he chose to); in his appeal to original sources, both biblical and patristic; in his use of rhetorical skills to communicate his message and to refute his opponents; in the promotion of his teaching through public media, especially printing; in his use of the vernacular in Bible translation and liturgy; in his appeal to academic freedom; in courting the great humanist scholars Erasmus and Reuchlin, and his alliance with others, especially in the early days of the reform; in his repudiation of allegory, etc., and his insistence on the literal sense in his biblical exegesis; and in his commitment to the identity of the German nation. Dost concludes that 'In many respects, Luther was as good a humanist as many who have borne this title.'[105]

Renaissance scholarship opened up a whole new world of knowledge, understanding and literary beauty. With the advent of printing, almost the whole corpus of ancient literature, secular and sacred, was made available in new editions by the end of the sixteenth century. The greatest humanist scholars, such as Valla and Erasmus, were the pioneers of critical study of the New Testament. They reconstructed authentic texts and attempted to do justice to the human element in biblical authorship.

The Reformers approached the text of the Bible and of the early Fathers as humanist scholars. They took humanist tools and applied them to Christian theology. Bousma suggests that we should see the Reformation as 'the theological fulfilment of the Renaissance.'[106] As accomplished humanist scholars, the Reformers looked down with effortless academic superiority on those who lacked their values and skills. The Reformers' disparagement of scholastic theology is partly attributable to a humanist contempt for superseded methods, the disdain of a brave new school of thought for what preceded it.

At first humanists hailed the Reformers as kindred spirits and gave them their support. But, as the violent parting of the ways between Luther and Erasmus over free will decisively shows,

---

[105]Dost, *Renaissance Humanism*, pp. 212, 217.
[106]Bousma, 'Renaissance and Reformation', p. 129.

humanists and Reformers were not really on the same wavelength.[107] Zwingli, a disciple of Erasmus, did something that Erasmus could not and would not ever do: he went out to battle, sword and battleaxe in hand; he was of another spirit to his master. Calvin was, as Trevor-Roper puts it, the heir of Erasmus and his early work reflects Erasmian, humanist methods. But Calvin's consent to the execution of Servetus shows how far he had moved from his intellectual roots.[108]

Erasmus was a teacher of the devout Christian life, the *philosophia Christi*. Christ 'desireth nothing else of us but a pure life and a simple'; a life that meditates on the mysteries of the faith and to which religious ceremonies are peripheral.[109] Erasmus remained within the church that he wanted to see purified in the light of early Christianity. He would not entertain schism and was unwilling to endanger his life, while the Reformers did both these things, though not willingly. Erasmus was a one-man industry, turning out not only a semi-critical text of the New Testament in 1516, but a new Latin translation, a commentary, biblical paraphrases, and translations and editions of the Greek and Latin Fathers. Erasmus was immersed in the Bible. Like Luther, he held a christological view of Scripture: Christ was the centre, Christ the teacher and example. Erasmus' scholarly ideal and model was St Jerome, translator of the Bible, guide of souls, reformer of morals. Erasmus was passionately inspired by Jerome, edited his works and wrote his life (Luther, by contrast, came to detest Jerome). The Erasmian approach was a profound influence on the Henrician reform in England.[110]

It was not only Protestants who diverged from Erasmus, but his own Roman Church. Humanism entailed an attack not only on metaphysical speculation and scholastic subtleties, but – more threateningly – on the principles of hierarchy and asceticism.[111]

---

[107]Luther, *Bondage of the Will*; id., *Luther and Erasmus on Freewill*. Cf. Léonard, *History of Protestantism*, vol. 1, ch. 4: 'Lutheranism Checked by the Humanist Reformation'.
[108]Trevor-Roper, *Religion, the Reformation and Social Change*, p. 26.
[109]Erasmus *Enchiridion*, pp. 7, 31.
[110]Hall, 'Erasmus: Biblical Scholar and Catholic Reformer', in *Humanists and Protestants*; Evans, *Language and Logic of the Bible: Road to Reformation*, p. 23; Reventlow, *Authority of the Bible*, pp. 39–47; McConica, *English Humanists*; Wooding, *Rethinking Catholicism*.
[111]Bousma, 'Renaissance and Reformation', p. 129.

Valla had exposed the pseudonymous authorship of *The Celestial Hierarchy* and *The Ecclesiastical Hierarchy* of 'Dionysius the Areopagite'. Humanist concentration on the biblical text posed a threat to the supreme authority of the teaching Church. The Council of Trent therefore intended to counteract Erasmus' subversive influence, while adopting many of his reform proposals, including the revision of the Vulgate, monastic reform and the decree on the use of images. The Roman Catholic reformers – Contarini, Sadoleto, Pole and Seripando – were deeply formed by Erasmian humanism: they did not prevail.[112]

The Reformers, on the other hand, were fervent evangelists, who clung to the promises of Scripture for dear life, who had rediscovered the gospel and were willing to see the outer fabric of the church disrupted in order that the gospel might have full sway. Their model was St Augustine of Hippo and his somber theology of human depravity, inscrutable divine election and free justification. Although some strands of medieval theology had privileged the literal sense of Scripture as the primary source of doctrine, the Reformers – humanist scholars as they were – came to the text with a new immediacy and freshness, uncluttered with glosses and generations of interpretation.

Thus, the priorities of the humanists and the Reformers were not identical. While the humanists loved the classical and patristic authors for their style, their eloquence and their learning, the Reformers went to the New Testament and the Fathers for the theology: they uncovered the authentic belief and experience of early Christianity. Nevertheless, the new learning was often the vehicle of reforming, evangelical ideas. In England, says H. C. Porter, the Reformation in Cambridge 'first appeared as an aspect of the New Learning. For the history of England, as well as for that of the university, it was the most important aspect.'[113]

Humanist sympathies did not necessarily bring with them adoption of reformed theology. Thomas More, writing in support of Henry VIII's tract on the seven sacraments against Martin Luther, used the phrase that the Council of Trent later rejected: *partim . . . partim* – that divine revelation was to be found partly in the Scriptures and partly in unwritten, oral traditions (what More

---

[112]Gilmore, 'Italian Reactions', p. 113.
[113]Porter, *Reformation and Reaction*, p. 41.

called 'the living word of God').[114] More urged Luther to recognize that God chose to transmit certain truths outside of the Scriptures and to accept that the Church had God-given authority and wisdom to discern and interpret these.[115] The conservative formularies of Henry VIII's reign, the *Ten Articles* (1535) and *The King's Book* (1543), lumped Canon, Creeds and Councils together as the word of God and made a place for oral tradition alongside Scripture. Albert Pigge (Pighius, 1490–1542), who contended against both Luther and Calvin on the subject of freewill, championed oral tradition and arrived at an explicit dualism between Scripture and tradition. Ironically, Pigge coined the phrase 'the Church alone' (*propter ecclesiam solam*).[116] In England, Stephen Gardiner, Bishop of Winchester and Cranmer's opponent, justifies the Church's role as the guardian and interpreter of Scripture on the grounds that Scripture is 'a pure, sweet flower, whereof spiders gather poison and bees honey'.[117]

The Reformers and the authority of Scripture

The Reformers, both Continental and English, were caught up as protagonists in these continuing debates.[118] They followed early medieval use by asserting the primacy of Scripture, but contemporary use in defining Scripture as limited to the canonical books.[119] Calvin identified the issue of binding oral tradition as the key point of contention between the theologians of the reform and the Roman Church: 'Here then is the difference. They place the authority of the Church without [outside] the word of God; we annex it to the word, and allow it not to be separated from it.'[120] Cranmer collected material on this issue, which was posthumously collated and published

---

[114]Tavard, *Holy Writ*, p. 132.
[115]Ibid., p. 133.
[116]Ibid., p. 150.
[117]Ibid., p. 213.
[118]For the connections see Ha and Collinson (eds.), *Reception of the Continental Reformation*.
[119]Ibid., p. 174.
[120]*Institutes*, IV, viii, 13.

as *A Confutation of Unwritten Verities*.[121] In addition to the major thrust indicated in his title, another of Cranmer's key points is that doctrine cannot be proved on the authority of the Fathers alone, but only from Scripture. For Luther, the primacy of Scripture was a critical principle to cut back radically the claims of the Church to elaborate the conditions of salvation and to impose heavy burdens on the consciences of Christian folk. In his attack on Henry VIII's vindication of the seven sacraments, Luther typifies Henry as among those who appeal to human authority rather to the divine Scriptures: 'And so when I exclaim: The Gospel, the Gospel, Christ, Christ; they reply, The Fathers, the Fathers, use, use, statute, statute!'[122]

Luther favours what he calls the 'grammatical-historical' sense: 'Everywhere we should stick to just the simple, natural meaning of the words, as yielded by the rules of grammar and the habits of speech that God has created among men'. He observes that all heresies and errors have come from despising the straightforward sense of the words and hankering after figurative interpretations and speculative inferences.[123] But for Luther, the literal sense is not mundane and pedestrian, but theological and spiritual.

For the Reformers, Scripture clearly taught the way of salvation; its central message of justification by faith alone without meritorious works was the criterion of all Christian doctrine. Luther insisted at the Leipzig Disputation (1519): 'No believing Christian can be coerced beyond Holy Writ. By divine law we are forbidden to believe anything which is not established by divine Scripture or manifest revelation.'[124]

Because for Luther justification by faith was the benchmark of true doctrine, it was also the criterion of canonicity, a criterion that led him to marginalize certain New Testament books (James, 2 Pet., Jude, Rev.) as not sufficiently Christological and evangelical, though he did not propose that they should be formally removed from the canon. As we shall see later, the thrust of Luther's view of Scripture was echoed by Hooker in his teaching that Scripture is perfectly adapted to its divinely given purpose, namely to show

---

[121]Cranmer PS [vol. 1], *Remains and Letters*, pp. 1–67; MacCulloch, *Thomas Cranmer*, pp. 608–9, 633–6.

[122]Luther, *Martinus Lutherus contra Henricum Regem Angliæ*.

[123]*LW*, vol. 39, p. 181; *Bondage of the Will*, p. 192.

[124]*LW*, vol. 31, pp. 321–2; see further Althaus, *Theology of Luther*, pp. 3–8.

the way of salvation, but not to prescribe for all aspects of life, including the Church's worship and governance, as the Puritans insisted. Here the Puritans were the heirs of the Swiss Reformation (beginning with Zwingli, though not encouraged by Calvin) which had tended to take the Bible (both Testaments almost equally) as a body of prescriptive truths legislating for every aspect of Christian worship and discipline. In stressing the absolute perfection and all-encompassing sufficiency of Scripture, as for example, Heinrich Bullinger, successor of Zwingli in Zurich and semi-official doctor of the late Elizabethan Church, does, they were overreacting against the late medieval concept of oral tradition as a second source of divine revelation.[125] Luther, however, sat lightly to matters of church organization and ceremonial, emphasizing evangelical freedom and categorizing large areas as things indifferent – provided always that conscience was not imposed upon. Above all for Luther, the Scriptures are the matrix that presents Christ to us, the manger in which he lies, the swaddling clothes in which he is wrapped. 'Simple and lowly are these swaddling cloths, but dear is the treasure, Christ, who lies in them.'[126] Christology is the key to Luther's hermeneutic: 'all Scripture tends towards him [Christ]'.[127] God's truth is clearly revealed in Scripture as the Holy Spirit opens our eyes to it. Luther has something similar to Calvin's later doctrine of the internal testimony of the Holy Spirit authenticating biblical truth, a concept of external and internal clarity: 'the clarity of Scripture is twofold, just as its obscurity is twofold: one external and related to the ministry of the word, the other located in the understanding of the heart'.[128]

Luther does not deny that the Scriptures are frequently obscure, but he demonstrates with many biblical citations that the doctrine it contains is clear and luminous. The obscurity is due to our linguistic and grammatical ignorance, but the content or message of Scripture is as clear as day. For Luther, the perspicuity of Scripture is axiomatic: the first principle by which everything else must be tested.[129]

---

[125]Bullinger, *Decades*, PS, 1, pp. 61–4. On 'second source' theories see McGrath, *Intellectual Origins*, pp. 140–8; Tavard, *Holy Writ, passim*.

[126]*LW*, vol. 35, p. 236 ('Prefaces to the Old Testament').

[127]Ibid., p. 122. Siegfried Raeder in Saebø (ed.), *Hebrew Bible/Old Testament*, p. 377, argues that for Luther the Bible is gospel-centred, rather than Christ-centred.

[128]Luther, *Bondage of the Will*, pp. 73, 124–5 (= *LW*, vol. 33, p. 28).

[129]Ibid., pp. 71, 125–32.

Something very similar is found in Zwingli. God has created humankind with a hunger for his Word that cannot be satisfied in any other way. That Word is effective and has transforming power. Through the Holy Spirit, it brings its own inner illumination, clarity and assurance. 'When the Word of God shines on the human understanding, it enlightens it in such a way that it understands and confesses the Word and knows the certainty of it.' The clarity and sufficiency of God's word is matched by the inward work of the Spirit, bringing a certainty and assurance that cannot be found elsewhere. Zwingi's treatment is rhetorical and *ad hominem*; there is no systematic account of where the word is to be found, or whether it is written or spoken. Obviously, it is located in the Bible, but there is also a sense in Zwingli that the word is dynamic and free, and does its work best when preached or proclaimed.[130]

Calvin is the biblical theologian of the Reformation *par excellence*. The range and sophistication of his use of Scripture are unparalleled in his time. But that certainly does not imply that Calvin was always harping on about the Bible being divinely inspired or that he was some kind of forerunner of modern biblical fundamentalists. He was too competent a philologist to promote a doctrine of literal or verbal inspiration; it was primarily the persons through whom God spoke who were inspired. Calvin certainly believes that the Holy Spirit is the primary author of Scripture and that the prophets and Apostles were simply scribes (*amanuenses*), but humanist that he is, he is alert to the human element and, for example, he is not shy of doubting the Pauline authorship of Hebrews or the authenticity of 2 Peter. We need not worry about who wrote Hebrews, he says: 'I can adduce no reason to show that Paul was its author. . . . The manner of teaching and the style sufficiently show that Paul was not the author.' On 2 Peter Calvin treads carefully. The style is not Peter's, but the grace and power of the matter are clearly apostolic. 'If it is received as canonical,' writes Calvin, we are bound to accept Petrine authorship because the letter claims to be by Peter and pseudonymity would be unworthy of a minister of Christ – though there is no way that Peter could have written it in person. Probably

---

[130]Zwingli, *The Clarity and Certainty of the Word of God*, in *Zwingli and Bullinger*, pp. 49–95, quotation at p. 75. On Zwingli's use of the Old Testament see Opitz, 'Exegetical and Hermeneutical Work'.

as an old man, near to death, he commissioned one of his disciples to pen this testament. Such is Calvin's typical method: weighing up the evidence, with a command of the relevant sources, drawing nuanced, balanced and sometimes tentative conclusions and not fretting about what we cannot know.[131]

In his dedicatory epistle to the German classicist, theologian and reformer Simon Grynaeus (1493–1541) in the first of his commentaries, that on Romans (1540), Calvin spoke in an unusually personal vein about how he felt in tackling this Pauline letter, the key, as he said, to understanding the whole of Scripture.[132] The phrase 'lucid brevity' (perspicua brevitas) encapsulates Calvin's approach in all his commentaries. 'Although detailed philological examination, rhetorical analysis, and consideration of historical background, theological import, and the exegesis of others all provided tools for understanding, in the actual exposition they were kept to a minimum.'[133] Almost the only task of the interpreter, Calvin goes on, is to 'unfold the mind of the writer (mens scriptoris) whom he has undertake to expound' and not to be lured into digressions. Calvin next acknowledges his debt to 'the ancient commentators, whose godliness, learning, sanctity and age have secured them such great authority that we should not despise anything which they have produced.' Then, Calvin pays glowing tribute to his Reformation predecessors, to Melanchthon for his learning, industry and skill; to Bullinger; and to especially to his own mentor in Strasbourg, Martin Bucer, who had spoken 'the last word on the subject'. Calvin hails Bucer as the pre-eminent biblical interpreter of the day. But, he adds, Bucer is too 'verbose' to be read quickly by those in a hurry and too profound to be understood by less advanced readers. Finally, Calvin sets out his personal philosophy with regard to interpreting Scripture. We need to approach the sacred writings with 'great discretion and moderation', lest we diminish

---

[131]Calvin, Calvin's Commentaries: The Epistle of Paul the Apostle to the Hebrews and the First and Second Epistles of St Peter, pp. 1, 325. On Calvin's theological approach to Scripture, Niesel, Theology of Calvin, pp. 22–39 is still useful. An excellent account, with a comprehensive bibliography, is Pitkin, 'John Calvin and the Interpretation of the Bible'. See also Opitz, 'Scripture' and 'Exegetical and Hermeneutical Work'.

[132]Calvin, Calvin's Commentaries: The Epistle of Paul The Apostle to the Romans and Thessalonians, pp. 1–4.

[133]Pitkin, 'John Calvin', p. 353.

their innate majesty. To play around with Scripture and wrest its meaning to our own purposes, as some do, is 'presumptuous and almost blasphemous'. (In his writings Calvin frequently castigates those who concoct 'forced' interpretations.) As we undertake the task, he continues, we are to lay aside ambition, pride, hatred and rivalry, and to differ from others reluctantly and of necessity and for the good of the Church. Calvin had previously indicated that, like Luther, the interpreter was to look for the christological thread running through the Scriptures and, like Melanchthon, learn to know Christ in his benefits: 'This is what we should in short seek in the whole of Scripture: truly to know Jesus Christ and the infinite riches that are comprised in him and are offered to us by him from God the Father.' There is not a single word, even in the Old Testament, Calvin ventures to claim, that would not draw and bring us to Christ.[134] Calvin repeats the point a few years later in his commentary on Romans 10.4: 'Christ is the end of the law.' Justifying righteousness cannot be had through observance of the law, 'because the law has been given to lead us by the hand to another righteousness. Indeed [Calvin continues], every doctrine of the law, every command, every promise, always points to Christ. We are, therefore, to apply all its parts to him . . . the law in all its parts has reference to Christ. . . .'[135] This is not an artificial construct, an example of the 'forced' interpretation that Calvin so detested: he means that the law points dialectically to Christ by teaching us our need of his saving grace.

It is Calvin who introduces the idea that Scripture is *autopistos*, self-authenticating or self-convincing, into Reformation theology. This concept was destined to have a long and troublesome history. It would be embraced by some Anglican divines, though rejected by others, as we shall see. It was a polemical move, designed to avoid attributing the authority of Scripture to the Church, though the witness of the Church to Scripture is by no means excluded. Henk van den Belt has made an exhaustive study of Calvin's deployment of *autopistos* in the *Institutes* of 1559 and Calvin's other writings, comparing Calvin's own use with the wider Reformed tradition.[136]

---

[134]Calvin, Preface to Olivétan's French translation of the New Testament (1535): *Calvin: Commentaries* (LCC), pp. 58–73 at p. 70.
[135]Calvin, *Calvin's Commentaries: Romans*, pp. 222–3.
[136]van den Belt, *Authority of Scripture* is the source for what follows here.

The key to Calvin's use of *autopistos* is the profound insight (one that later governed Karl Barth's theology) that God can only be known through God. Only God can enlighten our minds to see God's own truth and seal it to our conscience to give peace with God. Our salvation cannot be dependent on merely human authority, as it would be if we had to trust the Church alone for Scripture's authority. Here we see the Reformers' extreme sensitivity to attributing any divine qualities to the Church as a corporate body or institution. Taught by experience, they were all too aware of its propensity to go astray and become corrupt.

Calvin insists in his *Reply* to Cardinal Sadoleto that the Roman error is to substitute the Church's teaching authority, supposedly inspired by the Holy Spirit, for the word of God. In his later writings against the 'spiritual' Libertines and 'enthusiasts', Calvin charges them with substituting their own fancies and feelings for God's revealed truth. Both make the same mistake: separating the Spirit from the Word, bypassing Scripture. Since the Spirit is the author of Scripture, it must be the Spirit who teaches our hearts through the Scriptures. The witness of the Church has a confirming role. However, in his contest with the sceptics in around 1550, Calvin finds it expedient to place more weight on the supporting *argumenta* – the dignity, eloquence, etc., of the biblical text. This change of emphasis is reflected in the 1559 edition of the *Institutes* where the internal testimony of the Holy Spirit to the self-evidencing character of Scripture is balanced by an account of the external proofs (*probationes*) that should be sufficient to convince even those who lack the gift of faith. But only the Spirit can give *certitudo*. Calvin claims that every believer can testify to the truth of this from experience.

Richard Hooker noted the powerful combination of theological exposition (the *Institutes*) and biblical commentary in Calvin's *oeuvre*, but he paid Calvin a backhanded compliment by seeming to suggest that Calvin forced the interpretation of Scripture to fit his theological system: 'Two thinges of principall moment there are which have deservedly procured him honour throughout the worlde: the one his exceeding paynes in composing the Institutions of Christian religion; the other his no less industrious travailes for exposition of holy Scripture according unto the same institutions.'[137]

---

[137]*EP*, Preface, ii, 8 (Folger, vol. 1, p. 10).

Here Hooker hit below the belt: the relation between biblical exposition and systematic doctrine in Calvin's case was actually reciprocal and, as we have noted, his objectivity is remarkable.

The *Institutes* (or 'Instruction') went through several editions in Latin and French until 1559. Calvin's definitive French edition helped to shape the French language, just as Luther's Bible shaped the German. The book grew and matured as Calvin's mind developed in dialogue with theologians, ancient and modern. Richard Muller's *The Unaccommodated Calvin* attempts to strip the *Institutes* of later dogmatically motivated anachronistic interpretations and to reveal its true nature, method and purpose, within the totality of Calvin's output.[138] Muller's aim is to liberate Calvin's theological achievement from modern interpreters and relocate it in its original sixteenth-century context; to relate it to its patristic and medieval forebears; and to show its critical connection with Renaissance Humanism and with the theological method of Luther's lieutenant Philip Melanchthon, among others. He does this by going back beyond the modern commentators and the critical editions of Calvin's text to the original sixteenth-century editions of the *Institutes*. In so doing, Muller scotches the popular caricature of Calvin as a stern, unbending predestinarian who logically extrapolated a grim theology from narrow dogmatic premises. Calvin could certainly be stern and uncompromising, but like all good theologians, he taught with a pastoral intent. Calvin was primarily a preacher and an expositor of Scripture. But instead of cluttering his commentaries with complex theological digressions on disputed questions, he provided a handbook, the *Institutes*, in which he set out a comprehensive, orderly exposition of Christian faith and practice, patterned on the Creed, and at the same time dealt with controversial points. Melanchthon's approach was rather similar: a complementarity of theological treatises, arranged in *loci communes* or commonplaces (topics), and biblical exposition informed by these theological themes and, like Calvin's, adorned with the skills of Renaissance hermeneutics developed from the medieval disciplines of the *Trivium* (Grammar, Rhetoric and Dialectic) of which Melanchthon was a master and prolific writer.[139]

---

[138]Muller, *Unaccommodated Calvin*.
[139]See further Wengert, 'Biblical Interpretation in the Works of Philip Melanchthon'. A selection of Melanchthon's *loci communes* (1521 edition) is available in *Melanchthon and Bucer*.

The Reformed tradition profoundly shaped Anglican theology in the sixteenth and seventeenth centuries – episcopal Calvinism was the unquestioned orthodoxy in the Elizabethan and early Jacobean Church – and lives on in some varieties of Anglican evangelicalism today. It is a tradition that is characterized by a biblical culture and reverent worship, a sense of the sovereignty of God, parity of ministers and therefore government by councils and synods, suspicion of hierarchy, shared leadership, respect for scholarship and veneration for the means of grace, and a concern to be involved on behalf of the Kingdom of God in the world. Such theological and pastoral virtues should not be the preserve of one member of the ecumenical family; nor should they be confined to a self-consciously Reformed constituency within the Church of England: they should benefit us all. In Hooker's day, the Presbyterian and Puritan manifestation of English Calvinism was a lethal threat to the Elizabethan settlement. Hooker reckoned it a serious possibility that the English Church, catholic and reformed as he believed it now was, might 'passe away as in a dreame'. Hooker's dread helps to explain his snide comments on Calvin in his Preface to the *Ecclesiastical Polity*.[140]

The authority of Scripture in the English Reformation

The way that Archbishop Thomas Cranmer grafted the Scriptures into his two Prayer Books sets the tone for the role of the Bible in the English Reformation. Cranmer saturated the liturgy with Scripture; it is a complex tissue of biblical quotations and allusions – 80 per cent of its text is taken from Scripture. Cranmer's 'basic operating principle', says John Booty, was to restore the Word of God to its central position in the common worship of the Church. He did this, Booty points out, by increasing both the quantity and the prominence of Scripture in the liturgy and by setting Word and Sacrament side by side in his 1550 Ordinal.[141]

---

[140]Hooker, 'A Preface, To them that seeke (as they tearme it) the reformation of Lawes, and orders Ecclesiasticall, in the Church of ENGLAND' (EP, i.1: 1, p. 1).
[141]Booty (ed.), Book of Common Prayer 1559, p. 360.

In Cranmer's 'Preface' in his Prayer Books of 1549 and 1552 (it was used again in 1559 after his death; in 1662 it was retitled 'Concerning the Service of the Church' and a new Preface was provided), certain key principles of the Reformation and its evaluation of Scripture can be detected: the principles of primitivism, edification, simplicity, authenticity, vernacular language and convenience:

> [H]ere you have an ordre for praier (as touchynge the readyng of holy scripture) muche agreable to the mynde and purpose of the olde fathers, and a greate deale more profitable and commodious, then that whiche of late was used. It is more profitable, because here are left out many thynges, whereof some be untrue, some uncertein, some vain and supersticious: and is ordyned nothyng to be read, but the very pure worde of God, the holy scriptures, or that whiche is evidently grounded upon the same: and that in suche a language and ordre, as is moste easy and plain for the understandyng, bothe of the readers and hearers. It is also more commodious, bothe for the shortnes thereof, and for the plaines of the ordre, and for that the rules be fewe and easy.[142]

Cranmer's own valuation of the Bible can be seen in his Preface to the Tyndale and Coverdale Great Bible (2nd edition) and in his Homily 'A Fruitful Exhortation to the Reading and Knowledge of Holy Scripture'. In the Preface Cranmer writes: 'In the scriptures be the fat pastures of the soul, therein is no venomous meat, no unwholesome thing; they be the very dainty and pure feeding. He that is ignorant, shall find there what he should learn. He that is a perverse sinner, shall there find his damnation to make him to tremble for fear. He that laboureth to serve God, shall find there his glory, and the promissions [i.e. promises] of eternal life, exhorting him more diligently to labor.'[143] The Homily begins: 'TO

---

[142]Cummings (ed.), *Book of Common Prayer*, p. 5.
[143]Cranmer, Preface to the Great Bible, 2nd edition. The Preface continues: 'Herein may princes learn how to govern their subjects; Subjects obedience, love, and dread to their princes; Husbands how they should behave them unto their wives, how to educate their children and servants; and contrary, the wives, children, and servants may know their duty to their husbands, parents, and masters. Here may all manner of persons, men, women, young, old, learned, unlearned, rich, poor, priests, laymen,

a Christian man there can bee nothing either more necessarie or profitable, then the knowledge of holy Scripture, forasmuch as in it is conteyned GODS true word, setting foorth his glory, and also mans duety. . . . And there is no trueth nor doctrine necessarie for our iustification and euerlasting saluation, but that is (or may bee) drawne out of that fountaine and Well of trueth.'[144] The reflective, recollected, comforting piety of the BCP is also present in what Cranmer says in this Homily about meditating on Scripture:

> Let vs night and day muse, and haue meditation and contemplation in them. Let vs ruminate, and (as it were) chew the cudde, that we may haue the sweet iuice, spirituall effect, marrow, hony, kirnell, taste, comfort and consolation of them (Psalms 56.4). Let vs stay, quiet, and certifie our consciences, with the most infallible certainty, trueth, and perpetuall assurance of them. Let vs pray to GOD (the onely authour of these heauenly studies) that wee may speake, thinke, beleeue, liue and depart hence, according to the wholesome doctrine, and verities of them.[145]

The collect that Cranmer composed for the Second Sunday of Advent breathes the same spirit, that of *lectio divina*:

> Blessed lord, which hast caused all holy Scriptures to bee written for our learnyng; graunte us that we maye in suche wise heare them, read, marke, learne, and inwardly digeste them; that by pacience, and coumfort of thy holy woorde, we may embrace, and euer holde fast the blessed hope of euerlasting life, which thou hast giuen us in our sauiour Jesus Christe.[146]

While it is abundantly clear that the English Reformers, like their continental colleagues, delighted to feed on the Scriptures as in rich

---

lords, ladies, officers, tenants, and mean men, virgins, wives, widows, lawyers, merchants, artificers, husbandmen, and all manner of persons of what estate or condition soever they be, may in this book learn all things what they ought to believe, what they ought to do, and what they should not do, as well concerning almighty God, as also concerning themselves and all other.' http://www.bible-researcher.com/cranmer.html

[144] http://www.anglicanlibrary.org/homilies/bk1hom01.htm

[145] Ibid.

[146] 1549 version: *The First and Second Prayer-Books*, p. 34.

pastures, some English Reformers already anticipate the Puritan approach of treating the Scriptures as legislation, legislation to be obeyed and to be implemented in society. While for William Tyndale the heart of the Bible is of course the gospel, the 'Evangelion [which] . . . signifieth good, merry, glad and joyful tidings, that maketh a man's heart glad, and maketh him sing, dance and leap for joy,' Tyndale's emphasis undoubtedly falls on the demands of the moral law for those who have been renewed by the gospel: Christians are empowered to keep God's law. The keeping of the moral law arises from grace: 'Deeds are the fruits of love; and love is the fruit of faith.' There is no works-salvation in Tyndale: salvation by works is 'that cankered heresy'. But deeply influenced by Erasmian humanism as he was, Tyndale stands apart from Luther in his stress on the thrust of the Bible being to reveal the ethical way of life required by obedience to God.[147]

But quite apart from the sympathies of some individual English Reformers, the official formularies of the English Reformation committed the Church of England only to the limited sense of *sola scriptura* advocated in their different ways by Luther and Hooker. Their whole emphasis is on things necessary for salvation – on the purpose of the revelation given through the prophets, Apostles and evangelists in the Bible. The historic Anglican formularies contain no definition of the nature of biblical inspiration or the extent of biblical authority – statements which would undoubtedly have embarrassed the Church in a later, critical, age. The distinction between things necessary to salvation and things not necessary, but nevertheless prudent and edifying to be followed, was made in the Ten Articles of Henry's reign.[148] The 'Bishops' Book' (1537) prepared the ground for the subsequent doctrinal reforms by asserting the supremacy of Scripture. The notion of truths necessary for salvation was articulated in the Ordinal that was published alongside Cranmer's First and Second Prayer Books (1549 and 1552). The presiding Archbishop asks the candidate for consecration to the episcopate:

Are you perswaded that the holy Scriptures conteine sufficiently all doctryne required of necessitie for eternall saluacion throughe

---

[147]Citations from Daniell, *Tyndale*, pp. 123, 165, 329. See also Trueman, 'Pathway to Reformation', pp. 11–29; id., *Luther's Legacy*, pp. 119–20.
[148]Dixon, *History*, vol. 1, pp. 409–11; Burnet, *History*, vol. 1, pp. 332–4.

the faith of Jesu Christ? And are you determined with the same holy scriptures to enstruct the people committed to your charge, and to teach or mainteine nothyng, as required of necessitie to eternall saluacyon, but that you shalbe perswaded may be concluded and proued by the same?[149]

The First Book of Homilies, written under Henry VIII but published under Edward VI, proclaims that 'there is no truth of doctrine necessary for our justification and everlasting salvation, but that is or may be drawn out of that fountain and well of truth', the holy Scriptures. The Second Book of Homilies, promulgated under Elizabeth, contends that the holy Scriptures contain 'all things needful for us to see, to hear, to learn and to believe, necessary for the attaining of eternal life'.[150]

In his *Apology* for the reformed Church of England, Jewel expounds the same principle. The English Church holds concerning the Scriptures:

> That they be the very might and strength of God to attain to salvation; that they be the foundations of the prophets and apostles whereupon is built the Church of God; that they be the very sure and infallible rule, whereby may be tried whether the church doth stagger or err, and whereunto all ecclesiastical doctrine ought to be called to account; and that against these scriptures neither law nor ordinance nor any custom ought to be heard.[151]

Like the Homilies, Jewel's *Apology*, together with his *Defence*, had quasi-official status in the sixteenth century, both sets of writings residing in parish churches and available for settling parish-pump theological arguments.

The Anglican Reformers insisted on the 'literal sense' of Scripture, but they were not literalists in the fundamentalist sense of

---

[149]*The First and Second Prayer Books*, p. 461. With the exception of 'mainteine', the same words are used in the ordination of priests. The words are the same in the 1662 Ordinal, which became strictly part of the Prayer Book for the first time then: Cummings (ed.), *Book of Common Prayer*, pp. 648, 786.
[150]*Sermons or Homilies Appointed to be Read in Churches*, pp. 1, 310.
[151]Jewel, PS, 3, p. 62.

the word. Like their continental counterparts, they had benefited from a humanist training; they were not merely engaged in bandying proof-texts taken out of context. According to Tyndale, 'The scripture hath but one sense, which is the literal sense. And that literal sense is the root and ground of all, and the anchor that never faileth.' Like Aquinas, Tyndale insists that only the literal sense can be used to prove doctrine, but the literal sense is not one genre over against others, but that to which all genres, including highly figurative ones, point, the natural force or content of the Bible.[152]

Whitgift, reiterating the standard Anglican position on the authority of Scripture, says that nothing may be put forward as necessary to salvation or as an article of faith which it is incumbent on Christians to believe 'except it be expressly contained in the word of God, *or may manifestly thereof be gathered'*.[153] A similar nuance may be detected in the Thirty-nine Articles' reference to proving or testing doctrinal claims by the Scriptures:

> Holy Scripture containeth all things necessary to salvation: so that whatsoever is not read therein, *nor may be proved thereby,* is not to be required of any man, that it should be believed as an article of the Faith, or be thought requisite or necessary to salvation. (Article VI, my emphasis)

As we shall see, the Articles also make the Scriptures the rule whereby all other forms of authority in the church are themselves to be assessed.

William Whitaker on the authority of Scripture

We turn now to note an outstanding exposition of the authority of Scripture among English Reformation writings, William Whitaker's *Disputation on Holy Scripture*.[154] Whitaker (1547/8–95) was

---

[152]Tyndale, PS, vol. 1, pp. 303–4, 306.
[153]Whitgift, PS, 1, p. 180, my emphasis.
[154]Trans. William Fitzgerald [Professor of Moral Philosophy, University of Dublin], PS, 1849; page references are inserted in my main text. For Whitaker's theology and role more broadly see Lake, *Moderate Puritans*, chs. 6 and 8.

regius professor of Divinity and Master of St John's College in the University of Cambridge, a Calvinist, of (conformist) Puritan sympathies, but one who had no time for those like Thomas Cartwright who sought to replace episcopacy in the Church of England with Presbyterianism. Whitaker was widely respected for his learning, moderation and impartiality. His *Disputation*, published in 1588, the year of the Spanish Armada, was the only one of his major works to appear in his lifetime. He indicates that it was part one of a proposed trilogy on the threefold office of Christ as Prophet, Priest and King – the three roles that received the anointing of God's Spirit in the Hebrew Scriptures. Here Whitaker is taking his cue from Calvin's exposition of the threefold messianic identity of Jesus Christ, which itself built on biblical, patristic and medieval precedents. Calvin, however, did not explicitly extend that threefold identity to the Church, in addition to the individual, and it is usually assumed that John Henry Newman was the first to do this in his preface, written as a Roman Catholic, to the revision of his earlier, Anglican work, *The Prophetical Office of the Church*, which was published under the title *The Via Media* in 1877.[155] But there seems to be a hint of this ecclesial application of the threefold office when Whitaker implies that Christ's prophetic office is exercised in his Church as he speaks through the Scriptures. Other treatises by Whitaker, on the Church, Councils and the power of the pope, remain in the obscurity of the original Latin in which they were published posthumously in Geneva in 1610. The *Disputation* was directed against two formidable Tridentine Roman Catholic controversialists, Robert Bellarmine SJ (1542–1621, later cardinal and archbishop; much later saint and doctor of the Church), who kept a bust of Whitaker, whose learning he could not but admire, in his study, and Thomas Stapleton (1535–98), who responded to Whitaker's robust defence. In Whitaker these two redoubtable Roman controversialists met their match. He has a vast command of patristic sources and deploys them along with the decrees of Councils and the works of approved Roman Catholic writers, though like other Protestant polemicists, he points out that the Fathers frequently do not agree among themselves, except on the basics of the faith (p. 455).

---

[155]Newman, *Via Media*.

Whitaker shares the standard view of the Tridentine Roman Catholic Church among the English Reformers; he does not have Richard Hooker's more nuanced and charitable perspective. For Whitaker, 'popery is nothing else but mere antichristianism' (p. 20). The claim of the Roman Church to give the Scriptures an authority that they supposedly would not otherwise have, that is to presume to sponsor and endorse the word of God, is 'the whole mystery of inquity' (p. 279). Nevertheless, Whitaker's argument is invariably calm, reasonable and courteous, never insulting or in bad taste.

In his *Disputation*, Whitaker takes as a sort of mantra and as an entrée to each major issue the words of Christ in John 5.39, 'Search the Scriptures' (in the imperative; modern translations put these words on the indicative, 'You search/study the Scriptures . . .'). The major areas of controversy that he addresses are (1) the extent of the canon of Scripture, that is whether those apocryphal books, formally accepted by the Roman Church at the Council of Trent, rightly belong within the canon; (2) whether the Scriptures should be available in the vernacular for all to understand; (3) whether the authority of the Bible is inherent in its inspiration or is awarded by the Church; (4) its clarity or perspicuity: can it be understood in essentials without ecclesiastical interpretation? (5) who has the right to interpret it and by what means; and (6) its sufficiency and perfection, that does not need to be supplemented by other ecclesiastical sources, least of all by the supposed unwritten apostolic truths, of which Roman Catholic apologists and polemicists made great play.

Of these six areas of contention, Whitaker considers (3), the question whether Scripture stands in its own authority or needs to receive it from elsewhere, to be the most important of the issues at stake between the Churches of the Reformation and the Roman Catholic Church of the Council of Trent (pp. 275, 279). His answer is at the same time moderate and uncompromising: we 'do not deny that it appertains to the church to approve, acknowledge, receive, promulge, [and] commend' the Scriptures to its members (p. 279). This is 'the illustrious office of the church', (p. 283). But we deny, he says, that the Scriptures receive their credibility solely on account of the Church's commendation. He follows Calvin in affirming, '[T]here is a more certain and illustrious testimony, whereby we are persuaded of the sacred character of these books, that is to say, the internal testimony of the Holy Spirit' (p. 279; cf. p. 290).

Whitaker also follows Calvin explicitly in enumerating the outward attributes of the Scriptures that reinforce the inward conviction of their truth: the majesty of their doctrine; the simplicity, purity and divinity of the style; their antiquity; the fulfilment of biblical prophecies; the miracles that attended the original revelation; the durability of the Scriptures, that is their ability to withstand the assaults of its enemies over time; the witness of the martyrs; and the transformation of unprepossessing biblical authors, shepherds, fishermen, etc. (pp. 293–4). Whitaker has something akin to a concept of the *sensus fidei* or *consensus fidelium* that would be promoted by Newman and figure in the teaching of Vatican II: all the faithful have received this testimony from the Spirit through the word. For by the Church, he points out, we mean, not the clergy, bishops, council and pope, as the Roman Catholics do, but 'the whole multitude of the faithful' (p. 280; cf. 448–9).

So authority to interpret the Scriptures also belongs to the Holy Spirit and to the Scriptures themselves: internally to the Spirit; externally to the biblical text (p. 415). 'Is it not the office of the Holy Spirit to teach all things necessary to salvation?' (p. 297). But Whitaker deplores 'enthusiasm' or claims to private revelations (ibid.). Scripture is self-authenticating, *autopiston* (p. 335). Whitaker assumes that the authority to interpret and make judgements is such that there can be no appeal; therefore, the judge cannot be the popes, whose authority has obviously often been challenged, and who have sometimes fallen into error and even heresy, but only the Holy Spirit (p. 448), the authority beyond all appeal.

However, means are needed to interpret the Scriptures aright; these are prayer for illumination; knowledge of the original languages; a sense of the genre of the passage: is it literal or figurative?; attention to the context and circumstances of the passage; comparing Scripture with Scripture to discover what the Holy Spirit means; the analogy of faith, which is the general tenor of Scripture where the sense is clear; and consulting learnt scholars and using their commentaries (pp. 466–73). With regard to the priority of the original languages Whitaker, professor of Divinity in the University of Cambridge and heir to the humanist ethic *ad fontes*, is at his most indignant:

[T]he synagogue of antichrist in their pretended council of Trent did that which the true church of Christ never in any council dared to attempt or think of, – namely, made the originals of scripture in both Testaments unauthoritative and non-authentic, and pronounced the authenticity of the vulgate Latin version, than which nothing can possibly be more faulty and corrupt. (p. 483)

To deprive Christians of the Scriptures in the vernacular is to take away the conversation of God with his people and theirs with him, and to interrupt the communion of God and humankind (p. 705).

On the old chestnut, St Augustine's remark against the Manichees that was invariably deployed in Protestant–Roman Catholic controversy, 'I would not believe the gospel if the authority of the catholic church did not move me,' Whitaker disarmingly replies: '[U]nless the church commended the sacred books to us, and led us, as it were by the hand, to the very fountains of divine truth, we should never emerge out of the darkest shades of error'; but the specific claims of the Roman Church do not follow from this premise (p. 322; cf. p. 319).

With regard to the patristic concept of the Rule of Faith (*regula fidei*) and its place in scriptural interpretation, Whitaker argues that the Rule of Faith is none other than Scripture itself or the epitome of Scripture or the Creed or the substance of the Creed and is engraved on the hearts of the faithful; it certainly does not refer to unwritten apostolic doctrines (pp. 328, 484). Here, Whitaker was following Irenaeus and Tertullian, rather than Clement of Alexandria and Origen.[156] There is an echo of Jewel's St Paul Cross Challenge Sermon: 'Let Stapleton, if he can, produce even a single passage from Augustine, wherein that holy father declares that the rule of faith contains any dogma which is not delivered in the scriptures' (p. 487).

On the perfection or sufficiency of Scripture, that is whether the Scriptures 'comprehend a full and perfect body of teaching', or whether unwritten traditions are needed to supplement it (p. 497), Whitaker enumerates the following items in Roman Catholic doctrine and practice: the oblation of the eucharistic sacrifice; the oil of chrism; invocation of the saints; prayers for the departed; the primacy of the Bishop of Rome; the consecration of the baptismal water; the sacraments of confirmation, orders, matrimony, penance,

---

[156]Kelly, *Early Christian Doctrines*, pp. 39–40, 43–4.

and extreme unction; the merits of good works; the need to make satisfaction for sins committed; and the requirement to enumerate one's sins to a priest (pp. 511–12). Trent's setting of unwritten traditions 'on a level with scripture in dignity, utility, authority, credit, and necessity' evokes Whitaker's indignation (p. 706).

Whitaker does not completely reject the medieval fourfold 'senses' of Scripture and has a place for allegory, etc. But he insists that actually there are not several *senses*, but only one. 'We affirm there is but one true, proper and genuine sense of scripture, arising from the words rightly understood, which we call the literal' or 'grammatical' (p. 406). Various legitimate figurative uses are not in fact other senses but derivations, corollaries, consequences, applications and accommodations of the one authentic meaning (pp. 404, 406, 408). Theological and doctrinal arguments may be drawn only from the literal, grammatical sense; the other so-called senses are too unstable (p. 409). On the question of the perspicuity or clarity of Scripture, Whitaker freely admits that, as he points out, Luther himself acknowledged that there are many obscure and doubtful passages, but all that is needed for saving faith and the Christian life is clear (p. 362). He also has Luther's biblical christocentrism: all parts of Scripture 'give plain testimony to Christ' (p. 25).

Richard Field on authority in theology

It makes sense to follow Whitaker with Field and not merely because of the agricultural connection of their names – white-acre and field! Field picks up several of the themes that Whitaker addresses in the *Disputation* and has his predecessor's moderation of tone and dialectical skill, though he is more prolix. Like Whitaker, Field's main antagonists are Bellarmine and Stapleton. Richard Field (1561–1616) is a frequently overlooked and generally underrated Anglican divine whose great treatise *Of the Church* was published in five books in the first decade of the seventeenth century (Books 1–4, 1606; Book 5, 1610).[157] Field was favoured by Queen Elizabeth I, becoming Chaplain in Ordinary and Canon of Windsor.

---

[157]Field, *Of the Church*; references in my main text are to volume and page.

James I made him Dean of Gloucester. James had him in mind for a bishopric, but left it too late; he famously said on Field's death, 'I should have done more for that man.' As I have written of him elsewhere, Field was one of the most stupendously learnt scholars of the reformed English Church in an age when its clerical scholars were becoming the wonder of the world (*clerus Britannicus stupor mundi*).[158]

Field was a close friend of Richard Hooker, but his overall approach is more typical of the Protestant Reformation than of the incipient Anglicanism of which Hooker, together with Lancelot Andrewes, is the forerunner. Both Hooker and Field use the phrase 'in which our fathers lived and died' of the medieval Church; unlike more extreme Protestant writers, they insisted that there was salvation for their forebears in the pre-Tridentine Western Church. Field regarded the pre-Tridentine Church as orthodox, though not of course perfect and, strange to say, more than once describes it as a 'Protestant' Church. But he saw the Council of Trent, with its considered, systematic rejection of the key tenets of the Reformation, as a watershed, and viewed the Roman Church of the Council as a schismatic and heretical faction within the history of the Latin Church and as really isolated within Christendom when one took the Orthodox and Reformation Churches into account. It might be said that his primary thesis in his great treatise was that 'none of the things wherein we at this day dissent from the present Church of Rome, were generally and constantly believed and received as articles of faith in the days of our fathers, in that Church wherein they lived and died'; so that, prior to Trent, Luther was in the same position as Augustine or Aquinas, standing for one point of view or school of thought among several on issues that had not been definitively resolved by the Church in Council (vol. 4, p. 510).

On the question of the 'apocryphal' books that Trent had decreed to be part of the canon of Scripture,[159] Field brings forward what he calls 'a cloud of witnesses, in all ages, and in all parts of the world . . . even till and after the time of Luther,' in support of the Protestant canon that lacked the Apocrypha (vol. 2, p. 125) – though

---

[158]On Field's ecclesiology see Avis, *Anglicanism and the Christian Church*, pp. 51–8 and id., *Beyond the Reformation?*, pp. 149–50.
[159]DS, #1502, p. 365; *Conciliorum*, p. 431.

the position of the reformed English Church was more nuanced, as we see in Article 6 of the Thirty-nine, dating in its present form from 1571, where the apocryphal books are said to be useful for 'example of life and instruction of manners', but not to establish doctrine.[160] Similarly – and this is typical of his method – Field cites a host of writers in support of the principle of the sufficiency of Scripture, that it contains all things necessary for salvation and does not need to be supplemented from tradition, particularly unwritten tradition. Field concludes on this point, '[T]he Church wherein our fathers lived and died, was, in this point touching the sufficiency of the scripture, an orthodox and true Protestant Church, as it was in the former, touching the canon of scripture' (vol. 2, pp. 126–40 at p. 140). Field goes on to cite similar precedents in favour of the Bible being available to the people in the vernacular (vol. 2, pp. 141–75).

Like the magisterial Reformers generally, Field affirms the indefectibility of the Church and expounds this in a nuanced, perhaps rather scholastic way. He has a strong sense that the whole Church, over time, cannot err in essential matters of faith, but of course it does not follow for him that the magisterium of the Church today cannot err – far from it: even General Councils are not exempt from error (vol. 2, pp. 392–408, esp. 406–7; 472). Field also has a profoundly catholic sense of the role of the Church in leading a person to Scripture and its teaching: we believe the Scripture because it is God's word; we believe it to be so because the Church testifies so; we believe the Church because it is guided by the Spirit of truth; altogether our faith is established on 'the authority of the catholic Church, led and guided by the Spirit' (vol. 2, p. 409), but that does not make the Church the ground of our faith; and this, Field believes, is what Augustine meant in the notorious quotation discussed above (vol. 2, p. 426; vol. 4, pp. 444–50).

Field freely admits that there are obscure places in the Bible and cites Luther to this effect, just as Whitaker does (vol. 2, p. 445; vol. 4, p. 483). He rejects the common Roman Catholic accusation that Protestants encourage rampant private judgement. On the contrary, those who follow their own fancies, neglecting received principles of interpretation and scholarly consensus, are guilty of

---

[160]This is also what the Irish Articles of 1615 say about the Apocrypha.

'enthusiasm'; them 'we accurse' (vol. 2, p. 447). We should be guided by the Fathers and may not depart from 'the main truth of doctrine which they deliver' in their various interpretations that in other respects diverge; but we may depart from their views, which were not in any case homogeneous, in details. We are to look for 'the true, literal, and natural sense' of the biblical text, even when we cannot find it in the Fathers (vol. 1, p. 450). Like Whitaker, whom perhaps he follows here, Field lists a range of rules or helps that are conducive to sound biblical interpretation: (1) spiritual illumination of the understanding; (2) a mind dedicated to the pursuit of God's truth; (3) knowledge of the rule of faith (the overall content and thrust of Scripture as received in the universal Church: vol. 2, pp. 442–3) and 'the practice of the saints according to the same'; (4) consideration of the consensus of interpretation and the implications of departing from it, together with awareness of the context and of biblical parallels; (5) knowledge of the relevant histories, arts, and sciences, because 'grace presupposeth nature'; (6) fluency in the original biblical languages. On these points, Field finds little or no difference with his adversaries (vol. 2, pp. 458–9; vol. 4. pp. 488–98).

In his analysis of various categories of tradition or traditions, Field insists that no article of the faith can be delivered by tradition alone, without scriptural support (vol. 2, p. 466). In a lengthy response to a critic, Field clarifies the rule whereby all controversies may be resolved: 'the written word of God, interpreted according to the rule of faith, the practice of the saints from the beginning, the conference of places [comparing one biblical passage with another], and all light of direction that either knowledge of tongues or any parts of good learning can yield' (vol. 4, p. 417; cf. p. 484).

Finally, we should note how close Field is to Luther in what he says about conscience, safeguarding the inner forum from ecclesiastical decrees that require obedience to rules and ceremonies on pain of eternal consequences, and attempts to prescribe inward actions of soul or spirit. Conscience cannot be bound by such authority, but is answerable to God alone. Human authority should not presume to rule in the conscience (vol. 2, pp. 528–9, 536).

What Whitaker and Field achieve is a deeply learnt, measured and judicious mediation of Reformation theology in the context of the reformed English Church. They go beyond the earlier English Reformers, such as Jewel, in their irenic perception of late medieval

Western Christianity (Field particularly), their systematic handling of the issues and in eschewing inflammatory language. So Hooker is not the only heavyweight English divine of the late sixteenth century who is worthy to be compared with the great scholastics of the high Middle Ages, the Tridentine apologists or the formidable scholars of Protestant Continental Europe.

2

Authority in the theology of the Reformation: II. History and tradition

Orientation to the Reformers on tradition

It is important not to read back into the sixteenth-century modern ecumenical concepts of tradition. The Reformers did not operate explicitly with the careful distinctions that have passed into the ecumenical consensus between three senses of the word 'tradition': (1) 'Tradition' as the apostolic faith or gospel; (2) 'tradition' as the living stream of belief, worship and spirituality that conveys Tradition and elucidates it in the history of the Church; and (3) 'traditions' as diverse specific practices on which churches differ.[1] The Reformers did not use the modern ecumenical language of tradition. This may explain why some standard expositions of Luther's theology have no index entry for tradition – or it may be a Lutheran blind spot! For the Reformers, 'tradition' or 'traditions' were usually negative terms, often referring to the medieval accretion of practices such as indulgences, meritorious works, pilgrimages, relics, masses for the dead, the cult of the saints and their images, that they wished to sweep away and referred to with disgust. However, some of the animus that the Reformers evinced against tradition in a broad sense should be attributed to the Renaissance scholars' contempt

---

[1]Rodger and Vischer (eds.), *Fourth World Conference on Faith and Order.*

for outmoded academic methods. The Aristotelian logic-chopping of the medieval schools and the layers of interpretation typical of the approach represented by Peter Lombard's *Sentences* and all those who commented on them were equally repugnant to men who had imbibed Erasmus' Greek New Testament and worked with what they believed to be authentic texts of St Augustine and other Fathers. But even here we should note that what the Reformers were doing at this point was to invoke authentic (original) tradition against more recent derivations and corruptions.

When the Reformers spoke of tradition or traditions, the overtones were generally pejorative. Tradition was suspect for them and called for what today we would call a hermeneutic of suspicion. Matthew 15.6 was ringing in their ears: 'For the sake of your tradition you make void the word of God.' The negative tone that the Reformers adopted with respect to tradition should not mislead us: it was no blanket rejection of the past; the reference was specific and limited. What they had in mind was certainly not everything that they shared with the ancient Latin Church: the Canon of Scripture, the Lord's Prayer, the creeds and other teachings of the early Councils (though Luther and the Reformers generally insisted that Councils could err and had done so), the ordered ministry, the need for structures of worship and oversight and for church law. As we shall see in more detail shortly, the magisterial Reformers honoured the Fathers of the early Church and studied them assiduously, appealing to their authority in confirmation of scriptural arguments or where Scripture was reticent. They regarded them as biblical theologians *par excellence*, as the witnesses who stood closest to the revelation inscribed in Scripture. At the least, as in the case of Zwingli, they employed their authority *ad hominem*, against opponents who relied on them.

The Reformers' polemic against 'tradition' or 'traditions' is directed at particular human practices ('human traditions') that the late medieval Roman church had made binding on the faithful. What roused the Reformers' indignation was not the fact that church authorities (the pope or the medieval councils) made laws or insisted on certain practices: the Church was bound to do this in the interests of good order and unity. What they objected to was the imposition of such rules on the consciences of the faithful and as necessary to salvation. What belonged to human right was elevated to divine right. What belonged in the earthly forum was falsely situated *coram deo* (before the face of God), and what belonged to 'things indifferent' (*adiaphora* – making no difference to one's salvation) was made necessary to salvation. For the Reformers, all things necessary to salvation were to be found expressed clearly in the text of Scripture: the Bible did not need the assistance of tradition to convey its saving message. It nowhere stated that auricular confession to a priest, confirmation, indulgences, obedience to the papacy, etc., were conditions of salvation. Luther and the first generation of Reformers did not have to contend with the Council of Trent's decree of 1546 that appeared to place unwritten traditions on a par with Scripture, twin channels of divine revelation, but Calvin among others, including English divines, later attacked it.

The criterion the Reformers applied in this context as elsewhere was that of justification by grace through faith alone. The keeping of human rules, rites and ceremonies could never justify the sinner in the sight of God. On the contrary, some of the requirements of canon law could not be kept without committing sin, as the Augsburg Confession (1530) claimed (ch. XXVIII).[2] In his *Apology of the Augsburg Confession* (Article XV, 'Human Traditions in the Church'), Philip Melanchthon made the distinction between the two uses of tradition, for justification and for edification, clear:

> Although the holy Fathers themselves had rites and traditions, they did not regard them as useful or necessary for justification. They did not obscure the glory or work of Christ but taught that we are justified by faith for Christ's sake, not for the sake of these human rites. They observed these human rites because they were profitable for good order, because they gave the people a set time to assemble, because they provided an example of how all things could be done decently and in in order in the churches, and finally because they helped instruct the common folk. . . . For these reasons the Fathers kept ceremonies, and for the same reasons we also believe in keeping traditions. We are amazed when our opponents maintain that traditions have another purpose, namely to merit the forgiveness of sins, grace and justification. What is this but honouring God "with gold

---

[2]Tappert, *Book of Concord*, p. 93.

and silver and precious stones," believing that he is reconciled by a variety of vestments, ornaments, and innumerable similar observances in the human traditions. (§20–21)[3]

Melanchthon added on behalf of the churches of the reform in Germany: 'We gladly keep the old traditions set up in the church because they are useful and promote tranquillity, and we interpret them in an evangelical way, excluding the opinion which holds that they justify' (§38).[4] Such opinions were, to quote St Paul, 'doctrines of demons' (§4, quoting 1 Tim. 4.1).[5] Similarly in the *Institutes*, Calvin attacked various decrees regarding forms of worship which lacked biblical authority as 'human traditions', but he made it clear that he supported lawful, useful church constitutions. Where liberty of conscience was flouted and human regulations were made necessary to salvation, 'a kind of Judaism' had been introduced.[6] The same point pervades the literature of the reform, for example, in Calvin's *The Necessity of Reforming the Church* (1544).[7]

Historical consciousness in the Reformation

To appeal to any aspect of tradition as a source of authority is to conjure up the past to serve the present, but selectively. There is paradox in invoking the authority of the past to justify the present, because the totality of the past cannot be present to us now, but only glimpses of it, always distorted by our contemporary perspective. History is truly in the eye of the beholder. Our historical vision can be corrected and purified by study and scholarly concourse, but it will always remain partial in every sense of the word. Here, I briefly sketch the state of historical study and historical consciousness in the sixteenth century as part of the context of the Reformation's view of Scripture and tradition.

---

[3]Ibid., p. 218.
[4]Ibid., p. 220.
[5]Ibid., p. 215.
[6]*Institutes* IV, x.
[7]Calvin, 'The Necessity of Reforming the Church', in *Tracts and Treatises*, vol. 1, pp. 121–234.

The weight of the Church's past hung heavily over sixteenth-century controversies. Roman Catholic claims leant strongly on history in the form of Church tradition because scriptural attestation for some of them was weak. However, deficiency in historical criticism and a poor sense of anachronism (which was characteristic of scholasticism) led Roman Catholic authorities, including at the Council of Trent, to claim more than could be justified from history.[8] Protestants, who were more strongly influenced by humanism, were wary of tradition as an authority and tended to assimilate it to particular 'traditions', which they believed had eclipsed the Word of God. But all parties, except the radicals, mined history for precedents that supported their position, and even the radicals took up a stance vis-à-vis history when some claimed that the true Church had ceased at the conversion of Constantine or even on the death of the last Apostle; the intervening centuries held no theological value for them, except as a dismal record of apostasy and persecution.[9]

A fully fledged genetic interpretation of history, with insight into complex multiple causation, was not available to sixteenth-century thinkers, but that is not to say that they were slaves to uniformitarianism. Protestants may have believed that the reformed churches faithfully replicated the primitive Church, and Roman Catholics may have held that the Apostles were the first bishops and Peter was the first pope – both sides insisting that their church had maintained or restored a divinely ordained pattern – but their sense of the past was not monochrome. The Reformation debates were not conducted in a historical vacuum, without a sense of what had gone before for good or ill. What was true in Germany was no less true in England. As O'Day remarks, 'On the face of it, it might seem that the Reformation of its nature rejected history. And so in a sense it did, or at least the force of recent precedent. . . . But is no less true that the English Reformation used history – an interpretation of the past – to justify its existence, its goals and its actions. It created its own historiography.'[10]

History can be interpreted either as a rolling story of change and development, in which new and unprecedented things emerge, or

---

[8]O'Malley, *Trent*, p. 249.
[9]See generally: Littell, *Anabaptist View of the Church*; George Hunstan Williams, *Radical Reformation*.
[10]O'Day, *Debate on the English Reformation*, p. 5.

as a uniform narrative where only incidental aspects change and the essence remains the same. For the medievals, the past was no different from the present and its great figures, whether Adam or Caesar, were seen as contemporaries. Generally, educated people in the middle ages did not construe their existence within a framework of historical development. Their lives were structured hierarchically rather than historically, in terms of being rather than becoming. The medieval historian or chronicler saw the world *sub specie aeternitatis*, setting forth an ordered cosmos and, even in the midst of war, famine, plague and early death, affirming ultimate universal harmony. The taken-for-granted methods of modern history – critical assessment of evidence, sensitivity to anachronism and concepts of multiple causation – were in their infancy.[11] But that had begun to change with Renaissance humanism.

The humanists were primarily lovers of ancient language and literature. Renaissance historiography was therefore a branch of rhetoric that looked to Cicero as both teacher and model. Humanist history remained didactic and was meant to be edifying. The past was full of *exempla*. Events would be simplified and their narrative presentation stylized without scruple because the historian saw himself as the servant of moral philosophy whose truths must be inculcated as persuasively as possible. The governing criteria were structure, symmetry and proportion. However, humanist historical methods were profoundly modified by Machiavelli, who injected a strong dose of political realism and local colour, and by his colleague Guicciardini in whom narrative control and sensitivity to the complexities of the historical process attained a new level. The methods of the humanist historians were not essentially inductive and they were not trying to get at 'what really happened.' Nevertheless, there was a new sense of the integrity of a cultural epoch and, although their approach was consciously Christian and catholic, they broke away from the providential schema of the medievals and embraced an alternative periodization that was structured by the fall of the Roman Empire and the rise of city states and a sense of nationhood. They were not enthused by the

---

[11]Selective references: Smalley, *Historians in the Middle Ages*; Haskins, *Renaissance of the Twelfth Century*; Morris, *Discovery of the Individual*; Southern, *History and Historians*; Ullmann, *Individual and Society*; id., *Medieval Foundations*; Louis Green, *Chronicle into History*; Avis, *Foundations of Modern Historical Thought*, ch. 1.

ages of saints, miracles and clerical dominance, so the medieval centuries were rather glossed over: it was Petrarch who dubbed them the 'dark ages'. What did impassion humanist historians was the sense of continuity between classical culture and their own age of cultural rebirth. While continuity was strong, the sense of transitoriness and loss was also apparent. History since the golden age was a record of declension; the lustre had faded over time, but was being reburnished in the new age of learning because it was bringing the glories of classical and Christian antiquity to light. The primitivist method, harking back to the pristine models of classical literature or to the doctrine and practice of the primitive Church, entailed a critique of the intervening centuries. For the humanist scholars, it meant rejection of scholastic methods; for the humanist theologians – that is to say the Reformers – it entailed a judgement on the doctrine and practice of the medieval Church, weighed in the balance against Scripture and the primitive Church.

An awareness of social change was beginning to dawn, and with it a sense of how one's own society had been shaped, what Ferguson calls 'a feeling for the uniqueness and organic unity of periods' and a consciousness that customs and institutions were relative to the changing circumstances of time and place.[12] Already concepts of process, period and contingency were in play, though not yet elaborated theoretically. The political character of the English Reformation led to a focus on the visible Church, the Church as (in Richard Hooker's phrase) a 'politic society', rather than as a *corpus mysticum*. The emphasis of debate in Tudor England on issues of polity – on governance, discipline, liturgy and ceremonial – lent itself to historical investigation on the human level. The major controversialists on behalf of the reformed English Church – Starkey, Jewel, Whitgift and to some extent Hooker – took their stand on the documentary history of the corporate *ecclesia*, with its customs, traditions and doctrines. Jewel's 'Challenge' adopted an overtly historical strategy. Although 'tradition' was suspect, 'custom' was venerated. While customs fell into the category of *adiaphora*, things that do not make a difference to salvation, they were not on that account to be treated as unimportant: customs were the outward expression of the inner life of the Church at a certain juncture and

---

[12]Ferguson, *Clio Unbound*, pp. ix–x. See also Fussner, *Historical Revolution*; Levy, *Tudor Historical Thought*.

signs of its continuity through time.[13] It was becoming possible to see the Church of the past in the round. Matthias Flacius Illyricus, the main author of the Lutheran historical *apologia*, the *Magdeburg Centuries*, insisted that Church history must incorporate Christian practice: prayers, devotions, worship and songs, as well as doctrine, 'for all these things are organically connected to one another'.[14]

Luther was forced to take history seriously by the challenge, voiced by Eck at Leipzig and by the Emperor Charles V, that 'a single monk must err if he stands against the opinion of all Christendom; otherwise Christendom itself would have been in error for more than a thousand years'. This jibe tormented Luther and he gave himself to the study of history, especially of Councils, and came up with an eschatological theology of history understood as a struggle between the minority, persecuted true church of the gospel and the dominant, triumphalist, persecuting false church of the pope. Such Protestant interpretations were of course 'venerable myths which the Reformers found irresistible because they defended the Reformation against the charge of irresponsible novelty'.[15] To innovate in doctrine was and remains, for all churches, thoroughly reprehensible.

Ambivalence about tradition

Tradition in its etymological New Testament sense (*paradosis*) means the act of handing something from one person to another for safe keeping, rather than the act of handing down something from one generation or one century to another, like passing on the baton in a relay race. This distinction suggests that the Reformers' relation to tradition was marked by a certain ambivalence about historical continuity. On the one hand, the driving force of the Reformation

---

[13]Cf. Ferguson, *Clio*, pp. 418–19, xiii, 425, 429.
[14]Grafton, 'Church History in Early Modern Europe', p. 25. See also, selectively: Cameron, 'Primitivism, Patristics and Polemics'; Burke, *Renaissance Sense of the Past*; Streuver, *Language of History*; Quinones, *Renaissance Discovery of Time*; Wilcox, *Development of Florentine Historiography*; Jacob Burckhardt, *Civilization of the Renaissance*; Gilbert, *Machiavelli and Guicciardini*.
[15]Dickens, Tonkin and Powell, *Reformation in Historical Thought*, p. 8. Headley, *Luther's View of Church History*; Glanmor Williams, *Reformation Views of Church History*, ch. 1.

was the attempt to retrieve in its integrity what had been handed on to the Church by Christ and the Apostles. The true gospel of the Church had been rediscovered. It was the true treasure, the pearl of great price, the one thing needful. To safeguard it, one must be willing to die a martyr's death. The act of rediscovering, safeguarding and handing on to faithful men leap-frogged the centuries and had little to do with ideas of succession (though some of the more radical Protestants elaborated an alternative apostolic succession, located in the dissident movements of medieval Europe). Unbroken continuity was not a virtue in itself. The received historical structures of papacy, episcopacy and canon law were dispensable. Saving faith was a timeless moment, so to speak.

On the other hand, the Reformers found themselves necessarily involved with matters concerning the handing down of teaching, of authority in oversight and of permanent structures of church life.[16] They were adamant that they were not setting up a new church. Their aim, on the contrary, was to renew the face of the one Church (as Calvin put it). They were not, they insisted, inventing new doctrines, but rather reinstating the apostolic teaching that had been held since the beginning but had become obscured. In sacramental theology and practice, they were clear that they were not innovating. In reforming the mass (e.g. giving Holy Communion in both kinds), they were restoring ancient practice. They insisted that authority to minister word and sacrament was not to be seized by the individual, but had to be given by constituted authority. In defending infant baptism, the magisterial Reformers were of course perpetuating longstanding tradition. Luther and Melanchthon claimed that it came down from the Apostles, from the pure time of the Church, before the rise of heresies. If infant baptism had not been true baptism, there would have been no Church for all those centuries, for the Church always remains in being by the promise of God, and without baptism there is no Church. On their own premises, Zwingli and Calvin could not appeal to tradition for

---

[16]A selection on the theological aspects of reforming the institution: Cranz, *Essay on the Development of Luther's Thought*; Pelikan, *Spirit Versus Structure*; Chadwick, *Early Reformation*; Witte, *Law and Protestantism*; Hendrix, *Recultivating the Vineyard*; Wright (ed.), *Martin Bucer*; Hall, 'Diakonia in Martin Bucer', in *Humanists and Protestants*; Bohatec, *Calvins Lehre*; Baur, *Gott, Recht und Weltliche Regiment*; Bieler, *Calvin's Economic and Social Thought*.

something as vitally connected with salvation as infant baptism, but found sophisticated biblical warrants for it.

Like their continental counterparts, from whom they tended to take their lead theologically, the English Reformers (whose views are reflected in the Thirty-nine Articles) held that Scripture contained all things necessary to salvation and that those invented human traditions that militated against the teaching of Scripture were to be abolished. Other practices could be maintained on their merits provided they were not imposed on the conscience or made necessary to salvation. These practices need not be the same everywhere; particular (i.e. national) churches had authority to legislate for themselves, but not for others, in rites and ceremonies. The approach that is typical of the English Reformers is clearly seen in John Jewel's *Apologia Ecclesiae Anglicanae* (1562) and in his extensive *Defence* of the *Apology*. Jewel's chosen field of battle, on which he prevailed, was the testimony of the early Church to scriptural truth. English Reformers such as Jewel felt themselves at one with the primitive Church, appealed to the consent of the Fathers and claimed that the Church of Rome had forsaken the fellowship of the holy Fathers and blessed martyrs.

The reformed English Church gave early tradition – the 'primitive Church' – a role in deciding matters concerning the outward ordering or polity of the Church, provided that they are 'not repugnant' to Scripture. This distinctive theme becomes pronounced, as we shall see in the next chapter, in Richard Hooker (1554–1600). Hooker attacked the contention of the Puritans in the Church of England that nothing could be done in worship and church government that did not enjoy explicit biblical warrant (therefore, for example, no surplices and no bishops). In place of 'things indifferent', Hooker spoke of 'things accessory' (i.e. accessory to salvation). While what was necessary to salvation was revealed only in Scripture, nothing in the life of the Church was entirely neutral. However, the role of tradition is only one element in Hooker's argument: sanctified reason and a sense of what is appropriate to the circumstances also play a part in clarifying God's will where Scripture does not inform us. Tradition is a rather crude term for what Hooker has in mind: collective practice and experience and the expressed mind of the Church, together with the consent of its members, are all involved. Hooker's balanced, integrated approach was distorted by some Anglican divines of the next century who took the appeal to 'antiquity' to an extreme, as we shall see in due course.

The uniformitarian assumptions of Western culture, unchallenged until the Romantic and historical movements of the late eighteenth and early nineteenth centuries, and common to Protestants and Roman Catholics alike, are evident in these debates. What enjoyed universal consent was right for all times and places. Oldest was best. The golden age lay in the remote past. Therefore, the Reformers were prejudiced against change, which should always be contemplated reluctantly and only when urgently called for and sanctioned by the magistrate (monarch). One could not improve on ancient wisdom and well-tried practice. To anticipate a little: Hooker's elevated estimate of human reason made possible a more urbane, sapiential approach than that of the Reformers themselves to the considerable area where God has placed responsibility for ordering its life firmly in the hands of the Church itself.

The authority of Fathers and Councils

The continental Reformers

The arguments of the Reformation, which went three ways, between the Magisterial Reformers, radical reformists and Roman Catholics, were fought out, not only on the battleground of the interpretation of Scripture, but also in the arena of the authority of the early Fathers of the Church. Controversialists on both sides set about proving, with immense labour, the agreement of their respective churches' positions with the teaching of the primitive Church. The Reformers were not content to appeal to the authority of Scripture, though Scripture was indeed the paramount and ultimate arbiter. Had they been setting out to create a church *de novo* rather than, as Calvin put it, to renew the face of the existing Church, they could have ignored tradition.[17] Had they believed, with some of the radical spirits of the Reformation, that the Church had apostatized

---

[17]Calvin, *Reply to Cardinal Sadoleto* in *Tracts and Treatises*, vol. 1, p. 37: 'All we have attempted has been to renew that ancient form of the Church' [which had been damaged under the papacy].

from the truth after the death of the last Apostle, the teaching of the Fathers would have been irrelevant. Steinmetz well describes the stance of the magisterial Reformers vis-à-vis the Christian centuries before them:

> The goal of the reformers was a reformed catholic church, built upon the foundation of the prophets and apostles, purged of the medieval innovations that had distorted the gospel, subordinate to the authority of Scripture and the ancient Christian writers, and continuous with what was best in the old church. . . . What the Protestants thought they offered was a genuine antiquity, one that stretched back to Peter and Paul and not merely to Lombard and Gratian.[18]

In fact the Reformers' appeal to patristic tradition was not merely *ad hominem*, to counter such an appeal by Roman Catholics, nor merely tactical, to undermine such radical innovations as the rejection of infant baptism by the Anabaptists. The Reformers' appeal to patristic tradition was integral to their theological method, even when they were debating among themselves.[19] It was an extension and practical application of the primacy of Scripture, for the Fathers were revered as biblical theologians who themselves deferred to the paramount authority of Scripture. The Reformers acknowledged that the guidance of the Fathers was needed, for while the message of salvation was clear to all on the surface of the biblical text, not all the teachings of Scripture were equally perspicuous.

Appeal to the authority of the Fathers and Councils was by no means a special or even unique characteristic of the English Reformers. They were following the polemical method pursued by both Protestants and Roman Catholics on the Continent. As Luther works towards his evangelical insight with regard to justifying faith, he does so in constant dialogue with the Fathers, especially 'blessed Augustine'.[20] If, as Althaus claims, 'there is no precedent for the way in which Luther, as an exegete and as a preacher, thinks in constant conversation with Scripture', it is equally true that the

---

[18]Steinmetz, *Luther in Context*, p. 129.
[19]Amy Burnett, 'According to the Oldest Authorities'.
[20]See especially the *Lectures on Romans*, LW, 25.

Fathers of the Church are his secondary dialogue partners, followed by the medieval schoolmen, but he can be rough with both.[21]

The career of Luther's lieutenant Philip Melanchthon was marked from beginning to end by assiduous study of the Fathers and deployment of their authority in support of the reform.[22] 'Melanchthon's earliest theological activities are accompanied by a steady stream of patristic references, historical studies, editions of ancient theological texts and assertions that they are a guide to the pure ultimate source of all theology, the Gospel.'[23] For Melanchthon, the reform and the renewal of patristic scholarship were simply two sides of the coin. One studied the Scriptures in the light of patristic theology and patristic theology in the light of the Scriptures. The return to the Scriptures is of a piece with the return to the Fathers: *ad fontes*. Renaissance humanist scholarship had made both possible. Melanchthon's *Apology of the Augsburg Confession* is a sustained appeal to the authority of the Fathers in support of the Lutheran Reformation. The Apostles, St Augustine, and the Reformers, he maintained, shared an identity of teaching.[24] For the Reformers, Rome and the radicals were guilty of the same error: innovating against the witness of the Scriptures and the Fathers.

The same ideological gambit of wrapping the Scriptures, the Fathers and the Reformers into a unified theological stance, while upholding the final authority of Scripture, is also typical of Zwingli, who read the Scriptures through the eyes of the Fathers (he had an extensive library of humanist editions, mainly by Erasmus).

For we teach not a single jot which we have not learned from the sacred Scriptures. Nor do we make a single assertion for which

---

[21]Althaus, *Theology of Luther*, p. 4. See also Schulze, 'Luther and the Church Fathers'. For Luther's relation to Aquinas, Biel, etc., see Oberman, *Harvest of Medieval Theology*; Steinmetz, 'Luther among the Anti-Thomists' and 'Luther and Calvin on Church and Tradition', in *Luther in Context*.

[22]For what follows here see Fraenkel, *Testimonia Patrum*.

[23]Ibid., p. 29.

[24]'We know that what we have said agrees with the prophetic and apostolic Scriptures, with the holy Fathers Ambrose, Augustine, and many others, and with the whole Church of Christ': *Apology*, Article IV (Justification) #389: Tappert, *Book of Concord*, p. 166.

we have not the authority of the first doctors of the Church – prophets, apostles, bishops, evangelists and expositors – those ancient Fathers who drew more purely from the fountainhead.[25]

As for Calvin, there are some uncertainties about his knowledge of the Fathers and the way that he deploys them.[26] From the first edition of the *Institutes*, in his 'Prefatory Address to the King of France' (Francis I, Calvin's sovereign), Calvin claims the authority of the Fathers for the reform. 'It is a calumny,' he protests, 'to represent us as opposed to the Fathers,' and goes on to cite numerous patristic sayings against common practices of the late medieval Church.[27] In his *Reply to Cardinal Sadoleto* (1539) Calvin refutes the 'calumny' that the Protestants do not defer to any authority but their own private judgement. While Fathers and Councils have authority only in so far as they agree with the Word of God, 'we still give to Fathers and Councils such rank and honour as it is proper for them under Christ to hold'.[28]

It is not always clear whether Calvin has used original patristic sources or whether he has made use of an anthology, a *florilegium*, of handy quotations. In doctrinal matters, he uses the Fathers mainly polemically; in biblical exegesis, mainly non-polemically. But there is evidence of a change of attitude approximately mid-career, when he moves from deploying patristic texts largely polemically in his theology, and in a rather *ad hominem* way, to treating the Fathers as genuine dialogue partners. Frequently he engages with patristic sources only to disagree with them. Intriguingly, he draws on patristic authorities more extensively for church order (especially Jerome and Eusebius) than for his defence of the doctrine of the Trinity. For Calvin, as for other Reformers, the works of the Fathers were a battleground for intra-Protestant arguments as well as for controversy with Roman Catholics.[29] Calvin probably used the Greek Fathers in Latin translation, but Chrysostom is undoubtedly his favourite patristic commentator on the Bible, admired and

---

[25]Zwingli, *An Exposition of the Faith*, in *Zwingli and Bullinger*, p. 278. See also Stephens, *Theology of Zwingli*, pp. 51–79; Backus, 'Ulrich Zwingli, Martin Bucer'.
[26]Concise introductions: Wendel, *Calvin*, pp. 123–6; Backus, 'Calvin and the Church Fathers'; Steinmetz, 'Calvin and Patristic Exegesis', in *Calvin in Context*; van Oort, 'Calvin and the Church Fathers'; detailed study: Lane, *John Calvin*.
[27]*Institutes*, vol. 1, p. 10 and following.
[28]Calvin, *Tracts and Treatises*, vol. 1, p. 66 (adapted).
[29]For example, Chung-Kim, 'Use of the Fathers in the Eucharistic Debates'.

emulated for his method of drawing out the 'literal' meaning of the text, that intended by the biblical writer.[30] However, Augustine holds pride of place for Calvin among the Fathers: the citations and allusions in the whole corpus of his work to Augustine's writings run into thousands. As Wendel says, 'He makes St Augustine his constant reading, and feels on an equal footing with him, quotes him at every opportunity, appropriates his expressions and regards him as one of the most valuable of allies in his controversies.'[31] Unlike some other humanists, Calvin may not have been at the cutting edge of patristic study, but he is immersed in the writings of the early Fathers; he does not defer uncritically to their authority, but they shape his mind.

Calvin's engagement with the Church Fathers is the tip of the iceberg of his interaction with various traditions of philosophy, theology and biblical exegesis from the past and the present – not only patristic, but classical, scholastic, late medieval, humanistic, Lutheran and varieties of Swiss Reformed. Calvin's contemporary dialogue partners are Lutheran, Roman Catholic, Anabaptist and Radical Protestant. Steinmetz's studies in this field bring out what he aptly describes as 'the corporate nature' of Calvin's biblical exegesis. Calvin may have been largely self-taught in theology – the *autodidact par excellence* – but he was no solitary thinker and of course no blinkered bigot. While he took even the most prestigious authors of the Church's tradition as dialogue partners to sharpen his pen on, rather than as authorities to be deferred to, the extent of the cross-confessional consensus that comes to light in Calvin's work is impressive.[32]

The English Reformers

The English Reformers deployed the Fathers from the first. Tyndale (1494?–1536) shows knowledge of Augustine and Jerome and

---

[30]Awad, 'Influence of John Chrysostom's hermeneutics'; Richard Burnett, 'John Calvin and the *Sensus Literalis*' (i.e. not fundamentalist literalism and not to the exclusion of allegorical exegesis, but concentration on the manifest content of Scripture, the revelation of God in Jesus Christ); for the philosophical aspects, Torrance, *Hermeneutics of Calvin* and see also id., 'Knowledge of God and Speech about Him according to John Calvin', in *Theology in Reconstruction*.
[31]Wendel, *Calvin*, p. 124.
[32]Steinmetz, *Calvin in Context*.

refers also to Cyprian, Chrysostom, Origen and others. But William Frith quotes from the Fathers even more frequently than Tyndale, referring especially to Augustine but also to Jerome, Ambrose, Athanasius and Chrysostom.[33] Trueman writes of Robert Barnes that 'The impact of patristic writers upon the work of Robert Barnes can scarcely be overestimated. His earliest work consists of a collection of quotations from early Christian writers in support of a series of Reformation propositions, not unlike the medieval *Sentences* in form.'[34]

True humanist scholar that he was, it was natural that Cranmer appealed to 'the consent of all the old doctors of the Church.'[35] In his draft canon law, the *Reformatio Legum Ecclesiasticarum* Cranmer wrote concerning the authority of the Fathers:

> Finally, we consider that the authority of the orthodox fathers is also not at all to be despised, for a great many things are said by them in a most clear and helpful way. Yet we do not allow that the meaning of Holy Writ can be determined by their opinion. For Holy Writ [*Sacrae Litterae*] must be our rule and judge for all Christian teaching.[36]

This high estimation of the Fathers was put into practice: the royal injunctions of Edward VI in 1547 instructed cathedrals that 'they shall make a library in some convenient place within their church, within the space of one year next ensuing this visitation, and shall lay [lay] in the same Saint Augustine's, Basil, Gregory Nazianzen, Jerome, Ambrose, Chrysostom, Cyprian, Theophylact, Erasmus, and other good writers' works'.[37]

For Jewel, a consensus of antiquity was to be sought where the Scriptures were obscure. The first 600 years of Christian history were normative; they provided a safeguard against the accretions of

---

[33]Trueman, *Luther's Legacy*, pp. 31–2.
[34]Ibid., p. 33.
[35]Thomas Cranmer, PS, II, p. 360. Cf. Dowling, 'Cranmer as Humanist Reformer'. See also Greenslade, *English Reformers and the Fathers*; Haugaard, 'Renaissance Patristic Scholarship and Theology in Sixteenth-Century England'. Middleton, *Fathers and Anglicans*, is a slightly romantic *apologia* for the patristic character of historic Anglicanism, but contains many good things.
[36]Bray (ed.), *Tudor Church Reform*, p. 183 (*Reformatio* 1, 15).
[37]Frere and Kennedy (eds.), *Visitation Articles*, vol. 2, p. 136 (no. 8).

tradition and untrammeled private judgement alike. But the Fathers were not to be awarded greater authority than they sought for themselves; it was as faithful and privileged interpreters of Scripture that their guidance was to be valued. 'They be interpreters of the Word of God. We despise them not, we read them, we reverence them,' Jewel insisted. 'Yet may they not be compared with the word of God. We may not build upon them; we may not make them the foundation and warrant of our conscience; we may not put our trust in them.'[38]

The reformed English Church inherited, via the medieval Church, the substance of the faith of the early Church in its integrity. The Church of England received, affirmed, preserved and defended the trinitarian and christological dogmas formulated by the early ecumenical councils and embodied in the Niceno-Constantinopolitan and 'Athanasian' creeds (*Quicunque vult*). These doctrines and the creeds that express them are inculcated assiduously in the Book of Common Prayer and upheld in the Thirty-nine Articles with the significant comment that 'they may be proved by most certain warrants of Holy Scripture' (Article VIII). The English Reformers, like their continental counterparts, presupposed the catholic faith and, in the best sense, took it for granted. Their writings were on the whole devoted to controversial matters arising from late medieval developments, which they maintained not to be of the catholic faith. The Reformers were, however, mistaken in supposing that aspects of medieval religion such as prayers for the faithful departed, veneration of the saints, the consecrated religious life, a form of eucharistic sacrifice and so on, could not be justified by appeal to primitive Christianity. When this became apparent through the post-Tridentine resurgence of Roman Catholic patristic scholarship, Lutheran and Reformed use of the Fathers became more critical and selective, while the Anglican response was to make a limited accommodation to such usages.

The Church of England did not set out to make new doctrines. It did not claim to have its own version of the Christian faith. It held that the message of salvation and the form of Christian life that was its appropriate response were clearly revealed in Scripture. The formulation and defence of the catholic faith at the

---

[38]Jewel, PS, vol. 6, p. 1173; cf. Booty, *John Jewel*, pp. 130–3, 147.

hands of the Fathers and first four (or six) General Councils was to be received as consonant with Scripture, though not infallible. Because I have discussed the place of councils in Reformation thought at length elsewhere,[39] I will simply touch briefly here on the theological or doctrinal role of councils, according to the English Reformers.

The English Reformers discuss councils of all kinds at great length (the general index entry of the Parker Society edition runs to 30 columns of small print), but they do so not to discuss the doctrines of the early Ecumenical Councils, but to rebut polemically the claims of their Roman Catholic adversaries that Councils were dependent on the pope and were authoritative sources of teachings not found in Scripture. Jewel claims on the basis of his patristic research that in both doctrine and practice the Roman Church had 'forsaken the fellowship of the holy Fathers'.[40] Cranmer summarizes the purpose of councils as being 'to declare the faith and reform errors'.[41] Jewel gives them a similar declaratory function: 'a council may testify the truth to be truth'; but he adds, 'it cannot make falsehood to be truth'.[42] Councils acknowledged themselves to be subject to Scripture and are still to be evaluated by the same standard. They appealed to Scripture and so should we. Their role is to articulate and defend the faith once for all delivered, not to make new articles of faith to be imposed on the consciences of Christians.[43]

The negative tenor of some of the English Reformers' comments on councils should not blind us to the underlying fact of their respect for and acceptance of the early Ecumenical Councils. They deplored the failure of the Councils of Constance and Basle in the early fifteenth century to reform practical abuses. Jewel in particular appealed from the conciliar principle in general to the early normative councils. However, for the Reformers only the Scriptures were infallible guides: councils were fallible and had erred in matters of substance. Cranmer insisted that 'general councils

---

[39] Avis, *Beyond the Reformation?*, pp. 134–41.
[40] Jewel, PS, vol. 4, p. 901.
[41] Cranmer, PS, vol. 2, pp. 76–7.
[42] Jewel, PS, vol. 2, p. 996.
[43] Whitaker, PS, pp. 434–5; Becon, PS, vol. 3, pp. 391–2; Rogers, PS, p. 210; Cranmer, PS, vol. 2, p. 36.

have erred, as well in the judgment of the Scriptures as also in necessary articles of our faith'.[44] The Thirty-nine Articles express the unanimous view of the English Reformers (and of the German and Swiss Reformers for that matter) when they assert (Article XXI) that Councils 'may err, and sometimes have erred, even in things pertaining unto God'. The Latin text of the Articles (1563) makes it clear that the expression 'things pertaining unto God' is a way of speaking about the substance or essence of Christianity as contained in the Church's traditional rule of faith (*in hijs quae ad normam pietatis pertinent*) – though it is imperative to note at this point that this does not mean that the Reformers had no doctrine of the indefectibility of the Church: they did indeed believe that the Church would not perish from the earth nor the true faith be lost; if councils, popes and bishops failed or went astray, the faith would be preserved in a part of the Church, even if by a persecuted remnant. Jewel asserted that 'the Church of God hath been ever from the beginning, and shall continue unto the end'.[45] Article XXI concludes by once again insisting that General Councils do not have an authority superior to, or complementary to Scripture, but 'things ordained by them as necessary to salvation have neither strength nor authority, unless it may be declared that they be taken out of Holy Scripture'.

But the Reformers will not allow that the authority of Scripture is in any way dependent on the Church, now or then, validating it. It stands on its own authority. To cite Whitaker, 'The sum of our opinion is, that the Scripture is αυτοπιστος, that is, hath all its authority and credit from itself; is to be acknowledged, is to be received, not only because the Church hath so determined and commanded, but because it comes from God, not by the Church, but by the Holy Ghost.'[46] In so far as 'the Church' has a role in commending Scripture, it is the Church in a particular sense: 'Now by the Church we understand not, as they [the Romanists] do, the pastors, bishops, councils, pope; but the whole multitude of the faithful. For this whole multitude hath learned from the Holy Spirit that this Scripture is sacred, that these books are divine.

---

[44]Cranmer, PS, vol. 2, p. 39; cf. pp. 11, 53; Fulke, PS, vol. 2, p. 231; Jewel, PS, vol. 3, pp. 176–7; 4, p. 1109; Ridley, PS, pp. 129–30, 134; Rogers, PS, pp. 207–1.
[45]Jewel, PS, vol. 3, p. 190.
[46]Whitaker, PS, pp. 279–80.

This persuasion the Holy Spirit hath sealed in the minds of all the faithful.'[47] What the Reformers take away from the hierarchy, they give to the whole body; they feel after the concept of the *consensus fidelium*.

The authority of the Church to order its life

The Reformers do not, as is often supposed, minimize the authority of the Church, but they do not necessarily accept the claims of an existing church to be the Church! Luther holds that the true Church is always hidden from profane sight ('The Church is hidden away, the saints are out of sight'), but nevertheless it cannot deviate from the true faith, for Christ abides with his Church until the end of the age (Mt. 28.20). God has always preserved for himself a Church 'among the common people'. When Christ was crucified, the Apostles deserted him and only Joseph of Arimathea, Nicodemus and the penitent thief remained faithful; but those who rejected him were supposedly the people of God. So, throughout history, perhaps those were called the people of God who were not so, while others, a hidden remnant, were in truth the people of God but were not so called. However, in practice we should follow the rule of charity and regard all the baptized as saints of God.[48]

Calvin often speaks about the 'form' of the Church. In his Address to Francis I of France, with which Calvin prefaced the *Institutes* from the first edition of 1536 onward, he rejects the Roman view that 'the form of the Church is always visible and apparent' and that the location of this form is Rome. The form of the Church cannot be known by outwardly impressive attributes of size and strength, which Calvin disparages as 'vain pomp', but only by the signs of the pure preaching of the word and the due administration of the sacraments. Calvin goes as far as to claim that, in extreme circumstances, the Church can exist without any external form and he gives many biblical examples to prove it. Like Luther, he holds that the Church may sometimes be hidden from

---

[47]Ibid.
[48]Luther, *Bondage of the Will*, pp. 119–23.

human gaze, being known only to God.[49] What makes it possible for Calvin to hold, paradoxically, that the visible Church may sometimes be invisible except to the eye of faith is his powerful sense of the mystical dimension of the Church, the elect people of God, which is partly on earth and partly in heaven. However, even when the Church may hardly be visible, it does not cease to exist, for 'God wondrously preserves his Church, while placing it as it were in concealment.'[50] (The catholic doctrine of the indefectibility of the Church is affirmed by the Reformers.) But for Calvin, unlike Luther, the obscurity of the Church is exceptional. Calvin discourses at length on the role and authority of the visible Church. She is Mother Church; her fellowship and nurture are indispensable: '[T]here is no other means of entering into life unless she conceive us in the womb and give us birth, unless she nourish us at her breasts, and, in short, keep us under her charge and government, until, divested of mortal flesh, we become like the angels.' We cannot graduate from this Dame School of the Church until we have spent our whole lives as scholars. We therefore heed her authority as dutiful members of Christ's flock. Like Luther, Calvin castigates the hyper-spiritual people, the fanatics, who disparage the external means of grace and claim direct revelations of the Holy Spirit. He echoes the old adage *Extra ecclesiam nulla salus*, Outside the Church there is no salvation.[51]

Article XXXIV of the Thirty-nine Articles of the Church of England upholds the authority of the Church: 'Every particular or national Church (*quaelibet ecclesia particularis siue nationalis*) hath authority to ordain, change, and abolish, ceremonies or rites of the church, ordained only by man's authority, so that all things be done to edifying.' In asserting the right of a church to make laws to regulate its worship, government and life, this article cuts two ways, first against Rome, which resisted the claims of national churches to reform themselves, and second against the extreme reformists who believed in a biblical blueprint for every aspect of life and that this blueprint was embodied in 'the best reformed churches', especially Calvin's and Beza's Geneva. Against both, the

---

[49]*Institutes*, vol. 1, pp. 14–17.
[50]Ibid., IV, i, 2: vol. 2, pp. 281–2.
[51]Ibid., IV, i, 3–5: vol. 2, pp. 283–5. See further on Luther's and Calvin's ecclesiology, Avis, *Church in the Theology of the Reformers*, Part 1; 'Church and Ministry'.

Church of England in its official formularies maintained the right and duty of a particular or national church to govern itself. There must be uniformity within the realm, but a uniformity imposed from Rome or Geneva is rejected: 'It is not necessary that Traditions and Ceremonies be in all places one, and utterly like; for at all times they have been divers, and may be changed according to the diversities of countries, times, and men's manners, [yet] so that nothing be ordained against God's Word.'

It was a fundamental plank of the English Reformation that, just as a particular, national church had the right and duty to undertake reforms without prejudicing its catholicity, so too a diversity of ceremonies and outward order between particular churches did not betoken a breach of unity in saving faith. The Henrician formularies declared that the unity of the 'one, catholic church is a mere spiritual unity', consisting in 'the unity which is in one God, one faith, one doctrine of Christ and his sacraments'. This essential spiritual unity is not destroyed by the various 'outward rites, ceremonies, traditions and ordinances' instituted by proper local authority. The churches of England, Spain, Italy and Poland 'be not separate from the unity, but be one church in God, notwithstanding that among them there is great distance of place, diversity of traditions, not in all things unity of opinions, alteration in rites, ceremonies, and ordinances, or estimation of the same.' Such outward differences are neither commanded by Scripture nor necessary to salvation; they make no difference to eternal destiny; they are *adiaphora*.[52] Philip Melanchthon's exposition of adiaphorism in the 1535 edition of his *Loci Communes* (Commonplaces), dedicated to Henry VIII, was imbibed by Thomas Starkey and thus became (notes Zeeveld) the direct ideological forebear of developed Anglican polity.[53]

Cranmer concluded his first (1549) and prefaced his second Prayer Book (1552) with a statement 'Of Ceremonies' which maintained that matters of 'discipline and order . . . upon just causes may be altered and changed and therefore are not to be esteemed equal with God's law.' And Cranmer added, 'In these our doings we condemn no other nations, nor prescribe anything but to our own people only.' For Cranmer, the corporate principle was

---

[52]Lloyd, *Formularies of Faith*, pp. 56, 246–7; Verkamp, *Indifferent Mean*, p. 139.
[53]Zeeveld, *Foundations of Tudor Policy*; for Thomas Starkey, even the papacy was an *adiaphoron* (pp. 151–6).

supreme. His stress was on the common good; communal activity was the highest good for man. Once again we see the continuity between the Henrican and Edwardian conception of the national Church, on the one hand, and the Christian political philosophy of Richard Hooker, on the other. Hooker would provide the philosophical principles underlying Anglican claims for the power of the Church to make laws, in his distinction between mutable and immutable positive law in the third book of the *Ecclesiastical Polity*, but in doing so Hooker stood in continuity with the stance of the English Reformers and – surprising as it may seem to some – John Calvin.

In asserting the power of the Church to make laws, the Thirty-nine Articles had Calvin on their side against the more biblicistic Protestants. While Zwingli, Bucer and German-speaking Swiss theology laid the foundations of the Puritan legalism that appealed to the Bible – and to both Testaments equally – as a book of laws and precedents, Calvin himself exhibited a humanistic reasonableness in this matter and operated with a tacit concept of *adiaphora,* things indifferent. In his treatment in the *Institutes* (IV, x) of the Church's power to make laws, Calvin employs the distinction, so crucial to Reformation theology, between things necessary to salvation and things indifferent, of merely human origin, which cannot bind the conscience. Calvin's attack is directed against laws of the Church enforcing rites, ceremonies and observances as an obligation of conscience and necessary to salvation, so laying burdens on Christian folk that are more than they can bear. He specifically excludes from his critique the 'sacred and useful constitutions of the church which tend to preserve discipline, decency or peace'. Hooker was able to make considerable play of the fact that Calvin had upheld the right of the church to make laws to regulate its life, in upholding the prerogatives of the Church of England against the radical reformers such as Cartwright who would have permitted nothing not explicitly laid down in Scripture. Calvin holds that while 'the whole sum of righteousness, and all the parts of divine worship, and everything necessary to salvation' is clearly revealed in Scripture, 'in external discipline and ceremonies' the Lord has not prescribed what should be done, foreseeing that this would vary with times and circumstances: 'in them we must have recourse to the general rules which he has given, employing them to test whatever the necessity of the church may require to be enjoined for order and decency'.

The Church has the freedom to change and abolish old forms and to introduce new to meet a changed situation. Calvin is impatient with the scrupulous legalism that continually intrudes on Christian liberty. 'What, is religion placed in a woman's bonnet . . .? Is her silence fixed by a decree which cannot be violated . . .?' In such matters, custom, humanity and modesty should be our guide.[54]

The Thirty-nine Articles also maintained that, besides her power to decide rites or ceremonies, the Church has 'authority in controversies of faith', though she cannot ordain anything contrary to Scripture or enforce any such decrees as necessary for salvation (Article XX). The English Reformers in their writings support this claim. The Church has authority not only in deciding rites, ceremonies and things indifferent,[55] but also in controversies of faith.[56] But she has no authority to make new articles of faith and cannot bind things left free by the gospel.[57] Nothing can be enforced by the Church that is not grounded in the word of God, and the church cannot forbid what the Apostles permitted.[58]

The doctrinal authority of the monarch

In this book, we are not really concerned with the 'political' structures of authority, the workings of conciliarity in the Church, but rather with the use of authority in theological method. However, we need to touch briefly on the question of what, if any, doctrinal authority the sovereign enjoyed in the reformed English Church – the monarch as interpreter of Scripture and tradition.[59] The nascent reformed Church of England appealed from the jurisdiction of the pope to the only available alternative source of ecclesiastical jurisdiction, that of its 'Supreme Head in earth, so far as the law of Christ allows' (Henry VIII and Edward VI) or 'Supreme Governor' (Elizabeth I and all subsequent monarchs to the present day). Henry,

---

[54]*Inst.* IV, *passim*, esp. 30–1.
[55]Rogers, PS, p. 184; Whitaker, PS, p. 507; Whitgift, PS, vol. 1, pp. 180, 222.
[56]Whitaker, PS, p. 190.
[57]Coverdale, PS, vol. 2, pp. 338, 418; cf. 422.
[58]Philpott, PS, pp. 344, 379; Rogers, PS, p. 201.
[59]See further Avis, *Church in the Theology of the Reformers*, chs. 9 ('The Godly Prince') and 10 ('The Royal Supremacy').

while repudiating any claim to headship in the mystical body of the church – his role, he insisted, was confined to the government of its outward order and to the headship of all estates of the realm, including the clerical estate – had certainly taken it upon himself to promulgate doctrine in consultation with his spiritual advisers. He had been encouraged in his theological ambitions not only by the civil lawyers but by Archbishop Cranmer himself.[60] Elizabeth, on the other hand, exhibited some diffidence – either out of conscience or political astuteness – about her supremacy in the church. Ostensibly at least, she declined any 'superiority . . . to define decide or determine any article or point of the Christian faith and religion.'[61] Appended to the queen's Injunctions of 1559 was an Admonition drawn up by Cecil which denied that 'the kings and queens of this realm may challenge authority and power of ministry of divine offices in the church' and added, 'Certainly her majesty neither doth, nor ever will challenge any other authority.' Her claim was only 'under God to have the sovereignty and rule over all manner of persons born within her realms . . . of which estate, either ecclesiastical or temporal . . . so as no other foreign power shall or ought to have any superiority over them.' Article XXXVII of the Thirty-nine Articles of Religion refers to these Injunctions when it says, 'Where we attribute to the Queen's Majesty the chief government, by which Titles we understand the minds of some slanderous folks to be offended; we give not to our Princes the ministering either of God's Word, or of the Sacraments . . . but only that prerogative, which we see to have been given always to all godly Princes in Holy Scriptures by God himself; that is, that they should rule all estates and degrees committed to their charge by God, whether they be Ecclesiastical or Temporal.' Richard Hooker and his near contemporary Richard Field reinforced this restricted interpretation of the royal supremacy. Hooker went beyond the facts in reducing the royal role to purely temporal matters. As Claire Cross has pointed out, while apologists made much of the distinction between jurisdiction and doctrine, 'the complexities of Tudor politics did not allow a monarch's actions to fit into these

---

[60]Scarisbrick, *Henry VIII*, pp. 364–5, 521–43. For Henry's personal religious policy see Bernard, *King's Reformation*.
[61]Haugaard, *Elizabeth and the English Reformation*, p. 237.

neat categories'.[62] The 'intuitive flashes of sagacity or caprice' which dictated Elizabeth's conduct of affairs baffled the theorists of the Elizabethan settlement.[63]

At the accession of Elizabeth I, Bishop Bonner presented to the Queen, on behalf of the Convocation of Canterbury, six resolutions: of these, the fifth specifically denied the right of the laity to handle or define matters touching the faith, sacraments and discipline of the church. It was the swansong of unreformed clericalism. The Elizabethan settlement of religion established a significant role for the laity in the Church of England. Elton called it 'the triumph of the laity'. The Church of England that emerged from the vicissitudes of the sixteenth century was a lay Christian's church in which, provided outward conformity was satisfied, a large area of private opinion and practice remained free. By the end of Elizabeth's reign, it had been established that the supremacy lay in the-Queen-in-Parliament. It is significant that the Act of Supremacy of 1559, which referred to the Scriptures and General Councils as the criteria of orthodoxy and heresy, went on to give Parliament, with bishops in the House of Lords as, so to speak, the synod of the Church, power to determine what was heretical 'with the assent of the clergy in their convocation'.[64] This Act took the determination of right and wrong doctrine out of the hands not only of the pope, but also of the queen and her successors – at least in theory.

To leap way beyond the scope of this chapter: in the twentieth century, with the so-called Enabling Act of 1919 and the creation of the General Synod in 1970, followed by the Doctrine and Worship Measure 1974, the Church of England would receive from a Parliament, which had long ceased to be in any meaningful sense the synod of the Church of England, her own decision-making bodies, with competence in the spheres of doctrine and worship. While a Reformation principle of the theological competence of the laity was carried forward from the sixteenth century as a permanent feature of the Anglican faith, it is worth noting at this point that there is nothing in the Church of England of

---

[62]Cross, *Royal Supremacy*, p. 18; cf. 69.
[63]Dixon, *History*, vol. 6, p. 3.
[64]Elton, *Tudor Constitution*, p. 368.

today, or in her sister Churches of the Anglican Communion, that corresponds even remotely to the theological office that Henry VIII appropriated for himself.[65]

The liturgical expression of doctrine

If there are liberties and privileges of the individual Christian under the gospel, there are also liberties and privileges of the Christian Church. It can regulate its life and adjudicate in theological debate. But this power is subject to two constraints: first, in all essential matters affecting salvation, the Scriptures speak with a clear and decisive voice, and second, the individual conscience is answerable to its Maker alone (in Luther's phrase *coram Deo*, before the face of God). There is a principle of moderation at work here which is opposed to any absolute authority that oppresses the conscience and eliminates doubt, and therefore trust, from our walk of faith; and there is a principle of reticence in the area of Christian dogma: what is revealed is what we need to know, no more. The Thirty-nine Articles (1563) reflect these aspects of the embryonic Anglican philosophy. They emerged from a continual process of replication and revision going back to the formularies of Henry's reign. As such they incorporated both the corporate, conservative principle that did not lightly depart from tradition, which characterized much of the English Reformation, and the progressive, critical principle, that judged tradition, including Fathers and Councils by the touchstone of Scripture, without which there could have been no Reformation.

The Thirty-nine Articles typify this approach: they are not only selective – addressing what needed to be addressed at the time – but also generally reserved in their assertions, speaking out sharply only when it was necessary to correct some specific error. The Articles do not prescribe the full range of Christian doctrines. The Victorian Church historian R. W. Dixon claimed that the Articles stood on a higher level than the argumentative Protestant confessions of the Continent (though he could not have intended to include the

---

[65]On Church-State relations in England in the twentieth century see Avis, *Church, State and Establishment*.

Augsburg Confession or many of the Reformation catechisms in that description) and the anathematizing tone of the Council of Trent. The Articles, Dixon, declared, 'dogmatise without arguing; they affirm without offering proof; they deal neither in expostulation nor rebuke. They are not apologetic. Completeness of form is their character.'[66]

It was nevertheless necessary (and still is) for the full orbit of Christian truth, as received by the reformed English Church, to be expressed. This role fell to the liturgy, to the Book of Common Prayer (BCP). The doctrinal limitations of the Articles, which are not accidental, cast more weight on the liturgy: on the doctrinal scales the Articles are light, the BCP heavy. The Articles do not stand alone, as the sole instantiation of Anglican doctrine; they stand alongside the liturgy and the Ordinal, all three being 'historic formularies' for the Church of England today.[67] There is a complementarity of doctrinal sources here.

For the Churches of the Anglican Communion, perhaps more than for any other church except the Orthodox, the liturgy in the broadest sense has a doctrinal and confessional function: it is the place where, particularly, Anglican beliefs are articulated, where a Christian theological worldview is expressed – expressed not in cut and dried propositions, but poetically and doxologically. The ancient principle *lex orandi, lex credendi* (the rule of prayer is the rule of belief) is of course not confined to Anglicans, for all Christians aspire to pray as they believe and believe as they pray.[68] But Anglican Churches are churches that conceive their relation to Christian doctrine liturgically.[69] They state their doctrines in the liturgical register. To understand historic Anglican teaching, we need to turn to the liturgy, rather than to the Thirty-nine Articles alone. The Anglican instantiation of the principle *lex orandi, lex credendi* in the successive editions of the BCP is a further aspect of Archbishop Thomas Cranmer's genius and perhaps his chief legacy,

---

[66]Dixon, *History*, vol. 5, pp. 394–5.
[67]Canon C 15. 'Preface to the Declaration of Assent'.
[68]*Lex orandi legem statuat credendi*: the rule of prayer establishes the rule of faith. Alternative version: *legem credendi lex statuat supplicandi*: Let the law of prayer establish the law of belief. The formula derives from Prosper of Aquitaine, c. 435–42. See further Wainwright, *Doxology*, chs VII and VIII.
[69]O'Donovan, *Thirty-nine Articles*, p. viii.

one for which we can never be sufficiently grateful.[70] The BCP has therefore been aptly described as the 'hermeneutical key' to the understanding of the Anglican tradition.[71]

The collects of the BCP, in the drafting and collating of which Cranmer played a major role, have a special significance in articulating Christian belief for Anglicans. Elegant and beautiful as the collects almost all are, they are condensed expressions of spiritual theology, addressed to God. Collects gather up – 'collect' – the spoken and unspoken prayers, hopes and longings of those using them to aid their worship; they rehearse God's gracious acts in salvation history or appeal to God's revealed character in Jesus Christ and on that premise seek good and salutary things from God. The salience of the collects in everyday Anglican spirituality, including their use in private devotions, highlights the fact that as Anglicans we aim to do our theology in a doxological way and we seek to pray with reflective theological integrity.[72]

---

[70]Ibid.

[71]Griffiss, *Anglican Vision*, p. 109.

[72]Cf. Dudley, *Collect in Anglican Liturgy*, p. 43. See also Nichols (ed.), *Collect in the Churches of the Reformation*. Further on this topic see Avis, 'Book of Common Prayer'.

3

Richard Hooker's theological method

'Learned', 'godly', 'judicious', 'eloquent', 'incomparable' – these are a few of the superlatives that have been applied, in the four centuries since his death, to Richard Hooker (1553/4–1600). Hooker's great work, *Of the Laws of Ecclesiastical Polity*, is a great deal more about heaven and earth than the 'polity' – that is to say the organization and governance – of the Church, that the title suggests. It traverses the landscape of the Church's faith and order as the reformed English Church had received it and reshapes it in stronger continuity with the resources of Western Christendom as a whole. Hooker's achievement was to strengthen the catholicity of the Reformation in England, helping to pull the Church of England back into balance after the excesses – the sacramental reductionism and devastating iconoclasm – of the Edwardian regime.[1] Hooker's contemporaries, both supporters and critics, saw at once that he had done a new thing. He had enlarged the envelope of official English theology. He had reinstated the beauty of holiness. He had begun to change how the Church of England thought about the Church. Although the reception of Hooker's work had a chequered history, he undoubtedly put his unique stamp on emerging Anglicanism, not least on its understanding of authority.[2]

---

[1]See generally MacCulloch, *Tudor Church*. For the iconoclasm see Duffy, *Stripping of the Altars*, ch. 13, and for local detail, id., *Voices of Morebath*, chs. 5 and 6.
[2]For Hooker's legacy and standing in the eyes of posterity see Eccleshall, 'Richard Hooker and the Peculiarities of the English'; Condren, 'Creation of Richard Hooker's Public Authority'; Lake, 'Business as Usual?'; Brydon, *Evolving Reputation*; MacCulloch, 'Richard Hooker's Reputation'; Kirby (ed.), *Companion to Richard Hooker* is probably the best comprehensive, in-depth introduction to Hooker. The most enjoyable brief account of Hooker is probably Trevor-Roper, 'Richard Hooker and the Church of England', in *Renaissance Essays*.

Understanding Richard Hooker

Richard Hooker is the prime architect of what later became recognizably 'Anglican' ecclesiology, the pre-eminent Anglican theologian of all time. Hooker has sometimes been credited with 'inventing' Anglicanism and its supposed 'middle way', but this is to speak crudely and anachronistically. Hooker does not use the term 'Anglicanism' and nowhere speaks of a *via media*.[3] To credit Hooker alone with the invention of what later developed into Anglicanism as we know it is to overlook the contributions of the English Reformers themselves, especially Archbishop Thomas Cranmer and his Prayer Books and Bishop John Jewel and his *Apologia*, not to mention the personal policy and example of Queen Elizabeth I. However, Hooker remains a primary source, along with these figures, of the profile of Anglican ideology that emerges in the mid-seventeenth century, and also something of a precedent since his work already contains strong intimations of that later platform. Hooker is the progenitor of several distinctive aspects of the Anglican expression of the Christian Church, not only ecclesiology in a narrow sense, but also sacramental theology and moral theology.[4]

Hooker's authorial *persona* – mild, irenic and reconciling – has often been taken at face value, but this is actually to be taken in. Hooker is a highly effective controversialist who knows how to manipulate his readers to gain his ends. Lee Gibbs presents Hooker as 'an Elizabethan polemicist. . . .'[5] To highlight this aspect seems unnecessarily narrow, though it counteracts the 'too-good-for-this-world' image of Hooker put out by Izaac Walton in his *Life* (1665) and followed by many writers on Hooker ever since. Perhaps it is still necessary, in spite of C. J. Sisson's work 75 years ago, to scotch the myths propagated by Walton of Hooker as a devoted parish priest forced to tend the sheep on his glebe land, rocking the baby's cradle while trying to read a book, henpecked by a shrewish wife, a man of 'humble, modest, dove-like character'.[6] In fact Hooker had married into wealth and his wife, Joan Churchman,

---

[3]MacCulloch, 'Richard Hooker's Reputation', p. 564.
[4]Joyce, *Richard Hooker and Moral Theology*.
[5]Gibbs in Kirby (ed.), *Companion*, p. 1.
[6]Walton, *Lives*; Novarr, *Making of Walton's* Lives; Martin, *Walton's* Lives; Sisson, *Judicious Marriage*.

was good to him. He did not always reside in his parishes. He may well have been saintly, but if so he was also 'as wise as a serpent' and certainly not 'as harmless as a dove'. Hooker was certainly polemical, but is that really what we remember him for? It is true that, as Patterson puts it, in that age 'Theologians of all points of view wrote in a venomous way that suggested violent intentions towards their adversaries.'[7] By this criterion, as Patterson points out, 'Hooker was unlike his contemporaries. . . . He stands apart from theologians who were intent on ridiculing, belittling or demonizing their opponents,' though he adds that Hooker had 'his own special kind of polemic'.[8] He did indeed, and he is not beyond a bit of ridiculing or belittling, though that is not his favoured register. Hooker was accused by his puritan adversaries (in *A Christian Letter*, 1599) of being (among other things) a 'rhetorician' – and so he was, immensely skilled in persuading and in fact manipulating his audience.[9] As Joyce points out, Hooker was capable of 'the most waspish, acerbic and irreverent assaults' on those he was taking to task, not only contemporary Puritans, but also Calvin himself.[10] But the fact that he employs rhetorical skills does not mean that he was not seeking a change of heart and mind, a genuine conversion of his opponents; only that he goes about it in a formidably effective way. So much so that, apart from *A Christian Letter* – an almost equally crafty attempt to traduce Hooker by deploying the writings of Reformation worthies, especially Cranmer and Jewel, against him and majoring on his rhetorical tactics – Hooker was not answered in his lifetime, though the gap between publication of his first five books and his death was short. The opposition got its revenge in the 1640s, in the years leading up to the English Civil War and the rule of Oliver Cromwell, when Parliament comprehensively dismantled the Church of England's episcopate, liturgy, Christian calendar and cathedral foundations, executing first the Archbishop of Canterbury (William Laud) and then the Church of England's Supreme Governor (Charles I). But for the time being, as the Bishop of Exeter, John Gauden, one of Hooker's later editors, put it in 1662,

---

[7] Patterson in Kirby (ed.), *Companion*, p. 89.
[8] Ibid., pp. 110–11.
[9] Hooker, Folger edn, vol. 4, pp. 1–79. See also R. P. Almasy in Kirby (ed.), *Companion*, pp. 121–50; Vickers, 'Public and Private Rhetoric'.
[10] Joyce, *Hooker and Moral Theology*, p. 51. See her whole discussion, pp. 45–66.

Hooker 'did cast the tortoise of Non-conformity upon its back'. I don't think that, as Joyce suggests, Hooker's formidable methods of argument make him any less 'judicious': to be judicious is not necessarily to be dispassionate and it is certainly not to be naive or innocent.

Because Hooker was little answered in his own time and since then has been deployed (and still is) tendentiously, it has taken until the late twentieth and early twenty-first centuries for Hooker's work to be subjected to rigorous, comprehensive and comparative analysis on the basis of a definitive text. There is no shortage of tendentious and idiosyncratic interpretations of Hooker's theology, the crux here often being Hooker's relation to the main-line Protestant theology of the magisterial Reformers, particularly Calvin. The main advocates of Hooker as a Reformed theologian are Nigel Atkinson, Torrance Kirby and, more subtly, Nigel Voak.[11] Their arguments should not be dismissed, as they are by some. These scholars have a point. Hooker was nurtured on Reformed theology and had deeply imbibed Calvin. He is no less a theologian of sovereign grace than Calvin himself.[12] But Hooker cannot be described as a Reformed theologian *tout court*. Of course, Hooker operates within the Reformation ambiance, but he ranges much more widely; he is eclectic, discriminating, and not an exponent of any one school of thought. We should let Hooker be his own man. Undeniably, Hooker (together with Lancelot Andrewes) speaks a different language from that of the English Reformers, but it is a language that is enriched and enlarged, not discontinuous with what went before. Hooker has a seminal place in the ongoing, unfolding English Reformation, which should not be seen as something complete before he arrived on the scene, a fixed benchmark against which he can be judged, but as an unfolding process, one that arguably continued at least until 1662. The fact that it has taken the direction it has up to the present owes much to Richard Hooker.[13]

There is nothing new in theological protagonists attempting to wrest Hooker to their own ends: he had been firmly appropriated

---

[11]Atkinson, *Hooker and the Authority of Scripture*; Kirby, *Hooker's Doctrine*; Voak, *Hooker and Reformed Theology*. A more extreme and less scholarly, example of forcing Hooker into a Reformed procrustean bed is Simuț, *Hooker and his Early Doctrine*.

[12]Cf. Rasmussen, 'Priority of God's Gracious Action'.

[13]Cf. Church, 'Bishop Andrewes', in *Pascal and Other Sermons*, esp. pp. 65–77.

for this role by the beginning of the eighteenth century.[14] The *Ecclesiastical Polity* was barely resisted at the time that it appeared: it is indeed 'incredible' that only one challenge – the so-called 'A Christian Letter' – was published in Hooker's lifetime.[15] Hooker had set out to be unanswerable and had succeeded. Nevertheless, Hooker achieved his position of pre-eminence among Anglican divines only gradually. He was claimed by the Laudians and by the group who foreshadowed the later liberal Anglicans, notably by Chillingworth; by Clarendon and Hammond in the period before the Restoration of the monarchy and Church. He was explicitly attacked by Scottish authors (George Gillespie) and by Richard Baxter. It was the high, Laudian estimation of Hooker that prevailed, though when the later books were published, their moderation with regard to episcopacy and monarchy was not palatable to the High Church victors of 1660–62.

Brydon repeatedly suggests that Hooker is intrinsically ambiguous.[16] It gives food for thought that, while some of our contemporary exponents of Hooker can claim him as a card-carrying Reformed theologian, King James II attributed his own conversion to Roman Catholicism to his reading of Hooker (which his father, King Charles I, had urged upon his sons at the end of his life). Brydon's phrase 'elusive and often idiosyncratic formulations' is apt.[17] Those Puritan critics who complained that Hooker was obscure had a valid point. Like the Bible and Shakespeare, Hooker provides an inexhaustible fund of interpretations. But that does not mean that we cannot establish clearly enough Hooker's intention, any more than that there is no coherent meaning running through the Scriptures or that Shakespeare is really 'a nose of wax' to be moulded to our whims.

Hooker on authority in theology

What is so impressive about Richard Hooker is the way that he welds together all available sources of knowledge and insight about things human and divine. Hooker combines a commitment

---

[14]Brydon, *Evolving Reputation*.
[15]Ibid., p. 22.
[16]Ibid., pp. 104, 156, 203.
[17]Ibid., p. 203.

to Scripture that is second to none with a recognition of other vital sources of authority that are needed either to interpret or to supplement Scripture. Hooker yields nothing to Calvin or the English Puritans in his knowledge and deployment of the Bible. But he does not think that the Bible is all that is needed. He sees the hand of God guiding the Church in other ways too. As Rowan Williams paraphrases Hooker: 'God teaches by many means, and we do no honour to God or to the Bible by imagining that all God might wish to say to us can be contained in one volume.'[18]

Hooker was a highly original thinker and one difficult to categorize (supposing that we wished to do that; some do). He cannot simply be recruited into the ranks of the 'magisterial' Reformers (Luther, Calvin, Bucer, Bullinger, etc.) on behalf of Anglicanism. On the other hand, he is no slavish follower of Thomas Aquinas, though his debt to the Angelic Doctor (and therefore to Aristotle) is immense, especially on natural law, moral reasoning, virtue and character. He calls Aquinas 'the greatest amongst the Schoole divines'.[19] He stands in the Erasmian tradition of Christian humanism: he has been called 'a God-centred Humanist'.[20] Hooker died, still only in his mid-40s, in 1600, his own man to the end, but with three of his eight books unpublished.

Hooker's learning is awesome: texts biblical and classical; theology patristic, medieval and reformed; law civil and ecclesiastical. He has a remarkable sense of history for his time and explicitly identifies 64 historians, though this number does not exhaust his historical sources. For Hooker, the English Church is the product of its own history. His method is historically perceptive: he sets events and concepts in a temporal perspective informed by documentary evidence. Like his Tudor predecessors and his eighteenth-century successor Edmund Burke, Hooker values custom as the embodiment of reason in particular circumstances and takes a preferential option for what is already established.[21]

Hooker's creative use of diverse sources led one of his modern interpreters to claim that 'Hooker's outstanding characteristic as a

---

[18]Rowan Williams, Foreword to Kirby (ed.), *Companion*, p. xix.

[19]*EP*, III, ix, 2: 1, p. 236.

[20]Willey, *English Moralists*, p. 102.

[21]Ferguson, *Clio Unbound*, pp. 207–22 (the chapter on Hooker incorporates the substance of Ferguson's article 'Historical Perspective of Hooker').

thinker is his eclecticism'.[22] But it seems to me that eclecticism is simply a condition of the richness and depth of Hooker's thinking, not the key to it. What is most striking is his unifying power as a synthesizer of ideas and traditions. Nearly a century and a half ago, the second-generation Tractarian R. W. Church designated Hooker's view of authority as 'the concurrence and co-operation, each in its due place, of all possible means of knowledge for man's direction'.[23] This gets closer to the heart of the matter, but Hooker goes further than cooperation and concurrence, as though various streams of thought merely existed in parallel in his mind and travelled in the same direction. Hooker achieves a unified worldview in which it is no longer easy – perhaps no longer possible – to disentangle the various contributory strands.

The idea that Anglican theological method draws on Scripture, tradition and reason, in roughly equal measure and in that order, is often attributed to Hooker. In reality, it is little more than an urban myth. The truth of the matter is much more subtle and a lot more interesting. For Hooker, the hierarchy of authorities was Scripture, reason and the Church. But how he understood the authority of Scripture, what he meant by reason, and where tradition fits in are questions that, if we allow Hooker to be our guide, take us into a disarmingly sublime realm of theological contemplation where we struggle to keep our critical faculties alert. If, as recent scholarship has highlighted, Hooker was a master of rhetorical manipulation, engaged in an ideological battle with Elizabethan Puritanism, that does not mean that he was wrong in what he taught.

The realm of law

Hooker grounds his argument in first principles; he finds these given in the realm of law, permeating the universe and reflecting the nature of God whose being is a law unto his working. And this realm of law is a unity. For Hooker (as in fact for the Reformers as much as for Thomas Aquinas), natural law and biblical (moral) law are 'all one' (*EP*, III, ix, 2: 1, p. 237). Torrance Kirby makes

---

[22]Thompson, 'The Philosopher of the "Politic Society",' p. 21.
[23]Church (ed.), *Book I Of the Laws*: http://www.archive.org/stream/a587912800 hookuoft/a587912800hookuoft_djvu.txt

the point strongly, though overstating it, when he claims that for Hooker, 'God is Law'.[24] To say as Hooker does, that 'the being of God is a kinde of lawe to his working: for that perfection which God is, geveth perfection to that he doth' (*EP*, I, ii, 2: 1, p. 59), is not the same as to suggest that God is law without remainder or that law is adequate to define the divine nature. As Hooker himself summarizes with regard to the role of law: 'her seate is the bosome of God, her voyce the harmony of the world' (*EP*, I, xvi, 8: 1, p. 142). However, Kirby is near the mark when he speaks of 'Hooker's reconciliation of a Neoplatonic ontology of participation with a Reformed soteriology'.[25] But I cannot follow Kirby when he goes on to refer to Hooker's 'difficulty in reconciling the authority of the natural law with the core assumptions of Reformation soteriology and scriptural hermeneutics'.[26] I think Hooker manages the synthesis very elegantly. As Kirby himself correctly points out, it is 'a commonplace of the exegesis of the reformers that the twofold obligation to honor God and deal justly with one's neighbor is taught by both natural and divine law. The interplay between the natural and the revealed knowledge of God gives shape to the magisterial reformers' complex, dialectical approach to the authority of natural law; and the theory of natural law in turn constitutes a critical link between theology and ethics in their thought.'[27] Hooker's difficulty was not with the legacy of the magisterial Reformers generally, but with the radically different biblical hermeneutic employed by the Puritans. As Grislis puts it, 'With regard to soteriology. . . . Hooker was close to the moderate Puritans. Ecclesiology, however, was a different matter.'[28]

Divine law is inscribed in the Scriptures and is interpreted by human reason under the guidance of the wisdom of the past. That wisdom is embedded in practices that have stood the test of time by effectively enabling the participation of Christians in the life of God the Holy Trinity (our fellowship with 'God, Angels, and holie men': *EP*, I, xv, 2: 1, p. 131). Nature and grace, the secular and the sacred, are not polarized as they are in some aspects of

---

[24]Kirby in Kirby (ed.), *Companion*, pp. 251–2.
[25]Ibid., p. 260.
[26]Ibid., p. 261.
[27]Ibid., p. 266.
[28]E. Grislis in ibid., p. 273.

the Reformers' theology, but are complementary and integrated. Ingalls demonstrates Hooker's continuity with the magisterial Reformers, in the tradition of Augustine of Hippo, but shows that this allegiance is not incompatible with Hooker's major debt to Aquinas.[29] The Incarnation is the touchstone. 'It would have been unthinkable to Hooker that reformed faith should represent a departure from Christological orthodoxy, as indeed it would have been to earlier magisterial reformers. It is therefore a mistake to approach Hooker with the assumption that the reformed doctrine of justification excludes the principle that grace does not destroy but perfects nature.'[30] For example, the Church herself is not purely the supernatural, mystical Church, but also a political body or society, with structures of governance that reflect the practical wisdom of political philosophy. It follows that it is inappropriate to look for precise biblical precepts or precedents for the outward ordering of the Church's life. Fundamental biblical principles are, so to speak, mediated by and embodied in human political forms, governed by positive law. Every particular (national) church has the authority within itself to regulate its life according to reason and a sense of what is appropriate to the circumstances, but in a way that is consonant with Scripture and not contrary to it.

Although Hooker is a deeply biblical thinker and his goal is the mystical participation of the Christian in the life and grace of God the Holy Trinity through the sacraments, there is undoubtedly an element of expediency and pragmatism in Hooker's approach, which is justified by his taxonomy of law: divine and human, natural and positive (and it is important to note that positive law as well as natural law can be given by God for a particular, temporary purpose). Thus, Hooker argues against the Presbyterian Puritans that episcopacy is to be retained in the Church, but concedes that the Church could survive temporarily without bishops in extreme circumstances. Again: the royal supremacy in church and state is, for Hooker, a God-given institution, but the sovereign rules by consent and is subject to the law of the land, so cannot act arbitrarily. Hooker is an inheritor and perpetuator

---

[29]Munz, *Place of Hooker*.
[30]R. Ingalls in Kirby (ed.), *Companion*, p. 183.

of the pre-Reformation Conciliar Movement which held that authority resides in the whole body of the Church, in principle laity as well as clergy, and is to be exercised in a constitutional and representative way.[31]

Hooker, Luther and the Puritans

It was in controversy with the radical Puritans within the Church of England that Hooker developed the foundations of an Anglican understanding of authority. It was an argument internal to the Church of England. Puritans, notably Hooker's opponents Thomas Cartwright and Walter Travers, took the Reformation 'Scripture principle' in a new direction, that of *sola scriptura*.[32] For Luther, Scripture was the only sure guide to the way of salvation, and justification by faith was the touchstone of scriptural meaning. Contrary to a common misconception, Luther also looked to Scripture to show how Christians should live the life of faith, the Christian ethic. He was not so obsessed with justification by faith without works as to forget, as not only Roman Catholic writers have tediously alleged, that if faith is present in the heart and life, Christ is present and where Christ is present all works of charity will follow. 'O it is a living, busy, active, mighty thing, this faith. It is impossible for it not to be doing good works incessantly.'[33]

The work of Tuomo Mannermaa and his colleagues in the so-called Finnish School of Luther studies is the antidote to the caricature of Luther's theology that has been perpetrated by scholars of all traditions over many years.[34] The fact that Luther articulated his theology by means of provocative and often outrageous paradoxes is no excuse for the failure of many scholars to make the basic effort of understanding that any creative thinker demands. The heart of

---

[31]See further Avis, *Beyond the Reformation?*, and with reference to Hooker and conciliarism, pp. 142–8.

[32]Pearson, *Thomas Cartwright*; id., *Church and State*: Cartwright rejected the Magisterial Reformers' concept of the godly prince governing the Church on the Old Testament model (p. 12); Knox, *Walter Travers: Paragon of Elizabethan Puritanism* (London: Methuen, 1962).

[33]*LW*, vol. 35, p. 370.

[34]See Mannermaa, *Christ Present in Faith*; Braaten and Jenson (eds.), *Union with Christ*.

Luther's theology was corrupted by the claim – popularized notably by Louis Bouyer (Roman Catholic) and Eric Mascall (Anglo-Catholic) – that Luther was in thrall to a 'vicious extrinsicism' in the matter of salvation. That is to say that he taught that justification was an external, forensic decree by God that put the penitent sinner in a right relationship with God without effecting any moral change or spiritual renovation in the person. It was, in effect, an act of sleight of hand, awarding the status of righteousness in the sight of God while allowing the Christian to continue to wallow in sin without the power to break free from it. That is not Christianity and it is not what Luther said. The revisionist Finnish school of Luther interpretation, stemming from the work of Mannermaa, has given us new spectacles with which to view Luther's theology, if we needed them. Mannermaa has reclaimed the dimension of *being* in Luther's theology and thus put into perspective the complementary dimension of *act*. In Luther, justification was never merely forensic and external (extrinsic), but always involved spiritual and moral transformation by the indwelling presence of Christ, which was nothing less than the content of faith. As Luther puts it, *in ipsa fide Christus adest:* in the event of faith, Christ is present – that is to say, present within the believer to impart his divine life, love and holiness.[35] Mannermaa argues that Luther's understanding of justification/sanctification, as a single act (not as a dualism or disjunction, which can only be an artificial conceptual construct), is analogous to the Orthodox idea of *theosis*, divinization. This reorientation has obvious immediate implications for Luther's ecclesiology, securing the inseparable connection between faith (in which Christ is present to the individual) and the Church (where Christ is present to the community), and for his ethics (where the recovery of ontology enables us to see the vital place that Luther, along with the other major Reformers, gave to natural law). These Finnish scholars have helped to challenge the assumption made by some Roman Catholic and some Anglican scholars alike, and still perpetrated with apparent impunity, that Luther was the prisoner of a sharply dualistic Nominalism that polarized nature and grace, justification and sanctification, natural law and gospel freedom. On the contrary, the Finns have argued, Luther was no

---

[35] *LW*, vol. 26, p. 129 (1535 *Lectures on Galatians*).

dualist in ethics, any more than he was in justification: the scope of
the natural law embraced creation and redemption, the temporal
order and the Church, faith and reason, the nature of God and the
calling of the Christian. There is one law and principle of self-giving
sacrificial love that runs through the order of creation and the
order of salvation. The Finns have vindicated the instinct of many
nonspecialist readers of Luther who always knew that his wonderful
sense of the intimacy and inwardness of Christ's presence and of
the freedom of a Christian to stand before God and alongside the
neighbour, fully united with Christ, and fulfilling the law of love,
was fundamentally incompatible with the extraordinary dualism so
often attributed to Luther. Perhaps, at last, we can move on from
that caricature.

Although Luther had much to say about the relevance of
Scripture to the Christian life in bringing forth good works, he did
not take the Bible as laying down everything that should be done
in the church, in terms of worship, ministry and governance. As we
have noted previously, Luther was relaxed about carrying forward
many medieval practices, including images and vestments.

Calvin distinguishes the Church's power in relation to the
authority of Scripture in three areas: doctrine, where it is bound to
the word of God in the Bible; jurisdiction, where it has discretion,
but in obedience to biblical principles; and legislation. The Church
cannot make laws to bind the conscience, or require obedience
to laws that are merely of human authority, as though they were
necessary to salvation, as, he says, the Roman Catholic Church
does. 'Our consciences have not to do with men but with God
only.'[36] But Calvin allows wide scope to the church to regulate its
life and worship, provided that everything is done 'decently and
in order' (1 Cor. 14.40). In discipline, ceremonial and forms of
worship, God has not prescribed in every particular what should be
done: God knew that this would depend on circumstances and that
one form would not be suitable for all ages. Therefore, old things
can be abolished and new ones introduced, by the authority of the
Church, as necessity requires. For example, scriptural rules about
the place of women in church – that they should cover their heads

---

[36]*Institutes*, IV, x, 5.

and keep silence – are not binding. In such matters 'the custom and institutions of the country, in short, humanity and the rules of modesty itself' should be our guide.[37]

The radical Puritans could not claim Calvin's authority for their insistence that the Bible was the rule for every aspect of life, especially every aspect of church life. Cartwright went as far as to claim that matters of church discipline and government were necessary to saving faith and even that the Presbyterian polity was part of the gospel itself.[38] Hooker set out to refute the Presbyterian platform and to vindicate episcopacy. But in doing so he broke out of the circle of argument about church polity and took the controversy to a new level. In effect, he tackled the Presbyterian system as a symptom of deeper, underlying issues to do with sources of authority, the nature of the Church and biblical hermeneutics. He believed that the Puritan or extreme Protestant view that Scripture legislates for every detail of life was not only mistaken but dangerous and cruel to those who misguidedly try to practice it.[39]

In refuting the Puritan contention that Scripture alone was the rule governing all the things that might be done by humankind and that all such things are to be found in the Bible (*EP*, II, viii, 5), Hooker clarifies the Anglican view of prescriptive authority in matters of doctrine and practice. He shows the proper place of Scripture, reason, and something else that we broadly call 'tradition', but which for Hooker was more like the teaching, practice and witness of the Church over time; he does not favour the word 'tradition'. Hooker defines each of these discriminatingly and distinctively, but he does not treat them as of equal status, as the unqualified slogan 'Scripture, reason and tradition' might suggest. Reason and tradition minister to our understanding of the revelation of God's truth in Scripture; they can never supplant it. Moreover, he sets them within a perspective created by aesthetic and moral judgement, a cultivated sense of what is fitting in particular circumstances. Finally, he takes away all illusions of infallible certainty and stresses that probability, or moral conviction that falls short of certitude, is our guide to truth.

---

[37]Ibid., IV, x, pp. 30–1.
[38]See *EP*, III, ii, 2n; iii, 2n: 1, pp. 208, 210.
[39]Perrott, 'Hooker and the Problem of Authority'.

Scripture

Hooker's primary source for all his work is the Bible, and this is true even of his more philosophical discourse, notably Book I of the *Ecclesiastical Polity*, which is a philosophical treatise on law. In this short book alone he quotes the Old Testament 50 times, the New Testament 100 times, and the Apocrypha (in the form of The Wisdom of Solomon) six times.[40] The eight books of the *Ecclesiastical Polity* contain a total of 1,373 biblical references. As a Renaissance, humanist scholar, like the Reformers generally, Hooker focuses on the literal or plain meaning of Scripture (though Aquinas has this emphasis too, as we have seen). Hooker rarely interprets the Bible typologically. 'I holde it for a most infallible rule in expositions of sacred scripture, that where a litterall construction will stand, the farthest from the letter is commonlie the worst' (*EP*, V, lix, 2: 2, p. 252).

If Hooker's Prayer Book was the Elizabethan Prayer Book of 1559, a light revision of Cranmer's second book of 1552, which version was his Bible? The King James Bible had not even been thought of when Hooker died in 1600: interestingly, he mainly uses the Geneva Bible, favoured by the Puritans, rather than the official Bishops' Bible, though he sometimes makes his own translation.[41]

In Hooker we see the beginning of an historical understanding in the modern sense, an awareness of the dynamics of becoming and process, both in the cosmos and in history. He has a sense of the whole Church, continuing through the centuries in its various major traditions. Like Lancelot Andrewes, Hooker inhabits and is at home in this world of catholicity. Renaissance scholarship had taught him the importance of historical context for the practice of hermeneutics and he applies this method to the Bible as well as to Church history.[42] Every biblical book was generated by particular circumstances and for a particular purpose and its content is to be understood accordingly (*EP*, I, xiv, 3). I concur with Joyce's verdict on Hooker's use of the Bible: '. . . it remains overwhelmingly the case that the sophistication, subtlety, and originality exhibited by Hooker in his use of scripture, and in his

---

[40]Folger edn, vol. 6, part 1, p. 91.
[41]Ibid., p. 64.
[42]Ibid., pp. 88, 157; Kaye, 'Authority and the Interpretation of Scripture.'

understanding of its nature and purpose, are both remarkable and profound.'[43]

Hooker operates with the Thomistic and late medieval distinction between two complementary sources of knowledge for human life on earth: the light of nature (natural knowledge of God and natural law) and the light of divine revelation in Scripture, both interpreted by reason. Nature follows its ordered course according to natural laws ordained by its creator. When these natural laws are recognized, interpreted and followed by humanity, we have the law of reason. Though nature and reason cannot show us the way of salvation, they overlap with the revealed Scriptures in what they teach. Scripture and nature are neither mutually exclusive nor fundamentally opposed. 'The scripture is fraught even with lawes of nature' (*EP*, I, xii, 1: 1, p. 119).

Where does Hooker stand with regard to the Reformation principle *sola scriptura*?[44] As we have already noted, this slogan is not a particularly helpful key to the teachings of the Reformers with regard to the authority of the Bible: their views not only differed as between Lutherans and the Reformed, but were altogether much more nuanced. However, all the Reformers and Hooker agreed that the terms or conditions of salvation were stated in Scripture and that nothing was to be added from tradition or church practice as a requirement of salvation. Like the later Reformers, Hooker explicitly rejects the teaching of the Council of Trent that 'unwritten verities' should be accorded the same reverence as the Scriptures.[45] In this sense, they all accepted *sola scriptura* as a critical principle, to curtail the claims of tradition and to safeguard or circumscribe the way of salvation for all. '[T]hey which adde traditions as part of supernaturall necessarye truth, have not the truth, but are in error' (*EP*, I, xiv, 5: 1, p. 129).

In several respects, Hooker qualifies the role of Scripture, compared with views that were held by some Reformers and his own contemporaries. First, he does not accept that Scripture is self-authenticating, as Luther and the Reformed held. The Reformers were of course combatting the claim that the authority of the Church validates the Scriptures and that therefore the Church

---

[43]Joyce, *Hooker and Moral Theology*, p. 147; see the whole section, pp. 103–47.

[44]Cf. Voak, 'Hooker and the Principle of *Sola Scriptura*.'

[45]Hooker, *A Learned Discourse of Justification, Works and how the Foundation of Faith is Overthrown*, §11 (Folger edn, vol. 5, p. 119).

somehow stands over the Bible, legitimating it. Thus Luther says, 'The gospel is not believed because the church confirms it, but because one recognizes that it is God's word.'[46] Calvin's discussion of the self-authenticating power of Scripture takes its rise from the same polemical starting point. But Hooker does not intend to cross swords with the great Reformers. He interprets the view of 'grave and learned men' about the self-evidencing authority of Scripture to mean that without the witness of the Holy Spirit in our hearts we will never hear God speaking to us in the Scriptures, whatever factors may incline us to heed them in the first place (*EP* III, viii, 15: 1, p. 233). There is no getting away from the fact that reason must make a judgement. 'In vaine it were to speake anything of God, but [unless] that by reason men are able some what to judge of that they heare, and by discourse to discerne how consonant it is to truth' (*EP* III, viii, 11: 1, p. 230).

Hooker is not far from Calvin at this point and is certainly not contradicting him. Both recognize and affirm the roles of reason and of the Spirit. Calvin, arguing against the force of tradition and the claims of the Roman Catholic Church, prioritizes the work of the Spirit. Hooker, fighting against the biblical absolutism of the Puritans, stresses the role of reason. Calvin, the author of the doctrine of the *testimonium internum spiritus sancti*, writes in the *Institutes*: 'the testimony of the Spirit is superior to reason. For as God alone can properly bear witness to his own words, so these words will not obtain full credit in the hearts of men, until they are sealed by the inward testimony of the Spirit.'[47] But Calvin's insistence on the indispensability of the Spirit's witness does not prevent him, in the following chapter of the *Institutes*, from setting out persuasive arguments and evidence from human reason as to the divine origin of Scripture. Calvin concludes:

> Then only, therefore, does Scripture suffice to give a saving knowledge of God when its certainty is founded on the inward persuasion of the Holy Spirit. Still the human testimonies which go to confirm it will not be without effect, if they are used in subordination to that chief and highest proof, as secondary helps to our weakness.[48]

---

[46]*WA*, 30:2, p. 687, cited Althaus, *Theology of Luther*, p. 75.

[47]*Institutes*, vol. 1, p. 72 (I, vii, 4).

[48]Ibid., p. 83 (I, viii, 13). See further Helm, *Calvin's Ideas*, ch. 9.

For Hooker, Scripture alone cannot assure us of its divine origin. Without reason we cannot know which particular books convey divine revelation. We need to be 'perswaded by other meanes that these scriptures are the oracles of God' (EP, I, xiv, 1: 1, p. 126). And again: '. . . it is not the worde of God which doth or possiblie can assure us, that wee do well to thinke it his worde' (EP, II, iv, 2: 1, p. 153). But that does not make reason supreme: it remains instrumental, a means to an end – the understanding of what is revealed. Reason alone cannot attain to the mysteries disclosed by revelation, but the Holy Spirit acts not apart from reason but in conjunction with it.

However, in the order of experience, it is the living tradition of the Church, embedded in its practices of reading, studying and preaching Scripture, that first directs us to the sacred writings. We have received them, and their valuation as containing divine revelation, from our forebears and they from theirs, in a fiduciary regress to the beginning of Christianity. It is the universal testimony of God's Church that provides 'the first outward motive' leading us to value the Scriptures as the word of God (EP, III, viii, 14: 1, p. 231). Here we see very clearly the experiential basis of tradition in Hooker's thought; but in contradistinction to the prevalent understanding of experience in our own day, Hooker's concept of experience is a collective, social and historical one.

The proper office of Scripture is to teach those things 'required as necessarie unto salvation . . . so that without performance of them we cannot by ordinarie course be saved, nor by any means be excluded from life observing them. In actions of this kinde our chiefest direction is from scripture, for nature is no sufficient teacher what we shoulde doe that we may attaine unto life everlasting. The unsufficiencie of the light of nature is by the light of scripture so fully and so perfectly herein supplied, that further light then [than] this hath added there doth not neede unto that ende' (EP, I, viii, 3: 1, pp. 188–9). In things necessary to salvation, Hooker affirms, following Augustine and the Reformers, that the Scriptures possess a perspicuity that makes their message available even to the simple (EP, Preface, iii, 2: 1, p. 13). Altogether; 'Scripture teacheth us that saving truth which God hath discovered unto the world by revelation, and it presumeth us taught otherwise that it self is divine and sacred' (EP, III, viii, 13: 1, p. 231).

In 1603, 3 years after Hooker's death, William Covell published *A Just and Temperate Defence of the Five Books of Ecclesiastical*

Polity written by Richard Hooker.[49] Although in some respects, particularly with regard to the status of the Roman Catholic Church, Covell pushed Hooker's rather generous views further than the master himself,[50] in others he stressed Hooker's reformed credentials and his respect for Calvin. Covell underlines that 'the Holy Scriptures contain all things necessary to salvation', that the Scriptures stand 'above the Church', and he reinforces the inseparable connection between the Church and the Word of God ('neither can stand where both are not').[51]

In one respect, Hooker shows himself to be more 'biblical' than the Puritans, and that is on the value he placed on the reading of the text of the Bible in public worship. Luther held that the oral gospel was the primary form of the word of God: there was a dynamic power in the word when it was shared between believers, spoken from faith to faith. But Luther also believed that the printed book was God's last and greatest gift before the world would end. And Luther, the translator of the Bible and commentator on many of its books, could hardly be accused of devaluing the written word. The English Puritans, on the other hand, asserted that sermons or preaching were the word of God and therefore God's ordinary way of leading individuals to saving faith, so that (in the view of some, including Cartwright) persons could not be saved if they lacked sermons, that is extempore sermons, given with the living voice, not written ones. This predilection is of a piece with the Puritan prejudice against written prayers and the Puritan privileging of extempore effusions.[52] Like free prayer, extempore preaching gave wings to the word. Under the *afflatus* of the Holy Spirit, the words of Scripture could be applied dynamically and effectively to the soul. The power of the word remained latent in the biblical text. Preaching was the most important part of the ordained ministry. Clergy who could not preach, but could only read the Homilies were 'dumb dogs, that cannot bark'.[53]

Hooker is, of course, defending to the last ditch every aspect of the Elizabethan Church by law established that the radical Puritans

---

[49]Covell, *Just and Temperate Defence.*
[50]See Lake, 'Business as Usual?'.
[51]Covell, *Defence*, p. 19.
[52]For a slightly later period see Maltby, 'Extravagancies and Impertinencies'.
[53]Hunt, *Art of Hearing*, ch. 1.

challenged, in some cases making a virtue of necessity. But in the course of defending the indefensible, he insists on the unique office of Scripture: 'the word of God is his heavenlie truth touchinge matters of eternall life revealed and uttered unto men; unto prophetes and apostles by immediate divine inspiration, from them to us by theire bookes and writinges'. In sermons, the fallible human element is dominant. The Puritans give too much scope to 'the witt of man', attributing to human skill what rightly belongs to God alone (*EP*, V, xxii, 10: 2, p. 99). Hooker asserts as robustly as any Reformer, 'We therefore have no *word of God* but the Scripture' (*EP*, V, xxi, 2: 2, p. 84). When we read or recite the Scriptures, 'we then deliver to the people *properlie* the worde of God' (*EP*, V, xxii, 10: 2, p. 99). Sermons are therefore derivative.[54]

While some Puritans claimed that one required scriptural warrant for the meanest action, Hooker insisted that to consult the Bible about 'vayne and childish trifles', would be 'to derogate from the reverende authoritie and dignitie of the Scripture' (*EP*, I, xv, 4: 1, pp. 132–3). The immutable part of the teaching of the Apostles is not concerned with such secondary matters as ecclesiastical ceremonies and government, where we have the light of reason and experience to guide us and can exercise our sense of what is appropriate to changing circumstances.[55] Just as every book of the Bible was written for a particular purpose, so the whole Scripture is given to serve the purpose of God in leading humanity to salvation.

> The testimonies of God are true, the testimonies of God are perfect, the testimonies of God are all sufficient unto that end for which they were geven. Therefore accordingly we do receive them, we do not thinke that in them God hath omitted any thing needfull unto his purpose, and left his intent to be accomplished by our divisinges. What the scripture purposeth, the same in all pointes it doth performe. Howbeit that here we swarve not in judgement, one thing especially we must observe, namely that the absolute perfection of scripture is seene by relation unto that end wherto it tendeth. (*EP*, II, viii, 5: 1, p. 189)

---

[54]Italics original. Cf. Calvin: '. . . there is no word of God to which place should be given in the Church' except what is contained in the canonical Scriptures. (*Institutes*, IV, viii, 8)

[55]Harrison, 'Prudence and Custom'.

For Hooker, Scripture is not self-explanatory, except in its fundamental gospel of salvation; it requires the application of reason. Hooker contributed to the Anglican conception of authority in religion not only by clarifying the scope and purpose of biblical revelation, but also by injecting an appeal to rationality into the earlier Anglican appeal to Scripture and antiquity.

Reason

For Hooker, Scripture holds the place of paramount authority, but second place he gives not to tradition but to reason.[56] Scripture and reason are allies. As Neelands puts it: 'For Hooker, Scripture and reason are not in conflict, since both have their source in God.'[57] Hooker's hierarchy of authority is Scripture, reason and (in shorthand) tradition, in that order. In matters of doctrine and practice alike, he writes, 'what scripture doth plainelie deliver, to that the first place both of creditt and obedience is due; the next whereunto is whatsoever anie man can necessarelie conclude by force of reason'; after these 'the voice of the Church succeedeth' (*EP*, V, viii, 2: 2, p. 39). Like Augustine and Aquinas before him, Hooker is drawing on Scripture, tradition and philosophy to create a synthesis, a unified comprehensive body of truth.[58] The role of reason is not only to provide one of the components (the material constituent of philosophy), but also to serve as the formal principle by means of which the synthesis is constructed.

We should not imagine that Hooker's hospitality to reason was some new departure in the theology of the Reformation, or that the continental and English Reformers despised reason, or even that Luther was hostile to reason – that is an anti-Reformation canard that comes from not reading Luther aright. It is true that Luther makes what Gerhard Ebeling calls 'extremely contradictory assertions concerning reason', but these need to be understood within Luther's distinctive theological method which thinks and speaks in terms of opposed totalities.[59] Luther praised reason as one

---

[56]Cf. Voak, *Hooker and Reformed Theology*, p. 264.
[57]Neelands, 'Hooker on Scripture, Reason and "Tradition",' p. 76.
[58]John S. Marshall, *Hooker and the Anglican Tradition*, pp. 66–8.
[59]Ebeling, *Luther: An Introduction*, p. 92; see also pp. 144–8, 229–32.

of the greatest of God's gifts to humankind. Reason is the mother of all the arts and sciences, the source of good government and sound economics. The natural law is the voice of reason. Though reason is damaged by the Fall, there is still a natural knowledge of God's existence and his metaphysical attributes. Reason belongs in the earthly, temporal realm, the sphere of human relations (*coram hominibus*). But in the heavenly, spiritual realm, in relation to God (*coram Deo*), reason is blind and cannot fathom the mystery of God's purposes; God's saving work in Jesus Christ is foolishness to human reason. When reason presumes to dictate what God can and cannot do, it becomes 'the devil's whore'. But reason becomes regenerate through justification, in order to understand the things of faith, though it still needs to recognize its limits.[60]

What Calvin says about reason closely follows the same pattern, echoing Luther quite plainly. In the context of a generous assessment of post-lapsarian human arts, skills and achievements, Calvin says:

> . . . we have one kind of intelligence of earthly things and another of heavenly things. By earthly things I mean those which relate not to God and his kingdom, to true righteousness and future blessedness, but have some connection with the present life and are in a manner confined within its boundaries. By heavenly things, I mean the pure knowledge of God, the method of true righteousness, and the mysteries of the heavenly kingdom. To the former belong matters of policy and economy. All mechanical arts and liberal studies. To the latter . . . belong the knowledge of God and of his will, and the means of framing the life in accordance with them.[61]

There are, surprising as it may seem to some, remarkable convergences between Luther's and Calvin's views of reason, on the one hand, and Hooker's on the other, though they are obviously

---

[60]Gerrish, *Grace and Reason*; Althaus, *Theology of Luther*, pp. 64–71; Lohse, *Luther's Theology*, pp. 196–200. An accessible 'applied' discussion is Grosshans, 'Luther on Faith and Reason'.

[61]*Institutes* II, ii, 13. Cf. Wendel, *Calvin*, pp. 185, 188, 192–3, 238, 247–9; Steinmetz, 'Calvin and the Natural Knowledge of God', in *Calvin in Context*. On the consequences of the Fall for human reason, see Helm, *Calvin's Ideas*, pp. 237–40. See also Biéler, *Calvin's Economic and Social Thought*.

not located in the same register of discourse and are directed at different targets. Hooker was following a well-travelled trajectory of Reformation theology, though applying the tradition to a fresh challenge – the Puritan claim that Scripture was given to legislate for every aspect of life, especially everything that should be done in the Church.

For Hooker, reason has its function in the world of law – that ordered world that derives from the God whose being is a law unto his working. The vocation of reason is to bring human existence into conformity with the order and harmony in the nature of things: 'all good lawes are the voyces of right reason, which is the instrument wherewith God will have the world guided' (*EP*, V, ix, 3: 2, p. 45). 'The lawes of well doing are the dictates of right reason' (*EP*, I, vii, 4: 1, p. 79). Reason for Hooker is therefore not autonomous or individualistic or secular. His concept of reason is the antithesis of that of the scientistic, positivistic mentality of modernity. Reason is a divinely implanted faculty for apprehending the truth revealed by God both in nature and Scripture. The kind of reason that Hooker intends, he says in his response to the accusations of his rival Travers that he had introduced scholàstic distinctions and rational subtleties into the exposition of Scripture, is 'not . . . myne owne reason . . . but true, sounde, divyne reason . . . reson . . . proper to that science whereby the thinges of god are knowne, theologicall reason which out of princyples in scripture that are playne soundly deduceth more doubtfull inferences' and brings to light the true meaning of the 'darker places' of Scripture.[62] We interpret Scripture by means of reason.

Reason seeks the good for humanity and moderates between appetite and will. 'The object of appetite is whatsoever sensible good may be wished for; the object of wil is that good which reason doth leade us to seeke' (*EP*, I, vii, 3: 1, p. 78). 'And to will is to bend our soules to the having or doing of that which they see to be good. Goodness is seene with the eye of the understanding. And the light of that eye is reason' (*EP*, I, vii, 2: 1, p. 78). But reason alone, considered as the study of the light of nature, has manifest limits. It cannot reveal the ultimate destination of the theological virtues of faith, hope and charity: *faith*, 'the principall object whereof is

---

[62]Folger edn, vol. 5, p. 255: 'Answer to the Admonition'.

that eternall verity which hath discovered [revealed] the treasures of hidden wisedome in Christ' and that conduces to 'the intuitive vision of God in the world to come'; *hope* 'the highest object whereof is that everlasting goodnes which in Christ doth quicken the dead' and which, beginning with a 'trembling expectation' in this life, 'endeth with reall and actuall fruition of that which no tongue can expresse'; *charity*, 'the finall object whereof is that incomprehensible bewtie which shineth in the countenance of Christ the sonne of the living God' and which, 'beginning here with a weake inclynation of heart towardes him unto whom wee are not able to aproch, endeth with endlesse union, the misterie whereof is higher than the reach of the thoughts of men'. These matters are the sole prerogative of revelation: 'There is not in the world a syllable muttered with certaine truth concerning any of these three, more than hath beene supernaturally receyved from the mouth of the eternall God' (*EP*, I, xi, 6: 1, pp. 118–19).

Moral certainty and human weakness

Hooker's phrase 'certain truth' in the above quotation prompts the question of certainty and probability in his thought. Hooker addresses both the subjective (personal assurance of salvation) and objective (reliable grounds for faith) aspects of certainty.[63] He tackles the former issue in *A Learned and Comfortable Sermon of the Certainie and Perpetuitie of Faith in the Elect* in defence of his claim elsewhere, provocative to the Puritans, that the prophet Habbakuk had doubted God.[64] Hooker broadens the issue to the question, Why are faithful Christians '*so weake in fayth*'? Considered in themselves, he replies, the truths of Christian faith are more certain than any science. The articles of the Christian faith are more certain, in this objective sense, than sensory knowledge and logical demonstration. To put it another way, we may distinguish between a certainty of evidence and a certainty of adherence. Some things may be more evident but less certain. We have less certainty

---

[63]Grislis, 'The Assurance of Faith', in McGrade (ed.), *Construction of Christian Community*.
[64]Folger edn, vol. 5, pp. 69–82 for what follows. For questions of faith and assurance in Calvinism and Puritanism see Kendall, *Calvin and English Calvinism*.

of evidence concerning things that we believe than we do concerning things that we perceive with our senses: the latter are more real to us than the former. Other things may be less evident and more certain. Certainty of adherence pertains when 'the hart doth cleave and stick unto that which it doth beleeve' because it is drawn to what it apprehends to be good and longs to believe: the affective element more than compensates for the weakness of evidence.[65] The Calvinist doctrine of the 'final perseverance of the saints' could be rather triumphalist in some hands, but Hooker gives it a modest and realistic tone. God gives the degree of inward certainty that will carry the believer to ultimate salvation. But this certainty is never so great as to amount to perfection in this life: a person with perfect faith would not need to be saved. Even the prophets struggled to hold on to God's faithfulness. 'A greeved spirit therefore is no argument of a faithless mind.'[66] The faith of believers experiences many great and grievous downfalls, but it proves invincible and conquers in the end.[67]

In the *Lawes*, however, he turns his attention from the inward state of assurance of salvation to the external or objective grounds for faith, arguing cumulatively, on the basis of law, Scripture, the Fathers, the wisdom of the Church and the sense of what is appropriate in the circumstances, for the reasonableness of Anglican ecclesiology and its relation to the civil order. In doing so, he deliberately shifted the centre of gravity from private judgement to 'publique consent' (*EP*, Preface 6.6: 1, p. 34).

Hooker's probabilistic doctrine of reason would be taken up again by a succession of Anglican thinkers: Locke, Butler, Keble, Gladstone and others nearer to our own time. Against both the Roman Catholics with their appeal to the infallibility of the Church and of the pope, and the Puritans with their biblical totalism, Hooker insisted in the *Ecclesiastical Polity* that the highest form of certainty we enjoy is that of 'probable persuasions'.[68] Though the human mind craves 'the most infallible certainety which the nature of thinges can yeeld', Hooker insists, assent must always

---

[65]Ibid., pp. 70–1.
[66]Ibid., p. 75.
[67]Ibid., p. 76.
[68]See Voak, *Hooker and Reformed Theology*, pp. 71–7 for a detailed account of degrees of evidence and certainty according to Hooker.

be proportionate to the evidence. Neither direct intuition of supernatural truths nor demonstrative proof of them is given to humanity in its earthly pilgrimage (*EP*, II, vii, 5: 1, p. 179). It seems that Hooker may be representative of the transition from one meaning of 'probable' to another: from 'backed by authoritative sources' to 'indicated by persuasive but not conclusive evidence'. 'Probable' is a word he uses much. H. C. Porter suggests that the *Ecclesiastical Polity* might be thought of as 'an extended essay on probabilities'.[69] This emphasis betokens a different ethos to that of Calvin's theology, where the stress is on certainty and assurance, even though there is significant overlap between Calvin's, Hooker's and Aquinas' teaching in this area.[70]

Tradition

Though Hooker privileges the office of reason in the ascertaining of truth, he is no rationalist. D'Entrèves writes: 'His theory is divided from the rationalism of later days not only by the maintenance of the traditional theological background and the limits which he is careful to assign to the independence or autonomy of human reason, but also by his idea that rational constructs must stand the test of history and may not contradict the evidence of tradition and historical development.'[71] To this latter aspect of Hooker's conception of authority, the role of tradition, we now turn.

To understand Hooker's appeal to tradition, we have to forget the simplistic but not unfamiliar idea of tradition as a fixed body of truths, expressed in propositional form, that are valid for all time. Tradition for Hooker is emergent, communal and reflective. Tradition is what our forebears have said and done consistently over time – in Haugaard's words 'the consensus of human reason within the Christian community', and therefore to be taken very seriously and surpassed in authority only by Scripture and 'demonstrative' reason.[72]

---

[69]Porter, 'Hooker, the Tudor Constitution, and the *Via Media*', p. 85.
[70]*Institutes*, I, vii, 5; Helm, *Calvin's Ideas*, pp. 250, 257–63.
[71]D'Entrèves, *Medieval Contribution to Political Thought*, p. 120.
[72]W. P. Haugaard in Folger edn, 6, part 1, p. 167.

The context of Hooker's discussion of tradition was the Tridentine insistence that unwritten traditions were a source of divine revelation with regard to what ought to be believed and done in the Church and were to be held with an equal reverence to that accorded to Scripture (*pari pietatis affectu ac reverentia suscipit et veneratur*).[73] Although Hooker rarely use the word 'tradition', and when he does it is not usually in a favourable sense because of the Tridentine associations, the idea is richly present in his work and the term 'tradition' will serve us to designate this third component of Hooker's synthesis, though practice, experience and consent are all involved. Together they constitute the third and final test or touchstone of religious truth, after Scripture and reason.

Hooker elides 'tradition' as a principle of authority in theological method into 'traditions Ecclesiasticall'. The latter are (a) primitive; (b) established by proper authority; (c) *adiaphora*, things that make no difference to salvation; and (d) binding on the Church until abrogated by proper authority again:

> Least [lest] therefore the name of tradition should be offensive to any, consideringe how farre by some it hath bene and is abused, wee meane by traditions [*sic*] ordinances made in the prime of Christian religion, established with that authoritie which Christ hath left his Church for matters indifferent, and in that consideration requisite to be observed till like authoritie see just and reasonable cause to alter them. (*EP*, V, lxv, 2: vol. 2, p. 302)

Hooker brings together revelation, reason and convenience as a method of evaluating such traditions: 'Where neither the evidence of anie law divine, nor the streingth of anie invincible argument otherwise found out by the light of reason, nor anie notable publique inconvenience' are decisive, 'the verie authority of the Church it selfe . . . maie give so much credit to her own lawes, as to make theire sentence touchinge fittnes and conveniencie waightier then [than] anie bare and naked conceipt to the contrarie' (*EP*, V, viii, 5: 2, p. 40).

---

[73]DS, §1502, p. 365; *Conciliorum*, p. 431 (trans: '. . . it [the Council of Trent] receives and venerates with the same sense of loyalty and reverence . . .'); cf. Gibbs, 'Richard Hooker's *Via Media* Doctrine', at p. 332.

There is a fundamentally conservative principle underlying Hooker's thought at this point and it belongs to the uniformitarian presupposition that he shared with all European culture before the eighteenth century. Truth was eternal. What was right was right for all times and places. Universal consent was equivalent to nature itself, and the voice of nature was as the voice of God: 'The generall and perpetuall voyce of men is as the sentence of God himselfe. For that which all men have at all times learnt, nature her selfe must needes have taught; and God being the author of nature, her voyce is but his intrument. By her from him we receive whatsoever in such sort we learn' (*EP*, I, viii, 3: 1, p. 84). Let us be loath 'to chaunge, without verie urgent necessitie, the ancient ordinances rites and longe approved customes of our venerable predecessors' (*EP*, V, vii, 3: 2, pp. 35–6). It is 'levitie and want of experience' that is attracted to innovation. But 'antiquitie, custome, and consent in the Church of God, makinge with that which law doth establish are them selves most sufficient reasons to uphold the same, unless some notable publique inconvenience inforce the contrarie.' If and when it does, Hooker immediately goes on to say, the church has authority to respond by altering its practice (*EP*, V, vii, 3: 2, p. 37).

Antiquity

Hooker's appeal to Christian antiquity is largely pragmatic in the best sense of the word, born of respect, humility and prudence. It is what Rowan Williams, in essays on Hooker, calls 'contemplative pragmatism': '[H]e is pragmatic to the degree that the accumulation of historical precedent has real intellectual weight, in the light of our ineradicable folly, selfishness and slowness as human thinkers, and he is contemplative to the degree that his guiding principles are seen by him as received, not invented, as the uncovering of a pattern of "wisdom" in the universe, focused in and through the Word incarnate.'[74] So Hooker writes: 'Neither may we . . . lightlie esteeme what hath bene allowed as fitt in the judgement of antiquitie and by the longe continewed practise of the whole Church, from

---

[74]Rowan Williams, *Anglican Identities*, p. 38; cf. p. 56. The two essays on Hooker in that volume were first published as respectively 'Hooker the Theologian' and 'Hooker: Philosopher, Anglican, Contemporary'.

which unnecessarelie to swarve, experience hath never as yet found
it safe' (*EP*, V, vii, 1: 2, p. 34). Hooker has already established with
utmost clarity the principle that matters regarding the outward
government of the Church come within the category of mutable
positive law. There is then no question of antiquity and tradition
legislating absolutely for all future situations. Respect for what
has gone before is the fruit of wisdom, not of sheer obedience.
Moreover, the authority that Hooker accords to tradition is
subject to the constraints provided by Scripture and reason: first,
that tradition alone cannot deliver supernaturally revealed truths
that are necessary for salvation – these belongs only to Scripture;
second, tradition is not to be followed when it is contrary to reason:
'the authority of men' should not 'prevaile with men either against
or above reason' (*EP*, II, vii, 6: 1, p. 181).

It is in the context of the foregoing principles with regard to
the wisdom that is to be found in tradition, especially ancient or
primitive tradition, that Hooker's idealization of the General
Councils of the Church should be set – 'those reverend religious
and sacred consultations . . . whereof Gods owne blessed spirit was
the author', which were 'never otherwise then [than] most highly
esteemed of, til pride ambition and tyrannie began by factious and
vile endevors to abuse that divine invention unto the furtherance
of wicked purposes'. Hooker shows himself an exponent of the
late medieval conciliar catholicism which the Reformers, both
English and foreign, re-appropriated to fit their situation, when he
prays that 'so gratious a thing may againe be reduced to that first
perfection' that it enjoyed in the time of the Apostles (*EP*, I, 10, 14:
1, p. 109).[75]

What became in later Anglican thought an appeal to antiquity
as prescriptive for the later Church, in Hooker remains a prudent
regard for well-tried human practice and a deference to the wisdom
of the ancients – 'that which the habit of sound experience plainely
delivereth' (*EP*, V, vii, 1: 2, p. 35). One Hookerian version of the
'threefold cord' is 'nature, scripture, and experience it self' (*EP*,
Preface, vi: 1, p. 29). Custom is accorded a value that it is foreign to
modernity and utterly alien to postmodernity. Custom is made up
of the deposit of practical judgements and the ensuing practices that

---

[75]See further discussion of Hooker's place in the conciliar tradition in Avis, *Beyond
the Reformation?*, pp. 147–9.

a society has inherited from its forebears. Custom is the product of the exercise of prudence by past ages and is therefore fundamentally reasonable. There is an initial presumption as to the integrity of custom, a bias towards tradition. To value custom is to recognize that experience, over time, has much to teach us.[76]

The ethical dimension: Hooker, Aquinas, Luther and Calvin

Hooker's whole system is imbued with ethical awareness. For Hooker, humans inhabit a moral universe. As we have seen, there is an ethical aspect to every topic that he discusses. Hooker seeks the path of holiness; he charts the royal road to the vision of God. He integrates ethical perception and theological judgement. He values tradition, custom and *habitude* above legislation (positive law) and that has remained the tenor of English Anglicanism to the present day, in spite of some appearances to the contrary (particularly the penchant of the General Synod to be constantly legislating – but that legislation is always checked by independent authority for its compatibility with the existing common law and other laws of the land). Kenneth Kirk once commented that the Church of England has spoken mainly by custom, not by law.[77] Bishop Kirk spoke in the spirit of Hooker, for whom law is primarily the moral logic of the cosmos, reflecting the mind of God, and only secondarily specific positive laws, whether human or divine.

Hooker draws extensively, though not uncritically on St Thomas, as do his successors among the seventeenth-century divines, especially Robert Sanderson, Jeremy Taylor and Joseph Hall. Both Hooker and his successors distinguish sharply between Aquinas and Tridentine Roman Catholic theology. Kirk points out that, while Aquinas succeeded in holding authority and freedom in balance, avoiding being over-prescriptive, later Roman writers did not. 'The only successors of St Thomas who can fairly be said to have attempted to carry

---

[76]W. H. Harrison, 'Prudence and Custom', pp. 904–5.
[77]Kirk, *Ignorance, Faith and Conformity*, pp. 148–50, cited Dewar, *Outline of Anglican Moral Theology*, p. 173. See also for the theme of this paragraph McAdoo, *Structure of Caroline Moral Theology*; Joyce, *Hooker and Anglican Moral Theology*.

out his ideal of combining the principle of authority with that of freedom are the little group of Anglican divines of the seventeenth century – Hooker, Jeremy Taylor, Sanderson, Hall, and their fellows.' Kirk continues: 'They had no doubts whatever as to the authority and divine commission of the Church, yet they rejected with final-ity the tendency of the Roman communion to push that authority to extremes.'[78] If Hooker is to be seen as the proponent of a *via media*, it is not to be understood as a middle way between the theo-logy and practice of Rome, on the one hand, and the Reformation on the other – Hooker's thought is deeply indebted to both medi-eval and Reformation theology, perhaps in roughly equal measure (together with his knowledge of the Fathers) – but rather as a mid-dle path between authority and liberty. Apologists for the English Reformation believed that this form of moderation was the guiding principle of the reform. As McAdoo suggests, it bears a superficial resemblance to the state policy of compromise, within certain param-eters, under Elizabeth I, who would not make windows into men's souls. Sanderson wrote:

> The *Church of England* meant to make use of her *liberty*. . . . Yet to do it with so much *prudence* and *moderation*, that the world might see, by what was *laid aside, that she acknowledged no subjection to the See of Rome*; and *by what was retained*, that she did not *recede from the Church of Rome*, out of any spirit of contradiction, but as *necessitated thereunto* for the maintenance of her just liberty.[79]

Of course, this rhetoric invites ideological critique, but so does everything else, and that does not mean that there is no truth in it.

Hooker and the Jacobean and Caroline divines rejected the Tridentine divorce of ascetic theology (focusing on holiness of life and the goal of the Beatific Vision) from ecclesiastical discipline with regard to our sins and failings and pastoral guidance about the moral dilemmas that we face. McAdoo is forthright: '[I]t was the separation of ascetic theology, to which the idea of the [beatific] vision is central, from the theology of law and acts which

---

[78]Kirk, *Some Principles of Moral Theology*, p. xi.
[79]Robert Sanderson, Preface to the *XXXV Sermons*, cited McAdoo, *Structure*, p. 5; cf. p. 4.

led continental moralists into the wastes of casuistic sophistry and unredeemed legalism.'[80] (It was that 'casuistical sophistry' that Pascal pilloried in his *Lettres Provinciales, 1656–57*.)[81] Hooker's thought is antipathetic to the legalism both of Tridentine Roman Catholicism and of English Puritanism. In place of Puritan literalism and legalism with regard to Scripture and what may be appropriated from tradition, Hooker sets what was for his day a sophisticated hermeneutic for their interpretation, which is the application of scholarly skills and morally sensitive judgements. We must first ask, Hooker believes, In what circumstances was this particular portion of Scripture given and what role does it play in God's purpose of bringing many sons and daughters to glory? This hermeneutical assessment includes, in more modern terms, the question of the passage's genre and *sitz im leben*.

With regard to biblical laws, while the Reformers tended to distinguish, just as Thomas Aquinas did, between the moral, ceremonial and judicial laws, Hooker approaches the same issues through a taxonomy of natural law and positive law, pointing out that not all divinely given positive laws are intended to be binding on the Church in all circumstances or for all time. We need to be aware that, contrary to what is often asserted, the magisterial Reformers retain a concept of natural law – they needed to do so in order to critique the church of their day and to discriminate between binding and nonbinding positive laws – and with it the ideas of equity and moderation (*aequitas, epieikeia*) in the administration of the law.[82]

Martin Luther's riposte to the 'Judaizers' who wanted to impose Old Testament judicial or ceremonial laws on Reformation Christians was, 'God did not lead us [Christians] out of Egypt!'; and, in different circumstances and somewhat outrageously, 'Moses is nothing to us [Christians].'[83] Luther believed that a reasoned judgement was called for, in Christian freedom, with regard to the use of the Mosaic law:

Neither is it true that the Old Testament was abrogated in such a way that it must not be kept, or that whoever kept it fully would

---

[80]McAdoo, *Structure*, p. 26.
[81]Pascal, *Provincial Letters*.
[82]On the Reformers and natural law see Avis, *Beyond the Reformation?*, pp. 122–33.
[83]Avis, 'Moses and the Magistrate'; Eells, *Attitude of Martin Bucer*, pp. 35–6, 211–12; cf. Faulkner, 'Luther and the Bigamous Marriage'.

be doing wrong, as St Jerome and many others mistakenly held. Rather, it is abrogated in the sense that we are free to keep it or not to keep it, and it is no longer necessary to keep it on penalty of losing one's soul as was the case at that time . . . it is not wrong to ignore them and it is not wrong to abide by them, but it is permissible and proper either to follow or to omit them.[84]

Luther did not, of course, dispute the fact that the Mosaic law was given by divine revelation, but to those who claimed that this was an entirely sufficient ground for observing it, Luther replies, in *How Christians should regard Moses* (1525), that that does not settle the question. It is not enough to know who spoke the word, but also to whom it was spoken. The peasants and Thomas Müntzer had raised the cry, 'God's word, God's word'. 'But my dear fellow', Luther responded, 'the question is whether it was said to you.' God commanded Abraham to sacrifice Isaac: that does not mean that I should do the same with my children. God gave the commandments to those he brought out of slavery: but God did not lead us Christians out of Egypt. 'I listen to that word that applies to me. We have the gospel.'[85]

Equally significant is the agreement between Hooker and Calvin in their approach to the question of the status of the positive laws of the Old Testament. For Calvin, the ceremonial and judicial laws are decisively abrogated for Christians. The circumstances are different; there is no comparison. But where particular laws embody the natural or moral law, the law of equity (*aequitas*) consummated in love (*caritas*), they point to abiding principles of obligation.[86] Like Bucer who, in the introduction to his commentary on Romans, wrote that just as the law brings condemnation and death to those who lack the Spirit of Christ, so to those who have received the Spirit it brings salvation and life, Calvin held that the law remained valid for Christians, not in its office to convict and condemn, but in its office to guide and control.[87]

Luther and the early Melanchthon were more radical. All law, the Decalogue, as well as the ceremonial and judicial law, has been

---

[84]*LW*, vol. 45, pp. 96–8.

[85]*LW*, vol. 35, pp. 164–5, 170–1.

[86]*Institutes*, II, vii, 16; other references to Calvin and to secondary literature in Avis, 'Moses and the Magistrate', pp. 163–5.

[87]Wendel, *Calvin*, pp. 196–208, esp. p. 205.; Tait, 'The Law and Its Works'.

abolished in Christ. This theme is pervasive in Luther. Luther has a *duplex usus legis*, twofold use of the law: the first use is political or civil (*usus civilis*), to restrain wrongdoing in society; the second use, the theological use (*usus theologicus*), is to convict the individual of sin, to show us our need of repentance, forgiveness and renewal. The Decalogue has been abrogated in its character as *law*, that is to say, in its office of judgement and condemnation, but not in its character as showing what God requires of our life in this world. Although Christians by their new nature cannot help but bring forth good works abundantly, as Luther eloquently proclaims in *The Freedom of a Christian* (1520),[88] they remain justified sinners (*simul iustus et peccator*) and need to be continually reminded of what is right and pleasing in the sight of God. Thus, Luther takes the Decalogue as the framework for his teaching on the Christian life in his Large and Small Catechisms and in his *Treatise on Good Works* (1520). Whether this adds up to an incipient concept of the third use of the law in Luther, as Ebeling seems to suggest, remains a moot point. I think that Luther does not push the idea that far; he is working on different premises.[89]

Melanchthon introduced the substantive concept of the *triplex usus legis*, the threefold use of the law, in the *Loci Communes* of 1535, though not with that explicit formula. The form of words, which would have a considerable history, first appears in Melanchthon's writing in the early 1540s, though the term *usus legis*, use of the law, comes from Luther's *duplex usus legis*. Melanchthon suggests that the ceremonial law is the one easiest to keep and is therefore comparatively trivial: it is less trouble, he remarks, to slay a whole flock of sheep for sacrifice than to curb one's anger, passion, etc. But though the papists are continually manufacturing foolish new ceremonies and requiring the faithful to observe them, Christ has abolished the ceremonial law. In Christian freedom, we may use those ceremonies that are edifying and leave the rest. Melanchthon was not advocating antinomianism (complete freedom from law; living

---

[88]*LW*, vol. 31, pp. 333–77.
[89]See further Althaus, *Theology of Luther*, pp. 266–73; Lohse, *Luther's Theology*, pp. 181–4, 270–6; Ebeling, 'On the Doctrine of the *Triplex Usus Legis* in the Theology of the Reformation', in *Word and Faith*; Bornkamm, *Luther and the Old Testament*; Elert, *Christian Ethos*, pp. 294–303; Sick, *Melanchthon als Ausleger*, pp. 38–40; Kisch, *Melanchthons Rechts-und-Soziallehre*, pp. 102–4; Tappert, *Book of Concord*, pp. 342–5, 365–411; Luther, *Treatise on Good Works*, *LW*, vol. 44, pp. 15–114.

without law), though some Lutherans, notably Johann Agricola, did. Christians keep God's law because it is engraved on their heart, not because it is in the Decalogue. 'Therefore the law has been abrogated, not that it not be kept, but in order that, even though not kept, it not condemn, and then too in order that it can be kept.'[90] However, in the mid-1530s, Melanchthon proposed the third use of the law *(tertius usus legis)*, to guide and direct the Christian life, and in this he was followed by later Lutheran orthodoxy and by Calvin. *The Formula of Concord* (1580) described the law of God as a mirror of God's will for how we should live, a mirror into which we should look continually.[91] Calvin also uses the mirror metaphor and regards the *usus theologicus* as the primary use for the world and the third use as the principal one for Christians. What St Paul says about the abrogation of the law, Calvin argues, refers not to the law itself but to its power to constrain the conscience.[92] Both Calvin and the *Formula of Concord* make the point that Christians are not so perfect that they do not often fall short and therefore need the guidance of God's moral law as revealed in Scripture.

The most explicit endorsement of the *triplex usus legis* in the English Reformation is perhaps to be found in Bullinger's *Decades*, which by direction of Archbishop Whitgift and Convocation in 1586 was to be purchased and studied by the clergy. Bullinger has the three uses in the order: theological, to convict of sin and lead us to Christ; the 'third use', to guide and instruct the Christian life; the civil or political use, to restrain the ungodly in society.[93] Bullinger also distinguishes the moral, ceremonial and judicial laws of the Old Testament, *lex Dei*: the moral law is contained in the Ten Commandments; the ceremonial law has been abrogated, but at the same time fulfilled in, for example, the substitution of the sacraments of the Lord's Supper and baptism for sacrifices and circumcision; the judicial laws have been abrogated, but the equivalent is needed in every state. To try to apply the judicial laws today would be crazy, but the Mosaic capital laws against incest, sexual perversion, adultery, magic and witchcraft are natural laws and must stand. Bullinger rehearses at length the provisions of the Mosaic judicial law, commenting on how wise and instructive it

---

[90]*Loci Communes*, 1521: LCC, pp. 120–30, at p. 125.

[91]*Formula of Concord*, art. 6: Tappert, *Book of Concord*, pp. 563–8, at p. 564.

[92]*Institutes*, II, vii, 6–15: vol. 1, pp. 304–11.

[93]Bullinger, PS, vol. 3, pp. 236–45 (Third Decade, 8th Sermon).

is. There is ambivalence here, a certain wistfulness with regard to the penal regime of the Old Testament; but this is entirely of its time.[94] Luther was not without his harsh and vindictive side, but his ideas on law and gospel were too radical and paradoxical for the Church of England, though I think they are more Pauline. The English Reformation tends towards the Swiss, Reformed strand of Protestantism. The moral element will shortly blend with stronger patristic and medieval influences in Hooker, Andrewes and the Caroline divines.

Whether the convergences that we have noted between Luther, Melanchthon and Calvin, on the one hand, and Hooker, on the other – for all their differences of style and idiom – are evidence of what Nigel Atkinson, Torrance Kirby and other want to claim, namely that Hooker stands in the mainstream of Reformation theology, is extremely doubtful, though there is unquestionably extensive common ground between Hooker and the Reformers. But the consensus goes wider than that. The distinction between moral, ceremonial and juridical (or judicial) Old Testament laws is patristic and medieval and is expounded extensively by Aquinas.[95] In his approach to the threefold division of the law of Moses, Calvin is following well-established tradition and Hooker is little short of being St Thomas' disciple. The convergence is a sign of continuity through the disruption of the Reformation, not of partisanship on the part of anyone.

Reflection

What distinguishes Hooker's use of authority in matters of religion in his time is the absence of the literalism and legalism that belong to aspects of Puritanism. For Hooker, neither Scripture nor tradition

---

[94]Ibid., vol. 3, pp. 255–82; vol. 1, pp. 209–11; 342–3; 412–13; vol. 2, pp. 255, 217–36, 280–2; Paulus, *Hexenwahn und Hexenprozess*, pp. 162–4. An exception to the general neglect by scholars of the controversy over the Mosaic judicial laws in sixteenth-century England is George, *Protestant Mind of the English Reformation*, esp. p. 231, where it is described as 'one of the most curious and distressing features of clerical legal theory'. Alec Vidler, *Christ's Strange Work* is an interesting discussion of the three uses of the law, with extensive quotation from diverse sources and modern application.

[95]*ST*, 1a2ae, Qn 99, articles 2–4; Qn 100, article 8; Qn 103, article 3; Qn 104, article 3: vol. 29, pp. 34–263.

contains a set of binding prescriptions and precedents to govern the life of the Church. This is not because Scripture is in any way imperfect, but because that is not its function in the purposes of God: it is perfect, sufficient and perspicuous in showing the way of salvation, that is to say union with God the Holy Trinity through the sacraments, effective by faith. Again, it is not because tradition is not important, but because an ongoing act of discernment, informed by Scripture and reason, is required in order to use tradition aright.

Underlying Hooker's teaching on the authority of Scripture and tradition is the conviction that there is an intuitive moral and aesthetic discernment that judges what is appropriate in the circumstances, a sense of what is fitting, what is becoming.[96] In all outward aspects of the church's corporate life, what interests Hooker is the discernment of the 'conveniencie and fittnes, in regarde of the use for which they should serve' (EP, V, vi, 1: 2, p. 33). 'Signs must resemble the things they signify.' The outward deportment of the church in all its offices, ceremonies and discipline must be such as to convey and reveal the inward realities of worship and holiness. Though subject to the test of Scripture and reason, in the senses defined above, Hooker's characteristic requirement is that 'in the externall forme of religion such thinges as are apparentlie, or can be sufficientlie proved, effectuall and generallie fitt to set forwarde godlines, either as betokeninge the greatnes of God, or as beseeminge the dignity of religion, or as concurringe with cœlestiall impressions in the mindes of men, maie be reverentlie thought of; some fewe, rare, casuall, and tollerable, or otherwise cureable inconveniences notwithstandinge' (EP, V, vi, 2: 2, p. 34).

What Hooker lacks, in his appeal to tradition, antiquity and established practice, and could not be expected to have, is an awareness of the ideological function of social practices, how they serve powerful interests and hold in subjugation economically weak and socially inferior groups. Hooker loved the hierarchical structure of society and believed that it reflected the angelic, heavenly order (EP, I, iv, 1–2). Walton 'records' that Hadrian à Saravia visited the dying Hooker, as his confessor, giving him Holy Communion and, returning the next day, found Hooker in deep contemplation. On being asked by Saravia what his thoughts were, Hooker replied

---

[96]John S. Marshall, *Hooker and the Anglican Tradition*, pp. 24, 81.

(according to Walton): 'That he was meditating the number and nature of Angels, and their blessed obedience and order, without which peace could not be in Heaven; and oh that it might be so on Earth!'[97] But Hooker's belief in a divinely ordained hierarchical social order weakens his arguments in favour of tradition – though we need to remember that Hooker does not absolutize tradition: it can and should be critiqued from the standpoint of Scripture and reason. Hooker's overall concept of authority reflects his vision of the Church, which is, we may say in summary, incarnational, corporate, organic, sacramental and dynamic.

---

[97]Walton, *Lives*, pp. 224–5. See further Tillyard, *Elizabethan World Picture*, esp. ch. 2.

4

Classical Anglican theology: I. Method, Scripture and tradition

Richard Hooker and Lancelot Andrewes together are the hinge on which the development of a recognizable Anglican theological method turns, between the Elizabethan Settlement and the efflorescence of Anglican theology in the seventeenth century. According to T. S. Eliot, 'the achievement of Hooker and Andrewes was to make the English Church more worthy of intellectual assent. . . . No religion can survive the judgment of history unless the best minds of its time have collaborated in its construction: if the Church of Elizabeth is worthy of the age of Shakespeare and Jonson, that is because of the work of Hooker and Andrewes.' The writings of Hooker and Andrewes, Eliot pointed out, reveal a determination to stick to essentials, an awareness of the needs of the times, the desire for clarity and precision about essentials, and a certain 'indifference to matters indifferent' which was the religious policy of Queen Elizabeth herself. Their thought reveals a catholicity of both theology and European culture more broadly.[1]

Key aspects of authority

Certain key features that affected issues of authority in this period may be mentioned immediately. First, there was no let-up

---

[1]Eliot, *For Lancelot Andrewes*, pp. 17–18. I am not sure that Eliot got Hooker right on 'things indifferent' (*adiaphora*); Hooker prefers the phrase 'things accessory', which implies a different valuation.

in hostile polemics between Anglicans and Roman Catholics. Protestant–Roman Catholic controversy by no means came to an end with the sixteenth century. Basic Reformation issues were still being rehearsed in the seventeenth century, and these centred on questions of authority. Does Scripture contain all things necessary to salvation, or does it need to be supplemented with 'unwritten apostolic traditions'? Is the Bible self-interpreting and, if not, who has the authority to say what it means? What is the role of the Church, and especially General Councils of the Church, in defining doctrine? Is the Church of England a true Church in which salvation is to be had, or is it necessary to be in communion with the pope to be saved? Are the claims of the papacy cogent and credible and, if not, where is authority to be found?

Second, the influence of the monarch on the teaching and practice of the Church of England was unabated through the reigns of James I and Charles I, but was interrupted by the latter's execution in 1649 and continued overall to reduce. Just as the 1530s had seen an appeal from pope to king, a later generation appealed from king to Parliament. Although James I, who succeeded Elizabeth I in 1603, had a double portion of Henry VIII's confidence when it came to the finer points of theology, there could no longer be any question of the Supreme Governor of the Church of England almost alone dictating what Christian doctrine should be. James II had to vacate the throne in 1688 because of the religious policy, favourable to Roman Catholicism, that he was attempting to implement. Through Civil War, Restoration and the 'Glorious Revolution', it became progressively clearer that Parliament was the dominant partner in the governance of the Church.

Third, internal theological debate was frenetic and personal positions were fluid. The theological trajectories of individuals were often marked by development at the least and by volatility at the extreme. Hooker had moved from a Puritan milieu in which Calvinism was orthodoxy to a much more eclectic stance in which he drew from many sources without repudiating Reformation principles. Lancelot Andrewes (1555–1626), who with Hooker is often regarded as a progenitor of later Anglicanism, made a similar journey. Andrewes moved from Calvinist orthodoxy in his early years to an anti-Calvinist stance in the 1590s and from Puritan austerity in ceremonial to an elaborate conception of the beauty of holiness, reflected in liturgy, church architecture and

furnishing.[2] William Chillingworth, famous for his provocative
dictum, 'The Bible, I say, the Bible alone, is the religion of
Protestants', converted to Roman Catholicism and back again.[3]
There was no settled 'Anglican' platform in this period, let alone a
generally recognized concept of a *via media* between Rome and the
Reformation: the Church of England saw itself as within the family
of Protestant Churches, but also as the exemplar among them of
apostolic, primitive Christianity, liturgical and episcopal.

Fourth, and following from the situation of theological fluidity,
the internal traditions of the Church of England remained incho-
ate and lacking in clear definition in this period. There were no
recognizable 'parties'. The seventeenth-century divines maintained
a broad consensus on the question of authority, as on other matters, for partisan churchmanship groupings were still in the future
and there was much crisscrossing of ideas and relationships at
this time.[4] This consensus focused on the paramount authority of
Holy Scripture in all questions of faith, order and morals, and particularly as the only source of doctrines necessary for salvation.
It acknowledged the place of tradition, in the form of the consent of antiquity, as a guide in interpreting the Scriptures where
their meaning was not readily apparent. It allowed scope to reason, informed by experience and scholarship, to arbitrate in the
articulation of doctrine and to moderate issues of church order.
As McAdoo has written, this consensus involved 'the centrality of
Scripture and the visibility and continuity of the Church, both confirmed by antiquity, and illuminated by the freedom of reason and
liberality of viewpoint'.[5]

Finally, the moral thrust – the integration of theology and
holiness, of ecclesiology and spirituality – established by Hooker
and Andrewes remains characteristic of Anglican divinity
throughout the seventeenth century. Early in his career, as catechist
of Pembroke College, Cambridge, Andrewes lectured on the Ten
Commandments and the serious young men flocked to hear him. His
expositions of the Decalogue were not simply Christian morality,

---

[2]Lake, 'Lancelot Andrewes'; McCulloch, 'Absent Presence'.
[3]Chillingworth, *Religion of Protestants*, p. 463 (vi, 56). On Chillingworth's
ecclesiology see Avis, *Anglicanism and the Christian Church*, pp. 88–92.
[4]See ibid., pp. 72–7.
[5]McAdoo, *Spirit of Anglicanism*, p. 357.

but comprised a complete theology, a body of divinity. The lectures were published posthumously as *The Moral Law Expounded*.[6] The great seventeenth-century moral theologians, casuists and spiritual directors, among whom was Andrewes himself, followed St Thomas Aquinas in their understanding of conscience (*synteresis* and *conscientia*), though they could be impatient of the more speculative subtleties of scholastic theology. Jeremy Taylor's *The Rule and Exercises of Holy Living* and its companion volume *The Rule and Exercises of Holy Dying* epitomize the fusion of the devotional, moral and theological in Caroline ascetical theology, and show that this genre was by no means the preserve of the Puritans. Although rigorous – like William Law later, he searches into every corner of the soul and holds every facet of life up to examination – Taylor is not legalistic, nor does he promote scrupulosity. After laying down no less than twenty-three rules for using our time to the glory of God and the salvation of our souls, he adds: 'Let all these things be done prudently and moderately, not with scruple and vexation . . . the particulars are not divine commandments; and therefore are to be used as shall be found expedient to every one's condition.'[7] The two most outstanding works of spiritual counsel and the cure of souls in this period were Sanderson's *De Oligatione Conscientiae* and Taylor's *Ductor Dubitantium*. Their stress was on the sovereignty of conscience, distinguishing that principle from the Roman Catholic insistence at that time, later revised by Vatican II, that conscience must submit implicitly to the teachings and rules of the Church, especially of the pope. Scripture and reason, rather than collected opinions, canon law and the confessional, were the criteria for these Anglican moral guides.[8]

The broad working consensus of seventeenth-century Anglicanism, across these several areas, was artificially preserved by the growing formal breach with the Puritan constituency from the 1640s, making Anglican theology less diverse than it might have been and narrower, though hardly monochrome. Hopes that the breach could be repaired following the Restoration in 1660 were short-lived and the Great Ejection of 1662 made the separation definitive. Notwithstanding this haemorrhage of Puritan divines, the coherence of the Anglican conception of authority was challenged by several factors.

---

[6]Porter, *Reformation and Reaction*, pp. 391–2.
[7]Taylor, *Holy Living*, p. 12.
[8]McAdoo, *Caroline Moral Theology*, pp. 66–7, 70–1, 79, 82.

First, critical Protestant thought challenged the notions of the consistency, consensus and coherence of the Fathers. William Chillingworth and the Tew Circle, influenced by the French Protestant Jean Daillé's critique of the Fathers,[9] sat lightly to their authority. In *The Religion of Protestants* Chillingworth pointed out that there were 'popes against popes, councils against councils, some fathers against others, the same fathers against themselves, a consent of fathers of one age against a consent of fathers of another age, the church of one age against the church of another age'.[10] The more subversive Socinian approach (rational analysis of scriptural mysteries, anti-trinitarianism) that Hobbes promoted, Newton espoused and Locke flirted with, showed that the authority of Fathers and Councils was open to challenge on rational grounds. As, in reply, Anglican patristic scholars such as William Beveridge, John Pearson and George Bull burrowed into old folios of the Greek and Latin Fathers to dig out evidence for orthodoxy, the effect was to produce a disproportionate emphasis on the authority of antiquity.[11] The Nonjurors who, because of their oath of allegiance to James II, could not accept William of Orange as King in 1688 and went into the wilderness or into schism, depending on one's viewpoint, pushed the claims of tradition further. They were the High Church traditionalists of their day, patristic, conservative and sacramental in theology. They went out of communion on a genuine point of conscience, but in isolation some adopted extreme and unbalanced views. In their devotion to antiquity, the so-called 'Usagers' among the later Nonjurors added liturgical flourishes from the early Church to the Prayer Book order of Holy Communion: the mixed chalice, prayers for the faithful departed, the *epiclesis*, and a prayer of oblation. The Nonjuring schism fizzled out; some returned to the Established Church, while others died off. In the eighteenth century, there were devout and loyal adherents of the Established Church who were strongly Nonjuring in their sympathies, Dr Samuel Johnson being perhaps the most celebrated.[12]

---

[9]Daillé, *Traicté de l'employ des Saincts Peres*.
[10]Chillingworth, *Religion of Protestants*, p. 463 (vi, 56).
[11]Ibid., p. 405.
[12]See further Overton, *Nonjurors*; H. Broxap, *Later Non-Jurors*; Every, *High Church Party*. For a summary of the ecclesiological issues at stake see Avis, *Anglicanism and the Christian Church*, pp. 81–4, 147–51. For Dr Johnson's High Church, Nonjuring and indeed Jacobite (i.e. conscientious loyalty to the exiled royal House of Stuart) convictions see Clark, *Samuel Johnson*.

Second, triumphant Puritanism in the 1640s and beyond replaced the understanding of the scope and limits of biblical authority that we associate with Hooker, where it is our guide in faith, order and morals, showing the way of salvation, with a more all-encompassing notion that stemmed from the Swiss Reformation. For mid-seventeenth-century Puritanism, the Bible was given to prescribe for every aspect of life, worship and church governance (though not necessarily in detail), to the exclusion of tradition. The Westminster Confession of Faith (1647) does not go all the way with this tendency. But it is significant that the Confession treats of the doctrine of Holy Scripture as the first article or chapter, unlike the Thirty-nine Articles, where it is dealt with in sixth place, after trinitarian doctrine (the first three articles of the Apostles' Creed). The Thirty-nine Articles begin with the faith of the Church; they then treat of Scripture and the Creeds, the basis of that faith. The Westminster Confession, anxious to minimize the role of tradition, starts with the Bible:

> VI. The whole counsel of God concerning all things necessary for His own glory, man's salvation, faith and life, is either expressly set down in Scripture, or by good and necessary consequence may be deduced from Scripture: unto which nothing at any time is to be added, whether by new revelations of the Spirit or traditions of men.[13]

The Westminster Confession follows Calvin in affirming that the authority of Scripture is not dependent on human testimony, even that of the Church, but is self-validating, though once its authority has been accepted through the internal witness of the Holy Spirit, the various perfections that we see in Scripture reinforce our belief. The Confession acknowledges that there are some circumstances, concerning worship and governance, human actions and societies where 'the light of nature, and Christian prudence, according to the general rules of the Word', should be our guide.[14]

Militant Puritan hostility to tradition sometimes included disparagement of the Fathers. 'Who is ignorant,' wrote John Milton, 'of the foul errors, the ridiculous wresting of Scripture, the Heresies,

---

[13][Westminster] Confession of Faith, p. 22.
[14]Ibid., p. 23. See the discussion of this statement in Warfield, 'Westminster Doctrine of Holy Scripture', in Westminster Assembly, pp. 155–257, esp. pp. 224–30. Warfield also deals with the sources of this section of the Confession.

the vanities thick sown' throughout the writings of various Fathers?[15] However, Puritan divines did not hesitate to appeal to the Fathers when it suited them, especially in defence of the principle of parity of ministers. In truth, their attitude to antiquity was one of profound ambivalence.[16]

Francis Bacon

A Christian philosopher

Francis Bacon (1561–1626), the greatest philosopher of science of the early modern period, is a Christian thinker who deserves his place in any account of Anglican theological method. Bacon devised a methodological programme for the reform, reorganization, and renewal of learning in all its departments – the 'Great Instauration'. His proposed method was empirical, examining experience and proceeding inductively, but not in a naive sense: the purpose of induction was to test hypotheses. 'Bacon's induction is not a scientific, but a juridical process. . . . This procedure is not observational but strictly inquisitorial.'[17] The same method covered what we would call the natural and human sciences. However, for Bacon, divine revelation in Scripture was a given. Though hardly a theologian, Bacon was a Christian thinker and a beacon in the intellectual landscape of Jacobean England and its Church. He achieved high office under James I, eventually becoming Lord Chancellor and Viscount St Albans, but was disgraced for corruption. He wrote prayers, translated Psalms, and penned sacred meditations. In a prayer he says, 'Thy creatures have been my books, but thy Scriptures much more. I have sought thee in the courts, fields and gardens, but I have found thee in thy temples . . . my heart (through thy grace) hath been an unquenched coal upon thine altar.'[18] His *Essays* are a key source for his religious thought. Bacon also applied his method to historical study, in which it was

---

[15]Cited Quantin, *Church of England and Christian Antiquity*, p. 257, from Milton, *Of Reformation touching Church-Discipline in England* (1641).

[16]Quantin, *Church of England and Christian Antiquity*, p. 263.

[17]Cassirer, *Platonic Renaissance*, p. 48.

[18]http://quod.lib.umich.edu/e/ecco/004786805.0001.000/1:77.1?rgn=div2;view= fulltext.

intended to provide the raw material for a science of humanity. In his history of the reign of King Henry VII, Bacon established himself as the first analytical or explanatory English historian, though his methods were dubious by modern standards.[19] Bacon is a major influence on the preoccupation with method, the turn to reason and the ambiguity about tradition in seventeenth-century Anglican theology. We cannot hope to understand Anglican theology in this its 'classical' period unless we reckon with Bacon.

Bacon's essays significantly begin with the implied figure of Jesus Christ. The essay 'On Truth', which is placed first, starts with the famous epigram: 'What *is Truth;* said jesting *Pilate;* And would not stay for an Answer.'[20] Bacon's clear intention is that where – or rather, in whom – the answer is to be found should be unambiguous. In this essay, we have Bacon's scale of values and philosophy of life. The 'Soveraigne Good of humane Nature', he asserts, is to seek, to know and to enjoy the truth. It is 'Heaven upon Earth, to have a Mans Minde Move in Charitie, Rest in Providence, and Turne upon the Poles of *Truth*.'[21] What Bacon says in the essay 'Of Unity in Religion' speaks to the modern ecumenical movement. Because religion is the chief bond of human society, it is all the more vital that the Church should be united. Nothing so much keeps people out of the Church, or drives them from it, as disunity. Unity can be preserved if the distinction between things fundamental and substantive in religion and mere matters of opinion or preference is observed. Uniformity is not required for unity.[22] Bacon's comment in the essay 'Of Atheisme' is pertinent to the early twenty-first-century attack on religious belief by Richard Dawkins and others: 'It is true, that a little Philosophy inclineth Mans Minde to *Atheisme*; But depth in Philosophy, bringeth Mens Mindes about to Religion.' Bacon's verdict is that '*Atheisme* is in all respects hatefull.'[23] But superstition is the other extreme. One of its causes is the over-reverencing of tradition and another is over-indulgence in pleasing and sensual rites and ceremonies.[24] Bacon almost certainly has

---

[19]In this section I draw on some material from Avis, *Machiavelli to Vico*.
[20]Bacon, *Essays*, p. 1.
[21]Ibid., pp. 2–3.
[22]Ibid., pp. 8–11.
[23]Ibid., pp. 64–7.
[24]Ibid., p. 69.

Rome, but not only Rome, in his sights here. The Roman Church, 'under pretext of Exposition of Scripture, doth not sticke to Adde and Alter; and to Pronounce that, which they do not Finde; And by *Shew* of *Antiquitie*, to introduce *Noveltie'*.[25]

Dualism of science and theology

Renaissance and Reformation Christian though he is, Bacon's method presupposes a dualism of science and religion. Bacon intensifies the breakdown of the unified cosmos and integrated intellectual world characteristic of the Middle Ages. He was building on the gathering consensus that a preoccupation with providential first causes was incompatible with a scientific investigation of empirical phenomena at the level of second causes. He has no place for metaphysics. But Bacon went further even than Machiavelli in making absolute the division of things human and things divine, science and religion, what is the case and what ought to be. In *Cogita et Visa* (1607), Bacon attacked the synthesis of science and religion that was being attempted in the Christian Platonism of the Renaissance, as a dangerous tendency. 'No opinions are in such favour today,' he complained, 'as those which with solemn pomp seem to celebrate a legal marriage between Theology and Natural Philosophy, that is, between Faith and the evidence of the senses, and which charm the minds of men with a pleasing variety of matter while producing a disastrous confusion between the human and the divine.' There was more danger to science from 'this specious and ill-matched union' than from open hostility, he concluded. Bacon's objections were grounded in the fear that a synthesis of science and theology tended to freeze existing scientific knowledge. Religion is typically not interested in pursuing fresh lines of enquiry, only in assimilating to an existing theological system what it feels it must come to terms with: '[A]ll fresh growth, additions, improvements are excluded more strictly and obstinately than ever before. In fine, every development of philosophy, every new frontier and direction, is regarded by religion with unworthy suspicion and violent contempt.'[26]

---

[25]Ibid., p. 222.
[26]*PFB*, p. 78.

Bacon was fired by an intense personal vision, a vision that was both humane and humanistic. His aim was the well-being and glory of humanity. 'My purpose,' he declared in the *Novum Organum*, 'is to try whether I cannot in fact lay more firmly the foundations and extend more widely the limits of the power and greatness of man . . . to establish and extend the power and dominion of the human race itself over the universe.'[27] He set out to improve the lot of humankind and to make science serve human needs, to put philosophy at the service of work. The divine purpose of knowledge was, in Bacon's view, 'the benefit and relief of the state of man'.[28] As he asserted in the *Novum Organum*, revealing himself as the beneficiary of the alchemical tradition: '[T]he true and lawful goal of the sciences is none other than this: that human life be endowed with new discoveries and powers.'[29] Both natural science and historical science were intended to serve a practical purpose, contributing to a science of humanity. However, there is in Bacon's thought a check on the ruthless exploitation of nature for practical ends. For although the whole thrust of Bacon's system is concerned with intentional activity, he sometimes pauses to acknowledge the value of contemplation. As light is more beautiful to behold than all the uses to which it is put, 'so assuredly, the very contemplation of things, as they are, without superstition or imposture, error or confusion, is in itself more worthy than all the fruit of inventions'.[30]

Rejection of history and tradition

Like Descartes, Hobbes and Spinoza, Bacon is determined to tear up the past and to make a fresh start by means of his patent method. Like Descartes, he wants to begin with doubt, with questioning. '[I]f a man will begin with certainties,' Bacon writes, 'he shall end in doubts; but if he will be content to begin with doubts, he shall end in certainties.'[31] The traditions of Western philosophy and theology have little to offer the enterprise that Bacon has in

---

[27]*PW*, pp. 294, 300.
[28]Ibid., p. 188.
[29]Ibid., p. 280.
[30]Ibid., p. 300.
[31]*AL*, p. 34.

hand: he will begin *de novo*. In 1603, in *The Masculine Birth of Time*, Bacon asserted, 'It would not be a proper thing for me, who am preparing things useful for the future of the human race, to busy myself in the study of ancient literature.'[32] And in the *Novum Organum* (1620), he claimed, 'We should at once and with one blow set aside all sciences and all authors; and that too without calling in any of the ancients to our aid and support, but relying on our own strength. . . . For new discoveries must be sought from the light of nature, not fetched out of the darkness of antiquity.'[33]

The drive for method

To start from scratch in this way – to brush aside the intellectual traditions of two and a half millennia and to build again from elective first principles – Bacon, like Descartes, needed a robust methodology. Whereas Descartes found a suitable instrument in introspection of his mental processes, Bacon employed a simple and naive theory of perception, whereby we can have direct and undistorted knowledge of reality. 'All depends,' he says in *The Great Instauration*, 'on keeping the eye steadily fixed upon the facts of nature and so receiving their images simply as they are, for God forbid that we should give out a dream of our own imagination for a pattern of the world; rather may he graciously grant to us to write an apocalypse or true vision of the footsteps of the Creator imprinted on his creatures.'[34] Bacon is under no illusion that most people can attain this level of perception without preparation. In the present state of learning, 'the mind of man is far from the nature of a clear and equal glass, wherein the beams of things should reflect according to their incidence; nay, it is rather like an enchanted glass, full of superstition and imposture, if it be not delivered and reduced'.[35] But under the discipline of true method, perceptions can become clear, distinct and unequivocal. The various idols that warp our understanding of reality can be demolished. Bacon's view is the antithesis of the post-Kantian, Romantic idea of perception,

---

[32] *PFB*, p. 68.
[33] *PW*, p. 297.
[34] Ibid., pp. 253–4.
[35] *AL*, p. 132.

epitomized in Blake's saying that we should see, not *with* but *through* the eye.[36] Another phrase of Bacon's brings comparison with Kant to mind: 'What I purpose,' he declares, 'is to unite you with *things themselves* in a chaste, holy and legal wedlock.'[37] Indeed, Bacon's epistemology could be seen as a sort of preemptive strike against the views argued by Kant a century and a half later, including the notion that we cannot know things in themselves *(noumena)*, but only *phenomena*.[38] Bacon's claims are almost a calculated provocation to later theories of knowledge with their profound caution about claims to epistemological realism: 'I am building in the human understanding a true model of the world, such as it is in fact, not such as man's own reason would have it to be.'[39]

Bacon assumed the unity of the sciences and the comprehensive applicability of his method. All empirical studies concerned with experience are forms of 'history': natural history on the one hand, civil (ecclesiastical and literary) history on the other. The study of nature and the study of humankind are to be conducted according to the same empirico-inductive method. Bacon is the forerunner of Descartes, Hobbes, Locke, Hume and the later positivist tradition in assuming that the natural and human realms are equally amenable to his chosen method of investigation. There is no hint in Bacon of the later romantic and idealist thinkers' separation of the natural sciences *(Naturwissenschaften)* from the human sciences *(Geisteswissenschaften)*, no recognition of the view that informed the great flowering of historical study in the nineteenth century, that the life of humankind is resistant to merely analytical and quantitative methods of investigation. For Bacon, as later for Hobbes, politics and ethics are to be pursued by the same method as the study of nature and history. The scope of his science is the measure of the universe itself. 'For the world is not to be narrowed till it will go into the understanding (which has been done hitherto) but the understanding to be expanded and opened till it can take in the image of the world, as it is in fact.' And then, Bacon concludes,

---

[36]Blake, *Complete Poems*, p. 510 ('Auguries of Innocence', ll. 124–5), 810 ('The Everlasting Gospel', ll. 105–6).

[37]*PFB*, p. 72, original emphasis.

[38]Kant, *Critique of Pure Reason*, Part III; pp. 180ff.

[39]*PW*, p. 298.

'we shall be no longer kept dancing within little rings, like persons bewitched, but our range and circuit will be as wide as the compass of the world'.[40]

One aspect of this all-embracing scope of Bacon's method marks a clear break with the classical-humanist rhetorical tradition. It was an axiom of rhetoric that one confined one's discourse to things that were worthy of inclusion, the virtuous, noble and excellent. Bacon, following the Italian humanist Lorenzo Valla, challenges this assumption, pointing out that nothing, however humble, distasteful or squalid can be excluded from the province of scientific knowledge. 'There are to be received into this history, first, things the most ordinary, such as it might be thought superfluous to record in writing, because they are so familiarly known; secondly, things mean, illiberal, filthy . . . ; thirdly, things trifling and childish . . .; and lastly, things which seem over subtle, because they are in themselves of no use.' To the pure all things are pure.[41] The sunlight penetrates the sewer just as it does the palace, yet the sun 'takes no pollution'. In 'laying a foundation in the human understanding for a holy temple after the model of the world', Bacon adopts the principle that 'Whatever deserves to exist deserves also to be known, for knowledge is the image of existence; and things mean and splendid alike exist.'[42] Ironically, Bacon died as a result of catching a chill while out stuffing snow into a dead chicken to test refrigeration.

Bacon believed that he had discovered a technique that, put into the hands of any competent person, would produce results. This method, he declared, 'leaves but little to the acuteness and strength of wits, but places all wits and understandings nearly on a level'.[43] It was the instrument 'by means of which all things else shall be discovered with ease'.[44] Not that he claimed absolute finality for his method; he envisaged it being superseded by more refined procedures. But this was not modesty on Bacon's part, for he held that his method would lead not only to innumerable useful discoveries, but also to more advanced methods of discovery itself.

---

[40]Ibid., pp. 404–5; cf. p. 299.
[41]Ibid., p. 406.
[42]Ibid., pp. 295–7.
[43]Ibid., p. 270; cf. p. 297.
[44]Ibid., p. 300.

The 'art of discovery' would itself advance as discoveries were made.[45]

So what was the method for which Bacon claimed so much? Bacon himself believed that it consisted in the inductive logic operating on the endless tables of facts that he attempted to gather in every sphere of knowledge. But to make Bacon an exponent of the kind of pure inductivism advocated by J. S. Mill 200 years later, a notion that has been exploded by twentieth-century philosophers of science such as A. N. Whitehead, Karl Popper, F. S. C. Northrop and Michael Polanyi, to name a few, would be a caricature. Bacon insists that enumerative induction is puerile.[46] It is true that he lays the emphasis on gathering facts but he also stresses the importance of structuring and interpreting them. The traditional division of the sciences into those that are empirical and those that are rational creates a false dichotomy, he believes: the empirical and rational methods must be combined. 'The Empirics, like ants, gather and consume. The Rationalists, like spiders, spin webs out of themselves. The Bee adopts the middle course, drawing her material from the flowers of the garden or the field, but transforming it, by a faculty peculiar to herself.'[47] Experiment without method is futile: 'For experience, when it wanders in its own tracks, is . . . mere groping in the dark and confounds men rather than instructs them. But when it shall proceed in accordance with a fixed law, in regular order, and without interruption, then may better things be hoped of knowledge.'[48]

Though Bacon believed that inductive logic was his greatest contribution, commentators have pointed out that even Bacon himself never managed to use it; that is not surprising, because naked induction is unworkable. More valuable in the long run was Bacon's broad empirical approach, his quest for objective truth and interest in the phenomena of natural and human life. These things were not the sole prerogative of genius, but provided a programme for the broadly based scientific movement of two centuries. In this sense, Bacon was right to claim a levelling effect for his theories: 'My system and method of research is of such a nature that it tends

---

[45]Ibid., p. 301.
[46]Ibid., pp. 290–1; *PFB*, p. 89.
[47]*PFB*, p. 131; cf. *PW*, p. 288.
[48]*PW*, p. 289.

to equalize men's wits and capacities. . . . Men are very far from realizing how strict and disciplined a thing is research into truth and nature, and how little it leaves to the judgement of men.'[49]

Words and ideas

Bacon advocated a style of writing to match the rigour of his method. It was to be characterized by 'chastity'. Words were 'counters' and 'signs', and had an exact value. Bacon is the founder of the analytical view of language that has a long history through Descartes, Hobbes and Locke, Bentham in the nineteenth century, to the early Wittgenstein's *Tractatus*. According to the analytical view, language reaches its full potential only when metaphors are ironed out and a virtual univocity of meaning is attained, so that each word can be treated as an atomic unit, a counter of meaning: clarity itself will give us the 'simple' truth. This approach is an attempt to close language up, to 'desynonymise' (a Coleridgean word). It can be seen at work in Bacon's attempt to restrict metaphor to illustration and ornament, Hobbes's treatment of duty and inclination, love and lust as synonymous, and later, Bentham's view of poetry as misrepresentation. While Bacon is generally regarded as the originator of the analytical view of language, S. T. Coleridge, a close student and admirer, and leading representative of the alternative 'fiduciary' view of language, did not detect this tendency in him and a modern scholar has also defended Bacon against this charge.[50] Although Bacon describes words as 'counters', he also speaks of them as 'symbols', which perhaps points towards a less crude view. However, the doctrine that each word ideally represents a single object, concept or relation, and its accompanying assumption that the penumbra of allusion, imagery and ethos needed to be stripped away, was certainly regarded later as typically Baconian, and was prevalent among the Fellows of the Royal Society from the Restoration onward. It has been said of Locke, for example, that 'he is forever talking as if lucidity is the same thing as simplicity; he cannot see that the truth might be so complex, or so approximate, that only a complex or approximate statement

---

[49]*PFB*, p. 1181.
[50]Righter, 'Francis Bacon'.

might be accurate'.[51] Philosophical style for Bacon was to be brief, concise and chaste, stripped of all extraneous matter:

> Away with antiquities and citations or testimonies of authors; also with disputes and controversies and differing opinions; everything in short which is philological. Never cite an author except in a matter of doubtful credit; never introduce a controversy unless in a matter of great moment. And for all that concerns ornaments of speech, similitudes, treasury of eloquence, and such like emptinesses, let it be utterly dismissed.[52]

In Bacon, as in Hobbes later, we have an analytical approach to language that is the antithesis of the hermeneutical method that was pioneered by the eighteenth-century Neapolitan philosopher of history G. B. Vico, for whom metaphor and imaginative creations were the key to understanding ancient, alien texts and cultures.[53]

Modernizing knowledge

It is a familiar paradox that the Renaissance, which began as the humanist appeal to classical antiquity against the degenerate state of contemporary letters and learning, eventuated in a challenge to the assumptions and values of the classical world and an assertion of the merits of modernity. Similarly, the Reformation which was, ideologically speaking, an appeal to the primitive Church against the Church of the time, generated radical ideas that undermined many patristic and medieval assumptions. Bacon recognized the impetus that the Reformation had given to scholarship and enquiry when he commented in *The Advancement of Learning* that Luther, finding himself isolated, one man against Christendom, 'was enforced to awake all antiquity, and to call former times to his succors to make a party against the present time. So that the ancient authors, both in

---

[51]Watson, 'Joseph Butler'.

[52]*Parasceve ad historiam naturalem et experimentalem*, 1620: *PW*, p. 403. On the analytical and fiduciary concepts of language and metaphor see Avis, *God and the Creative Imagination*.

[53]On Vico see Avis, *Foundations of Modern Historical Thought*, ch. 6; Berlin, *Vico and Herder*.

divinity and humanity, which had long time slept in libraries, began generally to be read and revolved.'[54]

Others before Bacon had challenged some of the central themes that linked the ancient world with the Renaissance. Jean Bodin (1530–96), for example, had ridiculed the notions of the Golden Age, the Four Monarchies derived from the prophecy of Daniel, and the *translatio imperium ad Germanos*.[55] But Bacon's criticism of antiquity is remarkable for its attempt to neutralize the formidable authority of the classical–medieval tradition by a process of historical relativizing. In order to get a hearing for his radical programme, Bacon needed to undermine the massive prestige of the Platonic contemplative–speculative approach of the classical tradition. He was attempting to divert attention from the authority of the ancients to the study of the world. 'Science is to be sought', he declared in 1603, 'from the light of nature, not from the darkness of antiquity. It matters not what has been done; our business is to see what can be done.'[56] So alongside the assertion of his own principles, Bacon prepared a crushing indictment of the received philosophical tradition, accusing it of ignorance, irrelevance and aridity. It was essentially static and complacent, assuming that 'whatever has not yet been discovered is indiscoverable'.[57] The tradition could not boast a single experiment that had improved the human condition.[58] Classical philosophy was barren, lacking a principle generative of good. It was the boyhood of knowledge 'and has the characteristic property of boys: it can talk but it cannot generate; for it is fruitful of controversies but barren of works'. The present state of learning, as a result, is like the mythological figure of Scylla 'who had the head and face of a virgin, but her womb was hung round with barking monsters'.[59] The classical tradition was vitiated by the 'pernicious and inveterate habit of dwelling on abstractions'.[60] It was marked by 'professorial pomp' and 'sterile contentiousness'.[61] But what else, asks Bacon, could be expected from the infancy of

---

[54]*AL*, p. 23.
[55]Bodin, *Method for the Easy Comprehension of History*; Franklin, *Jean Bodin*.
[56]*PFB*, p. 69.
[57]Ibid., p. 74.
[58]*PW*, p. 276; *PFB*, p. 85.
[59]*PW*, p. 243.
[60]Ibid., p. 303.
[61]cf. Rossi, *Francis Bacon*, ch. 2.

science, when it was 'in matter of knowledge but as the dawning or break of day'.[62] We should put the limitations of the ancients into historical perspective: nations were self-contained; travel was minimal; there was no community of scholarship; men and states were motivated more by desire for self-aggrandizement than by aspirations to improve the life of humanity. The great philosophers of antiquity may have been colossal intellects (though Bacon is not over impressed), but their achievements were circumscribed by the conditions of the age:

> Whether then you reckon times or spaces, you see within what narrow confines the great intellects of those ages moved, or were shut in. A history worthy of the name did not extend over a thousand years. The rest was but legends and dreams. And of the wide regions of the earth how small a part they know . . . whole climates and zones, in which countless men breathe and live, were pronounced uninhabitable. The peregrinations of a Democritus, a Plato, a Pythagoras, which seemed wonderful in their eyes, were hardly more than suburban excursions.[63]

As Bacon surveyed the sad record of the past, it seemed to resolve itself into a cyclical pattern. Philosophers had been moving in circles, their speculative, sterile arguments covering the same old ground: 'carried round in a whirl of arguments', 'content to circle round and round for ever amid the darkest idols of the mind under the high sounding name of contemplation'.[64] The circle is for Bacon the image of futility.[65] The cyclical view of history is almost universal, but Bacon's position was defined by the Christian and classical tradition: he took the doctrine of the Fall of Man seriously, and believed too in a Golden Age from which man had steadily declined. In the light of these notions, his cycle of futility turned into a spiral of decay. Though there had been visitations of enlightenment and learning – the Greek, the Roman, the modern revival of letters – achievement in the arts and sciences had become steadily weaker.

---

[62]*PW*, p. 190.
[63]*The Refutation of Philosophies* (1608): *PFB*, p. 110.
[64]*PFB*, p. 82.
[65]Guibbory, 'Bacon's View of History'.

The river of time had carried down to us 'the light and windy and sunk the solid and weighty'.[66] Whereas in the mechanical arts such as painting, artillery and sailing, progress is cumulative, in 'sciences of conceit' the process is reversed: 'the first author goeth furthest and time leeseth and corrupteth'. Philosophy was strongest at the beginning, in the work of Plato, Democritus and Hippocrates, but degenerated through tradition.[67] Only one thing could break this spiral of decline and that was his own scientific method. Already the opportunities were there in the advances of Renaissance life and learning. 'When I set before me the condition of these times, in which learning hath made her third visitation or circuit, in all the qualities thereof. . . . I cannot but be raised to this persuasion, that this third period of time will far surpass that of the Grecian and Roman learning.'[68] If humankind would only grasp the instrument (*organum*) that Bacon was holding out to him, there would be no limit to what could be achieved.

Bacon condemned the defeatism of the view that the sciences, like all human endeavour, must inevitably follow a cycle in which they first flourish, then decline, and collapse. It is a fatal error to imagine that in the sciences there is a fixed upper limit of attainment and that this can be reached within the life of an individual who is capable of bringing his field of study to a state of definitive and absolute perfection. On the contrary, every science grows by the patient observations of many men, one grasping one truth, one another, and handing on their contributions like a relay of torch-bearers (a notion Bacon had learnt from the cooperative enterprises of the guilds of artisans).[69] In his optimism regarding the benefits of his method, religion and science seem to come together again. Bacon grounds his optimism in the revealed will of God: 'only let the human race recover that right over nature which belongs to it by divine bequest, and let power be given it; the exercise thereof will be governed by sound reason and true religion.'[70]

---

[66]*PFB*, p. 68; cf. *PW*, p. 191.
[67]*PFB*, p. 68.
[68]*AL*, p. 208.
[69]*PFB*, p. 126: *De Sapientia Veterum*, 1609; Zilsel, 'Genesis of the Concept of Scientific Progress'.
[70]*PW*, p. 300.

Visions of progress

Bacon's vision of scientific progress is not the secular utopia of the French Enlightenment[71] and the later positivist tradition, but is formulated in Christian and biblical terms. He takes as his text Daniel 12:4, 'Many shall run to and fro and knowledge shall increase,' which as he interprets it, signifies the conjunction of scientific discovery with the great voyages of exploration to the New World and the East. Bacon sees himself explicitly as the Columbus of scientific discovery.[72] If the expansion of knowledge could be seen as a fulfilment of prophecy, this was one more piece of evidence that the last age of the world was at hand. Bacon's vision of a beneficent future to be brought about by technological advance strikes an apocalyptic note: by God's appointment, the tree of knowledge will bear its finest fruit 'in this autumn of the world'.[73] Bacon's vision was eschatological: he believed that scientific movement would usher in a new and last age, stored in the womb of time, and ready, by divine decree, to be inaugurated. The age to come would constitute a restoration of man's prelapsarian state and powers, and secondly, the enjoyment of the eternal sabbath promised to the people of God. The true end of knowledge, Bacon asserts, is 'a restitution and reinvesting (in great part) of man to the sovereignty and power which he had in his first state of creation'. Just as Adam named the creatures and had dominion over them, science gives the power to call the creatures by their true names (i.e. natures) and once again command them. 'For man by the fall fell at the same time from his state of innocency and from his dominion over creation. Both of these losses however can even in this life be in some part repaired, the former by religion and faith, the latter by arts and sciences.' But in two ways the curse of the Fall cannot be reversed: first, 'that vanity must be the end in all human effects', and secondly, that humankind is destined to earn their bread by the sweat of their brow. In this interpretation of Genesis 3:19, Bacon takes the curse to refer to the labours of science and the mental effort involved, not to physical exertion which can be eased by inventions.[74]

---

[71]Becker, *Heavenly City*.
[72]*PFB*, p. 94; cf. *PW*, p. 287.
[73]*PW*, p. 188.
[74]*PW*, pp. 188–9, 386–7; cf. Guibbory, 'Bacon's View of History'.

This interpretation of a biblical metaphor links up with a further theme in Bacon's great vision of a restoration of all things (*instauratio magna*): the promise of a sabbath rest for the people of God, by analogy with the seventh day of creation when God rested from his work. In the form of a prayer Bacon says, '[I]f we labour in thy works with sweat of our brows thou wilt make us partakers of thy vision and thy sabbath.'[75] While the image of the sabbath rest is in apparent conflict with the dominant images of ceaseless progression, advancement and discovery, it points nevertheless to a more radically eschatological dimension of Bacon's thought in which scientific control of the elements has become complete and man can enter into an ultimate state of technological bliss. Bacon was perhaps the first to combine a utilitarian concept of knowledge and a notion of cumulative scientific research to create a doctrine of scientific progress. It was this aspect of his thought (as well as his clear demarcation between religion and science) that commended Bacon to the Enlightenment.

Bacon's philosophy of history

The myth of the Golden Age was linked with the myth of the 'matchless wisdom of the ancients' – the theory that a lost civilization, existing before Greece and Rome, had attained a level of knowledge as great or greater than our own and had enshrined its wisdom in myths and fables to preserve it for a later age.[76] Bacon's espousal of this theory reveals the limitations of his historical grasp. For him human nature was always the same, essentially rational and comprehensible. The relativistic, developmental assumptions of later historicism were not anticipated by Bacon. The real watershed in modern historical thought comes with G. B. Vico who, in challenging Bacon, one of his masters in philosophy, originated hermeneutical concepts that could accommodate the supposed wild irrationality of primitive humanity. In Bacon's successive publications, we observe a gradual warming to the notion of the wisdom of the ancients, until it becomes integral to his final philosophical position. In *The Advancement of Learning* (1605), Bacon had recognized the role of hieroglyphics and symbolic gestures in communication among

---

[75]*PW*, p. 254.
[76]Levin, *Myth of the Golden Age.*

primitive peoples, and had pointed out an analogy with the sign language of deaf and dumb people (though not, as later thinkers were to do, with the first attempts at speech of little children).[77] But in the *Refutation of Philosophies* (1608), Bacon is openly flirting with the myth of the wisdom of the ancients. He believes the fables to be 'the sacred survivals of better times' and conjectures that scientific projects even more advanced than his own may have been known to remote antiquity. But he must stand by his oft-repeated principle that 'truth must be discovered by the light of nature, not recovered from the darkness of the past'.[78] A year later Bacon came into the open with *De Sapientia Veterum* (1609) in which he purported to reveal the hidden meaning of classical myths. There were possibly two reasons for this change of mind. Undoubtedly, the idea of an occult wisdom had captured his imagination, and all the more so as he became increasingly convinced that the tenets of his own philosophy had been anticipated by the ancients. He was no longer a voice in the wilderness, working, as he had complained, in complete isolation. Secondly, he no doubt had a tactical motive for espousing the theory of the matchless wisdom of the ancients. Conscious of the difficulties of getting a favourable reception for his ideas, with their outrageous attacks on tradition, Bacon had withheld publication of the three tractates *The Masculine Birth of Time* (1603), *Thoughts and Conclusions* (1607) and *Refutation of Philosophies* (1608). To comment now on the myths and fables of antiquity would be a covert way of propagating his views. Accordingly, the leading themes of *De Sapientia Veterum* were the importance of separating science and faith, the advantages of scientific naturalism (study of secondary causes), the need for the right method, the function of research in advancing knowledge and, finally, a defence of political realism in the tradition of Machiavelli.

In line with this development went a change of mind on the question, 'Which came first, the fable or the meaning?.' In *The Advancement of Learning*, Bacon suggested that the fable was original and the interpretation subsequent. By the time he came to write *De Sapientia Veterum*, he had reversed his view. While not prepared to be dogmatic, he was so impressed by the close correspondence between a myth and its meaning that he 'cannot

---

[77]*AL*, p. 137.
[78]*PFB*, p. 1200.

help believing such signification to have been designed and meditated from the first, and purposely shadowed out'. Other stories are so absurd that, out of respect for the sagacious ancients, one has to suppose that they contain a hidden meaning. Bacon did not believe that humanity was ever savage and primitive, so he could not accept – and Vico would condemn him for this – that the myths of primitive man might have been spontaneous, imaginative responses to the universe brought forth by inarticulate beings under pressure of the emotions of awe, fear and appetite. It is summed up in Bacon's saying: 'As hieroglyphics came before letters, so parables came before arguments.'[79]

It is paradoxical then, that Bacon does reveal an almost Vichean sense of the inaccessibility of history, of the obscurity of the past and the extreme difficulty of recovering it in historical science. Bacon speaks of 'the deluge of time' and is startlingly modern in what he says about ransacking all available sources of information to get at a lost world. 'Uttermost antiquity', he remarks in *Valerius Terminus*, is 'like fame that muffles her head and tells tales'. But the historian must resist the temptation to imitate those cartographers who fill their ignorance with wastes and deserts.[80] Time is the river that carries down to us on the surface the trivia, the flotsam and jetsam of history, and allows things of substance to sink into its dark depths.[81] The task of the historian is to rescue those 'remnants of history' that, like the spars of a shipwreck, tell a tale. Although 'the memory of things be decayed and almost lost, yet acute and industrious persons, by a certain perseverance and scrupulous diligence, contrive out of genealogies, annals, titles, monuments, coins, proper names and styles, etymologies of words, proverbs, traditions, archives and instruments as well public as private, fragments of histories scattered about in books not historical – contrive, I say, from all these things or some of them, to recover somewhat from the deluge of time.' This is a labour of love for the true antiquary, for whom it is 'joined with a kind of reverence' for the human past.[82] But the research of the antiquary is only a beginning: it must be followed by interpretation and reconstruction.

---

[79]*PW*, pp. 822–4; cf. Rossi, *Francis Bacon*, ch. 3.
[80]*PW*, p. 190.
[81]*PFB*, p. 68.
[82]*PW*, p. 433.

In his stress on imaginative recreation and the role of historical judgement, Bacon could be a nineteenth-century historian of the school of Ranke, lacking only the facility of documentary criticism. His ideal is a noble one:

> To carry the mind in writing back into the past, and bring it into sympathy with antiquity; diligently to examine, freely and faithfully to report, and by the light of words to place as it were before the eyes, the revelations of times, of characters, of persons, the fluctuations of counsels, the courses and currents of actions, the bottoms of pretences, the secrets of governments, is a task of great labor and judgement.[83]

In Bacon's all-embracing scheme, history is the first of the three divisions of learning and corresponds to the mental faculty of memory. It is followed by poesy, corresponding to imagination, and by philosophy, corresponding to reason. Many commentators on Bacon have been led astray by this apparently simplistic demarcation into accusing Bacon of inconsistency, because his own historical efforts obviously involve both imaginative reconstruction and rational interpretation. Stuart Clark has warned against pressing the division too far, and has pointed out that in employing what was a commonplace of Renaissance faculty psychology, Bacon was safeguarding scientific history against imaginative inventions on the one hand and deductive generalizations on the other. But Bacon's identification of history with the faculty of memory does have several significant consequences in his thought.[84]

First, as we have seen, Bacon fails to attain the Vichean understanding of myths and fables as imaginative constructions, an intuitive response to the mystery of the cosmos, which can be relived by the historian through the faculty of *fantasia*. This would have brought the power of imaginative reconstruction to the heart of Bacon's historical method. Secondly, Bacon abandoned the rhetorical commonplace that history was philosophy teaching by examples. He transferred the aesthetic function of history to poetry and its didactic function to philosophy. For Bacon, imaginative or fictional history (*historia conficta*) serves better than factual history

---

[83]*PW*, p. 432.
[84]Stuart Clark, 'Bacon's *Henry VII*'.

to delight and elevate the mind, for 'Poesy seems to bestow upon nature those things which history denies to it; and to satisfy the mind with the shadows of things when the substance cannot be obtained.' He continues:

There is agreeable to the spirit of man a more ample greatness, a more perfect order and a more beautiful variety than it can anywhere (since the Fall) find in nature. And, therefore, since the acts and events which are the subjects of real history are not of sufficient grandeur to satisfy the human mind, Poesy is at hand to feign acts more heroical; since the successes and issues of actions related in true history are far from being agreeable to the merits of virtue and vice, Poesy corrects it, exhibiting events and fortunes as according to merit and the law of providence; since true history wearies the mind with satiety of ordinary events, one like another, Poesy refreshes it by reciting things unexpected and full of vicissitudes. So that this Poesy conduces not only to delight but also to magnanimity and morality.[85]

Unlike reason and history which buckle and bow down the mind to the nature of things, poesy accommodates the show of things to the desires of the mind (*rerum simulacra ad animi desideria*).[86]

Philip Sidney, in his *Apologie for Poetrie* (written: 1579–80, published: 1595) had already made the fundamental distinction between the particular truths of history and the universal truths of poetry. But whereas Sidney's aim was to instil the glory of poetry and the nobility of imagination, Bacon's use of the dichotomy was intended to disparage and trivialize poesy, for from a rigorously empirical point of view, fiction is synonymous with falsehood. Hobbes would take the argument a stage further by arguing that both empirical and imaginative truth was inferior to mathematical demonstration, thereby trivializing history as well as poetry. For Hobbes, history could only be illustrative of rational truth, and for that purpose 'typical' history will serve as well as the real thing. By distinguishing the task of history, which was to establish an accurate record of events, from the task of philosophy, which was to draw out precepts and generalizations from the facts as a basis for

---

[85]*PW*, p. 440.
[86]Ibid.

a science of humanity in society, Bacon completed his destruction
of the received view of history as philosophy teaching by examples.
Just as natural history, in Bacon's system, forms a foundation for
applied science or natural philosophy, so civil history forms a
foundation for a science of humanity comprising ethics and civil
philosophy (politics). These disciplines operate in an empirical and
inductive way on the basis of the facts provided by history. They
are thus solely concerned with 'what is', not with 'what ought to
be'. The philosopher, acting as midwife, can produce a 'Georgics of
the Mind', a science of human nature, and to do this he will find
that character and disposition are best studied in the histories of
Livy, Tacitus, Herodian, Comines, Machiavelli and Guicciardini.
Bacon has a special word of praise for Tacitus and Machiavelli.
While the ethics of Plato and Aristotle are much admired, 'the
pages of Tacitus breathe a livelier and truer observation of morals
and institutions'. Machiavelli too shows us humanity as it is, not
as idealists have imagined it to be.[87]

There is a rather chilling Machiavellian touch in one of Bacon's
Sacred Meditations (perhaps inaptly named in this case). Bacon
is underlining the need for a man of affairs, a reformer, to be
appraised of villainy, and remarks that 'wicked men, who have not a
wholesome thought in them, naturally assume that goodness springs
from a certain simplicity of moral character and ignorance and
inexperience of human affairs'. They must be made to realize that
'every recess of their wicked hearts lies open to the understanding
of him' (not God but the philosopher–statesman) with whom
they have to do. Those who seek to serve the public good should
acquaint themselves with what Scripture calls 'the deeps of Satan',
for 'there are neither teeth nor stings, nor venom, nor wreaths and
folds of serpents, which ought not to be all known and as far as
examination doth lead, tried: neither let any man here fear infection
or pollution; for the sun entereth into sinks and is not defiled'.[88]
Like Hobbes after him, Bacon complains that moralists have held
up a model of perfect moral rectitude, but have done little to help
those who are struggling with acute moral decisions, involving

---

[87]*PW*, pp. 57–8; *PFB*, p. 710.
[88]Bacon, *Works*, vol. 7, p. 245 ('Of the Innocency of the Dove and the Wisdom of
the Serpent').

compromise or a choice between evils. He attributes this to the disdain felt by philosophers in the classical–rhetorical tradition to soil their thoughts with what is common or mean – 'that hidden rock whereupon both this and so many other barks of knowledge have struck and foundered'.[89] Bacon's programme for the reform of learning was intended to culminate in a scientific ethical system, the crown of his science of humanity.

Bacon's *History of the Reign of Henry VII* was intended, like the *Essays*, as an exercise in Baconian psychology, a Georgics of the mind, providing the raw material for the science of human nature. As Stuart Clark has pointed out, this did not necessarily involve Bacon in any detailed research or criticism of documents. Bacon thought that 'it was historically quite valid simply to take the story that was readily available in existing accounts of the reign, purge it of its interpretative framework, and substitute one of his own'. It is not as a model of how to write history that Bacon has his place in the evolution of modern historical thought.[90] His true importance for historical studies is twofold. First, it lies in his progressive vision. In Bacon we have not yet reached a full-fledged rationalistic idea of progress such as the *philosophes* promoted. Nevertheless, Bacon is, as Quinton has put it, 'the most confident, explicit and influential of the first exponents of the idea of progress'.[91] Secondly, Bacon secured the integration of historical studies into the early scientific (empirico-inductive) movement, and provided theoretical grounding for a science of history.[92] From the *philosophes* to Macaulay and James Mill, and from Vico to Coleridge, that is to rationalists and Romantics alike, Bacon dominates historical thought: for the rationalists the undisputed father of historical science; for the Romantics a giant to be overthrown in the path of historical understanding. A notion of progress, once it is in the air, is conducive to concepts of development in doctrine and practice, even for those who, like Newman, loath all talk of scientific and technological progress. But Bacon's hostility to tradition would contribute to the liberal strand in Anglican thought.

---

[89]*PW*, p. 562.
[90]Stuart Clark, 'Henry VII', p. 116.
[91]Quinton, *Francis Bacon*, p. 29.
[92]Fussner, *Historical Revolution*, p. 264.

Scripture and tradition

'The place and authority of Scripture,' writes McAdoo, 'does not vary throughout the seventeenth century. . . . It is the criterion in all writing on doctrine, ecclesiastical origins and polity, and the deciding factor in all disputed questions, appealed to by, and equally cogent for moderates, Puritans and Laudians.'[93] But Scripture was not taken in isolation: its interpretative context was primitive tradition or 'antiquity' and the interpretative instrument was the sanctified human reason. Chillingworth is an exception to the general tenor in his brash biblicism: 'Propose me anything out of this book [the Bible], and require whether I believe it or no, and seem it never so incomprehensible to human reason, I will subscribe it with hand and heart, as knowing no demonstration can be stronger than this; God hath said so, therefore it is true.'[94]

Bishop Beveridge (1637–1708) is more subtle and nuanced. Beveridge expounded Article VI of the Thirty-nine Articles ('Of the Sufficiency of the Holy Scriptures for salvation') thus[95]:

> There is nothing necessary to be believed concerning God, nor done in obedience unto God by us, but what is here revealed to us; and therefore all traditions of men which are contrary to this word of God are necessarily to be abhorred, and all traditions of men not recorded in this word of God are not necessarily to be believed. What is here written we are bound to believe . . . and what is not here written we are not bound to believe.

But Beveridge adds a significant qualification: 'I say we are not bound to believe it, but I cannot say we are bound not to believe it; for there be many truths which we may believe, nay, are bound to believe, because truth, which notwithstanding are not recorded in the word of God.' This caveat liberates his approach to authority from an obsessive biblicism, but Beveridge is careful not to overstep the fundamental Reformation principle, insisted on in that Article,

---

[93]McAdoo, *Spirit of Anglicanism*, pp. 309–10.
[94]Chillingworth, *Religion of Protestants*, p. 463 (vi, 56).
[95]For what follows from Beveridge: More and Cross (eds.), *Anglicanism*, pp. 94–5.

that Holy Scripture contains all things necessary to salvation. He continues therefore:

> Though there be many things we may believe, yet is there nothing we need believe in order to our everlasting happiness which is not here written; so that if we believe all that is here spoken, and do all that is here commanded, we shall certainly be saved, though we do not believe what is not here spoken, nor do what is not here commanded.

The place that classical Anglicanism allocates to extra-biblical tradition is then favourable, though strictly circumscribed. Primitive tradition illuminates the biblical text. Patristic theology was assimilated into the Anglican way of thinking. Anglican scholars sacrificed great portions of their lives to the study of the Fathers. Most notably, James Ussher devoted 18 years to reading them systematically: his erudition was, for many then and since, beyond imagining.[96] Responding to the French Protestant Peter Moulin about episcopacy, Andrewes writes: 'Very glad I was to hear it from you, That the Authority of Antiquity should be ever in great esteem with you. I love you for that word. . . . For my part it hath been my opinion ever, I was ever of that mind.'[97]

In his *Discourse about Tradition* (1683), Simon Patrick refutes 'the calumny . . . that the Church of England rejects all tradition':

> No, the Scripture itself is a tradition; and we admit all other traditions which are subordinate, and are agreeable unto that; together with all those things which can be proved to be apostolical by the general testimony of the Church in all ages: nay, if any thing not contained in Scripture, which the Roman church now pretends to be part of God's word, were delivered to us, by as universal uncontrolled tradition as the Scripture is, we should receive it, as we do the Scripture.[98]

Patrick also upholds the authority of the inherited rule of faith (*regula fidei*) – which is not the same as 'unwritten verities', for

---

[96]Ford, *Ussher*, Introduction.
[97]Andrewes, *Of Episcopacy*, pp. 14–15.
[98]Patrick, *Discourse about Tradition*, p. 48.

these are ancient texts – in a way that would later be affirmed by Keble and by Newman and Manning in their Anglican period. 'The sum and substance of the Christian religion,' Patrick affirms, 'hath been delivered down to us, even from the Apostles' days, in other ways or forms, beside the Scriptures,' that is to say in the baptismal vows, the creed, in prayers and hymns.[99]

The role of primitive tradition, for Simon Patrick, is to guide our interpretation of Scripture:

> The sense of the whole Church . . . must be acknowledged also to be of greater or lesser authority, as it was nearer or farther off from the times of the Apostles. What was delivered by their immediate followers ought to weigh so much with us, as to have the greatest humane authority, and to be looked upon as little less than divine.[100]

In his *Exposition of the XXXIX Articles* (1699), Gilbert Burnet, Bishop of Salisbury under William III (and Queen Mary, while she lived), addresses the question of Scripture and tradition, especially supposed unwritten apostolic traditions.[101] Under Article VI, 'Of the Sufficiency of Holy Scriptures for salvation', Burnet notes where the Church of England and the Roman Catholic Church agree and where they disagree with regard to the rule of faith. Both recognize that the Scriptures are divinely inspired and are given by God. But Roman Catholics – whom he acknowledges elsewhere to belong to the Church and whose orders and sacraments he accepts – hold that the Scriptures are not a sufficient rule of faith on their own, but need to be supplemented by oral apostolic tradition, and that to identify precisely which such traditions are truly apostolic, an infallible defining authority in the Church is needed, that is, the papacy. The Church of England, on the other hand, holds the Scriptures to be a complete rule of faith, and although it makes much use of tradition, especially that which is most primitive and nearest the apostolic source, as a guide in interpreting the Scriptures, in matters of faith it rejects all oral tradition and refuses to accept

---

[99]Ibid., p. 18.

[100]Ibid., p. 7; cf. 22.

[101]Further on Burnet and on the attempted censure of his *Exposition* see Avis, *Anglicanism and the Christian Church*, pp. 100–6.

any doctrine that is not clearly contained in Scripture or may be clearly proved from it. Tradition was invoked against Christ, but he rebutted it from Scripture, charging the Jews with making the law of God of no effect by means of their traditions. We cannot enter into communion with a Church that imposes on the conscience doctrines or practices drawn from unwritten traditions, and this is the main ground of the Church of England's separate existence from the Roman Church.[102]

The appeal to the Fathers in the first half of the seventeenth century was not a kind of patristic fundamentalism or trading of texts, but was marked by moderation and liberality, as both McAdoo and Quantin agree.[103] Alongside the theological deployment of the Fathers at this time, we find a homiletical and rhetorical use of their writings in the sermons of Lancelot Andrewes (especially the Greek Fathers)[104] and a spiritual use in private devotion. Andrewes' *Preces privatae* are studded with quotations from and allusions to the Fathers (Irenaeus, Tertullian, Cyprian, Gregory of Nyssa and his namesake of Nazianzen, Chrysostom, Jerome and Augustine), the medievals (Alcuin, Anselm, Bernard, Peter Lombard, Thomas Aquinas, Bradwardine and Jean Gerson) and sixteenth-century Roman Catholic writers (Erasmus, John Fisher), as well as ancient liturgies – though (interestingly) not the Reformers.[105]

It was in the 1620s, with the work of Richard Montague, that the issues were sharpened. Calvinist theology was no longer the lens through which the Fathers were viewed; the Arminian framework began to take its place, and by the 1630s antiquity was seen as the preparation for reading Protestant divines, and not vice versa.[106] Where the Reformed theological paradigm persisted, it often favoured Augustine, rather than Calvin – John Davenant and Samuel Ward being cases in point. Ward's view of tradition (congenial to Ussher and Davenant) was that 'the perpetual Tradition of the Church is no way to be slighted, where it doth not

---

[102][Burnet], *Exposition of the XXXIX Articles*, pp. 79–87.
[103]Quantin, *Church of England and Christian Antiquity*, p. 150: 'The early seventeenth-century appeal to the Fathers was both irenical and liberal in character, in the Erasmian tradition of Christian humanism.'
[104]Lossky, *Lancelot Andrewes*.
[105]Andrewes, *Devotions*.
[106]Quantin, *Church of England and Christian Antiquity*, pp. 155–70.

cross the Scripture, but is consonant to general Grounds contained in them'.[107] Laud's rule of thumb was 'Scripture interpreted by the Primitive Church'. As with the Reformers, the supremacy of Scripture was not upheld to the exclusion of early tradition.[108]

Consensus of the Fathers?

What is meant by primitive tradition: the views of all of the Fathers, singly, one by one, or some amalgamation of them all; the lowest patristic common denominator or something much bigger but more elusive? This is the problem of the consensus of antiquity in seventeenth-century Anglican theological method.

The uncompromising High Churchman, Peter Gunning, Richard Baxter's nemesis at the Savoy Conference (1661)[109] and later Bishop of Chichester and then of Ely, reflected with distaste in 1662 on the theological turbulence of the Interregnum when anyone could interpret any biblical text according to their own fancies. On the contrary:

> Reason, and experience, and the direction of all wise men in the Church of God ancient and modern (the house of wisdom), Councils, reverend Fathers and writers, and our Church in particular, have directed and commanded us not to interpret Scripture in things of public concernment to the Church's rule of believing and doing, but as we find it interpreted by the Holy Fathers and Doctors of the Church, as they had received it from those before them.[110]

John Cosin offered a generously open-ended view of tradition in controversy with Roman Catholics, but one that remained firmly anchored in the consensus of antiquity. We agree with them, he said on 'The unanimous and general consent of the ancient Catholic Fathers and the universal Church of Christ in the interpretation of

---

[107]Ward to Ussher, cited Quantin, ibid., p. 183.
[108]Ibid., p. 193. For the uses of Church history in theological debate see Spurr, 'A special kindness for dead bishops'.
[109]Baxter, *Autobiography*, pp. 169, 223–4.
[110]More and Cross (eds.), *Anglicanism*, p. 91.

the Holy Scriptures, and the collection of all necessary matters of Faith from them during the first six hundred years, and downwards to our own days.'[111] The 'general, constant and perpetual consensus of the Fathers' was also championed by Matthew Scrivener in the early 1670s, but as Quantin correctly observes, such a consensus is an elusive and unstable basis for theological method.[112] However, in so far as English patristic scholarship in the second half of the seventeenth century attempted to reconstruct and to portray the faith and order of the early Church, as a weapon against both Roman Catholic claims and Dissenting challenges, it was continuing the work of the Reformers who used the same method against Rome and the Reformation radicals (Anabaptists). Appeal to antiquity was also a weapon in internal Anglican controversy. The massive researches of Joseph Bingham and others, including various Nonjurors, into early Christian teaching and practice informed the debate over the comprehension of Dissenters in the late seventeenth century. Dissenters did not have holy orders and were guilty of schism. Their ministers were equal to laymen. Dissenters had therefore received lay baptism. Were these valid baptisms, albeit uncanonically administered? If they were not valid baptisms, there was no chance of Dissenters being brought within a comprehensive national Church. Although Bingham's arguments for a principle of economy eventually shaped Anglican policy towards the baptisms administered by ministers lacking episcopal ordination, refuting the hard-line views of Roger Laurence, the Nonjuror, and some conforming High Churchmen, comprehension failed for other reasons.[113]

One aspect of that reconstruction and portrayal of the primitive Church was the research of such as Ussher and later Pearson in support of the true text of Ignatius' epistles to the churches of Asia Minor at the start of the second century with their assumption of monarchical or solo episcopacy. If Ignatius showed the apostolic origins of episcopacy, Cyprian demonstrated the independence of the bishops from the pope and showed their corporate solidarity, and Clement of Rome testified against the sin of schism.[114] Some

---

[111]Ibid., p. 55.
[112]Quantin, *Church of England and Christian Antiquity*, p. 338.
[113]Barnard, 'The Use of the Patristic Tradition'.
[114]Quantin, *Church of England and Christian Antiquity*, p. 341.

things were clear enough: as Bull put it, next to Scripture the
Church of England reveres and follows 'the unanimous judgement
of antiquity where it can be found (as it certainly is on all the most
important questions'.[115] Beveridge extended the scope of consensus
and unanimity to the mind of the Church through the ages: 'that
immense body of all Christians in all ages that is commonly called
the Catholic or universal Church' and whose consensus teaches
certain basic principles. As for the Fathers, Beveridge said, 'we do
not speak of each Father separately but of all of them together.' The
fact that they disagree about various matters makes their agreement
on others all the more convincing.[116]

Two centuries later, the Tractarians were able to appeal to the
consistent witness of the Anglican divines of this period to the
collective authority of the Fathers. In *Tract 78*, they were able
to produce a *catena* of forty-two authors or official sources that
appealed to the consensus of the Fathers. The extracts ranged
from Jewel in the mid-sixteenth century to Van Mildert, Bishop
of Durham in the early nineteenth, and took in writers of various
stripes, including Hooker on the one hand and some Nonjurors on
the other. The principle, for which they believed the earlier Anglican
divines, as well as they themselves, stood was 'Catholicity is the only
test of truth.'[117] This list, or Anglican 'succession', as the authors call
it, remains an impressive testimony to the power and coherence of
Anglican theology during this period, as well as to the principle
which it is meant to illustrate.

The Anglican appeal to tradition in the form of antiquity was
not, as McAdoo points out, 'an academic or antiquarian frame of
reference nor was it primarily a method of doctrinal equation'.[118]
What respect for tradition provided was the continuity that is
essential to catholicity, but it was a continuity that was not merely
external, a rigid straitjacket of enforced conformity to precedent
(which one?), but internal and one of a common mind and felt
spiritual affinity. It gave emerging Anglicanism, perhaps uniquely
among those churches that were shaped by the Reformation, a

---

[115]Ibid., p. 349.
[116]Ibid., pp. 350–1.
[117]*Tracts for the Times*, vol. IV (1836–37); pagination not continuous in the volume;
quote from p. 2.
[118]McAdoo, *Spirit of Anglicanism*, p. 318.

profound sense of the Christian past and anchored it in history, while at the same time serving to counterbalance the more unpredictable elements of rational enquiry and freedom of debate. It was owing to the balancing factors of reason, conscience and the Hookerian sense of what is appropriate to the circumstances, that tradition and antiquity were not permitted to become independent sources of authority, but were confined to the ancillary role of providing general guidance and sources of relevant evidence in doctrinal debate. The weakness of this position is, however, as McAdoo points out, that in some circumstances 'the appeal to antiquity can convey the impression of producing authorities rather than adducing evidence',[119] and this was not what Anglican theological method in this period normally intended.

Critique of a critique

Jean-Louis Quantin, writing perfectly in what is not his native language and deploying awesome learning, analyses the appeal to antiquity – one aspect of tradition – from the Reformation to the Nonjurors.[120] Quantin's work is a mine of information and indispensable in its sphere, but I find some of his sweeping judgements stimulating, rather than convincing. Quantin is essentially arguing that a *confessional identity* for the reformed English Church was being *constructed* in the seventeenth century and that the Anglo-Catholic movement, from the Tractarians to recent times, engaged in a similar construction, but that this was an ideological exercise in justification of their own stance, a manifestation of the Whig interpretation of history. I would say that there were always Anglican *identities* – a constellation of identities – rather than one identity and that the Church of England has never been *confessional* in the way that other reformed churches have been. And to say that identity was 'constructed' by theologians gives a little too much weight to the cerebral and intellectual in the life of a church. There is more to a church's identity than theology: it is a life-world. How much did the life-world of English people change in the sixteenth century? There was still prayer and sacrament, priest and parish,

---

[119]Ibid., p. 407.
[120]Quantin, *Church of England and Christian Antiquity*.

bishop and cathedral, even though the way that they manifested themselves varied from one reign to the next. The dynamic nature of emerging Anglicanism lies in the fact that, as Quantin puts it, 'The originality of the sixteenth-century Church of England was to have adopted a Reformed theology while retaining pre-Reformation structures.'[121]

Quantin warns that it is still too often assumed that deploying patristic quotations to support one's argument 'necessarily implies a commitment to tradition'.[122] But 'tradition' here is undifferentiated, lacking in profile. The Reformers and seventeenth-century divines were not committed to 'tradition' as such (who could be, given its bewildering diversity?), but to that normative part of it which they invoked as 'the primitive Church'. However, Quantin's charge against Anglican apologists then and now of massaging the past to give credibility to the present is a warning well taken – provided that we are all willing to apply it to ourselves as well.

In the late sixteenth century, the dominant theology in the Church of England was that of the Swiss Reformation, including Calvin but not limited to him. Quantin believes that there was a 'latent contradiction' between Protestant doctrine and pre-Reformation structures in the Elizabethan Church, a contradiction that would come home to roost in the conflicts of the mid-seventeenth century.[123] Because the Puritan-Presbyterian-Independent axis that temporarily destroyed the Church of England half a century later was identified with Calvinist theology, that theology was widely discredited when England emerged from the Civil War and Oliver Cromwell's Protectorate. The theological court of appeal shifted from Reformed to patristic sources (though that was certainly not the end of Calvinism in the Church of England).[124] It was that trauma that ensured that patristic authority became an essential part of what we may by now call Anglican apologetic.

Quantin dismisses as romantic twaddle the idea that there was such a thing as 'the Anglican mind' and exposes the *via media* project as a rhetorical strategy. Orthodoxy, he holds, was a construction and has now, thanks to recent research, been deconstructed.[125]

---

[121]Ibid., p. 88.
[122]Ibid., p. 22.
[123]Ibid., pp. 14–15.
[124]Hampton, *Anti-Arminians*.
[125]Quantin, *Church of England and Christian Antiquity*, p. 16.

He accuses McAdoo and Gary Bennett of idealizing the development of Anglican theology in this period, of a 'Whig interpretation' of Anglican history – everything was working together to produce the right, the definitive theology, that of scholarly, moderate Anglican Catholicism of the mid-twentieth century. Quantin is hostile to Anglo-Catholicism, describing it as 'a segment within a segment'.[126] Quantin shows how theological method was tactical, adaptive and ideological. In the seventeenth century, he alleges, 'the very identity of the Church of England was reinvented'.[127]

Quantin takes the role of antiquity in seventeenth-century apologetic as a pivotal indicator of theological method, which in his view lacked integrity. 'The Fathers were not regarded as sources of doctrine but as repositories of useful quotations to prove a doctrine garnered elsewhere, in theory from Scripture, in practice from the works of modern Protestant theologians.' But Quantin, adds, taking the words out of my mouth, as it were, 'Roman Catholic divines did not proceed otherwise.'[128]

Several questions keep cropping up. Is it true, as was often claimed, that the Church of England was more devoted to patristic study than other reformed churches? This is doubtful and we have already noted some evidence in the case. Which Fathers do we mean when we appeal to patristic theology: the ante-Nicene or the fourth and fifth-century writers? Preferences changed, from the earlier to the later as the century wore on. Was the true Church continuous through history, as Archbishop Laud argued, or episodic and largely underground in the form of medieval 'heresies', as Anglican Reformers up to Elizabeth's Archbishop Parker tended to insist – a mere dotted line through the centuries? Similarly, was the classic Anglican claim of continuity with the primitive Church mere rhetorical bluster, given that there was no fully-fledged concept of the apostolic succession in and of the Church, in the sense of the historic episcopate, until after the Civil War?[129] What

---

[126]Ibid., p. 10.

[127]Ibid., p. 17. Quantin seems kinder to the Church of England in his earlier short study, 'The Fathers in Seventeenth Century Anglican Theology'.

[128]Ibid., p. 83.

[129]The concept of apostolic succession and continuity of apostolic ministry certainly exists in embryo in Bilson, Hooker and Andrewes at the turn of the sixteenth century. The Tractarians were able to deploy them to start their *catena* of authorities in support of this doctrine: *Tract 74: Catena Patrum, No. 1: Testimony of Writers in the Later English Church to the Doctrine of the Apostolical Succession: Tracts for the Times.*

is the significance of the fact that, while it was standard to identify the pope with anti-christ until the mid-seventeenth century, this identification is not supported by the official formularies? Should students be put to read the Fathers before their minds were shaped by reading Calvin and other Reformed divines, or vice versa? What does the Protestant slogan *sola scriptura* mean – that the Bible contains precepts and precedents to govern every aspect of church life, or that it alone shows the way of salvation? These are some of the tensions and dilemmas of emerging Anglicanism: Quantin does not believe that they were resolved or apparently that they ever could be. *Au contraire*, without being complacent or triumphalist or engaging in 'effortless Anglican superiority', this present study upholds the integrity of the Anglican platform, its theology, ecclesiology and the methods that underpinned it.

5

Classical Anglicanism:
II. The authority of reason
and the validity of tradition

Richard Hooker had formulated, on the basis of first principles, what became the typical appeal of classical Anglican theological method to Scripture, reason and tradition (or antiquity), though with Scripture always (at least in theory) supreme among them. In the hands of the seventeenth-century Anglican divines (Jacobean, Caroline and Restoration), Hooker's method – albeit with some differences of emphasis between the 'liberal' Anglicans such as Hales and Chillingworth who endorsed Hooker's placing of reason above tradition, and the High Churchmen who tended to reverse Hooker's order, placing tradition above reason – produced what is often regarded as the finest flower of Anglican divinity, a monumental cumulative theological achievement. Hooker had also established the place of reason, which was merely implicit in the Anglican Reformers, as competent to interpret Scripture, adjudicate on tradition and instruct the Church as to what was and what was not binding in both. Against exaggerated forms of philosophical Nominalism, associated particularly with Gabriel Biel,[1] Hooker declared, following Aquinas, that God's being is a law to his working, that the structures of the world are rational and operate according to divinely ordained laws in their proper spheres, and that reason is God's highest gift to humanity. The seventeenth-century divines, following Hooker, had as McAdoo puts it, 'firmly grasped the truth

---

[1] See Obermann, *Harvest.*

that reason was the human characteristic and that its sphere was not simply speculation but the whole range of human activities'.[2]

The appeal to reason was by no means the preserve of one particular tradition within the seventeenth-century Church of England. Jeremy Taylor, a 'liberal catholic' Anglican (to use an anachronistic descriptor), asserts: 'Scripture, tradition, councils and Fathers are the evidence in a question, but reason is the judge.'[3] Simon Patrick (1625–1707, a prominent Latitudinarian bishop), later in the century, opposes reason to the mere assertion of authority, particularly an authority claiming infallibility for itself. God 'hath given us the use of reason', Patrick says, 'which if we will blindly resign to any pretended authority, what is it but to shut our eyes when we should open them'.[4] Gilbert Burnet, a 'liberal Protestant' Anglican (to use a convenient, though anachronistic label), sounds like one of the Cambridge Platonists when he announces, 'Reason is God's image in us.'[5] Among High Churchmen, William Laud speaks of the role of reason in a way that echoes Hooker (and therefore Aquinas), but which is actually not far from Calvin: 'Though reason without grace cannot see the way to heaven nor believe this Book [the Scriptures] in which God hath written the way, yet grace is never placed but in a reasonable creature.' According to Laud, grace refreshes the spiritual sight, enabling reason to see that which by nature it cannot see, but not to detract from reason in what it can understand. Faith is greater than either reason or knowledge in this life.[6] We may compare Laud's moderate 'reasonableness' with the more strident appeal to reason in William Sherlock in 1690: 'We must believe nothing that contradicts the plain and express dictates of natural reason, which all mankind agree in, whatever pretence of revelation there be for it.' However, Sherlock points out, this does not mean forcing one's personal interpretation on the text, but submitting to the sense and meaning of the text, rather than attempting to make Scripture submit to our rational speculation about matters beyond our ken, especially the infinite nature and essence of God.[7] This approach to Scripture is again close to Calvin.

---

[2]McAdoo, *Spirit of Anglicanism*, p. 312.
[3]Ibid., p. 74. See further on Taylor below.
[4]Patrick, *Sermon Preached before the King*, p. 25.
[5][Burnet], *Exposition*, p. 211.
[6]More and Cross (eds.), *Anglicanism*, p. 102.
[7]Ibid., p. 117.

Latitudinarians and Cambridge Platonists

Bishop Burnet recalls of the 'Latitudinarians', whom he had known personally: 'They loved the constitution of the church, and the liturgy, and could well live under them; but they did not think it unlawful to live under another form. They wished that things might have been carried on with more moderation, and they continued to keep a good correspondence with those who had differed from them in opinion, and allowed a great freedom both in philosophy and in divinity; from whence they were called men of latitude. And upon this men of narrower thoughts and fiercer tempers fastened upon them the name of *Latitudinarians*.'[8] The 'latitude men' generally, and particularly the Cambridge Platonists who had taught and mentored many of them, sought a harmony and coinherence of grace and nature, revelation and reason, theology and philosophy, and moral rigour and purified affections.[9] What we are seeing here is the rise and dominance of rational, moral religion in the Church of England, but that does not mean that the Latitudinarians neglected, either in their lives or in their teaching, personal devotion to Christ, prayer, use of the sacraments or love of the Scriptures.[10]

The Cambridge Platonists are principally Benjamin Whichcote, Nathaniel Culverwel, John Smith, Henry More and Ralph Cudworth. But we should not think of them as a sort of Sealed Knot of eclectics: De Pauley includes Stillingfleet among the Platonists and shows their affinities with Andrewes and Laud.[11] These divines did not work in separate silos; the theological community of the Church of England was open and permeable, though electric with

---

[8]Burnet, *History of his own Times*, pp. 128–9. Cf. [Patrick, Simon], *A Brief Account of the New Sect of Latitudinarians*.

[9]For the Latitudinarians see McAdoo, *Spirit of Anglicanism*, chs. 5 and 6; Spurr, 'Latitudinarianism and the Restoration Church'; Porter, *Reformation and Reaction*, pp. 414–29; Cragg, *Puritanism to the Age of Reason*, ch. 4; Rivers, *Reason, Grace and Sentiment*, vol. 1, ch. 2. For mainly the theology of the Cambridge Platonists see Tulloch, *Rational Theology: II The Cambridge Platonists*. For mainly the philosophy see Muirhead, *Platonic Tradition in Anglo-Saxon Philosophy*; Cassirer, *Platonic Renaissance*. See also de Pauley, *Candle of the Lord*; Powicke, *Cambridge Platonists* – not wholly reliable on the theological context. For a selection from their writings, see Patrides (ed. and intro.), *Cambridge Platonists*.

[10]C. F. Allison, *Rise of Moralism*.

[11]de Pauley, *Candle of the Lord*, pp. 245–6.

controversy. Whichcote insisted against his critics that he had read more of Calvin, Perkins and Beza than of pagan philosophers such as Plato.[12] Rivers makes the point that Wilkins, not a Cambridge man, was one of the most significant figures, alongside Whichcote, among the first generation of Latitudinarians, and that Tillotson, who was not particularly a Platonist, dominated in the second generation.[13] Latitudinarianism can be seen as the outer circle; Cambridge Platonism as the inner.

The question of theological authority is central for this group, as for others. The Cambridge Platonists deal in reason, the light of nature, conscience, commonly accepted notions, Scripture, the leading of the Spirit, tradition and antiquity, and philosophy ancient and modern. Their favourite biblical text is Proverbs 20.27: 'The spirit of man is the candle of the LORD' (KJB). This text had been a favourite of Lancelot Andrewes, so is not unique to the Platonists.[14] In every person there is a spiritual and intellectual endowment, not extinguished by the Fall, that is the human affinity with God. It is the organ by which we apprehend the truth, both in nature and in Scripture. Biblical revelation includes, builds on and transcends the 'natural light'. The work of the Cambridge Platonists and of the bishops and clergy who took part in the Royal Society 'made natural theology a fixture in Anglican theological method'.[15]

These men were not ivory-tower contemplatives. They directed their fire against a broad range of enemy targets: supposed atheists (like Hobbes), or those (the libertines) who lived as though there were no God; those whom they regarded as enthusiasts, fanatics and sectarians among the Nonconformists after 1660; and Calvinists among the Puritan Nonconformists, with their doctrine of predestination, their emphasis on the incapacity of the fallen intellect, and their denial of free will; and Roman Catholics, who exalted the authority of the Church above Scripture, reason and antiquity. The Latitudinarians as a group were collaborative, organized and worked purposefully to propagate their views and to shape the education and formation of the clergy.[16]

---

[12]Porter, *Reformation and Reaction*, p. 424.
[13]Rivers, *Reason, Grace and Sentiment*, vol. 1, p. 28.
[14]Porter, *Reformation and Reaction*, p. 394.
[15]McAdoo, *Spirit of Anglicanism*, p. 311.
[16]Ibid., p. 39.

The biblical image of the candle of the Lord unites for them the intellectual and moral dimensions of thought and feeling. Reason and conscience go together and the practice of the Christian virtues is necessary to see the light. The Cambridge Platonists were abused by Puritans as 'Moral Preachers' and 'meer Moral Men, without the power of Godliness', because for them the ethical dimension of the Bible was indispensable. Their preaching filled a moral vacuum at the height of Presbyterian doctrinal and speculative sermons under the Commonwealth. Burnet alleges that 'the way of preaching . . . among the divines of England before them was overrun with pedantry, a great mixture of quotations from fathers and ancient writers, a long opening of a text with the concordance of every word in it, and a giving all the different expositions with the grounds of them, and the entering into some parts of controversy, and all concluding in some, but very short, practical applications . . .,' so that 'all was piebald.'[17] They taught a moral road to spiritual enlightenment and deplored the preaching of naked faith without a life of obedience to God and the gospel. Whichcote reveals his continuity with Hooker (God's being is a law to his working) and embraces the Platonic tradition against the Nominalist stress on law and the ethical derived from the will of God and human authority: 'The *Moral* part of Religion never alters. Moral Laws are Laws *of themselves*, without Sanction by Will; and the Necessity of them arises from the Things themselves. All *other* things in Religion are *in Order to* These. The Moral Part of Religion does *sanctify* the Soul . . .'[18] The morally demanding religious life was also the way to happiness in this world and in heaven.

Although they were not at all unsympathetic to scientific research – Cudworth and More were members of the Royal Society and Glanville wrote a programmatic agenda for its work[19] – they repudiated Bacon's dualism of science and theology. Powicke says of Bacon that he 'honoured theology as the Jews honoured the Holy of holies: he thought it too sacred to enter'.[20] Cassirer says of the Platonists' disdain for Bacon's system: 'it was looked upon

---

[17]Burnet, *History of his Own Time*, p. 131; cf. Powicke, *Cambridge Platonists*, pp. 42–6; Rivers, *Reason, Grace and Sentiment*, vol. 1, p. 37.
[18]Whichcote, *Aphorisms*, no. 221 (orthography original).
[19]Cassirer, *Platonic Renaissance*, pp. 59–60.
[20]Powicke, *Cambridge Platonists*, p. 26.

by them as the absolute negation, subversion and perversion of all that in which they saw the meaning and true dignity of philosophic knowledge'.[21] Whichcote affirmed that 'There is nothing so intrinsically Rational as *Religion* is; nothing, that can so Justify it self; nothing, that hath so pure Reason to recommend itself, as Religion hath.' And again: 'A man's *Reason* is nowhere so much satisfied; as in matters of *Faith*' and nothing can be deemed to be revealed that is not made intelligible. Nothing without reason was to be proposed for belief and nothing against reason was to be accepted: 'Scripture is to be taken in a rational sense.'[22] Glanville protests that 'to decry, and disgrace *Reason*, is to strike up *Religion* by the Roots, and to prepare the world for *Atheism*'.[23] Tillotson, Archbishop of Canterbury, says 'Reason is the faculty whereby revelation is to be discerned.'[24] They acknowledged that there was much in Christianity that transcended reason, but insisted that it takes reason to know that.

Several characteristics of reason, as it was understood and deployed by the Cambridge Platonists, deserve to be noted. First, reason was the image of God in humankind, 'the candle of the Lord', not a searchlight but an instrument and the best that we have. It was the truly and uniquely human attribute and endowment and was not to be suppressed in the interests of authority or simple faith. But, secondly, this does not mean that the Cambridge Platonists set up reason in the place of Scripture, like the French Revolutionaries and their cult of reason personified as a sort of goddess: rather that reason must be our guide in understanding Scripture. Whichcote was emphatic that, on all necessary questions and taken as a whole, Scripture was 'clear, full and perspicuous'; 'the Revelation in Scripture is the only Rule in all matters of *Faith*'.[25] It was reason in the spirit of Richard Hooker, devout, prayerful and without hubris, that they espoused. Finally, their concept of reason was not merely analytical, but infused with moral and mystical intuition, the whole person reasoning. Its sphere was the whole world, as indicated

---

[21]Cassirer, *Platonic Renaissance*, p. 49.
[22]Whichcote, *Aphorisms*, nos 457, 880, 943, 1168 (orthography original).
[23]Rivers, *Reason, Grace and Sentiment*, vol. 1, p. 65.
[24]Ibid., pp. 66–7.
[25]Whichcote, *Select Sermons*, cited McAdoo, *Spirit of Anglicanism*, p. 89; id., *Aphorisms*, no. 778 (italics original).

by the affinity between the Cambridge Platonists and the new generation of natural philosophers (scientists) among whom John Ray was eminent.[26] 'The reason of things, the nature of things', was Whichcote's watchword. It was a cosmic vision.

Thomas Hobbes

Apostle of infidelity or pillar of the Established Church?

'Is Saul also among the prophets?' (1 Sam. 10.11). Is Hobbes also among the Anglican theologians of the seventeenth century? For students of the period, that is a question of endless fascination and divides interpreters of Hobbes. Was Thomas Hobbes (1588–1679) actually the arch-atheist of his age, or the staunchest supporter of the state Church – or possibly both at once? The evidence points both ways and in the end a judgement has to be made, or possibly suspended. When I studied Hobbes and history thirty years ago, I went along with the received 'politically correct' interpretation of Hobbes the secularist and atheist. But I have now changed my mind. We will review the main lines of the debate – in a word, godly or godless? – shortly. But of one thing there can be no doubt: Hobbes gave a massive impetus to the emerging rationalizing tendency in philosophy and theology in the second half of the seventeenth century. His method purported to be rigorously logical and deductive, on the model of mathematics and geometry in particular. Whether Hobbes succeeded in creating a completely coherent logical system is open to doubt, but that was his beloved model, and it set up a methodological paradigm for others to measure themselves against. The boldness of his ideas, the power of his reasoning and the penetrating pithiness of his language made him a force to be reckoned with. Hobbes had few disciples, but many antagonists: he set the age against himself, though his system was intended to support the status quo. The Latitudinarians, who leaned towards toleration and the Erastianism that could secure it, were forced to protest their innocence of 'Hobbism'. Others, like

---

[26] On Ray see McAdoo, *Spirit of Anglicanism*, ch. 7.

the Cambridge Platonists, who had their own way of privileging reason in theological argument, were compelled to adopt Hobbesian methods in order to attack him. Hobbes defined the debate, in the seventeenth century and well beyond, on religion, ethics and political philosophy. Hobbes cannot be omitted from any account of Anglican theological method in this period.

Indeed, Hobbes was, as Mintz puts it, the *bête noire* of his age, dubbed 'the Monster of Malmesbury' and 'the bug-bear of the nation', that is, a source of dread, a bogeyman.[27] In the minds of his contemporaries, Hobbes came to embody all that was opposed to Christianity and sound morals. To take one instance of many: Burnet says of Hobbes, 'He was a sceptic in religion; immoral in his philosophy; wavering in his politics; and a dogmatist in everything. A scoffer at Christianity, and at the belief of a future state; yet he is known to have frequently been a partaker of the eucharist; and to have been fearful of spectral appearances.' Burnet adds, 'So difficult is it to be consistent.'[28] Yet no one gave stronger intellectual support through his philosophy than Hobbes to the Church–State nexus. Hobbes's 'Leviathan' was a sovereign with absolute power in the state – a state that had absorbed the Church. There was no ecclesiastical function – defining doctrine, preaching, celebrating the sacraments, ordaining, administering discipline – that the sovereign could not perform.[29] This was Erastianism taken to its furthest extreme. But Hobbes had to live down – and write down, over and over again – the accusations of 'atheism' that he had brought upon himself by his philosophy.

Many modern scholars have taken contemporary assessments of Hobbes at face value – and we may say, largely out of their historical and intellectual context – and have portrayed Hobbes – an accomplished biblical scholar by the standards of his day and no mean polemical theologian – as the Apostle of secularism and atheism.[30] Leo Strauss led the way in 1936. While rightly pointing

---

[27]Mintz, *Hunting of Leviathan*, p. vii.
[28]Burnet, *History of his own Time*, p. 128n.
[29]*Lev.*, II, xviii: p. 233; III, xlii: pp. 570–1.
[30]Reventlow, *Authority of the Bible*, pp. 194–222, 524–38, provides a useful critical survey of German and English studies of Hobbes up to 1980. He locates Hobbes in the Anglican rational, ethical, royalist, humanist stream, but this would be basically Arminian, so Reventlow's theory, which contains elements of truth, does not explain Hobbes' pessimistic, Calvinistic view of human nature and human society.

to Hobbes's systematic opposition to all tradition (which is one reason why I locate the discussion of Hobbes at this point), Strauss infers that Hobbes denied the validity of received ethical norms altogether and therefore subverted the ethics of society. On this interpretation, Hobbes replaced traditional ethical norms with the mere command of the sovereign. Strauss also believes that Hobbes deduced his uncompromisingly cynical view of human nature from Aristotle (the content, not the method, for he abominated Aristotle's basically empirical method), rather than, as others suggest, from a Calvinist view of fallen humanity's total depravity.[31] In a later article, Strauss claims that Hobbes traced the downfall, as he saw it – having lived, as a self-confessed timid soul, through the savagery of the English Civil War – of the 'idealistic' (liberal) tradition of political philosophy, stemming from Aristotle, to one fundamental mistake: the assumption that 'man' is by nature a political or social animal. On the contrary, Hobbes insisted, the state of nature is one of a war of all against all. Paradoxically and unconvincingly, because it does not follow at all from Hobbes's bleak view of human nature, Strauss then hails Hobbes's thought as pointing 'necessarily and unmistakeably . . . to a thoroughly "enlightened," that is, a religious or atheistic society as the solution of the social or political problem.'[32] In fact, Hobbes's logical, deductive, ahistorical approach is the antithesis of the broadly empirical, 'experimental' methods of the Enlightenment.

Quentin Skinner's accomplished study of Hobbes' use of rhetorical devices presents a more subtle challenge to Hobbes's protestations of Anglican orthodoxy.[33] Skinner appears not to side explicitly with the 'atheistic' interpretation of Hobbes (unless he is taking this as read), but the drift of his argument is towards that view. He shows convincingly how Hobbes at first embraced the tradition of humanist rhetoric with all its arts of persuasion, then in his middle phase repudiated it, preferring to rely on the power of plain reason and naked logic to make his case, before in *Leviathan*, returning to his earlier stance and deploying the full panoply of rhetorical skills, particularly irony, to ridicule his adversaries and to debunk opposing beliefs. Clearly, Hobbes pillories scholastic philosophers,

---

[31]Strauss, *Political Philosophy of Hobbes*, esp. p. 97.
[32]Strauss, 'Spirit of Hobbes's Political Philosophy', pp. 3, 27.
[33]Skinner, *Reason and Rhetoric*, especially ch. 10.

papist priests, and fanatical 'enthusiasts': that is not debatable. But Skinner does not convince me when he suggests that certain possible ambiguities in some of Hobbes's language about the Bible and Christian doctrine are meant to scoff and sneer. I do not think that Skinner has made a case for Hobbes's unbelief – if that is part of what he intended to do.

Hobbes never publicly denies the existence of God and, *au contraire*, offers plausible arguments for the existence of a Supreme Being. So Jesseph follows Strauss in arguing that Hobbes's theistic discourse should not be taken at face value, but should be deconstructed by means of a hermeneutic of suspicion: Hobbes is speaking in a vein of arch-irony. '[T]he sincerity of these professions of belief is only apparent, and Hobbes was really a sly and ironic atheist who concealed his disbelief behind a screen of disingenuous theological verbiage while constructing a theological system that makes the concept of God inadmissible.' Jesseph argues that Hobbes 'explicitly and repeatedly endorsed principles that render the concept of God an absurdity'. He assumes that Hobbes's two principles, the principles of materialism (all that exists is corporeal) and of the incomprehensibility of God (God's essence cannot be known by humankind), utterly rule out the possibility that Hobbes was a Christian believer.[34] Mintz is another writer who advances the 'irony' interpretation of Hobbes's theological material. Hobbes's system, he writes, 'was not merely irreligious – it was barbed with irony. It delivered outrageously heretical/heterodox opinions at the same time that it professed to be orthodox. And it used the language of orthodoxy as a means of exploding orthodox beliefs.'[35]

Jeffrey Collins has a more interesting theory, while maintaining with Strauss and Jesseph that Hobbes was an unbeliever.[36] Collins

---

[34]Jesseph, 'Hobbes's Atheism', quotes at pp. 140–1. Cf. Strauss, *Political Philosophy of Hobbes*, p. 76.

[35]Mintz, *Hunting of Leviathan*, pp. 34–5. Cooke, *Hobbes and Christianity*, takes the same view. Hobbes attempts to deceive his Christian readers by a show of scriptural citations, but in reality he dethrones God and the Bible and puts 'man' and his rights in their place. Hobbes has no place for grace and merely wants to make the world a safe place for the natural man. Cf. equally decisively Willey, *Seventeenth Century Background*, ch. 6. Israel, *Enlightenment Contested*, p. 65, groups Hobbes with Spinoza and Bayle as the most subversive naturalistic thinkers of the early Enlightenment. As I will show, I believe that in two of these three cases – Bayle as well as Hobbes – Israel is mistaken in his interpretation of them, not as subversive, but as naturalistic.

[36]Collins, *Allegiance of Hobbes*.

portrays Hobbes as someone whose extreme Erastianism and anticlericalism led him to abandon the royalist cause during the Interregnum and to support Oliver Cromwell, the Lord Protector (King Charles II being in exile) as the best guarantee of national and social stability and security. According to Collins, Hobbes took this so far as to give his backing to the Independents, who formed Cromwell's main power base. Certainly, Hobbes's contemporaries interpreted *Leviathan* as a vindication of the Rebellion and as a betrayal of the monarchy. Collins suggests that Hobbes's main reasons for deciding to return to England in 1551–52 were not merely political, but ecclesiological. Of course, after the Restoration of the monarchy and the Church in 1660, Hobbes engaged in strenuous efforts at damage limitation, rewriting portions of *Leviathan* in the Latin version, and actually succeeded in ingratiating himself once again with Charles II, who was won over by his wit and sagacity.

Hobbes's Erastianism and anticlericalism draw on two well-established theological traditions: that of Reformation ecclesiology, which was anti-hierarchical and approached the inherited structures of the Church with suspicion and was violently anti-papal[37]; and that of Renaissance humanism infused with philosophical scepticism, which saw a politically controlled civil religion as an instrument of social renewal and stability. Collins believes that Hobbes's espousal of an ideal of 'neo-pagan' civil religion placed Hobbes outside the Christian, reformed, Erastian trajectory. Hobbes, he believes, held a 'psychological theory of religion', as an emotional response to the fear of death, and therefore did not believe in divine revelation. He developed his psychological understanding of religion and his instrumental view of religious authority, not (according to Collins) within a Protestant theological matrix, but in the context of Machiavellian civic humanism.[38] What Hobbes puts forward is, therefore, 'little more than a sanctified doctrine of worldly obedience'.[39]

However, Collins sees a further development in Hobbes's thought, following what he believes to be a broad shift in humanist thinking

---

[37]The second best-known saying of Hobbes is his description of the Roman Catholic Church as 'the *Ghost* of the deceased *Romane Empire*, sitting crowned upon the grave thereof' (*Lev*. IV:47: p. 712).

[38]Collins, *Allegiance of Hobbes*, pp. 14, 26, 29.

[39]Ibid., pp. 35–6. Cf. Richard Tuck, '"Christian Atheism" of Thomas Hobbes'', who argues – implausibly to my mind – that Hobbes' moved to atheism in *Leviathan* for purely political or ecclesiological reasons.

from a Ciceronian civic humanism, an ethic of civic involvement and *virtú*, to a more strategic political pragmatism, influenced by Tacitus, which sought to devise means to enable the political–intellectual elite to keep the vulgar herd at bay and in its place. These are elements that we see in Montaigne and we think that Hobbes had absorbed Montaigne's *Essais*. I suggest that, if Hobbes does indeed embrace civic humanism on the Italian model or a political pragmatism and cynicism that owes as much to Tacitus as it does to Machiavelli, it was his dualism of reason and revelation, politics and eschatology that enabled him to do so.

The question that Collins and others who take the line that Hobbes's theology was a smoke screen for political manoeuvreing have to answer is why should Hobbes bother to write a major work of political theology – *Leviathan* – if he was not only hostile to Christian belief, but a confirmed atheist? Collins proposes that the role of *Leviathan* was to provide a construction of Christian theology that would render it 'politically malleable', just as the pagan religions, the civic cults, had been in antiquity.[40] I find this a completely implausible theory to account for Hobbes the theologian. The last thing Hobbes would have done if he had wanted to provide a pliable religion for political ends was to advance outrageous theological positions – theological dynamite – and thus alienate the entire clerical establishment in England. It is not news that Hobbes's religious beliefs have perplexed interpreters – his philosophy also invites charges of irreconcilable contradiction[41] – but is it necessary to admit defeat and to confess with some writers that his personal beliefs 'remain a mystery'?[42] Let us see what can be offered on the other side of the equation.

One of the earliest modern exponents of the view that Hobbes was a sincere Christian believer was the redoubtable Anglo-Catholic philosopher A. E. Taylor, in 1936, whose views cannot

---

[40]Collins, *Allegiance of Hobbes*, p. 45. Collins speculates on likely influences on Hobbes's thought – besides Machiavelli and Montaigne, he suggests Bacon, Lipsius, Vossius, Selden, Grotius and Paulo Sarpi – while acknowledging that Hobbes was 'circumspect' about who influenced him (p. 48). Hobbes never mentions Machiavelli by name. On the other hand, the influence of Calvin and Calvinist theologians is crucial.

[41]James, *Life of Reason*, p. 21: 'a system which . . . is split from top to bottom.'

[42]Sutherland, 'God and Religion in *Leviathan*'; Pacchi, 'Hobbes and the Problem of God', p. 187; Springborg, 'Hobbes on Religion', p. 369.

be lightly dismissed. Taylor is concerned with Hobbes's ethical theory, rather than directly with his theology.[43] We should not be misled, says Taylor, by Hobbes's emphasis on the psychological motives for obeying the sovereign's commands: what lies behind the psychology is a 'deontological' theory of ethical obligation, akin to Kant's 'categorical imperative', an irreducible sense of 'ought'. In Hobbes's thought, our sense of obligation is not created by the sovereign's commands, backed by the threat of penalties, but evoked by them. The dictates of natural law in Hobbes are not, as some interpreters would have it, mere assertions of the sovereign's will, though for the untutored multitude, whom Hobbes despised and feared, that may be how they are received. For Hobbes, natural law is not merely the command of the sovereign, but the will and command of God. Taylor believes that 'a certain kind of theism is absolutely necessary' to make sense of the connection in Hobbes between duty, command and law.[44]

Taylor is scathing about the theological innocence of those who, misled by cries of 'atheism' on the part of Hobbes's contemporaries when 'atheism' meant pretty much anything that deviated from the writer's own theological position, fail to recognize the precedents in the Christian tradition of much that looks strange in Hobbes. (Calvinists called Arminians 'atheists' and vice versa; Protestants labelled Roman Catholics 'atheists' and vice versa; Milton calls the fallen angels in *Paradise Lost* 'the atheist crew'. Explicit atheism was very rare and almost untenable.)[45] Many aspects of Hobbes's system that have been attacked for 'atheism', Taylor points out, 'are so far from being necessarily expressions of atheism that they are the common stock-in-trade of orthodox Christian scholastics'. These arguments, he claims, would prove the atheism of most of the medieval schoolmen, including St Thomas Aquinas.[46]

---

[43]A. E. Taylor, 'Ethical Doctrine of Hobbes'.

[44]Ibid., p. 50.

[45]Milton, *English Poems*, p. 239 (Book VI, line 370). Bacon says, 'The Contemplative *Atheist* is rare': *Essays*, p. 66. Rivers, *Reason, Grace and Sentiment*, vol. 1, p. 44, claims that no seventeenth-century writer explicitly proclaims himself to be an atheist; the notorious libertine, the Earl of Rochester, told Gilbert Burnet that he had never known a complete atheist.

[46]Taylor, 'Ethical Doctrine', pp. 51, 53. The essay by Stuart M. Brown Jr, in the same volume attempts a refutation of Taylor.

Taylor is seconded in the same volume of essays by Willis B. Glover who points out that Hobbes not only devoted more than one-third of his overtly political writings to discussion of religion, but devoted several works to combating the charge of atheism and to proving that he was not only a Christian believer, but a loyal Anglican.[47] Hobbes confessed to being physically timid, but he was intellectually intrepid: intellectually he feared no man alive. Glover pillories those reconstructions of Hobbes's thought that leave out of account vast swathes of his writings on the grounds that they are not compatible with the interpretation that is being advanced. And he makes Taylor's point that a good many of the tenets for which Hobbes has been indicted of atheism by modern scholars are in fact close to important doctrines in the history of Christian thought.[48]

In 1955 Howard Warrender's analysis of Hobbes' theory of obligation broadly corroborated Taylor's argument, though with some minor demurs. Obligation, Warrender argued, cannot be merely a matter of the will of the subject answering to the will of the sovereign; it must have a deeper, prior ontological basis; it must run through all human life, including life in Hobbes's 'state of nature.' As Warrender puts it, 'A moral obligation . . . to obey the civil law cannot logically be extracted from a system in which man has *no* moral obligations before or apart from the institution of that law. Any view that assumes otherwise, contains a hiatus in the argument that cannot be surmounted, and if, in fact, this is Hobbes's position, he must be held to have failed in his main enterprise.'[49]

Although Warrender does not point the moral – like Taylor, he is reticent about the theological implications of his position – it is evident that a deontological doctrine of obligation, grounded in natural law, sits uneasily with a materialistic, secular, atheistic world view, but comports well with Christian theism.

The eminent historian of ideas, J. G. A. Pocock nicely comments that the attitude of many scholars towards the theological sections (books III and IV) of *Leviathan* is first, that they don't really exist,

---

[47]Glover, 'God and Thomas Hobbes'.
[48]Ibid., pp. 148, 157.
[49]Warrender, *Political Philosophy of Hobbes*, p. 6; cf. p. 7. For Warrender's minor disagreements with Taylor, see pp. 335–7.

and second, that Hobbes didn't mean them.[50] On any theory that Hobbes was an unbeliever, Pocock points out, 'the difficulty remains of imagining why a notoriously arrogant thinker, vehement in his dislike of "insignificant speech," should have written and afterwards defended sixteen chapters of what he held to be nonsense, and exposed them to the scrutiny of a public which did not consider this kind of thing nonsense at all'.[51]

Peter Geach, the Roman Catholic philosopher, was not someone to make that kind of mistake; he was not misled by some of Hobbes's more outlandish ideas into assuming that they were unprecedented in the Christian tradition. Geach concludes that Hobbes saw himself as a genuine member of the Established Church, but that in his Christology and therefore in his doctrine of God he was a Socinian – a rational theologian who applied critical reason to the interpretation of the Bible and did not accept the eternal deity of Christ.[52] In other words, for Geach, Hobbes was not an orthodox Anglican, though for almost all of his life he conformed to the Established Church. However, against Geach, I need to point out that it is Hobbes's doctrine of the absolute unity of Church and State which presents an insuperable barrier to his being seen as a Socinian: the Socinians were feared as a threat to national stability because they aimed to prise apart Church and State in the interests of toleration. However, Hobbes no doubt appropriated elements of Socinianism selectively.

The most thorough and most theologically competent (though sometimes a little naive) vindication of Hobbes as a Christian and an Anglican has been provided by Martinich.[53] For Martinich, Hobbes was 'a sincere and relatively orthodox Christian' and held 'a strong intellectual commitment to the Calvinist Christianity of Jacobean England'. He was doctrinally orthodox, a staunch Calvinist and a convinced episcopalian. His views were close to those of King James I, and parallels can be found in

---

[50]Pocock, 'Time, History and Eschatology in the Thought of Thomas Hobbes', in *Politics, Language and Time*, p. 160.
[51]Ibid., p. 162.
[52]Geach, 'Religion of Thomas Hobbes'. On Socinianism see Stromberg, *Religious Liberalism*; McLachlan, *Socinianism*, and Mortimer, *Reason and Religion*. See also Overhoff, 'Theology of Thomas Hobbes's *Leviathan*'.
[53]Martinich, *Two Gods of* Leviathan.

James's writings to some of the more startling expressions used by Hobbes. One of Hobbes's ostensibly most outrageous statements – to which Martinich adduces parallels in the writings of James I – is: 'that great LEVIATHAN, or rather (to speake more reverently) . . . that *Mortall God*, to which wee owe . . . our peace and defence.' But the atheist tendency in Hobbes studies needs to reckon with the full second part of the statement: 'to which wee owe, under the *Immortal God*, our peace and defence'.[54] It would be a rash interpreter who could claim to detect irony and scorn here.

Pointing out that, while Hobbes's contemporaries reviled him for 'atheism', our contemporaries today praise him for it, Martinich notes that 'At least 95% of Hobbes's remarks about religion are either obviously consonant with orthodox Christianity, typical of seventeenth-century Christianity, or directed specifically against Presbyterianism or Catholicism.'[55] Even if Martinich overstates his case with regard to Hobbes's doctrinal orthodoxy (what of the Trinity and Christology?), he has, I think, demonstrated that a knowledge of the medieval scholastic tradition and of sixteenth-century Calvinism makes sense of much of Hobbes's theology and his place in Anglican thought. Set this evidence alongside Aubrey's testimony that Hobbes was an intimate of Falkland, the presiding spirit of the Tew Circle of 'liberal' Anglicans, and that on his deathbed he received Holy Communion from John Pearson, the unimpeachably orthodox Bishop of Chester, and made his confession to John Cosin, the High Church Bishop of Durham, and we have compelling evidence of his genuine, if unique, form of Anglicanism.[56] I think there are ample grounds for treating Hobbes as an authentic Anglican philosopher–theologian and that is what I will do here, while acknowledging that his theology was over-rationalistic and often counterproductive in the impetus it gave to logico-deductive reasoning, the promotion of an anthropology modelled on motion and mechanism and the complete subservience of the Church to the State. Hobbes should be seen as an apologist, first for the absolute State that alone could provide security in times

---

[54]*Lev.*, II, xvii: p. 227; Martinich, *Two Gods of* Leviathan, pp. 1, 333–5.
[55]Ibid., pp. 9, 14.
[56]Aubrey, *Brief Lives*, pp. 317–18.

of turmoil and second for a Christian theology that was assimilated
to the new scientific paradigms pioneered by Copernicus, Galileo
and Harvey.[57]

Hobbes and his sources

Hobbes's most fascinating intellectual relationships, as far as we can
deduce since he is reticent about his sources, are with Machiavelli,
Bacon, Descartes, Montaigne, Galileo and Harvey – among the
most original and powerful intellects of the previous age. In his
undeceived estimate of human nature, his grasp of the individual's
drive for power and his strength of rational analysis, Hobbes has
a marked affinity with Machiavelli, though these derive also from
his Calvinist theology. D. G. James comments: Hobbes 'more than
any other great writer of the seventeenth and eighteenth centuries,
preached the power and scope of human reason'.[58] Hobbes's ethical
realism links him with both Machiavelli and Bacon. As Aubrey
tells us, Hobbes was Bacon's companion and the confidant of his
thoughts.[59]

In his mature work, Hobbes hailed Copernicus, Galileo and
William Harvey as founders of the new natural science, and his
worldview was deliberately intended to accommodate their
discoveries.[60] But Hobbes conspicuously failed to mention Bacon
and did not attempt to conceal his contempt for the experimentation
of the Royal Society along Baconian lines.[61] And while Bacon
weakened his case by not taking sufficient account of the role of
mathematics in scientific procedure, Hobbes went to the opposite
extreme, excluding as unscientific and therefore irrelevant anything
that could not be pressed somehow into a mathematical mould

---

[57]The view that Hobbes was a sincere Christian believer is also defended by Schneider,
'Piety of Hobbes', and Johnson, 'Hobbes' "Anglican Doctrine"', the latter on the
grounds of a radical dualism in Hobbes' thought between piety on the one hand and
philosophy and science on the other: never the twain shall meet. I am not convinced
that we need to resort to that desperate solution – Hobbes would not be the first
theologian, or the last, to hold that God and spirits have bodies.
[58]James, *Life of Reason*, p. ix.
[59]Aubrey, *Brief Lives*, pp. 308–9.
[60]Martinich, *Two Gods of* Leviathan, pp. 7, 15.
[61]*EW*, vol. 4, p. 437.

(history being a prime casualty). But the common ground between Bacon and Hobbes is significant and lies in the presuppositions rather than the content of their philosophies.

First, both Bacon and Hobbes, along with other outstanding thinkers of the time, especially Descartes, are obsessed by method. As Hobbes says, 'Most men wander out of the way and fall into error for want of method.'[62] Not only was method a reliable (even infallible) guide; it was also a short cut. As Hobbes puts it: 'Method, therefore, in the study of philosophy, is the *shortest way* of finding out effects by their known causes or of causes by their known effects.'[63] As this statement suggests, methods may be deductive or inductive, Hobbes strongly favouring the former, Bacon the latter. Both believed that their preferred methods would bring about a scientific reconstruction of the disciplines of ethics and politics. While Hobbes does not owe his passionate interest in method to Bacon (as a philosophical issue it goes back at least to Aristotle, and Descartes was a more recent exponent of a patent method), Bacon and Hobbes are the two most outstanding English methodologists of the seventeenth century before Newton.

Secondly, Bacon and Hobbes share the analytical view of language that became a salient feature of the English positivist tradition. They both refer to words as 'counters', fight shy of metaphor, and seek a one-to-one correspondence between a word and its meaning (see below).

Thirdly, Bacon and Hobbes share a concern to ameliorate the lot of humanity by the application of science to industry. For them both, knowledge is not virtue (as for Platonism) or salvation (as for Christianity), but power. 'The end or scope of philosophy', Hobbes claims, consists in use and application, 'as far as matter, strength and industry will permit, for the commodity of human life.' Purely intellectual triumphs are hollow victories and not worth the effort. The only philosophical game worth the candle is the one that presupposes that 'the end of knowledge is power'. All the commodities of civilized life are produced by those arts such as measurement, movement, construction, navigation,

---

[62]*EW*, vol. 1, p. 1. For the dispute between Hobbes and Descartes over the nature of light see Richard Tuck, 'Hobbes and Descartes', in Rogers and Ryan (eds.), *Perspectives on Hobbes*.
[63]*EW*, p. 66 (emphasis altered).

calculation and so on, that are created when philosophy is put to work.[64]

Bacon had initiated a revolution in the method of the sciences; Hobbes stood for a counter-revolution. Bacon's empirical approach, pruned of its extravagances, was prophetic of modern scientific and technological achievement. The protagonists of the European Enlightenment looked on Bacon, along with Locke and Newton, as a founding father. Hobbes, on the other hand, along with Descartes and Spinoza, represents a mathematical, *a priori*, deductive approach that, as a method, has been less central to modern thought, but in its substantive conclusions has been immensely influential. This distinction of method and content raises the question, touched on by Strauss and others, whether Hobbes's purported geometrical method was not largely incidental to a philosophical vision that was primarily the creation of imagination tempered by incisive observation of human nature. In any event, Hobbes's eccentric method was no handicap to the influence of his ideas which were taken to be – extremely ironically, if our earlier argument is correct, against Hobbes's intentions – fundamentally rationalist, secularist and relativist in their import.[65] Of Hobbes's influence, G. P. Gooch wrote: 'To a far greater degree than Bacon, he was the author of the atmospheric change which substituted the secular for the theological standpoint throughout the boundless realms of thought and speculation.'[66]

The link with Descartes is also paradoxical. While adopting and radicalizing Descartes's mathematico-deductive method, Hobbes uses it to establish opposite conclusions: for Descartes reality is essentially thought; for Hobbes it is basically material or corporeal (even God has a body). In common with Machiavelli and Bacon, Descartes is not mentioned in Hobbes's writings.

If it is appropriate to look back to Machiavelli to draw comparisons with the thought of Hobbes, it is also appropriate to look ahead to Vico. But surely Hobbes and Vico stand at opposite ends of the spectrum with regard to how we view the past: the one militantly rationalist, temperamentally averse to the contingencies of the historical process, distrustful of the conjectures and uncertainties

---

[64]*EW*, vol. 1, p. 7.
[65]So Martinich, *Two Gods of* Leviathan, p. 8.
[66]Gooch, *Political Thought in England*, p. 57.

of historical study; the other the originator of the method of imaginative reconstruction of the past, plunging with relish into the dark recesses of history? However, what Hobbes and Vico do have in common is a fundamental methodological principle: we can truly know only what we have made ourselves, which was expressed by Vico in the formula *verum factum convertantur* or *verum ipsum factum*, the true and the made are convertible. This is axiomatic for both philosophers, but they draw opposite conclusions from it. Both apply it to mathematics, principally geometry, but whereas Hobbes concludes that all the sciences must be made to conform to geometrical method in order to give assured results, Vico asserts that the self-evidencing character of geometry makes it a vacuous science that can tell us nothing that we really want to know. Again, while Hobbes bases his claim to have discovered an infallible science of ethics and politics on the grounds that we create the commonwealth ourselves, it does not occur to him that the same principle provides a foundation for historical science. For Vico, however, the *verum factum* principle constitutes the basis of historical understanding, for the creations of history are not pure mental constructs, like geometrical figures, but leave their tracks in time and can therefore be studied empirically. However, the extent of Vico's indebtedness to Hobbes on this matter is open to conjecture.

Hobbes's system

Hobbes's thought falls into two broad phases: first, the humanist phase in which his fundamental assessment of human nature was formed and which culminated in his translation of Thucydides in 1629; second, the rationalist phase, which stemmed from his discovery of Euclid, which struck him with the force of revelation, in 1630, and led to the attempted science of humanity on a geometrical model. This was the discovery that revolutionized his thinking and determined his mature system. He had already adopted the fundamentally materialistic and somewhat Machiavellian principles of his view of life, but he still lacked a method which would unify and mobilize those principles, turning them into a powerful political philosophy. Hobbes discovered his method on the occasion when, happening to catch sight of an open copy of the *Elements* of Euclid in a gentleman's library, he was fascinated to find that the proposition that seemed quite impossible was simply the inevitable outcome of a series of logical steps based on indubitable axioms.[67] But Hobbes was a philosopher, not a mathematician (in spite of his claims to have squared the circle!), and philosophy has a content of its own. Hobbes found this content in the notions of motion and generation. He owes these two fundamental concepts primarily to Galileo and to William Harvey, the discoverer of the circulation of the blood. Hobbes reveals his debt: 'Galileus in our time . . . was the first that opened to us the gate of natural philosophy universal, which is the knowledge of the nature of motion.'[68] And Harvey, adding to the category of motion (as in *The Motion of the Blood*), the category of generation (as in *The Generation of Living Creatures*), gave a genetic twist to the new method with his concept of recapitulation. We should note, however, that Hobbes did not take this genetic interest, as he might have done, in an historical sense, but in a logical sense. He was concerned solely with logical sequence understood in a quasi-mathematical sense as computation. Reasoning, or more accurately, ratiocination, was a question of adding or subtracting definitions. As Hobbes put it in *Leviathan*: 'In summe, in what matter soever there is place for *addition* and *subtraction*, there also is place for *Reason*; and where these have no place, there *Reason* has nothing at all to do.'[69]

Harvey had studied at Padua, the centre of Renaissance methodology, and probably Hobbes was influenced by Paduan thought through him. Paduan methodology focused on the time-honoured process of analysis and synthesis (there termed resolution and composition). But Galileo had introduced a refinement, a sort of middle term, in which the elements of analysis were idealized into quasi-mathematical formulae before being brought together again in a new synthesis.[70] Corresponding to this distinction in Hobbes's thought was the fundamental division of knowledge into rational and empirical sciences. Rational, deductive science proceeds synthetically, following the motions of men's minds; it operates in the realm of hypothetical (or 'conditional' as Hobbes calls it) knowledge and

---

[67] Aubrey, *Brief Lives*, p. 309.
[68] *EW*, vol. 1 [*De Corpore*], p. viii.
[69] *Lev.*, I, v: p. 111, original emphasis.
[70] *EW*, vol. 1 [*De Corpore*], p. 66 (original emphasis); Watkins, *Hobbes' System*, chs. 3 and 4. In this section I adapt some material from Avis, *Machiavelli to Vico*.

its judgements are infallible. Empirical, inductive, science proceeds analytically following the deliverances of sense; it operates in the realm of categorical (or as Hobbes says, 'absolute') knowledge and its findings are conjectural.[71]

In Hobbes's system, everything is ultimately reduced to motion. Just as there are motions of bodies, so there are also motions of minds. Physical motions in the natural world are generated by nature; they are external, so to speak, to us, and we can have only indirect, conjectural, empirical knowledge of them. The motions of the lines of geometrical figures are generated by human reason: they are the creations of the human mind and can therefore be known with demonstrable certainty.

The motions of political bodies or commonwealths would seem, according to Hobbes, to be in an intermediate position. They have a physical reality and are therefore susceptible of being studied inductively and empirically. But on the other hand, they are generated by human reason and will. In this respect, geometry and society come into the same category. They are our own creations: we can know their causes, generation and construction. There is no need, therefore, to resort to the painstaking empirical study of society: the nature of the commonwealth may be discovered by any man 'that will but examine his own mind'. Hobbes believed that on this basis he could construct rational, deductive sciences of politics and ethics.[72] In *Leviathan*, Hobbes asserts that 'the skill of making and maintaining commonwealths' is a matter of following certain rules of procedure, as in arithmetic or geometry, not a matter of practice or skill, as in playing tennis – 'which Rules, neither poor men have the leisure, nor men that have had the leisure, have hitherto had the curiosity, or the method to find out'.[73] In other words, Hobbes is revealing them to the world for the first time, thanks to his infallible method. 'Natural Philosophy is . . . but young, but Civil Philosophy yet much younger, as being no older . . . than my own book *De Cive*.'[74]

Here we are at the heart of Hobbes's system. While he concedes the theoretical possibility of an inductive approach to politics,

---

[71]*Lev.*, I, v: p. 117; ix: p. 147; EW [*De Corpore*], pp. 73–4; Peters, *Hobbes*, pp. 50–1.
[72]*EW*, vol. 1 [*De Corpore*], p. 74.
[73]*Lev.*, II, xx: p. 261.
[74]*EW*, vol. 1, p. ix.

moving from the interpretation of sense-data to the invention of principles, his whole emphasis is on the deductive, *a priori* approach. It is possible to attain, he affirms, 'the knowledge of the passions and perturbations of the mind, by the synthetical method, and from the very first principles of philosophy',[75] and then to project one's findings on to the commonwealth itself, which, after all, is but an 'Artificiall Man'.[76] In a word, 'the principles of the politics consists in the knowledge of the motions of the mind'.[77]

Underlying this position is Hobbes's extreme nominalist view of language and reasoning. In a system that attempts in the last analysis to reduce everything to motion, concepts are a matter of names produced by arbitrarily uttered sounds. But such ethical and historical relativism was unacceptable to Hobbes once he had come under the spell of geometrical method. He is convinced that he can offer a more excellent way that will supersede the uncertainties of traditional ethics. Like Bacon, he is profoundly dissatisfied with the theoretical and idealistic ethical teaching that was common to the classical and Christian traditions. In his humanist phase, he had been attracted to the Renaissance method of indirectly inculcating moral virtues through historical examples, but had repudiated this whole approach on his conversion to mathematics. Bacon wanted to reconstruct the humanist method through inductive historical study that would leave history strengthened by adherence to a rigorous method, while ethics would become the empirical study of how men do in fact behave. Hobbes, on the other hand, sought to short-cut all ethical uncertainties by appealing to the finality of logic.

Hobbes's concept of human nature derives from the assumption that natural life is basically motion: 'life is but a motion of Limbs'.[78] The whole of Hobbes's philosophy of man and society is made to appear to follow from this, though one would be hard put to find a commentator on Hobbes who believed that it did – all of it – logically follow. Not for nothing has Hobbes's system been called 'the politics of motion'.[79] But this is the only premise that Hobbes, given the method that he had espoused, could in fact adopt. As

---

[75]*EW*, vol. 1 [*De Corpore*], pp. 73–4.
[76]*Lev.*, 'Introduction', p. 81.
[77]*EW*, vol. 1 [*De Corpore*], p. 74.
[78]*Lev.*, 'Introduction', p. 81.
[79]Spragens, *Politics of Motion*.

Michael Oakeshott has proposed, Hobbes's doctrine of man and society should be seen as 'not the last chapter in a philosophy of materialism, but the reflection of civil association in the mirror of rationalistic philosophy'.[80]

Because life is motion, humanity has the ability to copy nature and construct mechanical devices, such as clocks, that ape his own physical construction. 'For what is the *Heart* but a *Spring*; and the *Nerves*, but so many *Strings*; and the *Joynts* but so many *Wheeles*, giving motion to the whole Body, such as was intended by the Artificer?'[81] The state is simply the projection of mechanistic man on an enormous scale. 'For by Art is created that great LEVIATHAN called a COMMON-WEALTH, or STATE, (in latine CIVITAS) which is but an Artificiall Man.'[82] In the state, sovereignty is the artificial soul, the heart of the great engine, imparting motion to the whole; the magistrates are the joints; rewards and punishments are the nerves because they provide the stimulus for movement of the limbs and organs; wealth constitutes the strength of the body; concord, the health; sedition, the sickness; and Civil War, the death.

The analogy of society, or sometimes the whole human race, as a corporate person, is a familiar one in the history of political thought, most familiar in the expression 'the body politic'. It was made much of by thinkers in the tradition of the Christian humanism of Hooker, Butler and Burke (reinforced by Romanticist idealism), such as Coleridge, F. D. Maurice and other liberal Anglicans. But they were working on totally different premises stemming from a radically different view of man. They saw the human person primarily as a spiritual being, endowed with creative reason by which she/he could transcend egotism and the bounds of sense and enter into a fellowship in which she/he would find true fulfilment. They operated with a view of language and metaphor radically opposed to that of Hobbes. For these thinkers metaphor was a vehicle of spiritual truth, not a corruption of univocal speech. Hobbes's ostensibly organic view of society has to be interpreted in the light of his mechanistic view of humanity.

For Hobbes, 'man' is a restless being, never satisfied with his lot, always seeking to improve his position at the expense of others. The

---

[80]Oakeshott, *Hobbes on Civil Association*, p. 26.
[81]*Lev.*, 'Introduction', p. 81, original emphasis.
[82]Ibid.

objects of all his striving are a series of receding mirages, for there is no static state of beatitude with which he would be satisfied.

The Felicity of this life, consisteth not in the repose of a mind satisfied. For there is no such *Finis ultimus*, (utmost ayme,), nor *Summum Bonum*, (greatest Good), as is spoken of in the Books of the old Morall Philosophers. Nor can a man any more live, whose Desires are at an end, than he, whose Senses and Imaginations are at a stand. Felicity is a continuall progresse of the desire, from one object to another.[83]

So far this is innocuous, reflecting a teleology of desire from Aristotle, through Aquinas to Hooker,[84] but Hobbes' anthropology now takes a grim turn – which is not to say that it is mistaken. What Acton attributed to Machiavelli – the discovery of the dynamics of power that govern history – is equally applicable to Hobbes. His doctrine of human motivation is perhaps narrower than Machiavelli's (whose *necessitâ* embraced the demands of avarice and pride as well as of survival), but it is more radical and more systematic. The fundamental human drive is the lust for power, born of fear and generating fear. 'I put for a generall inclination of all mankind, a perpetuall and restlesse desire of Power after power, that ceaseth only in death.'[85] And just as Machiavelli had argued that the only means of defence was attack, that the safety of the state entailed a commitment to continuous aggression, so Hobbes points out that those who possess power can only secure what they have by acquiring more.[86]

D. G. James entitled his discussion of Hobbes 'The Proud Mind' and characterized Hobbes's system as 'the zenith of the pride of the Renaissance'.[87] In his confidence in the unaided powers of man's natural reason, Hobbes is a true child of the Renaissance; but in applying those powers to the improvement of society, he is a successor of Bacon and a harbinger of the French Enlightenment. Renaissance historical and political thought had been shaped by a

---

[83]*Lev.*, I, xi: p. 160.
[84]Cf. Hooker *EP*, I, xi, 4.
[85]*Lev.*, I, xi: p. 161.
[86]Ibid.
[87]James, *Life of Reason*, p. 25.

robust confidence in humanity's ability to determine its own destiny. Both Machiavelli and Guicciardini, though they acknowledge the mysterious influence of *Fortuna*, assume that history is of our own making, rather than the unfolding of a predetermined providential scheme. But their grasp of human self-determination is crude and undeveloped since social and economic forces were barely understood at that time. In Hobbes, however, as in other theoreticians of a social contract, there is a fuller realization that society is a natural growth, that institutions are contingent, not necessary in the scheme of things, and are alterable by human decision. In addition, we find a firmer grasp of the social and economic factors that transcend the individual's impact on history.[88]

The Renaissance had inherited from antiquity the idea of a Golden Age in the past, from which civilization had steadily degenerated. The literary notion of the noble savage, the happy heathen, originates with Lucretius and became common coin. The myth of the Golden Age was exposed by Bodin, and although Bacon fell for it, a very different picture of human origins began to gain currency and held sway until Rousseau. The two philosophers who paint the bleakest picture of man in the state of nature are Hobbes and Vico. This is one more piece of evidence of common ground.

Hobbes's description of the state of nature serves his political polemic. Before any social contract, lacking the protection and sanctions of the state, human beings barely survived, isolated in a hostile environment. What a blessing the creation of Leviathan was! '[W]ithout a common power to keep them all in awe, they are in that condition which is called Warre; and such a warre as is of every man, against every man.'[89] In this condition of anarchy or 'absolute liberty', as Hobbes pointedly calls it,[90] all the amenities of civilization are lacking and even survival is barely secured. In words that have passed into the English language, Hobbes writes:

> In such condition there is no place for Industry; because the fruit thereof is uncertain: and consequently no Culture of the Earth; no Navigation, nor use of the commodities that may be imported

---

[88]Peters, *Hobbes*, p. 197.
[89]*Lev.*, I, xiii: p. 185; cf. *De Cive*, pp. 117–18, in Gert (ed.), *Hobbes: Man and Citizen*.
[90]*Lev.*, II, xxxi: p. 395.

by Sea; no commodious Building; no Instrument of moving, and removing such things as require much force; no Knowledge of the face of the Earth; no account of Time; no Arts; no Letters; no Society; and, what is worst of all, continuall feare, and danger of violent death; And the life of man, solitary, poore, nasty, brutish, and short.[91]

In the state of nature, there is no such thing as personal property or ownership of land: 'no *Mine* and *Thine* distinct; but onely that to be every mans, that he can get; and for so long, as he can keep it'.[92] How attractive that picture makes a strong and secure state, enclosing a stable Church! In search of authority indeed!

Did Hobbes believe that he was describing an actual historical period, as Vico, for one, certainly did? Some commentators seem to assume that the historicity of the state of nature was irrelevant to Hobbes's argument. Peters, for example, remarks that 'Hobbes did not take such a state of nature seriously as an historical hypothesis.' He was conducting an experiment of the type Galileo had pioneered: 'a resolution of society into its clear and distinct parts so as to reconstruct the whole in order of logical dependence rather than of historical genesis'.[93] G. P. Gooch notes that, in Hobbes, the necessity for absolute government is said repeatedly to lie in human nature itself as revealed in primitive societies, and points out that neither Hobbes nor his contemporaries knew anything of the actual way of life of primitive communities.

His terrifying picture of a war of all against all corresponds to no reality. No community lives or could live in the state which he describes. For Hobbes there is no middle term between anarchy and absolutism. He was not aware that custom preceded law, and that the sanction of the former is as potent as that of the latter. He rightly rejected sentimental rhapsodies on the noble savage and the golden age of innocence and virtue; but he was unaware that the elements of social life are never absent among human beings and that savages possess a rudimentary morality without any political organization.[94]

---

[91]*Lev.*, I, xiii: p. 186.
[92]*Lev.*, I, xiii: p. 188, original emphasis.
[93]Peters, *Hobbes*, p. 168.
[94]Gooch, *Political Thought*, p. 49.

Hobbes himself does not regard it as vital to his position to hold that all societies have emerged from this pre-social state. He cites the American Indians and the breakdown of public order (that was always uppermost for Hobbes, timid soul that he confessed himself to be) in times of Civil War. Beneath the veneer of civilized life, the primitive and aggressive instincts of humankind were always ready to break out. Hobbes assumed that he was describing historical realities, but it was not essential to his case that the state of nature was universal. The form of his account of the state of nature was historical but its function was that of an explanatory myth. Hobbes came to prefer, on methodological grounds, 'typical' to actual history.[95] Although, inevitably, he draws strongly on previous thinkers, the idea of inhabiting tradition, whether theological or philosophical, is antipathetic to him.

In Hobbes's mature system, historical study is relegated to an inferior position alongside all other 'conjectural' pursuits. According to Hobbes, the great bulk of human experience falls below the level of reasoning, including sense, memory, image, wisdom, prudence, purely inductive science, history and poetry.[96] History is specifically excluded from the realm of philosophy on the grounds that it does not lend itself to geometrical method: 'such knowledge is but experience, or authority, and not ratiocination'.[97] History is fallible: it can neither tell us with assurance about the past nor form a basis for prediction of the future. History is not capable of fulfilling its traditional humanist function of providing ethical *exempla*, or its new role of delivering the basic data of political science. Could it be, then, that Hobbes entertains a very modern conception of history for its own sake – answering to our insatiable desire to know what actually happened in the past? Hobbes affirms in a backhanded way that it is pleasing to recall the past: 'It is pleasing to represent the past, if it was good, because it was good; and if it was evil, because it is past.'[98] The ideal of modern historicism in the tradition of Ranke, to recreate the past as it actually was, is quite foreign to Hobbes. The more the ideal character of Hobbes's system became clear to him, the less he had

---

[95]Cf. Warrender, *Political Philosophy of Hobbes*, pp. 237–42.
[96]James, *Life of Reason*, p. 32.
[97]*EW*, vol. 1 [*De Corpore*], pp. 10–11.
[98]*De Homine* (Gert (ed.), p. 51).

to bother with history.[99] Typical history serves as well as actual history and this is precisely what he offers in his account of the state of nature and the genesis of Leviathan.

We can deduce from the fact that Hobbes lumps together history and poetry as unsatisfactory conjectural sciences, that a particular view of language underlies his position. We can take our cue in this matter from a striking contrast between Hobbes's view of the origins of speech and the theory later put forward by Vico. The disagreement is made all the more significant by the fact that, as we have already noted, Hobbes seems to anticipate Vico's celebrated *verum factum* principle. Vico sees language arising spontaneously out of the inarticulate cries and rhythmic utterances of primitive man under the pressure of strong emotion. He postulates a continuum of development from almost animal noises at the lowest level up to the highest achievement of poetic creation. Hobbes, on the other hand, has a profound distaste for the spontaneous, the irrational and the emotional. For him, there is a great gulf fixed between crude animal utterances and rational human discourse: 'Not by their will, but out of the necessity of nature, these calls by which hope, fear, joy and the like are signified, are forced out by the strength of these passions . . . burst forth by the strength of nature from the peculiar fears, joys, desires and other passions.'[100]

For Vico, however, metaphor and metaphorical expression, that is, poetry, was the primary form of the human apprehension of reality and a window into truth. For Hobbes, metaphor was at best an aberration, at worst the sign of a sick language. To employ metaphor is to use words in a sense other than the 'intended' one (the assumption being that there is a one to one relation between the sound and its meaning) in a way that can only lead into error. Hobbes deplored the use of metaphors, tropes and other rhetorical figures 'instead of words proper'.[101] 'Metaphors, and senslesse and ambiguous words, are like *ignes fatui*; and reasoning upon them, is wandering amongst innumerable absurdities; and their end, contention, and sedition, or contempt.'[102] Hobbes's basic objection to regarding primitive cries as worthy of the designation 'speech'

---

[99]Strauss, *Political Philosophy of Hobbes*, p. 97.
[100]*De Homine* (Gert (ed.), pp. 37–8).
[101]*Lev.*, I, v: p. 114.
[102]Ibid., p. 116.

is that they are spontaneous, not brought forth by an effort of will ('not by their will, but out of the necessity of nature'). For him, language is a matter of naming like that of Adam naming the creatures in the Garden of Eden. It is purely a product of will and therefore completely arbitrary. 'A name is a word taken at pleasure to serve as a mark that may raise in our minds a thought like some thought we had before.'[103] Out of names we construct definitions and by means of definitions we engage in rational thought. Hobbes's much vaunted method consists in reasoning from definitions by addition and subtraction. In a famous metaphor, adapted from Bacon, Hobbes asserts: 'Words are wise mens counters, they do but reckon by them: but they are the mony of fooles.'[104] He thus drags language also into his mathematical and specifically geometrical scheme, for, as he points out, 'in Geometry, (which is the onely Science that it hath pleased God hitherto to bestow on mankind,) men begin at settling the significations of their words'.[105] For Vico, by contrast, to understand a metaphor from then past was to gain an entrance into a distant world of human experience and the possibility of doing this vindicated historical science. For Hobbes, the metaphorical character of human utterance foreclosed once and for all the possibility that history, conjectural in its method, trivial in its conclusions, could attain the status of a true science. But this exclusion stemmed from a disastrously mistaken evaluation of metaphor.[106]

Hobbes and theological method

Whatever the proponents of the 'atheistical' interpretation of Hobbes would have us think, it seems abundantly clear to me that Hobbes fears God, reverences Christ as Saviour, and believes that he draws his theology from the Scriptures. Hobbes is a theologian to be reckoned with and a skilled interpreter – and sometimes manipulator – of the biblical text. But Scripture was not the only word of God for Hobbes. There is a 'Naturall Word of God, but also

---

[103]*EW*, vol. 1, p. 16.
[104]*Lev.*, I, iv: p. 106.
[105]*Lev.*, I, iv: p. 105.
[106]For further discussion see Avis, *God and the Creative Imagination*.

a Propheticall.' Reason is also in a sense the Word of God, for 'we are not to renounce our Senses, and Experience; nor (that which is the undoubted Word of God) our naturall Reason'. These are not to be (as in the Parable of the Talents) 'folded up in the Napkin of an Implicate [implicit] Faith, but employed in the purchase of Justice, Peace, and true Religion'. 'For though there be many things in Gods Word above Reason; that is to say, which cannot by naturall reason be either demonstrated, or confuted; yet there is nothing contrary to it.' Where Christian doctrine seems to fly in the face of reason, the cause lies in our faulty interpretation or bad reasoning. We are to submit our understanding to the text and be captive to the word. We are not to practise logic-chopping or to speculate about things beyond our ken, 'For it is with the mysteries of our Religion, as with wholesome pills for the sick, which swallowed whole, have the vertue to cure; but chewed, are for the most part cast up again without effect.'[107]

Hobbes is one of the first to insist that biblical inspiration did not override the human faculties of the prophets; in that sense it was not 'supernatural', above or beyond nature. Not even Moses could have spoken with God as God really is: revelation is always mediated. God inculcates theological truth in the same way as moral virtue, by many means and through sound habits.[108] Claims to direct or immediate inspiration (Hobbes was all too familiar with such claims among the sectaries of the Civil War and Commonwealth period) are to be debunked: when people claim that God has spoken to them through the Bible, what has happened is that they have been struck by the scriptural words of prophets or Apostles. And for someone to claim that God had spoken to them in a dream is simply to say that they dreamed that God spoke to them – and dreams may have all kinds of natural and trivial causes.[109] It is the role of reason to arbitrate these claims and reason does well to be suspicious of delusion, ambition and imposture.[110]

Why do we believe the Christian faith? Hobbes's answer is solidly Calvinist, stressing that faith is a gift of the sovereign God. However, 'the most ordinary immediate cause of our beleef' is that

---

[107]*Lev.*, III, xxxii: pp. 109–10.
[108]*Lev.*, III, xxxvi: pp. 462–3.
[109]*Lev.*, III, xxxii: pp. 410–11.
[110]*Lev.*, III, xxxvi: pp. 466–7.

we believe the Bible to be the Word of God. Why so? Hobbes takes issue with those who claim to 'know' that the Bible is true, when what they should say is that they 'believe' it to be true – 'as if *Beleeving* and *Knowing* were all one'. So some people ground their belief in the infallibility of the Church, others on private religious experience. But both of these convictions rest on anterior principles, whether it be the nature of Scripture or the influence of human teachers and mentors. 'Besides, there is nothing in the Scripture, from which can be inferred the Infallibility of the Church; much lesse, of any particular Church; and least of all, the Infallibility of any particular man.' There is no substitute for the reasoned, critical study of the Bible.[111]

Hobbes has a concept of the essence of Christianity. The one belief needful for salvation is that Jesus is the Christ. This was the heart of the preaching of the Apostles and is now sufficient for church communion. Faith in Christ and obedience to God's law, in the form of the rule of the sovereign, is all that is required in a Christian. Hobbes's concept of the essence of Christianity, of the *unum necessarium*, is not the bare, reductionist formula that it may appear: Hobbes shows that all the important Christian doctrines are contained in the confession of Jesus as the Christ.[112] In his theological minimalism, Hobbes was making common cause with the advocates of broader toleration or comprehension within the national Church, the Latitudinarians and Stillingfleet in his early work. But Hobbes not only wanted to see an end of religious strife and dissension, but also had an eye to his own standing and safety within the realm as a notorious 'heretic'.

In his dismissal of historical knowledge as a pathway to understanding, Hobbes negates a *sine qua non* of Christian theology and one that is quintessentially Anglican: the capacity to indwell tradition. Hobbes also injected into English theology a strangely reductionist and impoverished concept of reason. Reason was reduced to 'reasoning', to computation. Hobbes's mechanical, geometrical theory of knowledge led him to claim that reasoning was no more than working with propositions, basically adding and subtracting the names of things. Although he had begun as a humanist scholar and his first work was an edition of Thucydides,

---

[111]*Lev.*, III, xliii: pp. 613–14.
[112]*Lev.*, III, xlii: pp. 538–44; xliii: pp. 610, 615, 621–2.

Hobbes had no place in his mature system for history, tradition or experience; hermeneutical it was not. Reason was *a priori*, deductive and untouched by the contingent. Hobbes pushed Anglican theological method into an excessive rationalism, and an arid and unproductive use of reason at that. '[B]y his very provocation,' says Mintz, 'Hobbes endowed the thought of his critics with a strong rationalist impulse. . . . The critics were satisfied that they had cut Hobbes down to size; in fact they had yielded, slowly and imperceptibly but also very surely to the force of his rationalist method.' So, by the end of the seventeenth century 'the whole mental climate' had been altered.[113] Everyone was playing by Hobbes's rules; logical exactitude and rational demonstration came to dominate Anglican theological method.

Whether Hobbes should be regarded as a sincere Anglican thinker or as a destructive fifth-columnist, using irony to discredit the established religion – whether he should be classed as an Anglican theologian, albeit a maverick one, or an infidel – is a secondary issue. What is important is that he changed the rules of the game. His brand of rationalism pervaded much Anglican thought well into the next century. In fact, it was not until German idealist philosophy was imbibed by English Romantic thinkers, and especially Coleridge, that an alternative, more creative theory of reason became available to Anglican theologians.

Thorndike's vindication of tradition

Herbert Thorndike (1598–1672) was one of the many clergy who suffered deprivation (in his case his college fellowship as well as his parish) during the 1640s and 1650s. His enforced seclusion gave him the opportunity to write an exhaustive, systematic treatise in vindication of the Church of England, then suppressed, as a church both catholic and reformed.[114] This work, the first part of which, *Of the Principles of Christian Truth*, is the part that concerns us, sets out to heal the scandal of division within Western Christianity, but

---

[113]Mintz, *Hunting of Leviathan*, pp. 149–50.
[114]Thorndike, *Epilogue to the Tragedy of the Church of England*. The references inserted in my text are to the pages of the *LACT* edition, extended over two volumes (II/1 and II/2) but with continuous pagination.

in reality it is a devastating polemical broadside against schismatics, and one that is not without its casualties due to 'friendly fire' on Thorndike's own side. He sets out to challenge Reformers and schismatics alike.

Thorndike's theological method arises out of his ecclesiology: unity and truth are interconnected: in the present state of disunity it is difficult to see the truth. Thorndike's method combines the unquestioned supremacy of Scripture, the arbitration of reason and a reappraisal of the role of tradition in the interpretation of Scripture that effectively undermines a couple of Reformation shibboleths – that the Bible is self-authenticating and that all the truths necessary for salvation are clear to all on the page of Scripture.[115] Altogether, this work constitutes a powerful vindication of tradition as conveying to us 'the principles of Christian truth'. Quantin puts it in a nutshell: 'Thorndike's originality was to make tradition prior both to Scripture and the Church'.[116] But Thorndike never makes tradition superior to Scripture: tradition is the hermeneutical tool.

Thorndike wages a sustained attack on reductionism and minimalism, which was the response of some (Locke above all) to the internecine Christian conflicts of the seventeenth century. What fills his vision is a whole Church, extended through time and space, ministering a rich and full-orbed faith, through which the 'rule of faith', derived from the Apostles, runs like a golden thread. Thorndike contains remarkable intimations of modern concepts such as the Church as communion (which is the 'depository' of Christ's truth, p. 411) and the essence (or 'substance') of Christianity (which is located or contained in practice as well as theology). There is a profound sense in Thorndike that the Church of the present is indebted to and beholden to ('obliged to') the whole Church in time and space.

But Thorndike's style is convoluted, jagged and inelegant. I find him more difficult to read than Hooker, but without the compensation of the aesthetic pleasure and elevation of mind that we receive from his judicious predecessor – which is a little

---

[115]For an introduction to Thorndike's ecclesiology see Avis, *Anglicanism and the Christian Church*, pp. 141–4.

[116]Quantin, *Church of England and Christian Antiquity*, p. 353. Quantin provides a summary of Thorndike's Latin work *De ratione ac iure finiendi controuersias Ecclesiae disputatio* (1670).

surprising given that Thorndike had deeply imbibed Hooker's writings. In some cases – fortunately mainly matters of detail – it is not obvious what Thorndike is trying to say.

Thorndike's key thesis in his project of resolving conflicting accounts of Christianity and the Church is that the 'consent' or 'consensus' of the whole Church sets a boundary to biblical interpretation (pp. 7, 100, 192, 409). This consensus is received by us through participation in the practice of the Church, not simply through its teaching (p. 550). It is not easily quantifiable – not a matter of 'counting noses'; that method comes up against the fact, of which Chillingworth made great play, that the Fathers sometimes contradict each other. But Thorndike finds reassurance that the witness of the Fathers is coherent overall in the fact that erroneous teaching was always challenged and usually disciplined (pp. 124–5). The consensus of the Church is infallible with regard to what is necessary for salvation (pp. 410, 412), but beyond that limit the Church is fallible. Claiming the support of Jewel and Field, Thorndike lays down that no interpretation of Scripture is acceptable that runs 'contrary to the consent of the fathers' (p. 564).

Thorndike's key thesis lays great store by tradition, but it does not overlook the role of reason. Reason is needed to judge whether a particular teaching is of God (p. 18). Everyone accepts this, whether they admit it or not. Both those who claim private revelations and those who invoke the infallibility of the Church *give their reasons* (p. 97). To ascertain the consensus of the Church is the work of reason working on the materials of tradition.

While some radicals of the mid-seventeenth century brazenly appealed to private spiritual revelations and Roman Catholics invoked the authority of a Church that cannot err in order to establish what is true doctrine, neither carry conviction, for both sources already presuppose the truth of Christianity – and we receive that from the Church. It is (as Augustine famously said) the Church's witness through the ages that leads us to faith and this witness is cogent because the Church is a single communion (pp. 101–2). But the authority of the Church cannot guarantee the truth of the Christian faith, because the existence of the Church presupposes that faith (p. 548). Thorndike rejects 'both extremes': the bare appeal to Scripture on the one hand and a church that claims to be infallible in things not necessary for salvation ('a sacrilegious privilege of infallibility') on the other (pp. 523, 561).

Thorndike overtly, though perhaps not very enthusiastically, allies himself with the Reformation, while alleging that the Reformers' expressions were often inadequate (p. 562). The English Church's Reformation was a moderate one, led by those who esteemed Melanchthon above Luther (p. 564). Thorndike's boldest challenge to the fundamentals of reformed theology is to the doctrine of the perspicuity or clarity of Scripture. He goes beyond Jeremy Taylor in insisting that all things necessary to salvation are not clear in Scripture to all understandings. Scripture itself does not claim perspicuity and the consensus of Christians through the ages does not support it (pp. 76–100). If all that is necessary to be believed for salvation were clear on the page of Scripture, Christians would not disagree about it: it would be obvious to all (p. 90). Belief in the perspicuity of Scripture does not help us to decipher difficult places (p. 100). With relentless logic, Thorndike demolishes the argument of William Whitaker that what is necessary is clear to those who have the Spirit of God. They cannot have the Spirit, Thorndike rejoins, unless they already believe what is necessary to salvation (pp. 96–7). The instruction of the Church is needed, beyond the biblical text, to guide us to what is necessary for salvation (p. 504).

On the other hand – and this was the crucial negative safeguard of reformed theology against Rome – nothing that is not found in Scripture can be necessary for salvation (p. 542). However, there are matters of church order, concerning ministry, rites and customs, that are not in Scripture but may have existed before the Scriptures were written and are therefore presupposed by Scripture (p. 422). That does not mean that we are free to discard them (p. 413), though Thorndike insists with Hooker that positive laws are not necessarily binding. He rejects the claim that he attributes to Cartwright and other Puritans that a text of Scripture is needed to mandate any action. Christianity as lived has an infinity of aspects and the Bible cannot possibly cover them all. It is sufficient that all that a Christian does should be informed by scriptural teaching (pp. 544–5).

Saving truth, for Thorndike, is more than the mere belief in 'Jesus is the Christ,' coupled with a morally good life, later proposed by Locke in *The Reasonableness of Christianity* (1695).[117]

---

[117]Locke, *Reasonableness of Christianity*, p. 105.

The trinitarian formula of the Great Commission in Matthew 28.16–20 ('in the name of the Father and of the Son and of the Holy Spirit') demarcates the truths necessary for salvation (p. 83). What is required is the full orbit of Christian truth, what the Church has taught through the ages, 'our common Christianity' (p. 97). It comprises the 'rule of faith' and is identical with the summary of Christian belief that was delivered to the Church by the Apostles (pp. 99, 111). At one point, Thorndike insists that saving knowledge includes the creation of the angels and their fall, because without this we cannot understand the Fall (p. 119). In another place, he agrees with Whitaker that there is a sense in which the whole of Scripture comprises the rule of faith, because nothing not in Scripture can have that function (pp. 545–6). In any case, Thorndike is not obsessed with the text: it is the meaning or sense, in both the Scriptures and the Creed, that matters, not the exact words. It is the Socinians (who deny the deity of Christ) who appeal to the naked biblical text (p. 565).

However, there is an important difference between the rule of faith, which is the content or sense of the Creed, and the substance of Christianity which comprises not only belief but also behaviour ('manners and godly life') (pp. 117–18). The rule of faith is to be adhered to, but the substance of Christianity must be lived. With an eye to the Roman Catholic insistence on unwritten apostolic doctrines, Thorndike allows that the rule of faith is handed on orally from generation to generation – the rule of faith that leads to everlasting life and the communion of the Church (p. 586). This is to concede that the truths necessary to salvation are conveyed by oral tradition – though Scripture is still the safeguard and the litmus test of all that the Church holds to be necessary to salvation.

During the upheavals of the Civil War, the Independents, Separatists and other 'sectaries', encouraged by Oliver Cromwell for his own ends, as Richard Baxter noted, had gained the upper hand over the Presbyterians. Though he himself did not conform in 1662, Baxter did not conceal his contempt for those who had thus destroyed the unity of the Church; even the Quakers were 'the poor deluded souls'.[118] Locke later gave indirect support to the voluntarist tendency when in *A Letter Concerning Toleration* (1689) he defined

---

[118]Baxter, *Autobiography*, pp. 56, 82, 189.

a church as 'a voluntary society of men, joining themselves together of their own accord, in order to the public worshipping of God, in such a manner as they judge acceptable to him, or effectual to the salvation of their souls'.[119] In other words, each individual should make up their own mind what they believe and which Church (if any) best suits their convictions. That is, of course, the unchallenged ideology of our modern individualistic society in the West, but in the seventeenth century it was subversive of the concept of the national Church, whether Anglican or Presbyterian.

For Thorndike, the voluntarist or 'independent' polity, where individuals choose to opt in to a particular congregation ('a most poisonous doctrine') and each congregation is regarded as autonomous, excludes catholic authority: 'shall we not be thoroughly reformed till we renounce one Catholic Church, as visibly a corporation as the baptism we received upon acknowledgement of it is visible?' (pp. 395–7, at p. 396). Because we participate in common Christianity through practice as well as through teaching and texts, we cannot indwell the consensus of the Church through the ages in a state of separation. No wonder that the schismatics generate so many fanciful interpretations (p. 400). Disunity is doubly tragic, as well as culpable, because it makes the truth, residing in the consensus of the Church, hard to discern (pp. 401–2, 557). When every individual is free to choose their own Church, the great Reformation quest for the 'true church' has become meaningless (p. 403).

So where is the authority of Scripture in all this? It is assumed and unquestioned ('presupposed'). The controversy between the Reformers and the Church of Rome for the past century and a half (Thorndike observes) had been polarized into Scripture versus the Church. This is unhelpful: the question is how Scripture should be interpreted. To this end, there are two avenues open to us: 'tradition and argument, authority and reason, history and logic'. Even skill in biblical languages comes to us though tradition which conveys 'laws of speaking', though reason is clearly essential (pp. 459, 488). We must bring 'the faith of the Church' to the task of interpretation (p. 541). Of course, this is what the Reformers also affirmed, but their doctrines of the self-authenticating nature of Scripture and of its perspicuity with regard to the truths necessary to salvation

---

[119]Locke, *Letter Concerning Toleration*, p. 13.

somewhat undercut their appeal to the Fathers. In Thorndike, who demolished both of those Reformation tenets, the appeal to tradition is much more crucial and indeed operative. Theology, however biblical, cannot be done except in the context of tradition.

Thorndike had vindicated tradition in a holistic sense ('our common Christianity'), not merely antiquity, as the key to the interpretation of Scripture. But with the danger of toleration of Roman Catholics by James II in the 1680s and the consequent threat to the Anglican establishment, polemic against tradition, especially the claims of antiquity and particularly in the form of unwritten apostolic teachings, as affirmed by the Council of Trent, went up a gear. Daniel Whitby's *Treatise of Traditions* (1689) is notable among this genre. In the late seventeenth century, the centre of gravity of Anglican theological method began to shift from tradition/antiquity to reason and evidences. As Quantin points out, the problem with anti-Roman polemic was where to stop in the assault on tradition before it began to damage the Church of England's own credentials.[120]

---

[120]Quantin, *Church of England and Christian Antiquity*, p. 299.

6

Classical Anglicanism: Doubt, risk and probability

A discerned consensus of the Fathers, not about everything that concerns the Church in its life, worship and governance, but about the doctrinal fundamentals of faith and order, was still part of the Anglican platform, vis-à-vis the Roman Catholic Church and the Continental Protestant Churches in the seventeenth century. Of course, that stance raises the question of what is fundamental in faith and order and what is not, and that question could be answered only by searching the Scriptures in the light of the rule of faith of the early Church and by making reasoned and reasonable judgements. Those judgements would have the character of probable truths. Against Roman Catholic and Calvinist insistence that complete certainty or certitude was possible in an act of faith, such diverse Anglican writers as Chillingworth, Tillotson, Stillingfleet and Locke insisted, as Hooker had done, that moral certainty or probability was all that was available and moreover that it was sufficient. They had taken to heart the challenge of Pyrrhonian scepticism or what Popkin calls 'mitigated scepticism', that recognizes the limits of our knowledge, the element of uncertainty in all our beliefs, and the need therefore to proportion belief to the evidence.[1] At this point we need to look at the emergence of probability, in the modern sense of the word, in philosophical and theological argument.

---

[1] Popkin, *History of Scepticism.*

How sure can we be?

During the course of the seventeenth century in Europe, a methodological shift took place in connection with the question, 'How
can we know?,' which we have already looked at in relation to
the quest for an infallible method in Bacon, Descartes and Hobbes,
and the related or consequent question, 'Can we be sure?,' which
we come to now. With regard to this second question, it was a
shift from demonstrable, certain proofs by means of sure-fire
methods, of which Bacon, Descartes, Spinoza and Hobbes are the
great exemplars (though their methods are different), to probable
arguments used persuasively, of which Montaigne, Charron,
Pascal and Bayle are the past masters on the Continent. Across the
spectrum of intellectual disciplines, writers increasingly tended to
withhold certainty from all except mathematics, and perhaps also
metaphysics. As we have seen, Hobbes's metaphysics, as well as his
epistemology, was modelled on mathematics, particularly geometry,
and was therefore regarded by him as a system of certain truths. But
now rationality, across a range of disciplines, became increasingly
assimilated to the idea of lack of certainty and with it acceptance
of the notions of probability and fallibility. The change of climate
began with humanists like Erasmus who sought to weld together
rhetoric, philosophy and an ethical, spiritual and practical – rather
than preponderantly doctrinal – Christianity.

Three major factors in the intellectual life of Europe contributed
to this shift towards entertaining the uncertain, the unprovable. First,
religious controversy and conflict – a battle, with bloody weapons
as well as with aggressive words, over authentic Christianity,
between the Reformation and the Counter-Reformation – had the
effect of undermining confidence, among reflective minds, that
either side could be in such complete possession of the truth as to
warrant inflicting persecution, death and war on the other. Needless
to say, this weakening of confidence is not true of the scholastic
theologians, both Protestant and Roman Catholic, who perpetuated
the old deductive, systematic methods.[2]

The second factor at work was the revival of an ancient tradition
of philosophical scepticism with regard to the reliability of the

---

[2]Muller, *After Calvin*; Trueman and Clark (eds.), *Protestant Scholasticism*; Selderhuis
(ed.), *Companion to Reformed Orthodoxy*.

senses, the capability of our reasoning faculties and the solidility of received knowledge and wisdom. The sources of seventeenth-century scepticism were both pagan and Christian; they included ancient texts from Cicero, Sextus Empiricus, Diogenes Laertius and Augustine (*Contra Academicos*), and recent writings, including Erasmus's satirical *Moriae encomium* (*In Praise of Folly*, 1511), Pico della Mirandola's *Examination of Vanity of the Doctrines of the Pagans and of the Truth of Christian Teachings* (1520) and Henry Cornelius Agrippa's *On the Weakness and Vanity of all Sciences and on the Excellence of the Word of God* (1530).[3] The resurgence of scepticism about what reason could deliver was not normally anti-Christian and in fact was practised by devout Christians, including theologians (Roman Catholics and Protestants), and infused important areas of religious thought.[4] For example, Descartes' *Meditations* (1641), which begin with a radical exercise in scepticism and doubt, are premised on the existence of God as the guarantor of veridical knowledge. Pascal demolishes the pretensions of human reason and finds 'Certainty, certainty' only in his mystical experience of 1654.[5] Chillingworth is led from sceptical premises and a theory of degrees of knowledge to a bibliocentric theology, while Tillotson, Archbishop of Canterbury, elaborates an elegant, reasonable, moral form of Anglicanism on similar premises.[6]

Related to scepticism is the third factor, the maturing of empirical, experimental physical science in a direction away from the rather imperial visions of Francis Bacon towards a more workaday practical scientific ethic. As Shapiro puts it, 'An essentially Baconian research program was combined with a philosophy of science that substituted concepts of probability once associated with rhetoric for the demonstrative certainty traditionally associated with science and logic.'[7] Incompleteness of knowledge was a condition of scientific

---

[3]Erasmus, *In Praise of Folly*; Agrippa, *Vanity of Arts and Sciences*.
[4]Larmore, 'Scepticism'; Popkin, *History of Scepticism*; Schreiner, *Are You Alone Wise?*.
[5]Pascal, *Pensées*, p. 309 ('The Memorial').
[6]Popkin, *History of Scepticism*, p. xiii: 'Since the term "scepticism" has been associated in the last two centuries with disbelief, especially disbelief in the central doctrines of the Judeo-Christian tradition, it may seem strange at first to read that the sceptics of the sixteenth and seventeenth centuries asserted, almost unanimously, that they were sincere believers in the Christian religion.'
[7]Shapiro, *Probability and Certainty*, p. 10.

progress. Science and theology were on parallel paths to a less doctrinaire, more tentative overall method; they were moving in the same direction not only because they drew on common intellectual resources, including scepticism about the senses and the reason, but because as disciplines they were porous and many of the same personnel participated in both. In fact, the cross-fertilization was broader than theology and science. As Shapiro writes: 'the central intellectual phenomenon of the second half of the seventeenth century was the peculiar interaction between efforts to establish a rational basis for an historically-based, non-dogmatic, Protestant Christianity and comparable efforts to achieve a probabilistic basis for the factual assertions of scientists, historians, and lawyers.'[8]

Between them, these three developments undermined confidence that we can know the truth more than approximately, tentatively and provisionally. The concept of probability, and of degrees of probability, became central to intellectual endeavour, including theology. The idea that we cannot be sure provided the intellectual and emotional ground for developments in religious toleration in seventeenth-century England.

Montaigne, Charron and Pascal

Roman Catholic moderate or constructive sceptics include Montaigne, Charron, Mersenne, Gassendi and Pascal. Michel de Montaigne (1533–92) is the brilliant amateur, the lay sceptic. In spite of his sceptical tone and down to earth, man of the world manner, Montaigne is not a fully-fledged philosophical sceptic.[9] Through all his enquiries, he maintains some confidence in reason, but he acknowledges, indeed flaunts, its limitations. Faith is greater than reason. What is going on in Montaigne's *Essais* is a dialogue or dialectic between reason and faith, with scepticism refereeing. Montaigne expounds the wisdom of the ancients and elegantly plays off one classical writer against another, moving towards a fuller wisdom. The most thorough exposition of his sceptical-believing world view comes in his mammoth 'essay' on natural theology, the

---

[8]Ibid., p. 268; Shapiro exaggerates the 'non-dogmatic' aspect. Patey, *Probability and Literary Form*, ch. 1, provides many examples of changing uses of 'probability'.
[9]Hartle, 'Montaigne and Skepticism'. Popkin, *History of Scepticism*, speaks, in my view misleadingly, of Montaigne's 'complete' or 'total' scepticism: ch. III.

Apologie de Raimonde Sebond. In this work, Montaigne shows that he is neither a total sceptic nor a full-blooded fideist. Those who take Montaigne for a secular, naturalistic thinker could never have read the *Apology*. The book of nature teaches fallen humanity of the existence and power of God the creator (cf. Rom. 1.20, quoted by Montaigne). But the fallen mind cannot read this book aright without grace, without divine illumination. Nature also shows us how little we know and understand about the physical and spiritual worlds, and teaches us humility. Reason takes away excuse before God, but it cannot bring knowledge of divine mysteries. We see why Montaigne appealed so strongly to Pascal when we read, 'I . . . trample down human pride and arrogance, crushing them under our feet; I make men feel the emptiness, the vanity, the nothingness of Man, wrenching from their grasp the sickly arms of human reason, making them bow their heads and bite the dust before the authority and awe of the Divine Majesty, to whom alone belong knowledge and wisdom'; and again, 'Man is the most blighted and frail of all creatures and, moreover, the most given to pride.'[10]

Montaigne's motto, *Que sçay-je?*, 'What do I know?' is not an assertion, but a question, so that even his starting point is open enquiry; as he said himself, 'the world is but a school of enquiry'.[11] Montaigne is both an Epicurean, seeking pleasure and contentment in the good things of life in his own castle in a sunny climate and a fruitful land, and a Stoic, enduring with philosophical fortitude the agony of 'the stone' and other ailments. Montaigne has been taken as a sceptical agnostic, totally at home in this world. Sainte-Beuve said that he was *tout simplement la Nature . . . la Nature au complet sans la Grace*.[12] In fact Montaigne is a sincere Catholic believer who collects images, lights candles, says his prayers, and crosses himself frequently. His Christian practice goes well beyond outward conformity to the established religion and whatever his questions and reservations, he does not challenge orthodox Christian belief. As his *Journal* of his pilgrimage to Rome and his essay on prayer show decisively, Montaigne's scepticism is held within a life of faith.[13] The *philosophes* misconstrued Montaigne

---

[10]Montaigne, *Essays*, pp. 500–1, 505. Screech's introduction sets Montaigne firmly in a Christian, Catholic context.

[11]Larmore, 'Scepticism', p. 1150.

[12]Cited Willey, *Christian Moralists*, p. 192.

[13]Montaigne, *Journal de Voyage*; id., *Essays*, pp. 355–65 (Bk II, 56).

when they took him as a precursor, just as they did Bayle. The
Christian faith is spacious enough to include those who push their
doubts and questions to the brink.

Pierre Charron (1541–1603), in his banned but best-selling
sceptical work *De la Sagesse* (1601, 1604), develops common
ground with his friend and kindred spirit Montaigne. The extent of
his debt and of the overlap is contested.[14] Charron attacks Aristotle
and his scholastic interpreters who took the senses as the basis of
knowledge, when they are in fact unreliable and deceptive. Charron
adapts Montaigne's motto, *Que sçay-je?*, in a significant way to
become, *Je ne sçay* ('I don't know'), which is an assertion that
seems to be in tension with the method he espouses of dispensing
wisdom. Charron has been claimed as an atheist and to read
some accounts[15] you would never guess that he was a dedicated
priest, who published sermons and writings on the Eucharist,
was favoured and promoted by his bishop, and was an apologist
for Christianity and the Roman Catholic Church. In 1594, he
published a major apologetic work, *Les Trois Veritez*, in which he
sought to prove the three truths of God, Christianity and (against
the Calvinists) the Roman Catholic Church. Scepticism about the
human capacity to know the truth of God without the guidance
of the Church came together with the negative strand in Christian
theology – apophaticism – to form a strong version of fideism with
which to confront unbelievers, including non-Christian sceptics.
De la Sagesse begins with the dictum, '[L]a vray science & le vray
estude de'l'homme, c'est l'homme.' But this is not a manifesto of
modern secular humanism. Like the Renaissance humanists who
put 'man' at the centre of their reflection and like Pope in his 'Essay
on Man', for Charron the study of man led to the glory of God. It
was claimed that *De la Sagesse* won the support of Henri IV and a
bishop or two, though its sceptical method was attacked by Jesuits
as 'atheistical'.[16]

---

[14]Jean Daniel Charron, *'Wisdom' of Pierre Charron*, and Françoise Kaye, *Charron et
Montaigne*, defend the originality of Charron.

[15]Tullio Gregory, 'Pierre Charron's "Scandalous Book".'

[16]Horowitz, 'Pierre Charron's View of the Source of Wisdom', argues that Charron's
Pyrrhonism has been exaggerated by such as Popkin and that he should be viewed in
the Christian, Renaissance, wisdom tradition. For biographical issues and an attempt
to downgrade Charron's significance see Soman, 'Pierre Charron'.

Strange as it may seem, Blaise Pascal (1623–62) owed his 'conversion' partly to reading Montaigne. Although Pascal does not use the term 'probability', he is regarded as the founder of modern probability theory on two counts: first, by virtue of his demolition, in the *Lettres Provinciales* of the casuistical probabilism of the Jesuits, based on the medieval idea of the weighing up of authoritative texts and precedents; and second, his famous Wager in the *Pensées*, where he urges the candidate who is suspended between belief and unbelief to live and act as though Christianity were true: it is more of a commitment than a calculation.[17]

Gassendi explicitly heralds the idea of probability as we find it in Locke and Butler: an approach to, or homing in on, the truth. It was not for humans, he said, to gaze on the 'bright shining sun of truth', but rather to be content with the 'dawn of probability', in the form of credible but provisional explanations.[18] Pascal, a close reader of Montaigne (though of course his world view is vastly more profound and tragic than Montaigne's), deliberately employs the reasoning powers of a genius to show the finitude, littleness and weakness of humanity, before transcending doubt with a leap of commitment that will lead to faith. However, reason for Pascal the mathematician of genius was still demonstrative, given to devising proofs, rather than intuitive, which lends itself to probable persuasions and eventually to hermeneutical methods.

Descartes and Spinoza

Between the Renaissance and the Enlightenment, a new movement of thought intervened that was rationalist in character and deeply antipathetic to tradition. Its representatives were, on the Continent, Descartes, Spinoza and Malebranche, and in England, Lord Herbert of Cherbury and, supremely, Thomas Hobbes. The urge to discover irrefutable, logically intact systems was a reaction to the threat posed by the revival of scepticism, especially in its 'applied' form of Pyrrhonism, which taught that we must learn to live with radical

---

[17]Hacking, *Emergence of Probability*, pp. 23–5, 66, 69; Pascal, *Provincial Letters*; id., *Pensées*, pp. 149–53.
[18]Daston, 'Probability', p. 1118.

uncertainty. Descartes (1596–1650) set out to destroy and replace scepticism, to slay the dragon, but he did not escape its gravitational pull. Descartes had read Agrippa, Montaigne and Charron, and he began his famous journey of discovery towards solid knowledge by wholeheartedly embracing methodological doubt. This entailed rejecting all he had trusted from the senses, the intellect and received wisdom.[19]

It is, therefore, highly ironic that Descartes, the founder of a militantly anti-historical rationalism, and whose contempt for history is notorious, should have been singled out by interpreters of the historical movement for the impetus that his thought gave to historical consciousness and thereby to sensitivity to tradition. It was Troeltsch's view that, by his method of systematic doubt followed by reconstruction from a subjective centre, Descartes had provided the indispensable premise of an historical outlook: he had brought human consciousness into the forefront of attention. The principle of methodical doubt, whatever else it did or did not do, at least set a question mark against all traditional authorities and provided the critical independence of judgement that is a precondition of historical inquiry – we may say, of all critical thinking.[20]

Like the other post-Renaissance proponents of patent methodologies, Descartes believed that his favoured method had unlimited application and could be turned to tackle all outstanding scientific and philosophical problems. Together with Bacon, whose *Novum Organum* appeared in the year that Descartes made his great 'discovery' (1620), Descartes gave currency and credibility to the idea of rational scientific progress. Descartes is the fountainhead of the rationalistic, uniformitarian idea of human nature that we can trace through the thought of Hobbes (where it is unadulterated), Locke (where it is moderated by his stress on experience) and the *philosophes*, to the Utilitarians and rationalists of the nineteenth century.

The central feature of Descartes' system is the notion of clear and distinct ideas; its method is mathematical and deductive. Before he formulated his distinctive position, Descartes already had a low view of history; his method, when espoused, merely reinforced

---

[19]Popkin, *History of Scepticism*, chs. IX and X.
[20]Rubanowice, 'Ernst Troeltsch's History', p. 85; Flint, *History of the Philosophy of History*.

a basically ahistorical outlook. He reflected in the *Discourse on Method*:

> I thought I had already given enough time to languages, and even also to the reading of the ancients, to their histories and fables. For to converse with those of other centuries is almost the same as to travel. It is a good thing to know something of the customs and manners of various peoples in order to judge of our own more objectively. . . . But when one spends too much time traveling, one becomes eventually a stranger in one's own country; and when one is too interested in what went on in past centuries, one usually remains extremely ignorant of what is happening in this century.[21]

We find Malebranche, half a century later, drawing the same analogy between travel and historical study.

On that memorable day in 1620, shut up with (or on) a stove, Descartes began to examine his thoughts. His first meditation concerns the principle of development, a notion that he found highly questionable.[22] He began by observing that often less perfection could be discerned in composite works produced by several hands: 'So it is that one sees that buildings undertaken and completed by a single architect are usually more beautiful and better ordered than those that several architects have tried to put into shape.' Ancient towns with their layers of development, winding streets and asymmetrical layout are inferior to the planned orderly creations of a single mind. Similarly, with regard to society, those peoples who emerged gradually from semi-savagery, making their laws piecemeal as they went along in response to crimes and quarrels, 'could not be so well organised as those who, from the moment at which they came together in association, observed the basic laws of some wise legislator'. (It still remained, of course, for Vico to demythologize the great law-givers of antiquity and, in doing so, to turn Descartes's view of tradition on its head, reversing his values and finding the real springs of human society, law and culture ultimately in the obscure and fantastic products of primitive imagination.) It was only a short step for Descartes from the infancy of society to the

---

[21]Descartes, *Discourse on Method*, pp. 30–1.
[22]Ibid., p. 35.

childhood of the individual. Just as society had emerged, thanks to clear and articulate reasoning *de novo*, from the thralldom of instinct and the tutelage of tradition, into the ordered, rational states devised by the great legislators of antiquity, so children, ruled by their appetites and led astray by incompetent tutors, have their powers of reasoning permanently impaired. If only we had had the full use of our reasoning faculties from the moment of birth and had never been guided by anything else![23]

There is a striking contrast between Descartes's attitude to childhood and that of the Romantics, as exemplified in Wordsworth's 'Ode: Intimations of Immortality from Recollections of Early Childhood',[24] just as there is between the Cartesian and, say, the Vichean views of society. As Maritain asserted: 'If Cartesianism showed itself so savage a ravager of the past in the intelligible order, it is because it began by disowning in the individual himself the essential intrinsic dependence of our present knowledge on our past.'[25] Wordsworth's counterfoil to Descartes is: 'The Child is father of the Man;/And I could wish my days to be/Bound each to each by natural piety.'[26] Descartes's proposals involve, first of all, a stripping away of the accumulated prejudices of a lifetime – the 'tradition', as it were, of the individual mind – by a process of methodical doubt. But having attempted to doubt all that he already believes, Descartes finds one idea in his mind that is unassailable: the notion that he is actually doubting. *Cogito ergo sum* is a clear, distinct and indubitable concept. Now if Descartes can find other ideas that are equally clear and distinct, he can begin the process of reconstruction.

For Descartes, as for Plato and a long tradition of Western philosophy that includes Nicholas of Cusa, Leonardo da Vinci, Galileo, Kepler, Spinoza and Hobbes, mathematics is the model of certain knowledge; its terms are clear, distinct and self-contained. For them, all problems of natural knowledge could be solved by applying the method of pure logical reasoning. Whereas Descartes retains an interest in empirical, experimental inquiry,

---

[23]Ibid., pp. 35–6.
[24]Wordsworth, *Poetical Works*, pp. 587–90.
[25]Maritain, *Three Reformers*, p. 62.
[26]Wordsworth, *Poetical Works*, p. 79 ('My heart leaps up when I behold'). These lines also form the motto for the 'Ode: Intimations of Immortality'.

Spinoza pushed the method to its ultimate conclusion. It can be said of Spinoza that 'no other philosopher has ever insisted more uncompromisingly that all problems, whether metaphysical, moral or scientific, must be formulated and solved as purely intellectual problems, as if they were theorems in geometry', not even Hobbes.[27] Spinoza is regarded as a pioneer of biblical criticism, but we should note that his approach to the Bible was not so much historical–critical in the modern sense, as rational-deductive, in the manner of Descartes. Spinoza proposed to interpret the Bible as he studied nature: the method was virtually the same; no tradition or authority could dictate to the individual interpreter.[28] The fact that Spinoza's method led him to a naturalistic or pantheistic metaphysic, where the totality of reality is described as *deus sive natura* (God or you could say Nature), and Hobbes' method led him to a mechanistic, materialistic metaphysic, was a warning to the age of Newton and Boyle to eschew *a priori* speculation and stick to workaday, empirical investigation. Spinoza and Hobbes were coupled together in the popular mind as embodiments of satanic lies and delusions, intellectual anti-christs. Israel notes that 'Spinozisme' in France and 'Spinozisterey' in Germany were used loosely to denote the totality of deistic, naturalistic and atheistic systems. But at the very least it can be said that neither was an atheist and Hobbes indeed was a churchman of sorts.[29]

Concerning Descartes there are several qualifications that need to be made. First, while Descartes stakes all on the criteria of clarity and distinctness, a certain lack of these two attributes can be detected in his own principles, as his critics at the time pointed out. The *Cogito* formula is his model, but the clarity and distinctness here involves a movement of thought, instantaneous though it be, from premise to conclusion: *Cogito* ergo *sum*. But in the *Meditations*, Descartes employs his canons of clarity and distinctness more generally: not only to ideas that involve a train

---

[27]Hampshire, *Spinoza*, p. 62; Spinoza, *Ethics*.
[28]Spinoza, *Chief Works* (*Theologico-Political Treatise*), p. 99; Scholder, *Birth of Modern Critical Theology*, pp. 138–42; Popkin, 'Spinoza and Biblical Scholarship'; cf. Arnold, 'Spinoza and the Bible', in *Essays in Criticism*: Spinoza 'nowhere distinctly gives his own opinion about the Bible's fundamental character. He takes the Bible as it stands, as he might take the phenomena of nature, and he discusses it as he finds it.'
[29]Israel, *Radical Enlightenment*, p. 13; Colie, 'Spinoza in England'.

of reasoning, however implicit, but also to perceptions (his own example is a piece of wax). Second, in the *Cogito* the premise 'I think' is obviously drawn from experience, not from logic. This makes the *Cognito* a synthetic *a posteriori* statement (to put it in the received Kantian jargon). Here, we may contrast the method of Spinoza who does not rely on experience at all; his statements are all *a priori*. Third, Descartes does not hold that either clear and distinct ideas (the *Cogito*) or clear and distinct perceptions (the piece of wax) in themselves constitute objective knowledge of reality. The canons of clarity and distinctness prove that objects (which may be physical or mental) are present to the mind, not that they correspond to the actual state of affairs 'outside' the mind, in the 'real' world, for as Descartes so ingenuously says, it might all be a dream or a demonic delusion. To guarantee the veridical status of both our ideas and our perceptions, Descartes has to introduce the notion of clear and distinct judgements and, underlying these, the existence of God (proved by the clear and distinct reasoning of his ontological argument) – a God who would not permit his creatures to be fundamentally and permanently deceived.[30] For Spinoza, on the other hand, clear and distinct ideas, in and of themselves, provide a knowledge of reality. For according to Spinoza, thought is itself one of the two knowable attributes (out of an infinite number) of ultimate reality or God – the other being extension.[31] When looked at in this way, Descartes' methodological ideal based on clear and distinct ideas seems somewhat lacking in clarity and distinctness itself. His key criterion was open to sceptical attack and the Pyrrhonists were not slow to exploit its weakness. Popkin calls Descartes at the end of the day, 'Sceptique malgré lui.'[32] In its origins, complex and enmeshed with abstract metaphysical speculation in the form of the ontological argument, his model of philosophical discourse was destined to enjoy a long history and to exert huge influence on Western thought by way of either development or reaction. One recurrent theme of this long-running controversy concerns the nature of language. In the philosophical

---

[30]Keeling, *Descartes*, pp. 173–5; Ashworth, 'Descartes' Theory of Clear and Distinct Ideas'; Schouls, *Descartes and the Enlightenment*, p. 21. See the critique of clear and distinct ideas in Wittgenstein, *Philosophical Investigations*, nos 46–7, 88–90.
[31]Spinoza, *Ethics*; Donagan, 'Spinoza's Theology'.
[32]Popkin, *History of Scepticism*, ch. X.

tradition that stems from Descartes, the notion of clear and distinct ideas carries the corollary of a rationalistic, analytical view of language, similar to that of Bacon and later Hobbes. We find in Descartes himself a radical distinction between the cries of animals which are the product of nature (instinct) and the first articulate speech of men which is solely the creation of reason. 'One should not confuse words,' he asserts, 'with the natural movements which bear witness to the passions.' It follows 'not only that animals have less reason than men, but that they have none at all'.[33] Here again, Descartes' view contrasts markedly with the views of Montaigne about the abilities of animals and the later theory of Vico, worked out in explicit antithesis to Cartesianism, that there is a line of cognitive continuity between animal cries and the inarticulate expressions of primitive humankind.

Nicolas Malebranche (1638–1715) experienced a sudden and total conversion to Descartes' philosophy as a young Oratorian and devoted his life to forging a synthesis of Christian theology and Cartesian philosophy. Impressed above all by Descartes's concentration on method, Malebranche's *De la recherche de la verité* (1674–75) is a cumulative metaphysical argument for a method that is fully revealed only at the end of this hefty treatise.[34] But Malebranche's method is not indebted only to Descartes's rationalism (he is critical of the arbitrary aprioristic approach of the later Descartes), but also to Bacon's empiricism. He calls in the new world of empirical, inductive investigation to redress the weakness of the old world of deductive system-building, but recognizes that, in view of the threat from scepticism, we need an overall theory, not merely piecemeal bits of evidence. Malebranche's concept of truth rests on the twin pillars of rational and empirical demonstration and is overarched by a Christian moral purpose. It is applicable to every department of knowledge.[35]

History and tradition cut a poor figure in the light of Malebranche's rigorous conditions of truth. Knowledge of the past is neither capable of rational demonstration nor susceptible of experimental proof. The moral and religious import of history is often hard to detect. Taking up Descartes's remark that those who

---

[33]Descartes, *Discourse on Method*, p. 75.
[34]Malebranche, *Oeuvres*, vol. 2.
[35]Rome, *Philosophy of Malebranche*.

become absorbed in the history of other ages lose touch with the times in which they live, Malebranche pours scorn on the antiquarian mentality. Chronology, genealogy, study of the way of life and the languages of the ancients are all lost labour, *recherches inutiles*.[36] Malebranche's sustained polemic against historical research can be seen as a bridge between Descartes's principles, inimical to history, and the French *philosophes'* suspicion of 'pedantry'.

Liberal Anglicans

John Hales

With Lucius Cary (Lord Falkland), William Chillingworth, John Hales and the early Clarendon (Edward Hyde), we encounter a robustly critical, indeed sceptical view of the authority of the Fathers, that is to say of Christian antiquity.[37] Whereas the more mainstream and High Church Anglicans, following Jewel's *Apology*, would set store by the *consent* of the Fathers, Hales (1584–1656) and the other members of the intellectual circle that Falkland gathered at Great Tew in Oxfordshire doubted whether that consent was as cogent as was claimed. They subjected the appeal to antiquity to a critique from the point of view of reason.[38] Pointing to the unedifying arguments in the early Church over the date of Easter and the legalism on which he believed that it was based, Hales condemns the leaders of the Church for ignorance and the faithful for apathy and credulity: 'because through sloth and blind obedience men examined not the things which they were taught, but like beasts of burthen, patiently couch'd down and indifferently underwent whatsoever their superiors laid upon them'. And Hales points the moral for our concept of authority: if the leaders of the

---

[36]Malebranche, *Oeuvres*, vol. 2, pp. 62–3, 200–1.

[37]In what follows I take Hales as representative of this school; for Falkland and Chillingworth, and for more on Hales see Quantin, *Church of England and Christian Antiquity*, pp. 209–28; Avis, *Anglicanism and the Christian Church*, pp. 85–97.

[38]See Clarendon, *Miscellaneous Works*, pp. 218–20; Wormald, *Clarendon*, pp. 240–76. On the intellectual circle centred on Lord Falkland's residence at Great Tew see Trevor-Roper, *Catholics, Anglicans and Puritans*, pp. 166–230; Ollard, *Clarendon*, pp. 29–41.

Church failed to show wisdom and discretion in a point so plain and so trivial as the date of Easter, it would ill become us to look to such 'poor-spirited persons' as arbiters of the points now at issue between the churches.[39] In his sermon, 'Of Enquiry and Private Judgement in Religion', Hales passes in review the various claimed authorities in theology. In his remarks on antiquity he anticipates Locke, asking, 'What is it else . . . but man's authority born some ages before us?'

> Now for the truth of things, time makes no alteration; things are still the same they are, let the time be past, present or to come. Those things which we reverence for antiquity, what were they at their first birth? Were they false? Time cannot make them true. Were they true? Time cannot make them more true.[40]

Time is irrelevant to the question of truth. Reason is the judge of opinions, whether ancient or modern. Although Izaac Walton claims that Hales 'loved the very name of Mr Hooker', the spirit in which they viewed the past was very different.[41] The Tew Circle had been intellectually stimulated by the writings of Faustus Socinus (1539–1604); without endorsing his anti-Trinitarian doctrine, they had bought into the Socinian critique of Roman Catholic infallibility claims and the stress on critical reason and personal judgement in the interpretation of Scripture.[42]

So, for Hales, church councils are, equally with antiquity in general, simply 'human authority after another fashion'. Hales is happy for church councils to make their contribution and for their decisions to be bought to the bar of reason. It is when infallibility is claimed for them that he protests. Infallibility is not the prerogative of 'any created power whatsoever'.[43] All agree that individuals may err, but 'can Christians err by whole shoals, by armies meeting for defence of the truth in synods and councils, especially general, which are countenanced by the great fable of all the world, the Bishop of Rome?' In answering this question, Hales sets aside any

---

[39]Hales, *Tract Concerning Schism*, pp. 7–8.
[40]Tulloch, *Rational Theology*, vol. 1, p. 249.
[41]Walton, *Lives*, p. 161.
[42]Mortimer, *Reason and Religion*, ch. 3.
[43]Hales, *Golden Remains*, p. 25.

claim that promises are given to the whole Church that are not the prerogative of any individual except, as Roman Catholics hold, the pope. His reply is purely *ad hominem*: 'To say that councils may not err, though private persons may, at first sight is a merry speech; as if a man should say, That every single soldier indeed may run away, but a whole army cannot.' He remains totally unimpressed by the calibre of most members of church councils:

> Considering the means how they are managed, it were a great marvel if they did not err: for what men are they of whom these great meetings do consist? Are they the best, the most learned, the most virtuous, the most likely to walk uprightly? No, the most ambitious, and many times men neither of judgement nor learning.[44]

For John Hales. ecclesiastical history is largely the record of the 'factioning and tumultuating of great and potent bishops'.[45]

The note of *universality* (Vincent of Lerins' *ubique*) is no safer guide; indeed it is the weakest of all: 'universality is such a proof of truth, as truth itself is ashamed of; for universality is nothing but a quainter and trimmer name to signify the multitude'. To say that truth lies with the multitude, or even the majority, contradicts the lonely voices of the Old Testament prophets and the notion of the faithful remnant. Such grounds may perhaps serve to excuse an error but never to warrant a truth.[46]

Hales is no exception to the fact that Anglicans of all complexions in this period accepted the Holy Scriptures as the paramount authority in the Church. Hales refers us to Moses and the prophets, the Apostles and Evangelists, for the fundamentals of Christianity. But his prescription contains a restriction: it is indeed the function of the Scriptures to show the way of salvation and the fundamentals of the faith, but not to legislate for every area of life. Like Hooker, Hales restricts the authority of Scripture to the redemptive purpose for which it was given, while he sees others, on all sides, 'torturing them [the Scriptures] to extract that out of them which God and nature never put in them'.[47] Hales bears witness to the fact that anti-Calvinism and a sceptical stance towards the Fathers could go

---

[44]Hales, *Works*, vol. 1, p. 65.
[45]Hales, *Tract Concerning Schism*, p. 12.
[46]Tulloch, *Rational Theology*, vol. 1, pp. 250–1.
[47]Hales, *Golden Remains*, p. 3.

hand in hand at this time; anti-Calvinism was not the prerogative of High Church thinkers only.[48]

Edward Stillingfleet, in his *Irenicum* (1661), quotes both Chillingworth and Hales against excessive deference to antiquity. Stillingfleet warns that 'as to matters of fact not clearly revealed in Scripture, no certainty can be had of them, from the hovering light of unconstant tradition'.[49] Stillingfleet has a rather rose-tinted view of the early Church: although at this stage he believes that it offers no blueprint of church government (he is advocating comprehension of Dissenters), it provides a model of moderation, toleration and liberty in both practice and opinion. Later he would argue on the basis of antiquity against the sin of schism: there were no adequate grounds for separation from the Established Church.

Jeremy Taylor

The case of Jeremy Taylor (1613–67) shows that among churchmen, an appeal to reason pursued by open debate was not the sole prerogative of liberal spirits, such as Falkland, Hales and Chillingworth, or of eccentric thinkers like Hobbes. Taylor is impossible to pigeon-hole and could be discussed at several points in our study of seventeenth-century Anglican theology, but although he is an apologist for episcopacy and a sacramental theologian, aspects usually associated with the High Church, he is also a powerful advocate of spiritual freedom, guided by reason. In the main part of *The Liberty of Prophesying* (1647), Taylor exposes the inadequacy of the various authorities typically advanced within the churches to settle controversies. Tradition, Councils, Fathers, popes – none is infallible. 'They that are dead some years before we were born, have a reverence due to them, yet more is due to truth that shall never die.'[50] Where the teachings of the ancients and the views of the moderns are evenly balanced, he gives the benefit of the doubt to tradition. But 'where a scruple or a grain of reason is evidently in the other balance', we should go with that.[51]

Even Scripture unaided is not a clear guide, except in the essential truths of salvation ('things plain, necessary and fundamental'), for

---

[48]Quantin, *Church of England and Christian Antiquity*, p. 209.
[49]Cited ibid., p. 286 [*Irenicum*, p. 320].
[50]Cited McAdoo, *Eucharistic Theology*, p. 31.
[51]Ibid., p. 341.

it is often obscure and gives rise to different interpretations. Taylor has a dash of the sceptic in him: 'men do not learn their doctrines from Scripture, but come to the understanding of Scripture with preconceptions and ideas of doctrines of their own'. The Scriptures are like those portraits that seem to look at you wherever you stand.[52] It comes to this: no individual or church is free from error on the one hand, or 'malice, interest and design' on the other; nothing is certain except the divine authority of Scripture, 'in which all that is necessary is plain' and much that is not necessary to salvation is 'very obscure, intricate and involved'. Therefore, we must either rest satisfied with the fundamental articles of faith grounded on the plain statements of Scripture, or we must find some other guide. And in this search, reason is our best guide and judge.[53]

Needless to say, Taylor is not advocating letting our reason run riot to speculate about mysteries beyond our ken or to construct doctrines *de novo*. The function of reason is to adjudicate in disputed questions of theology where Scripture itself is unclear. He is substantially echoing Chillingworth, but though his tone is just as bold, Taylor operates in a context of a received catholicity that preserves him from the brashness of the author of *The Religion of Protestants*. It is worth pointing out, however, that both Chillingworth and Taylor are free from the sort of secular rationalism that we associate with the French Enlightenment. As Tulloch points out, 'It never occurred to them to doubt the reality of revelation, and its supremacy over the conscience and reason.'[54] Taylor does not forget that probability is as much rational assurance as we can expect: in things not necessary to salvation, where we are 'left to our liberty', he wrote, we rely upon 'right reason proceeding upon the best grounds it can, viz. of divine revelation and human authority, and probability is our guide'.

Clarendon

In his essay 'Of the Reverence Due to Antiquity'[55] Clarendon, who as Edward Hyde had been a member of the Tew Circle and of one

---

[52]Taylor, *Works*, vol. 8, pp. 1, 7.
[53]Ibid., pp. 91–3.
[54]Tulloch, *Rational Theology*, vol. 1, p. 404.
[55]Clarendon, *Miscellaneous Works*, pp. 218–40.

heart and mind with Falkland, insisted that 'the too frequent appeal and the too supine resignation of our understanding to antiquity' was the greatest obstacle to truth and knowledge. It is false modesty that holds back from questioning the wisdom of the Fathers. No one follows them in everything. In particular their cosmology – pervaded by angels, devils and expectations of the coming millennium – is obsolete. 'He who will profess all the opinions which were held by the most ancient Fathers, and observe all that was practised in the primitive times, cannot be of the communion of any one church in the world.' Parties who differ most in their opinions and practices appeal with equal confidence to the so-called 'sense of antiquity' in support of their 'mutual contradictions'. We should indeed 'stand upon the old paths' – inform ourselves of what was said and done in the past – but not lie down in them! This does not mean that Clarendon advocates a simplistic appeal to Scripture. No current controversy, he asserts, could be settled purely by appealing to Scripture. It is sufficient for its purpose but is not an adequate guide to untangling fruitless controversies. 'It informs us sufficiently of all that we are obliged to think or to do; and whatsoever is too hard for us there to understand, is in no degree necessary for us to know.' It is clear that where there is this frank recognition of the plurality of interpretations of Scripture and tradition, reason must be the arbiter.

However, just as the authority of Scripture and tradition, respectively, were discriminatingly defined and restricted to their proper province, so too the role of reason was carefully limited. It was not so much constructive as critical, and found its role in the interpretation of Scripture and tradition. Clarendon shared an element of scepticism about the sources of authority with Chillingworth, Hales and others. As Chillingworth had argued against his Jesuit opponent, in the Roman Church tradition has acquired a disproportionate authority, not only eclipsing Scripture but also stifling reason:

Following your church I must hold many things not only above reason, but against it, if any thing be against it; whereas following the scripture I shall believe many mysteries, but no impossibilities; many things above reason, but nothing against it; many things which had they not been revealed, reason could never have discovered, but nothing which by true reason may be confuted; many things which reason cannot comprehend how they can be, but nothing which reason can comprehend that it cannot be. Nay I shall believe nothing which reason will not convince that I ought to believe it.[56]

Sir Thomas Browne

Sir Thomas Browne (1605–82) is a singular mind. Natural historian, antiquary, doctor and moralist, he qualifies also as an Anglican divine with some significance for theological method in the seventeenth century. But it is difficult to know where best to locate him on the map of Anglican thought. A layman, a physician and both deeply cultured and profoundly devout, Browne is an independent-minded biblical scholar, a lover of curiosities and antiquities, if not of antiquity, charitably disposed towards Roman Catholics and non-Christians overseas, and a man of stout reliance on his own reason and experience. Reason and experience in the manner of Francis Bacon are the key to Browne's approach both to the Bible and to natural and historical knowledge. The background to Browne's theological writings is the theological chaos of the Civil War and Protectorate, and the iconoclasm that devastated churches in his native Norwich. In *Religio Medici* (1642–43), Browne identifies himself as both catholic and reformed: 'I am of that reformed new-cast Religion, wherein I dislike nothing but the name; of the same belief our Saviour taught, the Apostles disseminated, the Fathers authorized, and the Martyrs confirmed', but which through the machinations of princes and the 'ambition & avarice of Prelates' needed Reformation in order to 'restore it to its primitive Integrity' (p. 3).[57] But, with regard to the Roman Church, 'we have reformed from them, not against them' (p. 4). As there were many Reformers, so there were many Reformations. But it is the Church of England, he says, that satisfies his conscience and reason best of all. He adheres loyally to her Articles and constitution. Beyond the formularies are 'points indifferent' and these 'I observe according to the rules of my private reason, or the humor and fashion of my devotion, neither believing this because *Luther* affirmed it, or disproving that

---

[56]More and Cross (eds.), *Anglicanism*, pp. 105–6.
[57]Sir Thomas Browne, *Religio Medici*; page references in my text.

because *Calvin* hath disavouched it. I condemne not all things in the Councell of *Trent*, nor approval all in the Synod of *Dort*. In briefe, where the Scripture is silent, the Church is my Text; where that speakes, 'tis but my Comment; where there is joynt silence of both, I borrow not the rules of my Religion from *Rome* or *Geneva*, but the dictates of my owne reason' (p. 6). There are many common inferences from Scripture to which Browne does not subscribe, for he would 'never betray the libertie of [his] reason'; what is not of faith 'may admit a free dispute' (pp. 52–3). While in philosophy he gives himself liberty of speculation, 'in Divinity I love to keepe the road; and though not in an implicite, yet an humble faith, follow the great wheele of the Church', so avoiding any 'taint or tincture' of 'Heresies, Schismes, or Errors' (pp. 11–12). He relishes the challenge of reasoning about the Trinity, the Incarnation and the Resurrection, but knows the limits of reason: 'I love to lose my selfe in a mystery to pursue my reason to an *oh altitudo*' (p. 17). Since he came to know that we know nothing, his reason has become more pliable to the will of his faith (p. 19) and he now counts it 'no vulgar part of faith to believe a thing not only above, but contrary to reason' (p. 20).

There is a methodological parallel between the way that Browne studies the natural world (natural philosophy) and the way that he studies the Bible. 'Thus there are two bookes from whence I collect my Divinity: besides that written one of God, another of his servant Nature, that universall and publik Manuscript, that lies expans'd uto the eyes of all; those that never saw him in the one, have discovered him in the other: This was the Scripture and Theology of the Heathens . . . nature is the Art of God' (pp. 32, 35).

Browne approaches Scripture as the formidable amateur: scholarly, critical, down to earth, not intimidated by Church doctrine or venerable tradition. His biblical researches have been described as 'diverse, labyrinthine, pedantic, encompassing and sometimes baffling' – and always central to his writing.[58] In 1646, he published the *Pseudodoxia Epidemica: Or Enquiries Into many Received Tenents And commonly presumed Truths* (known in brief as the *Vulgar Errors*).[59] Although Browne's biblical enquiries occupied

---

[58]Killeen, *Biblical Scholarship*, p. 107.
[59]Sir Thomas Browne, *Pseudodoxia Epidemica*.

only a fraction of this vast emporium of curious knowledge, the work was in part a diatribe against the rough handling of the Scriptures by the common people in the theological free-for-all of the Interregnum when the flood-gates of private judgement were opened. Selden said of the text *Scrutamine Scripturas* ('Search the Scriptures', Jn 5. 39): 'These two words have undone the world.'[60] Browne has something in common with the Pyrrhonists in his sceptical approach to received beliefs, superstitions and legends – he takes it all with a hefty grain of good-humoured salt – but he also has Bacon's passion to interrogate the evidence of nature and history to arrive at reliable knowledge. In matters of belief, Browne states at the end of a multitude of curious enquiries, the understanding is swayed by the authority of the person from whom we receive it and the probability of the object of belief. Even though we may have confidence in the former, we require satisfaction with regard to the latter: 'nor can we properly believe untill some argument of reason, or of our proper sense convince or determine our dubitations'.[61] Nevertheless, Browne's scepticism and sanity in so many areas does not prevent him believing in witches and alchemy.

Pierre Bayle

Pierre Bayle (1647–1706) is a major factor in the European intellectual environment. His *Dictionnaire historique et critique* was translated into English in 1710 and made an immediate impact. Israel states that Bayle 'exerted an unprecedented impact right across Europe. . . . No one else, not even Locke, was a staple of so many libraries or had so wide a general influence, his writings being everywhere acknowledged to be a prime cause of the tide of skepticism, atheism, and materialism sweeping the west of the continent.'[62] Popkin says that Bayle 'launched the Enlightenment' and describes the *Dictionnaire* as a 'Summa Sceptica that deftly undermined the foundations of the seventeenth-century intellectual world.'[63] Bayle punctured the hubris of speculative, deductive

---

[60]Killeen, *Biblical Scholarship*, p. 16.
[61]Browne, *Pseudodoxia Epidemica*, vol. 1, p. 605.
[62]Israel, *Enlightenment Contested*, p. 87.
[63]Bayle, *Historical and Critical Dictionary*, p. xi.

reason and demolished naive confidence in supposedly trustworthy historical records.

Yet what Bayle's own religious and philosophical beliefs were has puzzled interpreters. He has sometimes been taken for a total sceptic, whose method of systematic doubt, applied to all authorities, and of playing off one piece of documentation against another, one philosophical school against another, was radically corrosive of all doctrine.[64] On that interpretation, Bayle's protestations (even on his deathbed) of sincere Christian faith have to be understood as a smokescreen, as camouflage, as Israel does. Bayle's Dutch rational Arminian opponent, Jean le Clerc, said that Bayle sought to 'renverser la religion chrétienne, en feignant de la défendre.'[65] We have been here before, with Montaigne and Hobbes. It is implausible to say, as Israel does, of accomplished theologians and practising churchmen, such as Hobbes and Bayle, that they set out to destroy the received theological worldview and were opposed to all supernaturalism.[66]

The fact is that Bayle is well embedded in Christianity and Protestantism. What have been taken as attacks on Christianity *tout court* are aimed at the Roman Catholic Church. His hostility to rational religion, whether of the Dutch Arminian *rationaux*, such as le Clerc, or the deists, stems from a Calvinist view of fallen human reason, not from infidelity. Although Israel links Bayle with Spinoza as the fountainhead of corrosive scepticism, Bayle is vitriolic about Spinoza's monistic, pantheistic doctrine, dubbing it, in various respects, 'une absurdité prodigieuse', 'une abomination execrable' and morally dangerous.[67]

Of Huguenot stock, son of a minister, and resident for a while in Geneva, Bayle underwent a double conversion, like Chillingworth and Gibbon: from Protestant to Roman Catholic and back again, before settling as a member of the Reformed congregation in Rotterdam. He was deprived of his chair in the university because of his subversive views. As Labrousse suggests, he belongs not in the trajectory from Montaigne to Voltaire, subversive thinkers within a

---

[64]For a survey of views up to the mid-1970s, see Heyd's article review, 'A Disguised Atheist or a Sincere Christian?.'
[65]Quoted Israel, *Enlightenment Contested*, p. 92.
[66]Ibid., pp. 43, 65.
[67]Bayle, *Dictionnaire historique et critique*, p. 208 (art. 'Spinoza').

Roman Catholic ambit, but in the Genevan succession from Calvin
to Rousseau, an intellectual reformer. The acute psychological
insight into human motivation that characterizes the Augustinian
tradition, from Augustine's *Confessions* through Jansenist theology
and Pascal's *Pensées* to Rousseau's *Confessions*, informed Bayle's
analysis.[68]

Should Bayle then be classified as a fideist, who having
demolished the claims of reason and shown the contradictoriness
of the history of thought, casts himself into the arms of faith and
surrenders to divine revelation, or as an early liberal, minimalist
in religious belief, sitting lightly to the historic traditions of
Christendom, thoroughly tolerant and open to new knowledge?
Was he a thoroughgoing Pyrrhonist, never happier than when
deconstructing and demolishing, or did he have a constructive
intent? His method of systematic doubt was applied remorselessly
to the claims of reason and authority. He took on the rational
systematizers of the seventeenth century, undermining all the
certainties of their reasonable universe. Whereas Descartes had
applied his method of systematic doubt to sense knowledge and
to tradition, Bayle targeted the Cartesian confidence in reason
itself. By piling example on example in the *Dictionnaire historique
et critique*, Bayle showed that rationalism, taken to an extreme,
will self-destruct. His questioning method embraced also biblical
interpretation and the history of the Church. That does not make
him an unbeliever but rather an anticlerical and anti-rationalist
polemicist. But some have seen him as a dogmatic Phyrronist
even with regard to the empirical realm, revelling in pitting one
piece of evidence against another, without attempting to come to
a conclusion. Others, notably Devolvé, have seen Bayle as the first
positivist, forerunner of the *philosophes*, with faith in the ability
of critical science to establish firm conclusions, not only in history,
but in ethics, politics and so on.[69] But Bayle's sceptical, critical
method could not find rest in any form of secular ideology, but
only in Protestant faith. He is neither a seventeenth-century *érudit*,
a massively learnt compiler of facts, not an eighteenth-century
philosophe, like the authors of the *Encyclopédie*. Neither his

---

[68]Labrousse, *Pierre Bayle*, vol. 2, pp. 609–10. See also id.,'La mèthode critique', and
id., *Bayle*. Cf. Augustine, *Confessions*; Pascal, *Pensées*; Rousseau, *Confessions*.
[69]Devolvé, *Religion, Critique et Philosophie Positive*.

aims, his beliefs, not his methods were the same as theirs.[70] The eighteenth-century *Philosophes* tended to claim Bayle as an enemy of religious belief, as does Jonathan Israel today; but that is to misunderstand what Bayle is trying to do. For him, as for Pascal, scepticism is a tool or a tactic to undermine the claims of reason in order to make room for faith: Bayle is – like Pascal – a passionate fideist; he is not ashamed to speak of Jesus Christ in his work. But whether, logically, Bayle was engaged in cutting off the branch that he was sitting on is a moot point.

As a scholar, Bayle is a man of many parts: I select three. First, he is an empiricist. He has a passion for the particular, concrete fact, the contingent context and the give-away detail. He takes for himself the title *minutissimarum rerum minutissimus scrutator*, most minute explorer of most minute things. This is both a strength and a weakness: a strength because it enables him to expose the errors, bias and sheer wrong-headedness of previous authors; a weakness because, as Cassirer points out, he has no worked-out principle or system that enables him to take possession of the empirical world and to master it intellectually. For Bayle, the empirical world is a mere concatenation of miscellaneous facts – and he luxuriates in this.[71]

Second, Bayle is a critic: he is an unsparing critic without being a rationalist. Bayle may well be the inventor of *critique*, the deployment of internal, immanent, reasons to expose the falsity of a position. Rational of course he is – what is his method but the application of reason to documents, ideas and ideologies? His reason is deployed, not in constructing an intellectual system, but in truth-seeking. Objectivity is his goal – an objectivity to be attained by setting passion and prejudice aside.[72] Here I find at least an analogy with the method of Joseph Butler, for whom, as we shall see, the pursuit of truth – moral truth – is the highest calling of humans made in God's image. Butler teaches us to see that 'Everything is what it is and not another thing.' And Butler, like Bayle, leaves no hiding place, but exposes all human weaknesses, follies, evasions, and pretences.

---

[70]Bayle, *Dictionnaire historique et critique*, p. 7 (editor's introduction): 'Ni les intentions, ni l'idéologie, ni la methode ne sont les mémes.'
[71]Cassirer, *Philosophy of the Enlightenment*, pp. 202–4; cf. Wade, *Intellectual Development of Voltaire*, p. 467.
[72]Labrousse, *Pierre Bayle*, ch. 2.

Butler says that we cannot imagine greater human depravity than disinterested cruelty. As the literary scourge of human cruelty and superstition, Bayle has the same ethical motivation. He puts us in mind of the epitaph that Jonathan Swift composed for his tomb in St Patrick's Cathedral, Dublin: *Ubi sæva Indignatio Ulterius Cor lacerare nequit* ('Where fierce indignation can no longer tear the heart').

Third, it follows that Bayle is a moralist, imbued with what Labrousse calls 'Calvinistic moralism'.[73] He sits in judgement on the authors whom he interrogates. He is not moved by the aesthetic merits of their works. In the ancient historians, he finds contradictions, facts that do not match up, and dates that are completely wrong. He is no model historian himself, but a critic of history. Bayle's quarrel was with the whole of recorded history. He puts the human race itself in the dock, setting himself to expose its ignorance, crimes and follies. He could be Pascal when he says, 'l'histoire n'est autre chose que le portrait de la misère de l'homme'.[74] Paul Hazard comments that Bayle's catalogues amount to the most damning indictment ever drawn up by one human being to the shame and confusion of his fellows.[75]

Changing concepts of probability

Other notable Protestant sceptics are Hugo Grotius in the Low Countries, and William Chillingworth and Joseph Glanville in England. Chillingworth falls back on 'the Bible alone', without support from tradition, or so he pretends. In reality, he stands in a salient tradition of interpretation and he privileges reason as a tool. Glanville develops a concept of 'practical certainty', a certainty that cannot be doubted, but rejects the Aristotelian idea of 'infallible certainty', where all possibility of error has been eliminated.

The idea that we can know best what we have ourselves made surfaces at this time in Montaigne, Hobbes, Sanchez and Mersenne. It represents the beginning of a hermeneutical concept of knowledge,

---

[73]Ibid., p. 10.
[74]Bayle, *Oeuvres diverses*, vol. 3, p. 548; cf. Wade, *Intellectual Development of Voltaire*, p. 459.
[75]Hazard, *European Mind*, p. 131; cf. Brush, *Montaigne and Bayle*, p. 330.

where we seek to enter into the mind of the author, however strange, however alien, that may seem at first. It is the germ of the method of the human sciences. What it has is enthralling human interest; what it lacks is precision and certainty. A sophisticated account of this principle of *verum factum* is developed by Vico.

The idea of the 'probable' was changing its meaning from opinion warranted by authority to the degree of belief or assurance that was proportionate to the evidence. In Thomas Aquinas in the thirteenth century, influenced as he was by the newly available ancient Greek and Arabic texts, what was 'probable' was an opinion based on an appeal to authorities, especially Aristotle and Augustine. Because there were conflicting authorities, there were various probabilities and these needed to be weighed up and a judgement had to be reached – this is the heart of Thomas's method in the *Summa Theologiae*. Pascal lampooned the debased form of the weighing of probabilities in sixteenth-century Jesuit casuistry in his *Lettres Provinciales*. Early in the next century, a sense of the futility of seeking certainty in the moral realm began to prevail. Locke, however, gives probability an ethical edge, reshaping it as moral probation in this life. Instead of a putative certainty based on the weight of authorities, there was a continuum of degrees of assurance relative to the subject and the relevant evidence. All this sets the stage for Joseph Butler's apologetic doctrine of probability. However, the notion of probability, in its numerical rather than morally persuasive sense, requires the emergence of the idea of evidence and methods of collecting and evaluating it.[76] Bacon had pioneered the empirical methodology and it would come into its own among the Encyclopaedists of the French Enlightenment.

---

[76]Cf. Hacking, *Emergence of Probability*, p. 32.

7

Aspects of the Anglican Enlightenment

In its impact on theology, including Anglican theology with its distinctive methods and approaches, the Enlightenment at least equals the Reformation in significance. Some interpreters argue that the Enlightenment exceeds the Reformation and the Renaissance combined in shaping the modern Western world and that it belongs to a different order of magnitude.[1] The great surge of critical thinking and intellectual exploration, that we rather lazily call the Enlightenment, took its rise in late-seventeenth-century England and culminated in the pre-revolutionary programme of the French *philosophes*. But the Enlightenment was a cultural commonwealth that traversed Europe and spanned the Atlantic. The prestige of Locke and Newton secured English predominance, but the *philosophes* turned their methods and theories into a subversive ideology. A major bridge between English and French Enlightenment ideas was the publication of Voltaire's *Lettres Philosophique*, following his visit to England in 1726–9, on his release from a second spell in the Bastille. The letters described the British constitution, way of life and religious traditions, beginning with the Quakers and going on to depict Anglicans and Presbyterians, neither of them at all flatteringly. Voltaire commended British freedom and tolerance.[2] As Roy Porter puts it, 'All the shibboleths of Enlightenment were familiar to English lips: reason and experience; law, liberty and justice; happiness, humanity and nature; knowledge is power is

---

[1]Israel, *Radical Enlightenment*, pp. vi–vii.
[2]Voltaire, *Letters on England*; id., *Lettres Philosophiques*.

progress; *sapere aude,* and the rest . . . the baby Enlightenment's
first words were spoken in an English nursery.' Porter also notes
that that nursery was a Christian one: 'Enlightenment goals – like
criticism, sensibility or faith in progress – throve in England *within*
piety.'[3] To understand eighteenth-century Anglican theology, we
need to grasp the key points of the Enlightenment programme.

Let there be light!

Light was the deliberately adopted symbol of the movement.
Alexander Pope's proposed epitaph for Newton is not too strong:
'Nature and Nature's laws lay hid in night. God said, "Let Newton
be!" and all was light.'[4] James Thompson, in his adulatory *Poem
Sacred to the Memory of Sir Isaac Newton,* compares this 'first
of men' to the sun rising in its glory: 'When Newton rose, our
philosophic sun!.' Newton's discoveries in optics symbolized
enlightenment. 'Ev'n Light itself, which every thing displays,/
Shone undiscover'd, till his brighter mind/Untwisted all the shining
robe of day. . . .'[5] In his prospectus for the *Encyclopédie,* Diderot
referred to 'the general enlightenment that has spread throughout
society'. The *philosophes* themselves spoke of 'le siecle des lumieres'
and Gibbon, who was not ideologically naive, referred to his own
'enlightened age'. Voltaire claimed in the introduction to his *The Age
of Louis XIV* (1751) that he was depicting 'the most enlightened
century [the seventeenth] that ever was'.[6] The term *Aufklarung* was
in common use in Germany in the 1780s. Thinkers with, shall we
say, a dialectical relationship to the prevailing intellectual paradigm
could speak ironically of the Enlightenment, as when Vico refers to
'our own enlightened times'.[7] The image of light was also favoured
by unambiguously Christian writers, just as it had been in the early
Church when enlightenment was virtually a synonym for baptism
(cf. Heb. 6.4; 1 Pet. 2.9). But those whose orthodoxy was doubtful

---

[3]Roy Porter, 'Enlightenment in England', pp. 6–7.
[4]Pope, *Poetical Works,* p. 371.
[5]http://www.poemhunter.com/poem/a-poem-sacred-to-the-memory-of-sir-isaac-newton/
[6]Stern (ed.), *Varieties of History,* pp. 40–1.
[7]Berlin, 'Alleged Relativism in Eighteenth-Century Thought', in *Crooked Timber,* p. 85.

or explicitly suspect also employed it. Lessing, an unconventional Lutheran, wrote: 'The ultimate purpose of Christianity is . . . our salvation by means of our enlightenment.' It is in this enlightenment, Lessing continued, that 'in the last analysis, our entire salvation consists'.[8] (Augustine and Aquinas could equally have said this.) Joseph Priestley, a Dissenter and Unitarian, praised 'this enlightened age', but his compliment won him no friends among orthodox churchmen.[9] As we shall note, the opposite of enlightenment was not simply darkness but 'barbarism'. It is a word that peppers writings of the eighteenth century, whether rationalist or religious. The contrast between barbarism and enlightenment entailed an idea of progress on various fronts.

We are concerned with the relevance of the Enlightenment to questions of theological authority, that is to say method, knowledge, reason, approaches to Scripture, views of the past, historical perspective, tradition, development (or not), understandings of human nature, questions of truth, certainty and probability. The Enlightenment was a cultural revolution of great diversity, including internal tensions and contradictions, and it therefore defies simple definition.[10] There were significant differences between the English, Scottish, French, Dutch and German (*Aufklärung*) forms of the Enlightenment, to look no further afield. The Scottish Enlightenment excelled in 'philosophic history' and political economy; it was not overtly anti-Christian and among its sources of inspiration were Jacobite, Roman Catholic and Episcopalian influences.[11] The German scholars of the *Aufklärung* were earthed, in a way that the *philosophes* of France were not, in a body politic that was corporate, not internally polarized, an economically backward German countryside and the Lutheran Church. They tended therefore to be more realistic, more Christian and more organic in their thinking than the French, more integrated, less mechanical, presupposing in their researches the intimate connection of all events, their causes and motives.[12] In Britain, Enlightenment figures

---

[8]Henry E. Allison, *Lessing and the Enlightenment*, p. 66.
[9]Young, *Religion and Enlightenment*, p. 2.
[10]See Crocker, 'Enlightenment: What and Who?', p. 336.
[11]For an amusing introduction see Trevor-Roper, 'Scottish Enlightenment', in *History and the Enlightenment*.
[12]Reill, *German Enlightenment*.

such as Locke, Thomas Browne, Hutcheson, Addison, Shaftesbury, Chesterfield, William Law and Butler, excelled in the exploration of human psychology, the delicate dissection of emotions, passions, reasonings, motives, scruples and excuses in a way that lent itself at the hands of some (supremely Law and Butler) to the promotion of Christian morals and Christian apologetics.[13]

An age of reason?

For all the constant invocation of reason, the Enlightenment was also an age of credulity, superstition, interest in the occult, alchemy, quack remedies and masonic mythology.[14] The Enlightenment was the opposite of intellectually monochrome. It included Diderot's penchant for the gothic and the macabre; Hume's insistence that passion will trump reason every time – his undermining of the authority of reason in philosophy and theology; Rousseau's intense, deliberately cultivated subjectivity and attack on the *philosophes'* doctrinaire rationalism; Burke's hatred of abstract ideology and reverence for antiquity, including – unfashionably – the Middle Ages and for what has stood the test of time; Vico's *Scienza Nuova* which founded modern empathetic history – the method of imaginative indwelling of the past; and J. G. Hamann's sensual, imaginative philosophy. (Hamann said: 'God is a poet, not a mathematician' and held that poetry was the mother tongue of the human race.) All these aspects are intimations of Romanticism, deep within the Enlightenment.[15] Therefore, the Enlightenment should not be mainly identified with the *philosophes*, as Peter Gay wanted to do.[16]

---

[13]See Willey, *English Moralists*. Willey does not include Butler in this gallery of moralists, but discusses him in *Eighteenth-Century Background*, ch. 5.

[14]Redwood, *Reason, Ridicule and Religion*; Jacob, *Radical Enlightenment*; Pagliaro (ed.), *Irrationalism in the Eighteenth Century*.

[15]E.g. Diderot, *The Nun* [*La Religieuse*]; cf. Furbank, *Diderot*, ch. 12; Rousseau, *Reveries*; Vico, *New Science*; Berlin, *Magus of the North*; id., 'Counter-Enlightenment', in *Against the Current*.

[16]Gay, *Enlightenment*; id., 'Why was the Enlightenment?.' Cassirer, Hazard, Crocker and others attack the narrow identification of the Enlightenment with the *Philosophes*: Cassirer, *Philosophy of the Enlightenment*; Hazard, *European Mind*; Crocker, 'Enlightenment', p. 337. Hulliung, *Autocritique of Enlightenment*, insisting that Rousseau belongs to the Enlightenment and not to pre-romanticism, and pointing to his defence of the Enlightenment values of freedom, individual autonomy and toleration, suggests that Rousseau founded an 'alternative Enlightenment' (pp. 2, 4, 242).

The *philosophes* were simply the most secular thinkers of an age that also included devout Lutheran, Anglican, English Dissenting, Calvinist and Roman Catholic scholars who also consciously identified with the Enlightenment. There was, in truth, a family of Enlightenments, displaying both family resemblances and family quarrels, some bitter and bloody, so that it is distorting to speak of a single Enlightenment as a 'unified and universal intellectual movement', as Pocock puts it.[17]

The 'reason' that was invoked and praised *ad nauseam* by the Enlightenment was not the metaphysical, speculative, deductive reason of Descartes, Hobbes and Spinoza, but the empirical, 'experimental' method of Bacon, Locke and Newton (though the contrast should not be exaggerated, as though Descartes was opposed to the method of observation and experiment). The mantras of the eighteenth century, 'sufficient reason' and 'right reason', referred not to abstract principles, but to the constitution of the world as revealed by Newton and Locke (though their assumptions were far from identical). Their theories (which were regarded as facts) pointed to universal order and natural law and to the identity between nature and reason. Reason and nature must be made to coincide in every area of life and thought. Montesquieu and those who followed him (including the Scots William Robertson and John Millar) tended to assimilate the study of society to the successful and prestigious study of nature by Newton and the Newtonians. Montesquieu was hailed as the Newton of the social, historical world. He begins *L'Esprit des Lois* by defining laws as 'the necessary relations arising from the nature of things.'[18] It is easy to parody this sort of language and Samuel Johnson does precisely that in *Rasselas;* the prince and his sister sit at the feet of a supposedly wise old philosopher until they realize that his 'wisdom' is vacuous verbiage: 'To live according to nature, is to act always with due regard to the fitness arising from the relations and qualities of causes and effects; to concur with the great and unchangeable scheme of universal felicity; to co-operate

---

[17]Pocock, *Barbarism and Religion*, vol. 1, pp. 9, 13. For an anthology of texts that describe and define the Enlightenment see Schmidt (ed.), *What is Enlightenment?*. For the Enlightenment among English Dissenters see Haakonssen (ed.), *Enlightenment and Religion*. For aspects of the Roman Catholic Enlightenment see Lehner and Printy (eds.), *Companion to the Catholic Enlightenment*.
[18]Montesquieu, *Spirit of Laws*, Bk I, ch. 1: http://www.constitution.org/cm/sol.txt. See also Berlin, 'Montesquieu', in *Against the Current*.

with the general disposition and tendency of the present system of things'.[19]

The standard heuristic scientific model of the Enlightenment was mechanical, not organic: working parts could be taken out and examined separately, but how they comprised the whole eluded these scholars. The historians of the Enlightenment were not driven by a passion to discover the unique character of a society or a period for its own sake, but for the sake of deriving general laws that could then be universally and prescriptively applied. Lacking a concept of historical continuity from one stage of society to another, they were not able to arrive at an organic understanding of society and natiohs and the notion of growth and development eluded them. Hume partly grasps the social complexion of the individual, their embeddedness in society, and he does justice to the nonrational drivers of individual psychology, the emotions or passions. But without the concepts of continuity, organic growth and development, the depths of human history remain an inexplicable enigma to him. In Britain, only Burke transcends these limits. No wonder that tradition was a foreign country to the Enlightenment.[20]

The Enlightenment was methodologically self-conscious. The *Encyclopédie* defined method as 'the architecture of all sciences', fixing their scope and limit.[21] It is well said that 'Reason was the method and nature the high court of appeal for all eighteenth-century arguments.'[22] 'First follow Nature', urged Pope in the *Essay on Criticism* (1711), 'and your judgement frame/By her just standard, which is still the same.' He was referring to the canons of classical literature. 'Those rules of old discover'd, not devis'd,/Are Nature still, but Nature methodiz'd.' What Pope means by nature is 'sense' or 'good sense', the opposite of the wit and elaborate artifice of the Metaphysical Poets such as Donne. For 'True wit is nature to advantage dress'd,/What oft was thought, but ne'er so well express'd'. But this is still a far cry from Wordsworth's idea of nature a century later.[23]

---

[19]Samuel Johnson, *Rasselas*, p. 54.
[20]See Gossman, *Medievalism*; Sabine, 'Hume's Contribution'.
[21]Cited from art. 'Methode' by Schargo, *History in the Encyclopédie*, p. 17.
[22]Redwood, *Reason, Ridicule and Religion*, p. 12; Wade, *Intellectual Origins*, p. 22.
[23]Grierson and Smith, *Critical History*, p. 191.

James Thompson's *The Seasons* (1730) brings together Nature, Nature's explorer ('awful Newton'), and Nature's Author, God ('Hail, Source of Being, Universal Soul/Of heaven and earth! Essential Presence, hail!'). Thompson has a sense of the immanent, pervasive presence of God that is far removed from the remote deity of Newton and the deists, and akin to Wordsworth and Coleridge: 'boundless spirit all/ And unremitting energy, pervades,/ Adjusts, sustains, and agitates the whole'. Thompson equates 'fancy' and 'imagination' (Coleridge opposes them) and does not divorce them from reason and emotion: '. . . the soul,/Where, with the light of thoughtful reason mixed,/Shines lively fancy and the feeling heart'. But Thompson's predilection for ornamental periphrasis ('finny race' for fish; 'glossy kind' and 'soft tribes' for birds, etc.) shows him a long way short of Wordsworth in the depiction of nature.[24] *The Seasons* provided the inspiration for the libretto of Joseph Haydn's oratorio of the same name (just as Milton's *Paradise Lost*, along with the Book of Genesis and the Psalms, informed Haydn's *The Creation*). Burke included society in his concept of what is natural, not because it follows inexorable laws, but because it has grown, undergone development, not been manufactured. For Burke 'Nature' is not other than human nature. Descartes, by contrast, thought that what was constructed (by the power of reason) was superior to what had grown of its own accord.

Rather than 'The Age of Reason', the Enlightenment was a revolt against rationalism – precisely as a form of authoritarian dogma. It was the age of questioning, of criticism, of 'common sense' – the first age of Western civilization that claimed the right to do that, without constraint or limit. 'Reason' did not mean, as it did for the Christian tradition, a participation in the mind of God, but rather tracing of the hand of the Supreme Being in his works; not indwelling the truth as a given in divine revelation, but finding it out through ceaseless exploration of the physical, social and human world. Hazard points to the 'restlessness' of the Enlightenment mindset.

---

[24]James Thompson, *Seasons*, quotations from 'Spring'. On changing interpretations of nature in the Enlightenment see Willey, *Eighteenth-Century Background*, passim and esp. p. 237; see also Thompson's *Poem Sacred to the Memory of Sir Isaac Newton*, cited above.

The Enlightenment, especially in France, meant an attitude of suspicion with regard to received authority, especially of the Roman Catholic Church – a critical stance towards inherited orthodoxy. On his deathbed Diderot said, 'The first step towards philosophy is incredulity.'[25] This was not a universal 'baseless suspicion', like that of Nietzsche, but one born of bitter experience of the impediments to enquiry erected by the Roman Catholic Church (obscurantism, dogmatism, censorship and the persecution of dissidents) and the rather less formidable but no less real intolerance on the part of the Lutheran, Reformed and Anglican Churches. The Enlightenment thinkers, in France and elsewhere, looked for non-theological, natural or human explanations in nature and history. They rejected scholasticism, system-building and speculative metaphysics. Descartes' method of systematic doubt was a model, as was Bayle's unremitting interrogation of sources – though both Bayle and Descartes were figures whom, as Voltaire put it, one studied only to disagree with (Descartes, because doubt was only the first stage of speculative system-building; Bayle, because his method was subversive of all intellectual enterprises).

Distrusting external authority, the Enlightenment asserted the autonomy of the individual intellect working by empirical reasoning. Descartes' method of systematic doubt was a bid for freedom from prejudice and therefore error, prejudice being understood as any belief that was not authorized by reason.[26] (For Burke, in contrast, 'prejudice' stood for the wisdom of the ages and, when embraced by the enquirer, was heuristic of truth.) According to Kant, 'Enlightenment is man's emergence from his self-incurred immaturity' – immaturity meaning 'the inability to use one's own understanding without the guidance of another'; and 'Dogmas and formulas . . . are the ball and chain of his permanent immaturity.' All that is needed is the freedom to use one's own reason and to use it in the public domain.[27] Kant called for freedom; and 'freedom, mastery and progress' are three watchwords that point to the heart

---

[25]France, *Diderot*, p. 29.
[26]Schouls, *Descartes and the Enlightenment*, p. 11.
[27]Kant, *Political Writings*, pp. 54–5. Cf. O'Neil, 'Enlightenment as Autonomy', p. 185: 'no thinker of the Enlightenment was more deeply aware that reason might be an illusory and self-destroying authority than Immanuel Kant'.

of Enlightenment thought.[28] While the imagery of light suggests the realm of theory, of knowledge or contemplation, rather than of practice, it was accompanied by a novel confidence in the human ability to understand the world and to change it. Peter Gay styles the Enlightenment 'a recovery of nerve'.

Nevertheless, a vein of scepticism, inherited from the Pyrrhonists of the previous two centuries, gnawed away at Enlightenment pretensions. Some thinkers whom we associate with the Enlightenment were subversive of it: Rousseau subverted it from within.[29] It has been said of David Hume that he 'saw through the Enlightenment'.[30] Nevertheless, in spite of the contrary evidence, Voltaire clung to the faith that reason can pull us through and his ethical imperative, the scourge of human malignancy, never wavered. One aspect of the ethical imperative of the *philosophes* was their passionate commitment to the improvement of the human condition. They were, as Gay insisted, 'the party of humanity',[31] where *humanité* equalled *bienfaisance* (benevolence). Condorcet's battle cry was 'reason, tolerance, humanity', a variant of the general invocation of the *philosophes* to reason, humanity and justice. On the other hand, the French clergy seemed to have been oblivious to glaring social and economic injustice and inequality before the Revolution: they reaped the whirlwind at the Revolution.

The protagonists of enlightenment lacked a theory to account for the unexpected, the imaginative, the emotional and the irrational in human nature and its history. Their anthropology was two dimensional and uniformitarian. Reason and imagination were often seen as opposed, rather than as two sides of a single experience. The imaginative products of intellectual life – legend, fable, myth, even metaphor – were disdained and excluded. In his *Dictionnaire philosophique* (1764), Voltaire warned against the harmful effects of metaphor, as militating against truth and clarity. To that extent, the *philosophes* were the legatees of Descartes and Hobbes and Locke.

---

[28]Schouls, *Descartes and the Enlightenment*, p. 3.
[29]Hulliung, *Autocritique of the Enlightenment*. Garrard, *Rousseau's Counter-Enlightenment*, calls Rousseau 'the first enemy of the Enlightenment' (p. 120).
[30]Ginsberg, 'Hume versus the Enlightenment'.
[31]Gay, *Party of Humanity*. See also McCloy, *Humanitarian Movement*.

Tradition and development

The Enlightenment is often seen as an onslaught on tradition. Paul Hazard wrote: 'The Past abandoned; the Present enthroned in its place! . . . a whole section of Europe's *intelligentsia* suddenly dropped the cult of antiquity.'[32] Meinecke said: 'Never had there been an age that looked back on the past with such an autonomous attitude and with such complete self-assurance.'[33] A particularly egregious example of disdain for the past is provided by Thomas Warton (1728–90), no freethinker, but a clergyman of the Established Church and Poet Laureate. In the Preface to his three-volume *History of English Poetry* (1774–81), Warton wrote: 'We look back on the savage condition of our ancestors with the triumph of superiority; we are pleased to mark the steps by which we have been raised from rudeness to elegance.' He noted with complacency 'the infinite disproportion between the feeble efforts of remote ages and our present superiority in knowledge'.[34] Warton's smug sentiments could be paralleled in many writers of the time.

But the Enlightenment's rejection of tradition was highly selective. It was partly a case of the substitution of traditions. For some classicism (comprising Greek philosophy and pagan attitudes) replaced the Western Christian tradition of the Fathers, the schoolmen and the Counter-Reformation. Voltaire dismissed all philosophy between Plato and Locke and looked on the Middle Ages with repugnance. The 'Dark Ages' were for him 'a tissue of crimes, massacres, devastations' and the founding of monasteries (which was not much better), all of which arouses 'horror and pity'.[35] Voltaire and Gibbon each identified the same three ages of enlightenment, represented by Erasmus, Bacon and Newton – nothing between the ancient Greeks and the Renaissance.[36]

Enlightenment thought was an eclectic mixture of Cartesian, Lockean and Newtonian assumptions. Voltaire said of Descartes

---

[32] Hazard, *European Mind*, p. 47.

[33] Meinecke, *Historism*, p. 55.

[34] Cited Black, *Art of History*, p. 28.

[35] Cited Gooch, *Catherine the Great*, p. 231 ('Voltaire as Historian').

[36] Trevor-Roper, *Religion, the Reformation and Social Change*, pp. 199–200 (ch. 4: 'Religious Origins of the Enlightenment'); on his thesis and its context in his work see Robertson, 'Hugh Trevor-Roper'.

that he was 'born to uncover the errors of antiquity but to substitute his own', and that he was 'spurred on by that systematizing mind which blinds the greatest of men'.[37] Thanks to Voltaire, Newton enjoyed the highest prestige, but probably Locke had the greatest intellectual influence, though his theory of knowledge was simplified by the *philosophes* to mean that all ideas come from sense-experience. For more than a century, Locke's *Essay* 'determined the course of European thought'.[38] Newton and Locke stood for nature and mind, respectively (both spheres being approached empirically). Newtonian science was greeted like a new gospel, good news for all humanity.[39] Fontenelle (1657–1757) who was sometimes called the first of the *philosophes*, though he was a creative thinker in his own right, popularized Newtonian science and its method, at the same time intensifying the mathematical paradigm in the spirit of Descartes when applying the scientific method to human society. 'The geometrical spirit,' he wrote, 'is not so tied to geometry that it cannot be . . . transported to other branches of knowledge . . . morals or politics or criticism. . . .' Fontenelle's methodological ideals were 'order, clarity, precision and exactitude'.[40] He pursued Cartesian physics (but without God as a guarantee of veridicality), within a mechanical universe, while not subscribing to all of Newton's doctrines. Technological advancement would come and with it the amelioration of the human condition, but for Fontenelle this did not include ethical improvement. He is said to be the first to formulate the idea of indefinite, continuous progress, though even Pascal believed in scientific progress, for the human race was like a single man who learns continually as he grows (an image echoed by Turgot). Fontenelle's influence was profound and helped to shape the approaches of Montesquieu, Voltaire and the *Encyclopédists*.[41]

Other influences that contributed to belief in progress were Leibniz's unique speculative system and the Scottish philosophical historians and thinkers William Robertson, John Millar, Adam Ferguson and

---

[37]Voltaire, *Letters on England*, p. 63.
[38]Cragg, *Puritanism to the Age of Reason*, p. 114.
[39]Cobban, 'The Enlightenment', pp. 87–8.
[40]Cited from Fontenelle, 'The Utility of Mathematics' by Butterfield, *Origins of Modern Science*, p. 157.
[41]Marsak, *Bernard de Fontenelle*, pp. 23, 46; Edsall, 'Idea of History and Progress'.

Adam Smith, though for the Scottish school progress was understood as an observed law of society, rather than as an article of faith, held with sober realism and without dreams of perfectibility, indeed with a degree of pessimism.[42] So we find a growing confidence that progress – intellectual, social, technological and even moral – was possible and a prevailing atmosphere of optimism and complacency that infected Anglican theology too. English ideas of progress grew independently of French influence and differed from those of the *philosophes* in including religious growth and advancement and preparing the ground for concepts of the development of doctrine.[43] However, there was undoubtedly a tension between belief in social progress and looking on the past – in Gibbon's words – as 'the register of crimes, follies, and misfortunes of mankind'.[44]

The optimistic belief in progress was not un-nuanced and was challenged by some, among them American President John Adams (1735–1826), 'probably the most caustic critic of fatuous optimism that the age of Enlightenment produced'.[45] Voltaire himself was ambivalent: his historical work made him cynical about the human capacity for cruelty, ignorance and stupidity. Human history was nothing but a catalogue of mendacious acts. *Candide* is simply the most popular of Voltaire's expressions of pessimism, resignation and, one might say, philosophical defeatism, triggered as it was by the Lisbon earthquake of 1755, which killed 60,000 people.[46] It is said that the 'enlighteners' were often men of simple views who proposed simple solutions.[47] In the face of natural disaster and human wickedness, the deists had no theodicy; natural and human evil remained inexplicable.[48] They would not deserve to be criticized for that – all theodicy, all attempts to 'assert Eternal

---

[42]Forbes, 'Scientific Whiggism'; Heilbroner, 'Paradox of Progress'; Spitz, 'Significance of Leibniz'.

[43]Spadafora, *Idea of Progress*. Spadafora establishes that Bury, *Idea of Progress*, is misleading in suggesting that English belief in progress was dependent on French influence.

[44]Gibbon, *Decline and Fall* (hereinafter *D&F*), p. 44; this edition includes Gibbon's substantive discussions of Christianity. Frankel, *Faith of Reason*; Besterman, 'Reason and Progress'; F. C. Green, *Rousseau and the Idea of Progress*.

[45]Gay, *Enlightenment*, vol. 2, p. 99. See also Vyverberg, *Historical Pessimism*.

[46]Voltaire, *Candide*.

[47]Lovejoy, *Great Chain of Being*, pp. 7ff: an age of *esprits simplistes*.

[48]Wade, *Intellectual Origins*, pp. 26–7.

Providence, And justify the ways of God to men', as Milton put it,[49] falls short – if it were not that they preened themselves on having better answers than traditional Christianity. Nevertheless, there is a vein of historical pessimism even in Hume and Gibbon.

Christian scholars like Johnson and Butler were totally undeceived about the generally cruel nature of the world and the usually miserable condition of human life, but they held on to faith, hope and love, the three traditional theological virtues, as an antidote to cynicism and despair. Johnson explores the theme of the failure of earthly hopes and ambitions in *The Vanity of Human Wishes* (1749). The inevitable fate of humankind is unsparingly evoked: 'Nor think the doom of man revers'd for thee'. But in contrast to Voltaire, Johnson's advice is 'nor deem religion vain' and he ends by recommending prayerful supplication:

Yet when the sense of sacred presence fires,
And strong devotion to the skies aspires,
Pour forth thy fervours for a healthful mind,
Obedient passions, and a will resign'd.[50]

Ten years later (1759) Johnson published *Rasselas*, a philosophical or moral novel on a similar theme, with similarities to Voltaire's *Candide* which appeared in the same year. *Rasselas* includes a recognition of the fragility of reason: 'Of the uncertainties of our present state, the most dreadful and alarming is the uncertain continuance of reason.'[51] Johnson was a man deeply versed in mental distress who sometimes felt his reason, which the age prized above everything, slipping from him.[52] At times of profound despondency, Johnson would turn to Pascal's *Penseés*, which took the measure of human misery. Pascal divided the reasonable

---

[49]Milton, *Paradise Lost*, Bk I, lines 25–6, *English Poems*, p. 114.
[50]Samuel Johnson, *Selected Writings*, pp. 139–48.
[51]Samuel Johnson, *Rasselas*, p. 96 (ch. XLIII).
[52]Boswell, *Life of Johnson*, pp. 47–9, 342, 387, 400; Krutch, *Samuel Johnson*, pp. 1–2, 19, 107–8; Clifford, *Young Samuel Johnson*, pp. 124–5. Boswell also suffered from profound melancholia, accompanied by with fear of insanity: Sisman, *Boswell's Presumptous Task*, pp. 5–7. Johnson referred to Boswell's affliction as 'the *black dog*' (a form of words usually associated with Winston Churchill) and gave advice, drawn from his own experience, on how to combat it: Boswell, *Life of Johnson*, p. 1042.

thinkers of the eighteenth century. In contrast to Johnson, Voltaire saw Pascal as a principal antagonist and did his best to demolish his arguments. When the French Revolution broke out, Pascal's stock rose as Voltaire's plummeted.[53]

The expedition to the Inner Hebrides, that Johnson undertook with Boswell in 1773, was a venture into one of those regions of 'barbarism' that both repelled and allured the intelligentsia of the eighteenth century, as the antithesis of the ideal of rational, civilized order. In this and in his 'horror' of the wide, barren spaces, the 'naked' mountains and their 'horrid chasms', Johnson reflects the sentiments of his age, the very reverse of the thrill that the Romantics would derive from these features (the antithesis of Coleridge's 'deep romantic chasm' in *Kubla Khan*).[54] But in what he says about the fragility of oral tradition and the enshrining of tradition in ceremony, Johnson shows remarkable insight. Seeking reliable information about the history of castles and churches and the origin of social customs, Johnson is frustrated by the contradictory answers that he receives from the islanders. He reflects that these are a people without written records and whose history had not yet been written (though William Robertson had published a history of the country up to the reigns of Mary Queen of Scots and James VI in 1759).[55] '[O]ne generation of ignorance effaces the whole series of unwritten history,' Johnson pronounces; '. . . memory, once interrupted, is not to be recalled. Written learning is a fixed luminary. . . . Tradition is but a meteor, if once it falls, cannot be rekindled.'[56] He regrets that there was no time to visit the two small islands where the Roman Catholic faith had survived the Reformation ('the Popish Islands'), because 'Popery is favourable to ceremony; and among ignorant nations, ceremony is the only preservative of tradition' – a remarkable anthropological insight, albeit from someone who had little time for the 'philosophic' historians of his age.[57]

---

[53]Barker, *Strange Contrarieties*, pp. 163, 198–204.
[54]For the revolution in attitudes to mountains in the late eighteenth century see Macfarlane, *Mountains of the Mind*, pp. 17ff.
[55]Samuel Johnson, *Journey to the Western Islands*, pp. 17–18, 26, 29, 36, 69, 44.
[56]Ibid., p. 101.
[57]Ibid., p. 115.

Bernadetto Croce said that the eighteenth-century rationalists' view of progress was 'progress without development'.[58] And that is progress without an internal rationale. The *philosophes'* axiomatic uniformitarianism was inimical to developmental and evolutionary ideas: human nature, especially human reason, was the same in all cultures and at all times, and the intellectual ideal was to grasp clear and distinct ideas, which were assumed to be universal. The concept of uniformity as a criterion of truth militated against the emergence of the idea of development in theology as much as in history. When the deists, such as Matthew Tindal in *Christianity as Old as the Creation*, put forward their theories on the basis of universal truths and unchanging nature, many orthodox theologians were paralysed in response because they also operated on these assumptions. It was Joseph Butler who countered deist arguments by showing that our knowledge of divine revelation was partial, incomplete, varied and unequal – just like our knowledge of nature.[59]

The appeal to 'nature' presupposed uniformity and was related to the motifs of primitivism (the idealization of supposedly undeveloped and uncorrupted societies) and cosmopolitanism ('I take the whole world as my parish', boasted both George Whitefield and John Wesley). Cosmopolitan and uniformitarian ideas suggested to eighteenth-century thinkers that they could identify with all humankind in an attitude of painless benevolence. Montesquieu claimed: 'I prefer my family to myself, my country to my family, but the human race to my country' and Diderot echoed him in his article on cosmopolitanism in the *Encyclopédie*. Leibniz stated, 'I will only the good of all mankind.'[60] Gibbon suggested that a philosopher should consider the whole of Europe as one great republic whose inhabitants had attained almost the same level of politeness and cultivation.[61]

Turgot (1727–81) is dubbed by Manuel 'the apotheosis of Cartesianism'; he 'was led by his worship of reason to prefer the purest mathematical abstraction over any other form of knowledge and to look upon the metaphors and images in which the ancients

---

[58]Croce, *History*, p. 244.
[59]Crane, 'Anglican Apologetics'.
[60]Cited Schlereth, *Cosmopolitan Ideal*, pp. 47, 77, xxiv–xxv. See also Whitney, *Primitivism*.
[61]Gay, *Style in History*, p. 50.

communicated their ideas as a sort of baby-talk. . . .'[62] Condorcet believed that the study of history would yield 'fixed, immutable and certain principles'.[63] Fontenelle asserted that 'all men resemble each other so much that there is no people whose stupidities ought not to make us tremble'.[64] Hume held that reason was 'grounded in the nature of things, eternal and unyielding'.[65] Mankind, said Hume, are so much the same in all times and places that history cannot produce any surprises. The same motives always produce the same actions. To understand the ancient Greeks and Romans, we should study the French and English of today.[66] Hume cannot explain irrational or wayward actions in history. His characters, writes J. B. Black, are not real people, but 'a dexterously poised, mechanically sustained assemblage of divergent, disconnected or conflicting qualities'.[67] Hume's fellow Scottish historian William Robertson asserted that 'A human being as originally shaped by the hand of nature is everywhere the same.' Consequently, the wild, the extreme and the fanatical (e.g. Ignatius Loyola) was unworthy of notice by the historian.[68] The *philosophes* resisted Montesquieu's *L'Esprit des Lois* where his method – inductive, comparative and ultimately relativistic – was most explicit and seemed to undermine the dogma of the 'constant and immutable principles of human nature'.[69] Montesquieu posited that every society was a spiritual union (*union d'esprit*) with a common character which evolved over time, as a result of the action of an infinite number of causes.[70] Hume, Gibbon and Burke are his disciples in this respect. Hume postulates the uniform character of 'the whole fabric of human life' for methodological reasons – it gives us insight into the lives of people long ago and so makes the writing of history possible – but

---

[62]Manuel, *Eighteenth Century Confronts the Gods*, pp. 305–6; see also id., *Prophets of Paris*, pp. 13–51.

[63]Stromberg, 'History in the Eighteenth Century'.

[64]Cited from Fontenelle, *De l'Origine des fables* (1724) by Marsak, *Fontenelle*, pp. 49–51.

[65]Meinecke, *Historism*, p. 157, citing Hume's *Enquiry Concerning the Principles of Morals*.

[66]Hume, *Enquiry Concerning Human Understanding*, cited Black, *Art of History*, p. 96.

[67]Black, *Art of History*, p. 101.

[68]Ibid., p. 197.

[69]Becker, *Heavenly City*, pp. 100–1.

[70]Vyverberg, *Historical Pessimism*, pp. 161–2, citing the fragment *On Politics*.

Hume recognizes the diverse characters of nations, giving priority to 'moral' over 'physical' factors.[71] Voltaire distinguishes human nature, which is everywhere the same, from human customs, which vary. He insists that 'God has endowed us with a principle of universal reason' which remains constant and triumphs over passion, tyranny and clerical superstition.[72] Hume, Voltaire and Rousseau have what amounts to a superstructure of relativism on a foundation of uniformity.[73] The platform of equality of rights, so important for the French and American revolutions, presupposed a uniformity in human nature in all times and places. When the revolutionary slogan *Liberté, egalité, fraternité* led to the Terror, the idea of equality lost support. Burke's identification of the excesses of the French Revolution with egalitarianism effectively undermined uniformitarianism.[74]

Nevertheless, although research into ways of life, mores (Voltaire's *moeurs*), crafts and industries (the *Encyclopédie*), a genuinely historical perspective began to emerge and with it the raw materials for a notion of historical, cultural relativism.[75] For Diderot, facts are what matter, but when numerous pieces of factual evidence are assembled and set out side by side, differences and discrepancies emerge. It was Bayle's achievement to show this to devastating effect. Voltaire depicts the intellectual or cultural character of an age, but he is not interested in setting forth the ethos of a period in its integrity.

---

[71]Hume, 'Of National Characters', *Essays*. For discussion of Hume's philosophic history see Pocock, *Barbarism and Religion*, vol. 2, chs. 11–16. For Montesquieu's influence in Britain see Trevor-Roper, 'David Hume, Historian' and 'The Idea of *The Decline and Fall*', in *History and the Enlightenment*. D'Alembert recognized a particular 'spiritual disposition' in each nation in his article 'Caractère des nations' in the *Encyclopédie*.

[72]Cited Rosenthal, 'Voltaire's Philosophy', p. 167.

[73]Wertz, 'Hume, History and Human Nature'; Becker, *Heavenly City*, p. 87: Rousseau distinguishes between 'variety' and 'essentials' in human nature.

[74]Manuel, 'From Equality to Organicism'.

[75]Berlin, 'Alleged Relativism in Eighteenth-Century Thought', in *Crooked Timber*, usefully distinguishes between (1) relativism with regard to facts – we cannot ever fully know the truth – a notion that Berlin disdains; (2) relativism with regard to cultural values – a pluralism of ends – which he endorses; and (3) a relativism that is deterministic – we have no choice – which he also, needless to say, rejects. He rightly claims Vico as the pioneer of the idea of cultural, historical relativism: 'Giambattista Vico and Culural History', in ibid. See also Bourgault and Sparling (eds.), *Companion to Enlightenment Historiography*.

Though he often speaks of 'the spirit of an age', 'in the end, the spirit of the age . . . was nothing but the assessment of its balance sheet in terms of reason and unreason according to the currency valid at the time of the Enlightenment.'[76] Voltaire's historical work was not motivated by respect for the sanctity of facts: he expressed contempt for detail, for erudition. In the footnotes (8,000 of them) to the *Decline and Fall*, Gibbon is vitriolic about Voltaire's cavalier disregard for factual truth. Voltaire was dismissive of minute particulars, *petits faits*. The Reformation fares no better than earlier ages, owing to Voltaire's detestation of monks, including former monks like Luther.[77] Gibbon, on the other hand, respected detail and devoted 20 years of his life to a single, vast research project. He combined the erudition of the antiquaries (*érudits*) of the previous century with the 'philosophic', that is, reflective, generalizing, moralizing approach of the Enlightenment, emulating Voltaire and Hume in this respect. 'Gibbon learned from Bayle to blend malice and erudition.'[78] What the philosophic historians, supremely Hume and Gibbon, were doing was to bring reason and history together, to free reason from Cartesian rationalism, and to liberate history from mere antiquarianism. Notwithstanding their anti-Christian animus, they were forging a new, salutary hermeneutic of the past.[79]

Hume and Gibbon

It is necessary to challenge the common assumption, reinforced by partisan historians and certain modern theologians, that the Enlightenment was essentially anti-Christian. True, it took an anti-religious and anticlerical form in France, where hostility was particularly directed against the Jesuits, and there were 'enlightened' free-thinkers in all countries, including England.[80] But the animus of

---

[76]Meinecke, *Historism*, p. 80.
[77]Trevor-Roper, 'Historical Philosophy of the Enlightenment'; Gargett, *Voltaire and Protestantism*; Brumfitt, 'History and Propaganda'; Voltaire, *La Philosophie de l'histoire*, p. 27; Wade, *Intellectual Development*, pp. 451–510.
[78]Momigliano, *Studies in Historiography*, p. 43 ('Gibbon's Contribution to Historical Method').
[79]Weinsheimer, *Eighteenth-Century Hermeneutics*, p. 227.
[80]Champion, *Pillars of Priestcraft*.

those who were overtly hostile to Christianity was directed at least
partly against oppressive ecclesiastical authority and the obscurantism and censorship that went with it. Hostility to religion, therefore,
took a mainly anti-Roman Catholic and anti-Calvinist form. In
the case of Pierre Bayle, his unrelenting scepticism is directed against
the Roman Catholic Church and against rationalistic Protestantism
and deism, not against Calvinism, because he was grounded in Calvinism himself. Even the deism that stripped Christianity of much
of its credal content was not always anti-supernaturalistic. Then,
beyond deism, there was a small but significant element of atheism
and a surge of subversive literature that was not philosophically
sophisticated; it was journalistic, brilliant propaganda.[81] Diderot's
La Religieuse, which tells of an innocent girl forced into convent life
against her will and of the sadistic methods employed to keep her
there, is perhaps his most damaging attack on the Roman Catholic
Church. But even here Christ is honoured, the girl's faith survives
her ordeal, her prayers are touched with pathos, and she is not the
only saintly person in the story. Rather, it is twisted, bigoted, fanatical religiosity that Diderot exposes.[82] We shall see a similar form of
discrimination in Gibbon immediately.

The most deadly weapon against the entrenched ecclesiastical
monopoly under the *ancien regime* in Europe, including Britain, was
not argument but ridicule and mockery.[83] Hume and Gibbon were
the past masters of this art. When asked what he had to say about
Gibbon's account of early Christianity in the notorious Chapters 15
and 16 of the *Decline and Fall of the Roman Empire*, Archdeacon
William Paley replied, 'Who can refute a sneer?' and made the same
comment in print.[84] Both Hume and Gibbon were getting their
revenge on narrow authoritarian forms of Christianity, to which
they had been exposed in their impressionable youth – in Hume's
case, Scottish Calvinism, in Gibbon's (briefly) Roman Catholicism.
Hume snidely named his enemies as 'Stupidity, Christianity and

---

[81]Cobban, 'Enlightenment', p. 87.
[82]Diderot, *The Nun*.
[83]Redwood, *Reason, Ridicule and Religion*, p. 14. Cf. McManners, 'Enlightenment:
Secular and Christian', pp. 267, 282.
[84]Paley, *Principles of Moral and Political Philosophy*, vol. 1, p. 296, cited Cole, 'Who
can refute a sneer?', p. 65.

Ignorance'.[85] Gibbon, it has been well said, practised 'supremely artful modes of insinuation'.[86]

But their joint onslaught amounted to a great deal more than innuendo: the most brilliant philosopher of the eighteenth century and the historian whose fame will never die combined to make Christianity intellectually and historically problematic. They struck at the rational superstructure of Christian ideology that had taken centuries to construct – Hume undermining the standard arguments for the existence of God and belief in miracles, and Gibbon turning an inherent strength of Christianity, as an historical religion, into a liability (achieving a 'moral inversion' of Christianity).[87] Like those sea creatures that eat into a great coral reef that has taken millennia to form, they eroded the foundations of Christian theology, causing serious structural damage. But Hume undermined philosophy as well as theology; his scepticism wounded reason itself, seeing it as the slave of the passions, and gave an impetus to Romanticism and to certain forms of irrationalism, especially in Germany where Hamann and Jacobi seized on his demolition of reason.[88] Not that Hume was an absolute sceptic in the manner of the ancient Academicians who held that we cannot know anything. Commenting on Descartes' methodical doubt, Hume alleged that it was a method with no exit: 'The Cartesian doubt . . . were it ever possible to be attained by any human creature (as it plainly is not) would be entirely incurable; and no reasoning could ever bring us to a state of assurance and conviction upon any subject.'[89] Hume's methods of deconstruction assumed faith in reason, but in a chastened reason, a reason that knows its very considerable limitations.

Hume provided the philosophical weaponry – the epistemological scepticism and the common-sense anti-supernaturalism – which

---

[85]Gay, *Enlightenment*, vol. 1, p. 20.

[86]Foster, *Melancholy Duty*, p. 1.

[87]Ibid., p. 333. But Foster is surely mistaken in equating 'philosophic history' as such with an anti-Christian stance (p. 331), because this cannot apply to the eminent minister of the Kirk, William Robertson, the third figure of the triumvirate that Gibbon himself identified. See further, Trevor-Roper, 'The Historical Philosophy of the Enlightenment'.

[88]Isaiah Berlin, 'Hume and the Sources of German Anti-Rationalism', in *Against the Current*.

[89]Hume, *Enquiry Concerning Human Understanding*, Section XII, cited Popkin, *History of Scepticism*, p. 213.

Gibbon applied to ecclesiastical history, and there are many echoes of Hume in the *Decline and Fall*'s treatment of Christianity. Hume was a stronger influence on Gibbon's history than was Bayle or Voltaire. But Gibbon did not need to borrow his detestation of ecclesiastical power, clerical abuses, superstitious practices, censorship and obscurantism from anyone. Neglected by his idle Oxford tutors ('steeped in port and prejudice'), he had fallen prey to plausible arguments for the absolute authority and doctrinal infallibility of the Roman Catholic Church. His subsequent (first) spell in Lausanne among Protestant divines, enforced by parental authority, had the intended effect: Gibbon converted back. But the double conversion left him with a profound ingrained scepticism with regard to the grandiose claims, unverifiable dogmas and portentous rituals of institutional religion. In Chapters 15 and 16 and elsewhere in the *D&F,* he described the follies and iniquities of primitive Christianity in a tone of sardonic irony. Gibbon could not forgive Christianity, in its institutional form, for the part it had played, as he believed, in bringing down the civilizing structures of the Roman Empire that held barbarism at bay. Emperors who ruled well, bringing order and stability to a turbulent world, are praised – even if, like Decius and Diocletian, they were persecutors of the Church. Credulity, intolerance, bigotry, lack of civic virtue, carelessness about human well-being, masochism and deleterious internal strife about matters of little consequence – these were what he hated about the Church, not to mention fraud and deceit. It could all be summed up in two words that Gibbon had borrowed from Hume: 'superstition' and 'enthusiasm'. Both Hume and Gibbon seem nervous and fearful of passion. Both believed that humans were motivated by their passions; that passions easily got out of control and wreaked havoc; that self-restraint and moderation were to be esteemed; and that enthusiasm and superstition were the antithesis of these virtues. For both Hume and Gibbon, Christianity, in its historical manifestation, was an enemy of human freedom and well-being. When Gibbon castigates the medieval papacy as a system, it is because the source from which popes were drawn and the style in which they were maintained were 'the most adverse to reason, humanity and freedom'.[90]

---

[90]*D&F,* p. 888.

The publication in 1776 of volume 1 of the *Decline and Fall*, which included those chapters, stirred up a hornet's nest of condemnation and abuse, to which Gibbon replied in his *Vindication* (1779). His comments on his incompetent adversaries (excepting Richard Watson, the liberal divine, later Bishop of Llandaff, for whom he professed heartfelt admiration) are among the most delicious and malicious in his *Memoirs*. 'A victory over such antagonists was sufficient humiliation.'[91] 'Never, in literary history, has there been such a rout,' comments Trevor-Roper.[92] However, his critique of early Christianity seems to me to be largely fair comment. Who can deny the elements of credulity, fanaticism, intolerance, self-harm and anti-civil behaviour on the part of the early Christians? Gibbon took it as his 'melancholy duty' as an impartial historian to describe 'the inevitable mixture of error and corruption' which an originally pure Christianity 'contracted in a long residence upon earth, among a weak and degenerate race of beings'.[93] As Gibbon summarizes: 'Credulity performed the office of faith; fanaticism was permitted to assume the language of inspiration, and the effects of accident or contrivance were ascribed to supernatural causes'.[94] Gibbon's hatred of inhumanity, cruelty, bigotry, irrationality and mindless fervour goes a considerable way to explaining his authorial stance. Gibbon was a compassionate, humane man and when he praises an early Christian figure, such as Justin Martyr, it is for his 'humane temper', but he did not find human fellow-feeling pervasive among the early Christians or their medieval successors.[95]

Neither Hume nor Gibbon was an atheist. Hume held a form of sceptical or, as one interpreter puts it, 'attenuated deism', or perhaps we should say impersonal or minimal theism.[96] Although Hume couched his discussions of the philosophy of religion in a mode of 'prudential irony', he makes apparently heartfelt affirmations of the existence of God. He could not quite dispose of the argument

---

[91]Gibbon, *Autobiography*, p. 151. See also McCloy, *Gibbon's Antagonism*, for an account of the religious controversy caused by *D&F*.

[92]Trevor-Roper, 'Gibbon and the Publication of *The Decline and Fall*', in *History and the Enlightenment*, p. 146.

[93]*D&F*, p. 143.

[94]Ibid., p. 162.

[95]Ibid., p. 149.

[96]Gaskin, *Hume's Philosophy of Religion*, pp. 219–23; id., 'Hume on Religion', p. 321; Costelloe, 'In every civilized community'; Yandell, 'Hume on Religious Belief'; Nathan, 'The Existence and Nature of God'.

from design – it continued to bother him. He declared at the beginning of *The Natural History of Religion*, 'The whole frame of nature bespeaks an intelligent author; and no rational enquirer can, after serious reflection, suspend his belief a moment with regard to the primary principles of genuine Theism and Religion.'[97] Note the word 'rational': Hume is not merely saying that religious belief is a universal phenomenon (though he makes considerable play of this, emphasizing the motives of ignorance, hope, fear and imagination in generating early polytheistic religion). He is saying that rational enquiry supports it – and in this work, unlike the *Dialogues*, Hume is speaking in his own voice. His vitriolic shafts are aimed at debased forms of institutional religion, corrupted by superstition and enthusiasm. At the conclusion of this short treatise Hume reiterates, 'A purpose, an intention, a design is evident in every thing.' When we envisage the origin of the universe, 'we must adopt, with the strongest conviction, the idea of some intelligent cause or author'. The universal propensity to believe in an original, intelligent power behind the world 'may be considered as a kind of mark or stamp, which the divine workman has set upon his work; and nothing surely can more dignify mankind, than ... to bear the image or impression of the universal Creator.' But this authentic belief has been corrupted and debased by the superstition or frenzy of religious devotees into 'sick men's dreams'. unworthy of rational beings.[98] As a conservative political thinker and historian, Hume believed that a stable society needs a religion.

Gibbon stood at less of a distance from Christianity than Hume. Pocock, the supreme exponent of Gibbon as an historian, regards him as neither a theist nor a deist, but a mere sceptic; this is not a tenable view, though scepticism was a major factor in his approach to religion. The young Gibbon had been inoculated with scepticism with regard to the miraculous by his reading of the lethally polemical clergyman Conyers Middleton's subversive *A Free Inquiry, into the Miraculous Powers that are supposed to have Subsisted in the Christian Church, from the Earliest Times* (1749).[99] Later, Gibbon explicitly identified himself with Chillingworth and Bayle, both

---

[97]Hume, *Natural History of Religion*, in *Dissertation on the Passions; The Natural History of Religion*, p. 33.
[98]Ibid., pp. 85–6.
[99]On Middleton see Trevor-Roper, 'From Deism to History', in *History and Enlightenment*.

of whom had escaped, as he had, from Roman Catholicism to a
sceptical mode of Protestantism. 'I can never blush if my tender
mind was entangled in the sophistry that seduced the acute and
manly understandings of CHILLINGWORTH and BAYLE, who
afterwards emerged from superstition to scepticism.'[100] Trevor-
Roper more justifiably calls him a deist.[101] Bagehot thought, 'He was
no doubt a theist after the fashion of natural theology,' which seems
to me to be a paraphrase of deism, but I think there was a bit more
to Gibbon's faith than that.[102] D. M. Low remarked in 1960, 'It is
a facile mode among some writers to speak of Gibbon's antipathy
to Christianity' and we may add that the same facile mode has
continued to the present day.[103] Indeed, it is all too easy to view
Gibbon through secular, atheistic spectacles, along with similar
prejudices with regard to Montaigne, Charron, Hobbes, Swift and
Bayle. As with those enigmatic and ambiguous authors, there is
much to be said on the other side. As Foster puts it, 'That Gibbon
was harshly critical of Christianity is undeniable; that he had no use
for it is certainly not the case.'[104] Gibbon, who had been at certain
times a Freemason, undoubtedly believed in a 'Supreme Being',
which he also refers to as the 'First Cause', the 'Great Author', and
the 'Infinite Being'.[105]

It is striking that Gibbon never sneers at Jesus of Nazareth or
mocks 'the pure and simple maxims of the Gospel'.[106] He traces
the 'gradual corruption of Christianity' from apostolic purity.[107]
Internal conflicts and external exclusivism, he argues, 'infused a
spirit of bitterness into a system of love and harmony'.[108] He pays
honour to Christian ethics. Gibbon writes as a moralist, and the

---

[100]Gibbon, *Autobiography*, p. 55.

[101]Pocock, *Barbarism and Religion*, vol. 2; Trevor-Roper, intro., Gibbon, *The Decline and Fall of the Roman Empire and other selections*, p. xxvi. B. W. Young, 'Scepticism in Excess', concludes that Gibbon was a mere sceptic in religion. The phrase 'scepticism in excess' was applied by Coleridge to Gibbon.

[102]Bagehot, 'Edward Gibbon' (1856) in *Literary Studies*, vol. 1 (London: Longmans, Green & Co., 1898), p. 234.

[103]Low in, *D&F*, intro., p. xiv.

[104]Foster, *Melancholy Duty*, p. 19.

[105]McCoy, *Gibbon's Antagonism*, pp. 42–8.

[106]*D&F*, p. 337.

[107]Ibid., p. 507.

[108]Ibid., p. 160.

standards by which he judges bishops and popes who, by virtue of their profession and office, assumed the moral high ground are stringent. But he is generous in praise of such consecrated figures as Cyprian, Athanasius, Leo I, Chrysostom and Gregory I (Gibbon endorses the appellation 'Great'; esteems him as 'the Father of his country'; and describes his pontificate as 'one of the most edifying periods in the history of the church').[109] Gibbon esteems missionaries, ancient and modern, who brought comfort to the needy and distressed. He admires the compassion of those early Christians who rescued unwanted infants, exposed to the elements and the wild beasts. He gives credit where Christians showed 'humility, meekness, and patience' and exhibited 'mutual charity'.[110] The same sardonic contempt that he directs to Christian excesses he also applies to Roman polytheism. He is scathing not only about monkish obscurantism but also about female intelligence; it was weak-headed, impressionable women who provided the power-base for deluded fanatics or unscrupulous ecclesiastics as they flocked around them, hanging on their words, cherishing their tangible presence. The 'grave and temperate irony' that is his *metier* was learnt from Pascal's *Lettres Provinciales* which, Gibbon recalled, 'almost every year I have perused with new pleasure'.[111] Furthermore, Gibbon's great work does not lack pious references to the Creator: 'The God of nature has written his existence on all his works, and his law in the heart of man.'[112] Gibbon detested the *philosophes* for their intolerant views about religion and regarded Voltaire as a bigot for his dogmatic, anti-Christian deism.

There is contemporary testimony that Gibbon entertained a warmer, more positive attitude to Christian faith and worship than is normally assumed. In his *Memoirs,* he pays tribute to the spiritual and intellectual qualities of William Law, his father's tutor at the family home in Putney.[113] Friends testified that he died a Christian with the name of God on his lips. He attended both Protestant and Roman Catholic services. We discover from his *Journal* that Gibbon was a churchgoer and something of a

---

[109]Ibid., pp. 211–13, 323–36, 461–6, 491–2, 587–91.
[110]Ibid., p. 165.
[111]Gibbon, *Autobiography*, p. 72.
[112]*D&F*, pp. 665–6.
[113]Gibbon, *Autobiography*, pp. 17–18.

connoisseur of sermons. In his pew at Burriton Church twice each Sunday, he followed the Lessons in Greek, using the Septuagint for the Old Testament and Apocrypha, and meditated on them. The *Decline and Fall* shows Gibbon as something of textual critic of the New Testament. He read and annotated the family Bible. He held firm views about sermons: they should employ learning and eloquence and not omit to move the hearts of the hearers to virtue and to civic responsibility. In this requirement, Gibbon was frequently disappointed.[114]

In conclusion, Gibbon was a rational, unorthodox, professing Christian who held an ethical, rather deistic faith. He stresses the humanity of Jesus and has no time for supernatural special effects like miracles or for speculative dogma, least of all for intolerant, damnatory pronouncements. But that does not mean that his emotions were not exercised as well or that he had no religious feeling, as some have suggested: he was coolly passionate in his faith. But what is clear is that Gibbon cannot be claimed for the anti-Christian brigade of secularism, naturalism and atheism.

The triumph of enlightened civilization over barbarism (including unenlightened religion) is a recurring motif in Gibbon and in other writers. Gibbon confessed, 'I am ignorant, and I am careless, of the blind mythology of the barbarians,' and famously said at the end of his mighty project that he had described 'the triumph of barbarism and religion'.[115] The two substantives are not sarcastic synonyms. '[T]he phrase clearly indicates that if, in the dramatic history of Rome's fall, the two phenomena contributed to the same result, they nevertheless remained distinct. Religion helped barbarism to win, but it was not itself barbaric.'[116]

But Gibbon also regarded the French revolutionary thinkers, who were anti-Christian, as the new barbarians, who sought to undermine the order and happiness of society. Hume alleged as a major objection to belief in miracles that it abounds 'among ignorant and barbarous nations'; and homing in on the Bible, he attributes the Pentateuch to 'a barbarous and ignorant people'.[117] So Hume dismisses with Enlightenment arrogance the writers

---

[114]Turnbull, 'Supposed Infidelity of Gibbon'; Smith, 'Gibbon in Church'.
[115]*D&F*, pp. 659, 893.
[116]Furet, 'Civilization and Barbarism', p. 8.
[117]Hume, 'Of Miracles', *Essays*, pp. 519–44, at pp. 529, 543.

of both the New Testament and the Old. Voltaire contrasted the 'barbaric rusticity' (read superstition and credulity) of the Middle Ages, with the urban refinement (read scepticism about religious doctrine) that was available in the eighteenth century. He derided those historians who had 'nothing else to say but that one barbarian succeeded another barbarian on the banks' of some obscure river.[118] The contrast between Enlightenment and barbarism took Christian as well as secular forms. The pious poet James Thompson disdains those 'barbarous nations, whose inhuman love/Is wild desire, fierce as the suns they feel'.[119] The historian William Robertson charted the transition from 'confusion and barbarism' to 'order, regularity and refinement'.[120] But here the men of Enlightenment were burnishing a well-worn theme: Erasmus had deplored the barbarism (*rusticitatem*) of the medieval scholastics. Pope echoes this when he says that Erasmus 'Stemmed the wild torrent of a barb'rous age,/And drove those holy Vandals [monks] off the stage.'[121] Swift dreaded a return to the 'Gothic barbarism' of the fanatical sects under Cromwell's Commonwealth. Without using the term 'barbarism', Joseph Butler reveals in his state sermons the fear and horror that the anarchy, political and religious, of the Commonwealth period still inspired, nearly a century later.[122]

The Christian Enlightenment

However, the fact remains that the Enlightenment was largely a Christian, even an ecclesiastical and theological phenomenon, especially in Germany and England.[123] It tended to flourish where

---

[118]Cited Schargo, *History in the Encyclopédie*, p. 35.

[119]Thompson, *Seasons*, p. 33 ('Spring', ll.1130–1).

[120]On Robertson's histories see Stewart J. Brown (ed.), *William Robertson*; Smitten, 'William Robertson'; Pocock, *Religion and Barbarism*, vol. 2, ch. 19.

[121]Pope, *Poetical Works*, p. 50 (*Essay on Criticism*).

[122]Butler, *Works*, vol. 2, pp. 317–38 (Sermon 3 of the *Six Sermons Preached upon Public Occasions*).

[123]Cassirer, *Philosophy of the Enlightenment*, pp. 134–96; Gilley, 'Christianity and Enlightenment'; B. W. Young, *Religion and Enlightenment*; Aston, 'Horne and Heterodoxy'; Pocock, *Barbarism and Religion*, esp. vol. 1; Clark, *English Society*; Sorkin, *Religious Enlightenment*; Rosenblatt, 'Christian Enlightenment'.

Protestant semi-tolerance was replacing Protestant semi-bigotry and where rigid Calvinism was on the decline.[124] It found the Lutheran and Anglican milieus conducive. In the Protestant music of the period, the Lutheran, Johann Sebastian Bach and the Lutheran who worshipped as an Anglican, G. F. Handel, are supreme – and might both be described as musical expositors of Scripture. There is a lot to be said for the view that no one understood Luther better than Bach.[125]

In the English poetry of the 'Augustan Age', Dryden and his successor Pope were both Roman Catholics, Dryden being a convert from a Church of England family with Puritan leanings. Pope's theology was rather shaky: he was so carried away by the vague deistic ideas that he had heard from Bolingbroke that in the *Essay on Man* (1732),[126] he was (as Johnson said) 'in haste to teach what he had not learned' and had to be rescued by Bishop Warburton, who put an orthodox gloss on the work, which Pope received thankfully. He had not meant to be unorthodox, but rather (echoing Milton, of course) to 'vindicate the ways of God to man'. Like the sceptics, especially Pascal, Pope seeks to humble human pride of reason: 'In pride, in reas'ning pride, our error lies. . . . From pride, from pride, our very reas'ning springs.' But egregious Leibnizian, Panglossian sentiments abound: 'All discord, harmony not understood;/All partial evil, universal good:/ And, spite of pride, in erring reason's spite,/One truth is clear, Whatever is, is right'). Of this work Johnson pronounces, '[H]e tells us much that every man knows, and much that he does not know himself. . . . Never was penury of knowledge and vulgarity of sentiment so happily disguised.'[127] So much for Pope's essay in apologetics!

Some of the most ostensibly subversive thinkers, including Descartes, the French Oratorian, Richard Simon (1638–112), the pioneer of biblical criticism, and Vico were devout Roman Catholics. Simon had a wide grasp of Protestant as well as of Roman Catholic pre-critical biblical scholarship, which he evaluated impartially. His biblical work aimed to defend orthodoxy against

[124]Trevor-Roper, *Religion, the Reformation and Social Change*, ch. 4.
[125]Bainton, *Here I Stand*, p. 301.
[126]Pope, *Poetical Works*, pp. 193–229.
[127]Samuel Johnson, *Lives of the Poets*, vol. 2, p. 226.

Spinozism, but it also served to undercut the Protestant platform
sola scriptura.[128]

In literary biography, lexicography and criticism, Samuel Johnson,
an extremely devout Anglican High Churchman with Nonjuring
and Jacobite sympathies, reigned unchallenged, 'the Great Cham of
Literature', as Tobias Smollett called him. Johnson was just as much
a man of reason as the *philosophes*, but he told Boswell, who had
courted Rousseau abroad, that if he had his way, he would have
the man transported to the plantations. And when pressed to rank
Rousseau with Voltaire, replied, 'Why, Sir, it is difficult to settle the
proportion of iniquity between them.'[129]

The greatest satirist of the century, the sardonic Jonathan Swift,
Dean of St Patrick's Cathedral Dublin, is often seen like Montaigne,
Hobbes and Vico, as a secular thinker. He was derided as a man
who used his genius to obtain preferment in the Church, but did
not believe what he was compelled to profess. Dr Johnson was
prejudiced against him and censored him in his *Life of Swift* for
reasons that are not entirely clear – perhaps because they were too
much alike: the balance between reason and passion was precarious;
pathological moods threatened both; and both were highly sensitive
to indignity and given to *amour propre*.[130] Johnson took every
opportunity to deride Swift, but confessed that he was 'a man of
great parts [abilities, talents]' among the Irish clergy and had done
much for that country.[131] Sir Walter Scott described *Gulliver's Travels*
as 'severe, unjust and degrading'. Thackeray, while admiring the
humour of *Gulliver*, found its moral dimension 'horrible, shameful,

---

[128]Brevard Childs, 'Biblical Scholarship in the Seventeenth Century'. Israel, *Radical Enlightenment*, pp. 664–70, and *Enlightenment Contested*, ch. 20, is surely mistaken in claiming Vico among the leading subversive anti-Christian thinkers, alongside Spinoza. Vico has a subtle doctrine of a merciful and beneficent divine providence shaping human destiny and turning barbaric customs to beneficial ends (see Vico, *New Science*, and Momigliano, *Essays in Ancient and Modern History*). But for Israel the *Scienza Nuova* is an interpretation of purely human, this worldly reality; Vico's system is non-theological and severs the link between theology and history and politics. The 'divine Providence' that Vico so often invokes is taken by Israel to be a cipher for immanent historical processes and the human belief that they are divinely guided (*Radical Enlightenment*, pp. 668–9). I find this a unnatural gloss on Vico's theology of history.

[129]Boswell, *Life of Johnson*, p. 359.

[130]Warncke, 'Johnson on Swift'. Samuel Johnson, *Lives of the Poets*, vol. 2.

[131]Boswell, *Life of Johnson*, p. 448.

unmanly, blasphemous'. Macaulay called Swift a 'ribald priest'.
Leslie Stephen, Churton Collins and Augustine Birrell found parts
of *Gulliver* disgusting and repulsive.[132]

Like Bayle, Swift is often regarded as an ironist of profane
imagination, whose mordant wit has nothing of the spirit of
Christianity. But in fact Swift's religious sincerity was too strong for
outward show; he strove to conceal his piety. His prayers are devout;
his sermons are orthodox; he was a hammer of the deists, whose views
disgusted him. He was not taken in by the prevailing Newtonian
'mechanical philosophy', which he regarded as reductionist and
inimical to a spiritual understanding of the world.[133] Swift did
not help his reputation by his scurrilous, sometimes scatological
wit, but his Christian commitment was as strong as anyone's. As
Swift said of himself: 'Humour and mirth had place in all he writ;/
He reconciled divinity with wit.'[134] Addison regarded him as 'the
greatest genius of his age'.[135] Although *Gulliver's Travels* is his best
known satirical work, one of the most bitingly effective of his tracts
for his profane times is *An Argument to Prove that the Abolishing
of Christianity in England May, as Things Now Stand Today, be
Attended with Some Inconveniences, and Perhaps not Produce
Those Many Good Effects Proposed Thereby* (1708).[136] I single out
a passage near the beginning that shows that the Anglican (and
Reformation) appeal to the primitive Church was still in use and
that Swift has no hesitation in deploying it, albeit tongue-in-cheek:
'I hope no reader imagines me so weak to stand up in the defence of
real Christianity, such as used in primitive times (if we may believe
the authors of those ages) to have an influence upon men's belief
and actions. To offer at the restoring of that, would indeed be a wild
project: it would be to dig up foundations; to destroy at one blow
all the wit, and half the learning of the kingdom; to break the entire
frame and constitution of things; to ruin trade, extinguish arts and
sciences, with the professors of them; in short, to turn our courts,
exchanges, and shops into deserts. . . .'

---

[132]Swift, *Gulliver's Travels*: on Swift's chequered reputation see Michael Foot's
Introduction.
[133]See the powerful vindication by Hall, '"An Inverted Hypocrite": Swift the
Churchman', in *Humanists and Protestants*.
[134]Grierson and Smith, *Critical History*, p. 197.
[135]Stephen, *Swift*, p. 57. On Addison and Swift see Glendinning, *Jonathan Swift*.
[136]Swift, *Argument to Prove that the Abolishing of Christianity*.

The greatest essayist, Joseph Addison (1672–1719), 'endeav-our[ed] to enliven morality with wit, and to temper wit with morality'.[137] Addison traced the debased mores of the day to the exalting of fashionable wit above morals; he embarked on a crusade to reform manners according to the principles of 'nature and reason' and to some extent he succeeded. The historian J. R. Green said of the influence exerted by *The Spectator* that for a century it had 'greater weight on moral and religious opinions than all the charges of the bishops'.[138] Addison was the first lay preacher, so to speak, to reach the ear of the rising middle classes, to both reflect and articulate their values and aspirations. But Addison was more than a moralist: he was an Anglican churchman and a something of a Christian apologist. His creation in *The Spectator*, Sir Roger de Coverley, 'a whimsical country knight' is a dutiful churchgoer and a frequenter of Westminster Abbey.[139] The Church of England was the right church to be in, given the superstition of the Roman Catholics and the enthusiasm of the Dissenters. Addison is not ashamed to hold up a life of faith, prayer and devotion in his essays and speaks of the friendship of God.[140] He is scathing about the freethinking, scoffing *habitués* who frequented the coffee houses that he also patronized. He repeatedly claims that the best and greatest men of all ages and nations have been religious: Francis Bacon is his supreme example: he refers to Bacon's famous prayer as 'rather the devotion of an angel than of a man'.[141] Addison's tractate 'Of the Christian Religion' (published in 1721) considers the historical evidence for the authenticity of the Gospels. It is conventional, orthodox, credal, non-critical and recognizes the role of episcopal succession in the transmission of faithful witness in the early Church.[142] Addison's poem, now a well-known hymn, 'The spacious firmament on high,' looks rather deistical at first glance, but it is simply a paraphrase of the first half of Psalm 19. Haydn used it in *The Creation*. His paraphrase of Psalm 23, 'The Lord my pasture shall prepare,' is still sung in church. On his deathbed, Addison summoned a young nobleman of dissolute life, whom he

---

[137]Addison, *Works*, vol. 2, p. 253.
[138]Cited Willey, *English Moralists*, p. 233.
[139]Ibid., pp. 427, 446.
[140]Addison, *Works*, vol. 2, p. 413.
[141]Ibid., pp. 57, 225.
[142]Addison, *Miscellaneous Works*, vol. 2, pp. 407–45.

had tried to reclaim, and told him, 'I have sent for you, that you may see how a Christian can die.'[143] Johnson sums up Addison's faith and morals: 'His religion has nothing in it enthusiastic or superstitious; he appears neither weakly credulous, nor wantonly sceptical; his morality is neither dangerously lax, nor impracticably rigid. All the enchantment of fancy, and all the cogency or argument, are employed to recommend to the reader his real interest, the care of pleasing the Author of his being.'[144]

The greatest Scottish historian of the age, William Robertson (1721–93), was a Church of Scotland minister, Moderator of the General Assembly of the Kirk and Principal of Edinburgh University. His first published work was *The Situation of the World at the Time of Christ's Appearance* (1755). His Christian profession did not prevent him enjoying the friendship of Hume and the admiration of Voltaire and Catherine the Great. Several bishops of the Church of England were members of the Royal Society for the Promotion of Science. Enlightenment presuppositions also pervaded theology, both in the Established Church and among Dissenters.[145] Theology consequently saw a shift from debate over dogmas to debate over the foundations of the faith and the credibility of the Christian revelation, with appeal to the 'two books' of Scripture and nature. The same scholars worked simultaneously in natural science, philosophy and theology.

---

[143]Samuel Johnson, *Lives of the Poets*, vol. 1, p. 346.

[144]Ibid., p. 367.

[145]Philip Doddridge stated, 'It is certainly the duty of of every rational creature to bring his religion to the strictest test, and to retain or reject the faith in which he has been educated, as he finds it capable or incapable of rational defence': cited Stromberg, *Religious Liberalism*, p. 9.

8

Founders of the
Enlightenment attitude

John Locke

Rationality beyond Hooker and Hobbes

John Locke (1632–1704), a notable political thinker, is also a
lay theologian within the Anglican spectrum. His influence, on
philosophy, theology, ethics and politics in his time and subsequently
is matched only by Newton's.[1] Locke's theological method is
founded on the rational, reflective interpretation of experience; he
has little place for history or tradition.[2] Locke is definitely a post-
Hobbesian thinker, working both by way of continuity and by way
of reaction in the intellectual context created by Hobbes' powerful
and daring works. Locke plays down his positive debt to Hobbes –
it was politic to do so – and plays up his counterpoint to him.
There is not one acknowledged reference to Hobbes's writings in
the whole Lockean corpus, though there are echoes.[3] Like Hobbes,
Locke was a passionately rational thinker, though his is not the
a priori deductive rationalism of Hobbes. Like Hobbes, he is also a
militantly anti-historical thinker, averse to the contingencies of the
historical process and distrustful of the conjectures and uncertainties
of historical study.

---

[1]On Locke's theological influence see Sell, *John Locke*.
[2]See further on Locke and Anglicanism, Avis, *Anglicanism and the Christian Church*,
pp. 97–100.
[3]Peter Laslett, 'Introduction' to Locke, *Two Treatises of Government*, pp. 80–92,
102–5.

Locke is much closer to Hooker than to Hobbes. Initially, Locke did not take well to Hooker's *Ecclesiastical Polity* and managed to read only the first book, but later he plundered Hooker for supportive quotations.[4] Although in some respects Locke continues in the trajectory of Hooker, he does not have Hooker's sense of a Church shaped by all that has gone before and Hooker's awareness of historical context. It can be fairly said of Locke that his work remains untainted by historical perspective. In argument, he does not appeal to history or tradition, but thinks things out for himself purely on the basis of experience. Laslett comments on the treatises on government: 'Neither Machiavelli, nor Hobbes, nor Rousseau succeeded in making the discussion of politics so completely independent of historical example, so entirely autonomous an area of discourse.'[5]

Locke is one of the instigators of that obsession with the rationality of Christian belief and of reason as the primary instrument of theological method that characterized Anglican thought in the late seventeenth and early eighteenth centuries. Locke's much vaunted 'historical plain method', in his *Essay Concerning Human Understanding*, was not historical in the modern sense at all, but empirical – and empirical in a simplistic way, a mere reading off of the conscious operations of the mind.[6] In his later *The Reasonableness of Christianity, as delivered in the Scriptures* (1695) and his paraphrases of some Epistles of St Paul, Locke expounds what he believes to be the plain meaning of the text: this is an example of exegesis without metaphysics, a kind of textual empiricism, rather than an anticipation of the later historico-critical approach. We may say that at the end of his life Locke was, according to his lights, a biblical, though not a historical thinker.[7] But was he an orthodox thinker? In *The Reasonableness of Christianity*, he attacks the metaphysical elaboration of Christian doctrine in, for example, the 'Athanasian Creed' (*Quicunque Vult*) as tritheistic, and a deviation from the 'simple' teaching of Christ. There can be little doubt that he was influenced by the Socinian tendency of applying rational criteria to belief, but then so were many others: that is not the issue.

---

[4]Ibid., p. 70 & n.
[5]Ibid., p. 91.
[6]John Locke, *Essay Concerning Human Understanding*, vol. 1, p. 5.
[7]John Marshall, *John Locke*, chs. 9 and 10.

Locke protested his innocence of Socianianism in doctrine, but as his biographer comments, '*The Reasonableness of Christianity* is a Unitarian or Socinian book in everything but name.'[8] Whether Locke crossed the narrow line between brave rational reflection and explicit denial of the Creeds is debatable. What is certain is that in public Locke remained a practising Anglican and in private fervent in his devotions.

Reason versus tradition

In theological argument, as in political doctrine, free enquiry, combined with tolerance of different opinions (with some exceptions), is Locke's highway to truth, not the study of antiquity. Locke had imbibed Falkland and Hales on authority in the Church.[9] Truth is truth in the light of reason, not because it is hallowed by centuries of history. Tradition casts no mantle of respectability over error and superstition. Locke is scornful of those who expect opinions 'to gain force by growing older'.

> What a thousand years since would not . . . have appeared at all probable, is now urged as certain beyond all question, only because several have since said it one after another. Upon this ground propositions, evidently false or doubtful enough in their first beginning, come by an inverted role of probability, to pass for authentic truths; and those which found or deserved little credit from the mouths of their first authors are thought to grow venerable by age and are urged as undeniable.[10]

No, it is reason that must be 'our last judge and guide in everything',[11] but that raises no problems for religion because reason has an affinity to revelation and vice versa:

> *Reason* is natural *revelation*, whereby the eternal Father of light and fountain of all knowledge communicates to mankind that portion of truth which he has laid within the reach of their

---

[8]Cranston, *John Locke*, p. 390. Cf. Sell, *John Locke*, pp. 273–4.
[9]John Marshall, *John Locke*, pp. 45, 95 n31.
[10]Locke, *Essay*, vol. 2, p. 258.
[11]Ibid., p. 289.

natural faculties; *revelation* is natural *reason* enlarged by a new set of discoveries communicated by God immediately, which *reason* vouches the truth of, by the testimony and proofs it gives that they come from God. So that he that takes away *reason*, to make way for *revelation*, puts out the light of both . . .[12]

Although it is ultimately all we have to go by, reason ('understanding') in Locke is not arrogant, hubristic and speculative, but workmanlike, serviceable and modest. It is more down to earth than Hooker's reason, but equal to his in its combination of moral confidence and intellectual humility of a kind. Locke has a profound sense of the limitations of our condition, our 'darkness', short-sightedness and liability to error.[13] We should be aware of the shortfall in the reach of reason. There are many things that it cannot attain to. True knowledge is sparse. Speculation is discouraged as unprofitable, an attempt (as it were) to pull ourselves up by our own bootlaces:

All those sublime thoughts, which tower above the clouds and reach as high as heaven itself, take their rise and footing here: in all that great extent wherein the mind wanders, in those remote speculations it may seem to be elevated with, it stirs not one jot beyond those *ideas* which *sense* or *reflection* have offered for its contemplation.[14]

Locke has Hooker's realistic sense of the nature of things as they are in reality, not as we fancy them to be in our pet theories (this intellectual disposition is accentuated in Joseph Butler, as we shall see). Locke echoes Hooker's teaching on the degrees of certainty, his insistence on proportioning assent to the strength of the evidence, and his conclusion that in matters of divine truth infallible certainty is not granted to us and we must be guided by what Hooker called 'probable persuasions'. To defy these conditions of our knowledge is 'enthusiasm'.[15] Locke sets the keynote of his work in the introduction when he remarks that, if we can come

---

[12]Ibid.
[13]Ibid., vol. 2, pp. 164, 248.
[14]Ibid., vol. 1, p. 89.
[15]Ibid., IV, xix: vol. 2, pp. 288–96.

to a just appreciation of both the extent and the limitations of our knowledge, 'we may learn to content ourselves with what is attainable by us in this state'.[16] We cannot expect to fathom 'the vast ocean of *Being*'.[17] Our knowledge is enough to live by and our reason is sufficient for all necessary purposes. 'The candle that is set up in us shines bright enough for all our purposes.'[18] It is futile to crave certainty, where only probability is available and is actually sufficient.[19] In the majority of human affairs, God has 'afforded us only the twilight, as I may so say, of *probability*, suitable, I presume, to that state of mediocrity and probationership he has been pleased to place us in here, on our earthly pilgrimage to a more perfect state'.[20] Locke has the modern concept of probability, a probability based on evidence that is intrinsic to the matter in hand – that is to say, how it fits with our previous knowledge, confidence in what we observe, our own direct experience, and the number and credibility of testimonies – not on the accumulation of venerable authorities. '[T]here cannot be a more dangerous thing to rely on, nor more likely to mislead one, since there is much more falsehood and error among men than truth and knowledge,' than 'the opinion of others,' he says.[21]

Assessment of Locke on theological method

One main source of falsehood and error, according to Locke, was a mistaken view of words and ideas. It follows from Locke's notion of thinking as explicit, conscious cogitation that the units of human thought for him are the Cartesian and Hobbesian 'clear and distinct ideas'. However, Locke pushes this nominalist view of language a step further when he substitutes 'determinate' or 'determined' for Descartes' 'clear and distinct'. By this usage, Locke means that when we have an idea, we know exactly what we mean by it.[22] What makes it possible for him to hold this tenet is his Hobbesian

---

[16]Ibid., pp. 6–7.
[17]Ibid., p. 8.
[18]Ibid., p. 7.
[19]Ibid.
[20]Ibid., vol. 2, pp. 247–8.
[21]Ibid., IV, xv, 6: vol. 2, pp. 251–2.
[22]Ibid., vol. 1, p. xxxviii; cf. pp. 306–7.

emphasis on the arbitrariness of the meaning that we attach to words: 'sounds have no natural connection with our ideas, but all their signification from the arbitrary imposition of men'.[23] Locke's analytical doctrine of language follows from his neglect of the realm of implicit, subliminal thinking, where connections are made and metaphors are created. For Locke, as for Hobbes and later Bentham, metaphor was a superfluous accretion to language, at best a piece of nice ornamentation. Not that Locke denies that words are often vague in their import; but he sees this as an imperfection that the philosopher can remedy.[24] What we need to do, he says, is to *'fix in our minds clear, distinct and complete* ideas, as far as they are to be had, *and annexe to them proper and constant names'*.[25] We should not take words for things, Locke warns, or suppose that names in books correspond to real entities in nature, until we can 'frame clear and distinct ideas of those entities'.[26] In Locke's view of ideas and the words that make them up, there are no unfathomed depths, there is no aura of mystery, no shades of nuance, difficult to quantify. Locke's doctrine here is the antithesis of Coleridge's doctrine that we may comprehend what we cannot properly understand, or Michael Polanyi's dictum, 'We know more than we can tell.'[27]

Locke's place in the formation of Anglican theological method is indicated by his twofold appeal to Scripture and to reason: to Scripture in the plain meaning of the text, uncorrupted by ecclesiastical glosses; and to reason, not as high-flown and speculative, but as empirical, reflective and serviceable, guided by probability and a sense of the limitations of our condition, which is one of moral probation. In his sceptical attitude to tradition and antiquity, Locke makes common cause with Hales, Falkland and Hyde (Clarendon). In his appeal to reason he, as it were, looks back to Hooker for intellectual humility and to Chillingworth and Hobbes for fearlessness. In his appeal for a greater breadth of toleration, he stands with the Latitudinarians.[28] In his stress on probability and the moral conditions of the search for truth, he points ahead to

---

[23]Ibid., vol. 2, p. 77; cf. pp. 12–14.
[24]Ibid., vol. 2, pp. 76–7.
[25]Ibid., vol. 2, p. 239; original emphasis.
[26]Locke, *Conduct of the Understanding*, Section 29.
[27]Polanyi, *Personal Knowledge*; id., *The Tacit Dimension*.
[28]John Marshall, 'Locke and Latitudinarianism'.

Butler in the mid-eighteenth century and to Keble and Gladstone in the mid-nineteenth. The legacy of Locke's view of words and ideas was perverse, but he remains a seminal and pivotal Anglican thinker and a founder of the Anglican Enlightenment.

Isaac Newton

Diverging methods

In the seventeenth century, two distinct methods of philosophical and scientific inquiry competed for allegiance. One, represented by Descartes and Hobbes, took mathematics as its model, deduction as its method, and clear and distinct ideas as its epistemological ideal. The other, represented by Bacon, aimed to be rigorously empirical in its approach, to eschew speculation, and to proceed *a posteriori*, by pure induction. The first, the rationalist approach, was unconducive to history, poetry and other imaginative arts. The second, the empirical approach, though almost equally antipathetic to imaginative, creative expression, did, however, provide a rationale and a method for a more objective investigation of the past. In the thought of Locke and Newton, these two methods converge in an unstable but productive synthesis. Locke's 'plain historical method' and Newton's method of observation and experiment, strengthened by belief in a rational, mechanical universe, was embraced by the historians, social philosophers and theologians of the Enlightenment. Voltaire called Newton the greatest man who ever lived and regarded Locke as the greatest philosopher since Plato.

Newton combined a critical appropriation of the mathematical rationalism of the Continent with the inductive empiricism of the Royal Society. While the scientific programme set out by Bacon had been hampered by lack of adequate mathematics, Newton turned the labour of observation and experiment into mathematical terms. In the first phase of the Renaissance, some scholars had aspired to grasp the whole content of the physical world and of human life in all its particularity in directly empirical terms – a Promethean task, but one that did not seem impossible then.[29] Bacon's

---

[29]Ullmann, *Medieval Foundations*; Pocock, *Machiavellian Moment*; Southern, *Medieval Humanism*.

endless tables of data represent the furthest development of this approach – but at the same time a confession of failure, empirical overload. An alternative, streamlined method, employing the so-called resolutive–compositive formula refined at the University of Padua, recognized the need radically to simplify the data by converting it into mathematical codes. Leonardo, Kepler and Galileo handed on this approach to Descartes, in whose hands, however, it becomes the instrument of rationalistic systematization rather than a tool of discovery. Set against this tradition, Newton marks a fresh departure. For him, there is no *a priori* certainty, such as Kepler, Galileo and supremely Descartes possessed, that the world is inherently mathematical in its constitution, still less that its secrets can be fully unlocked by mathematical methods. As far as Newton is concerned, the world is what it is, a datum, and mathematics is therefore solely a method for solving problems presented by sense experience.[30]

Newton had been exhilarated by reading Descartes's *Géométrie*, but developed his own approach in conscious opposition to that of Descartes. As Koyré points out, the *Principia Mathematica* is anti-Cartesian to the core.[31] Newton's frequent critical remarks on the function of 'hypotheses' in science are directed at the rationalism of the Cartesians and Leibniz. Newton is not attempting the impossible task of contriving a science independent of what Bacon called *anticipationes naturae*, exploratory theories set up for observational or experimental testing. For Newton, especially in his later phase, 'hypotheses' were synonymous with unfounded and superfluous speculations, such as Descartes's celebrated vortices and Leibniz's monadology.[32] The second edition of the *Principia* was edited by Newton's disciple Roger Cotes, who also contributed a preface in which he clearly segregated the Newtonian and the Cartesian methods. The Cartesians (not mentioned by name), while they rightly assume that matter is homogeneous (and not, as the scholastics supposed, composed of specific and occult qualities) and that the variety of the universe can be explained

[30]Burtt, *Metaphysical Foundations*, pp. 208–9.
[31]Koyré, *Newtonian Studies*, p. 95.
[32]Newton, *Newton's Philosophy*, pp. 6–7; Koyré, *Newtonian Studies*: 'Concept and Experience in Newton's Scientific Thought'; Manuel, *Religion of Newton*, pp. 70, 75, 98.

in terms of simple fundamental principles, go astray when they attempt to construct, with whatever intellectual rigour and ingenuity, fanciful theories on the basis of erroneous principles. The result is merely a 'romance'; '. . . the true constitution of things . . . is not to be derived from fallacious conjectures when we can scarce reach it by the most certain observations.'[33] The Newtonians, by contrast (Cotes continued), seek to be faithful to experience alone, assuming no principles that are not drawn from the phenomena. 'They frame no hypotheses, nor receive them into philosophy otherwise than as questions whose truth may be disputed.' Their method, he explained, consists of the twofold procedure of analysis and synthesis (a common tradition in Western philosophy, and central to the approaches of Descartes, Hobbes and Locke also).[34] 'From some select phenomena they deduce by analysis the forces of nature and the more simple laws of forces, and from thence by synthesis show the constitution of the rest.' It is worth noting that too much should not be made of the incongruous expression 'deduce' here; Newton himself was prepared to use 'derive' or 'infer'.[35] In the *Optics* (1704), Newton expanded on this aspect of his method:

As in mathematics, so in natural philosophy, the investigation of difficult things by the method of analysis ought ever to precede the method of composition. This analysis consists in making experiments and observations, and in drawing general conclusions from them by induction, and admitting of no objections against the conclusions but such as are taken from experiment, or other certain truths. For hypotheses are not to be regarded in experimental philosophy. And although the arguing from experiments and observations by induction be no demonstration of general conclusions, yet it is the best way of arguing which the nature of things admits of, and may be looked upon as so much the stronger by how much the induction is more general.[36]

---

[33]Newton, *Newton's Philosophy*, p. 117.
[34]Schouls, *Imposition of Method*.
[35]Newton, *Newton's Philosophy*, pp. 117–18; cf. pp. 182–3.
[36]Ibid., pp. 178–9.

In this way, Newton concludes, we proceed from effects to their causes and from particular causes to more general ones, 'till the argument end in the most general'. The second stage, the stage of synthesis or composition, 'consists in assuming the causes discovered and established as principles, and by them explaining the phenomena proceeding from them and proving the explanations'.[37] It is not our business at present to ask how Newton's understanding of his method stands up in the light of the modern critique of the myth of inductive reasoning, most notably perhaps by Karl Popper and even more radically by Paul Feyerabend.[38]

Theology and the Newtonian paradigm

The prestige that accrued to Newton's method as a result of his success and fame led other areas of enquiry, including philosophy, theology and history, to absorb and adopt it. The historians of the eighteenth century were inspired by the glamour of the Newtonian vision to undertake vast (albeit selective) surveys of empirical data, issuing in general laws. In philosophy, Locke's 'plain historical method' insisted that the truth about human nature was to be discovered, not by *a priori* definitions and deductions in the manner of Christian scholasticism or even of rationalist systematizers like Descartes and Hobbes, but by observation and experience, resulting – it was believed – in uniform laws of human life, individual and social.[39] The Enlightenment's programme for an historical science of humankind, including its arts, technology and science, reflected the grandeur of the 'coherence, consistency and continuity'[40] of the Newtonian universe, and was informed by a uniformitarian conception of human nature. Humanity was necessarily always and everywhere the same in its fundamental constitution – by analogy with Newton's deistic God who 'exists necessarily; and by the same necessity He exists always and everywhere'.[41] But theology held to a similar metaphysic according to the rule of St Vincent of Lerins

---

[37]Ibid.
[38]Popper, *Logic of Scientific Discovery*; id., *Conjectures and Refutations*; Feyerabend, *Against Method*.
[39]Cf. Koyré, *Newtonian Studies*: 'The Significance of the Newtonian Synthesis'.
[40]Wade, *Intellectual Origins*, p. 534.
[41]Newton, *Newton's Philosophy*, p. 44.

in the fifth century that the true faith was what had been believed always, everywhere, and by all (*semper, ubique at ab omnibus creditum est*). But ironically, by its relentless application to the facts of the case which often would not be forced into the procrustean bed of uniformitarianism, the certainties of the Enlightenment's worldview began to be undermined and to suffer the destabilizing effects of historical relativism.

Newton's own obsessive, lifelong historical research – resulting in 4,000 folios of manuscripts on biblical chronology and the fulfilment of prophecy – was untrammelled by any such anachronistic hesitations.[42] Exhaustiveness, exactitude and precision were its attributes. By the standards of his contemporaries, Newton was a critical historian who applied the canons of the new inductive physical science to biblical history. His interpretations of the Old Testament show some glimmers of a critical approach: the creation narratives were expressed as an accommodation to uneducated people; the historical books had been compiled out of lost documents; the poetical books are to be interpreted according to their genre; prophetic symbolism needs to be understood in the light of ancient parallels. It was certainly not the case that Newton's rigorous empirical method in physics gave way, in his biblical computations, to undisciplined speculation. But his method turned the past into a pale reflection of the Newtonian universe – cold, colourless and indifferent to human hopes, with absolute space and time grinding on their way.

In the end his passion for factual detail shrivelled the past to a chronological table and a history of place names. His history was sparse; specific as a businessman's ledger, it allowed for no adornments, no excess. It had the precisionism of the Puritan and his moral absolutism; existence was stripped to a bony framework . . . there were hardly any conscious subjects in Newton's historical world, only objects. An interest in man's creations for their own sake, the aesthetic and the sensuous, is totally absent.[43]

All that was irrational, primitive, extravagant was beyond his ken. Vico sent Newton a complimentary copy of the first version of his

---

[42]Wiles, 'Newton and the Bible'.
[43]Manuel, *Isaac Newton, Historian*, p. 10.

Scienza Nuova (1725). It is not known whether Newton received and read it, but as Manuel comments, 'he would not have remotely comprehended its meaning' in any case. 'When confronted by the more complex manifestations of mankind – polytheist idolatry, luxury and lies, the poetical, the cabalistic, the emotive, the fabulous, the philosophical conceit, the cruel and the lustful – he either pushed them away with repugnance or dropped them into the eighteenth-century catchalls known as error and deception.'[44] Even the chronology, to which Newton had brought powers of intellect and intuition that his contemporaries regarded as superhuman, was nothing more than 'a magnificent rationalist delusion'.[45]

Newton's religious beliefs are controverted. On the one hand, he was a conforming churchman whose Anglican orthodoxy was unchallenged in his lifetime; he funded the distribution of Bibles to the poor and the building of London churches. On the other hand, he privately held heterodox, anti-trinitarian views, partly driven by his antipathy to speculative thought, and believed that trinitarian doctrine was the product of a conspiracy to derail authentic Christianity.[46] Were his deism and Socinianism an intentional embrace of heresy or simply a modification of the Anglican creed of the time, refracted by the obsession with empirical method? He believed that his theological work could purify revealed religion, just as his scientific work had purified natural philosophy. Manuel insists not only that Newton never held a simplistic mechanical view of the universe and was never a partisan of plain deistic natural religion, but also that he was always a firm believer in Christian theism.[47]

While the Enlightenment thinkers were more profoundly influenced by Descartes than they cared to acknowledge – the mirage of clear and distinct ideas, the analytical view of language that could be reduced to univocal counters, the penchant for simplistic, reductionist explanations – Newton was supremely their man. Newton and Descartes became symbolic, paradigmatic figures. Newton was seen

---

[44]Ibid., p. 193.

[45]Ibid., p. 49.

[46]Westfall, *Never at Rest*, pp. 309–20.

[47]Manuel, *Isaac Newton, Historian*, p. 8; id., *Religion of Newton*, pp. 6–7. Manuel's views are challenged by Newton's biographer: Westfall, 'Changing World of the Newtonian Industry'.

as embodying the ideal of modern, progressive and useful science, firmly based upon experimental and observational data which it subjected to precise mathematical treatment. Descartes became the symbol of a reactionary attempt to subject science to metaphysics, disregarding experience and computational precision, and replacing them by outlandish, unprovable hypotheses. Fontenelle, whose long life (1657–1757) bridges the seventeenth century and the Enlightenment, said in his *Eulogium* for Newton:

> One of them [Descartes], soaring aloft in daring flight, sought to take his stand at the fountain-head of all things in the light of a few clear and fundamental ideas, so that when he came to deal with the phenomena of Nature he would be able to treat them as necessary consequences thereof. The other [Newton], less daring, or more modest, in his aims, beginning with phenomena as his starting point proceeded therefrom to unknown principles, resolved to treat them as the logic of the consequences might require. The one starts from a clearly formulated idea to ascertain the cause of what he sees; the other starts from what he sees and goes on to seek out its cause.[48]

However, Descartes and Newton, as the beneficiaries of Galileo, were at one in the fundamental view of the world that they passed on to the Enlightenment. In terms of 'the Newtonian universe', humanity was purely peripheral.

> The world that people had thought themselves living in – a world rich in color and sound, redolent with fragrance, filled with gladness, love and beauty, speaking everywhere of purposive harmony and creative ideals – was crowded now into minute corners in the brains of scattered organic beings. The really important world outside was a world hard, cold, colorless, silent, and dead; a world of quantity, a world of mathematically computable motions in mechanical regularity.[49]

In such a climate, theology, philosophy, ethics and history could only be cramped. Although the Enlightenment saw the development

---

[48]Cited, Hazard, *European Mind*, p. 358.
[49]Burtt, *Metaphysical Foundations*, pp. 236–7.

of more objective methods in history and Newtonian assumptions profoundly affected the direction taken by literature, especially poetry,[50] theology became mesmerized by the 'plain historical [i.e. empirical] method'. The world ran according to the mechanical laws of God. Nature and reason were at one, so that to say that something was reasonable was to say that it was natural, and vice versa. Human nature was uncomplicated and did not vary. The truth of Christian theology could be proved by amassing evidence, biblical and historical; this was the primary task of theologians. A more profound understanding of God, the world, human nature and theological truth than the Newtonian paradigm could provide awaited the Romantic movement's onslaught on the major presuppositions of the Newtonian universe. This was the first great battle to which Blake, Coleridge, Wordsworth and Carlyle, to name but a few, addressed themselves.

The deists

Even when the Enlightenment was not theologically orthodox, it was almost always at least theistic, acknowledging a Supreme Being and often a good deal more. Atheists and materialists, like Helvétius, d'Holbach and Diderot, in France and (according to one school of thought, not ours) Hobbes in England, were very exceptional. Theology, popular as well as scholarly, was a major industry and was not confined to 'confessional' positions. Voltaire, Diderot and Rousseau each had his own 'theology', though not of course a Christian one.[51] Although 'Deism' is notoriously difficult to define, it is the label now irreversibly attached to the bewildering range of semi-Christian or sub-Christian theologies that were advocated across Europe in roughly the century between the mid-seventeenth and the mid-eighteenth.[52] There is a spectrum of positions among

---

[50]Nicholson, *Newton Demands the Muse.*
[51]Wade, *Structure and Form*, vol. 1. On the English freethinkers and deists see Rivers, *Reason, Grace, and Sentiment*, vol. 2, ch. 1; Israel, *Radical Enlightenment*, ch. 33.
[52]For discussion of the definition of deism and of its range see Byrne, *Natural Religion.* Reventlow, *Authority of the Bible*, pp. 289–334, is a useful survey which brings out the contribution of the deists to the rational, Enlightenment mind set, including a more detached, critical approach to the Bible.

those called 'deists', from rational theologians, through religious non-churchmen who still believed in a providential God, divine revelation, miracles and the afterlife with rewards and punishments, to subversive freethinkers who were hostile to all genuine religious feeling.[53] We engage briefly and selectively with these views purely for their relevance to mainstream Anglican theological method in defence of the faith.

Deistic writers attacked Christianity and the Church on three fronts.[54] First, on the philosophical front they called in question the proofs of Christian belief from alleged miracles, as contrary to the standards of probability that we rely on in everyday life, a weight of probability that outweighs any appeal to historical 'evidence' in principle. Secondly, the deists posed an ethical challenge to the moral worthiness of many, if not most, of the miracles contained in the Bible, even those of Jesus, alleging that they often did not reflect the justice and universal benevolence of God. As Byrne puts it, miracles, far from supporting the authority of Scripture, become reasons for distrusting it, 'not indications of divine warrant but of human error, superstition, and enthusiasm'.[55] Thirdly, deistic writers, not least the influential and elegant Shaftesbury, developed the rudiments of an historical and critical approach to the Bible, building on the early work of, for example, Spinoza and Simon.[56] They brought out the human and historically conditioned nature of the Bible, treating it like any other set of ancient texts, probing the literal sense and consequently calling into question the stock proofs of Christian apologetics from the fulfilment of Old Testament prophecy in the New. While this critique was external to the Church and hostile to it, the substance of it was gradually absorbed into mainstream theology: the historical–critical method is now universally approved by the major churches, and arguments from miracles and prophecy have disappeared from contemporary apologetics.

---

[53]Waligore, 'Piety of the English Deists'. Crocker, 'Enlightenment', p. 340, makes a similar point in general terms, and Brinton suggests that 'the faith of the Enlightenment is a kind of Christianity, a development out of Christianity': *Ideas and Men*, p. 407. Stromberg, *Religious Liberalism*, has stimulating, broad-brush judgements and interesting, out-of the-way pieces of documentation.

[54]See Byrne, *Natural Religion*, esp. ch. 4.

[55]Ibid., p. 100.

[56]On Shaftesbury's biblical comments see Reventlow, *Authority of the Bible*, pp. 308–21; for Spinoza, *Works*, vol. 1.

An aggressive deism was powerful in France between 1715 and 1750, but in England, while some deists, such as Charles Blount and Anthony Collins, were aggressive freethinkers, others were devout in their deistic way. Many deists were professing Christians, 'Christian deists', which is what Matthew Tindal, author of *Christianity as old as the Creation, or the Gospel a Republication of the Religion of Nature* (1730), called himself. His subtitle is virtually a paraphrase of one of Butler's axioms. But, as Byrne points out, Tindal's God and that of the English deists generally is impersonal, a function of the need to secure human happiness, and his religion is ahistorical and individualistic, prescinding from both a religious tradition and a community of faith. Religious truth must be available to all people at all times, or the character of God is impugned. Therefore, it cannot be conveyed by Scriptures or by tradition, which are available only to a few, but can be known by reason only.[57]

Lord Herbert of Cherbury

Lord Herbert of Cherbury (1582–1648), the so-called father of English deism, was not unique among rational thinkers in being a man of deep personal devotion, who found the Bible a source of inspiration and comfort and believed in prayer, signs, angels and special providences.[58] Edward Herbert was the elder brother of George Herbert, but he is devoid of the priest–poet's fervent devotion to Jesus Christ. Lord Herbert believed, with the deists after him, that to be true to divine justice and benevolence, the way of salvation must be universally clear and available: there is no place in his system for 'the scandal of particularity'. He attacks the Christian scheme (especially in its strong, Calvinist form) for its basis in divine election and foreknowledge, for a revelation given to one nation only, for a unique incarnation and redemption and sacraments of salvation reserved to comparatively few.

Lord Herbert's *De Veritate* (*On Truth*, 1724) is a work of general epistemology that was intended to rescue truth from the sceptics and was the first study of its kind in English.[59] In a sort of appendix

---

[57]Ibid., ch. 3.
[58]Herbert of Cherbury, *Life*.
[59]Herbert of Cherbury, *De Veritate*; Bedford, *Defence of Truth*; Popkin, *History of Scepticism*, ch. VIII; Peter Harrison, *'Religion' and the Religions*, ch. 3; Byrne, *Natural Religion*, pp. 22–37.

to *De Veritate*, Herbert sets out five fundamental religious truths ('Common Notions Concerning Religion') which he believes are innate principles that are implanted by God in every normal human being of all ages and confirmed by universal experience. They are: God exists; it is our duty to worship God; virtue is the best part of worship; we should repent of our sins; there will be rewards and punishments after death. (Locke attacked Herbert's claim on both counts: they are not innate and they are not universal.)[60]

The five assured truths are prefaced by a scathing attack on the kind of ecclesiastical authority that demands implicit faith, disparages reason and condemns private judgement. Herbert affirms the reality of revelations to the individual (sleeping or waking) and of grace (in the form of particular providences) and endorses prayer, penitence and worship, but he subjects everything to the test of reason and conscience.[61]

There is nothing intrinsically objectionable about submitting religious truth claims to the bar of reason: Butler says much the same, as do many other Anglican and Dissenting divines of the period. And Herbert is not a rationalist: reason is not dominant in his system. Divine initiative, implanting the Common Notions in our minds, has priority. His God is the God of religious pluralism: 'that which is everywhere accepted as the supreme manifestation of deity, by whatever name it may be called, I term God'.[62] Herbert often speaks like a Christian and claims to fully accept the Bible – but in the passages where does so, he does not mention the name of Jesus Christ.[63]

John Toland

Even John Toland's notorious *Christianity Not Mysterious* (1696) seems fairly tame.[64] Toland, however, knew that it was dangerous stuff: he published it anonymously and even the names of the printer and bookseller were withheld. Ostensibly Toland was replying to Edward Stillingfleet's sermon 'Christianity Mysterious, and the

---

[60]Locke, *Essay Concerning Human Understanding*, vol. 1, pp. 36–43 (I, iii, 15–27).
[61]Herbert, *De Veritate*, pp. 308–13.
[62]Ibid., p. 291.
[63]Ibid., pp. 314–15.
[64]Toland, *Christianity Not Mysterious*. On the context and responses see Champion, *Republican Learning*.

Wisdom of God in Making it So' (1694). Toland claims to write as a sincere Christian and against atheists, infidels and all enemies of revealed religion. He speaks of his 'conversion', but attributes it to reason, rather than the Holy Spirit. He declines to defend 'all those jarring Doctrines, ambiguous Terms, and puzzling Distinctions' that have exercised scholars over the centuries, but aims to vindicate the gospel of Christ and the Apostles.[65] He echoes Chillingworth in exposing the contradictions among Fathers and Councils, before plumping for reason as the only guide and authority in theological truth.[66]

Toland extrapolates from Descartes', Hobbes' and Locke's principles of rationality and founds reason on 'simple and distinct Ideas', so that 'what is evidently repugnant to clear and distinct Idea's [sic], or to our common Notions, is contrary to Reason'.[67] Part of the subversive nature of the book was its overt appeal to ordinary, uneducated people by the use of plain speech (foreshadowing John Wesley): let them work religion out for themselves, untrammeled by clerical authority. Religious freedom would lead to political liberation (Toland was a republican). But in contrast to Locke, who stressed the limitations of our knowledge and affirmed probability as a light in the darkness, Toland equates 'reasonable' with 'not mysterious' and insists that 'there is nothing in the Gospel contrary to Reason, nor above it; and that no Christian Doctrine can be properly call'd a Mystery'.[68] He reduces belief to acceptance of empirically informative statements. Toland reserves some of his most scathing comments for the rites and ceremonies of the Church, which cunning priests have devised to mystify the simple by deliberately making them 'downright unintelligible'.[69]

Writers on deism sometimes assert that deists deny revelation, or have no place for it; some make rejection of revelation a formal identifying mark of deism.[70] But this criterion is not generally sustainable. Toland tells us that part of his aim is to demonstrate that Christianity is not of human origin, but is divinely revealed and

---

[65]Ibid., Preface.
[66]Ibid., pp. 1–6.
[67]Ibid., p. 10.
[68]Ibid., p. 6.
[69]Ibid., pp. 172–3.
[70]For example, Peter Harrison, *'Religion' and the Religions*, p. 62.

he takes the New Testament as divine Scripture, though he insists that, to interpret it aright, the Bible should be read like any other book. For Tolland, the hallmark of revelation is that it fully accords with human reason: Jesus Christ is peripheral to his platform and Toland's view of salvation is Pelagian. He saw himself as a loyal member of the Church of England, but his principles, if pressed to their logical conclusion, would undermine all Christian faith (as we see pretty conclusively in Matthew Tindal's *Christianity as Old as the Creation* (1730), where reason and 'nature' are all in all).[71] Locke was appalled at *Christianity not Mysterious* and Peter Browne, an exponent of Lockean philosophy, retorted to Toland, '*I adore what I cannot comprehend.*'[72] It was the success of such deistic notions as these that called forth one of the greatest theological works in the English language: Butler's *Analogy.*

---

[71]Cragg, *Puritanism to the Age of Reason*, ch. 7. See further on Toland, Weinsheimer, *Eighteenth-Century Hermeneutics*, ch. 2: '"Toland on Reason."' Tindal, *Christianity*.
[72]Champion, *Republican Learning*, p. 81.

9

Exponents of the Anglican Enlightenment

In this chapter, I discuss four more major figures from the Anglican Enlightenment from the point of view of their theological method: William Law, John Wesley, Joseph Butler and Edmund Burke. I do not claim, in defence of this meagre selection, that they are adequately 'representative', but that they are different, that they are fascinating and that they interacted. Law was a profound influence on the younger Wesley, though later they fell out. Wesley and Butler clashed. Butler was a strong influence on Burke. Between them they display facets of the Anglican Enlightenment. They reveal both its strengths – they were possessed of formidable intellect, spiritual power and controversial skill – and its limitations, as will be become clear in each individual case, I trust. Although in the previous chapter and in this one, I have merely skimmed the surface of the Anglican Enlightenment and have not brought in other major figures such as Edmund Law, William Warburton, Richard Watson and Samuel Horsley, to name but a few, I hope that I have done enough to justify my contention (and that of other writers, notably Roy Porter and recently B. W. Young)[1] that in Britain the Enlightenment was a largely Christian phenomenon and in England was largely Anglican in location and character, though Dissenters were caught up in it too. Interestingly, Jonathan Israel, in his massive work *Enlightenment Contested*, in which he distinguishes between an early radical Enlightenment and a later moderate, mainstream one, does not mention Law, Wesley or Butler (Burke is outside his period but is mentioned incidentally).

---

[1]B. W. Young, *Religion and Enlightenment*; see ch. 6 for a treatment of Warburton.

If it still seems paradoxical, if not perverse, to speak of a 'Christian and Anglican Enlightenment', I think we do well to remember that Christian and Anglican writers adopted the pervasive vernacular imagery of the enlightened mind and enlightened society. They also learnt to appeal to reason rather than to received authority. They believed in progress, even if, as in the case of Wesley it was progress in the spread of the gospel, renovated lives and a purified nation, or as with Burke it was material and intellectual improvement, refinement of manners and constitutional development that they had in mind.[2] I do not find it helpful to distinguish, as Israel does, between an original 'radical', secular Enlightenment in Holland, France and England, and a later 'moderate', mainstream, ecclesiastical and monarchical Enlightenment; or as others do, between Enlightenment and Counter-Enlightenment.[3] The Counter-Enlightenment belongs to early in the next century with the conservative, Romantic theorists and idealists of Germany, France and England. Those in the eighteenth century who attacked the sub-Christian or anti-Christian stance of the *philosophes* were just as much inhabitants of the Enlightenment and saw themselves as such; they fought their battles with the same weapons of rational discourse. The Enlightenment was many-faceted, but it was, to a significant extent, a Christian cultural movement.

William Law

Mystical and polemical

The Nonjuror William Law (1686–1761) was regarded by Dean Inge as 'perhaps the greatest of our mystical divines'.[4] His two most eloquent, most fervent pieces of mystical devotion are *The Spirit of Prayer* (1749) and *The Spirit of Love* (1752).[5] Law was indebted to the German mystical writer Jacob Boehme, rather than to the English mystical tradition, whether medieval, or

---

[2]Weston, 'Burke's View of History', pp. 208–9.
[3]Israel, *Radical Enlightenment*; id., *Enlightenment Contested*; Aston, 'Horne and Heterodoxy'.
[4]Inge, *Studies of English Mystics*, p. 125.
[5]Law, *Works*.

contemporary in the form of the Cambridge Platonists, especially John Smith. But Law is not 'merely' a mystic: he is also a polemical ecclesiologist (against the ultra-low church, barely orthodox Bishop Hoadly), a polemical ethicist (against Bernard de Mandeville (1670–1733, author of the cynical and vicious *The Fable of the Bees: or Private Vices, Publick Benefits*, 1714, 1723, 1734), and a polemical apologist in his writings against the deists.[6] In these various genres, Law is an exponent of Anglican theological method in the age of Enlightenment, appealing to the harmony of reason and revelation, but not at the expense of the Scriptures and divine revelation. He was a formidable antagonist and no unorthodox writer was safe from attack. He goes for the equally formidable Bayle, for example, depicting him as an atheist and a contradictory one at that.[7]

Law's riposte to the egregious deist Matthew Tindal's *Christianity as Old as the Creation* conformed to the *zeitgeist* in being entitled *The Case of Reason, or Natural Religion Fairly and Fully Stated* (1731).[8] Tindal has been called 'the Voltaire of England without Voltaire's genius'. Tindal appeals vacuously to 'the reason and nature of things'. He will not allow that revelation could exceed natural religion or that there could be a revelation made to some that was not given to all. The thrust of Tindal's argument is to negate the reality of revelation altogether. Law anticipates Butler's argument in the *Analogy*, 5 years later, when he insists against Tindal that human reason cannot either prescribe or predict the nature and content of divine revelation. Reason is flawed and corrupted and is no fit judge of infinite wisdom. Law followed this diatribe with a broader and more gently persuasive work of apologetics, *An Appeal to all that Doubt, or Disbelieve the Truths of the Gospel*, addressed particularly to *Deists, Arians, Socinians, or Nominal Christians* in which *The True Grounds and Reasons of the whole Christian Faith and Life are plainly and fully demonstrated* (1740).[9] It is an exposition of the essentials of the faith, presented with a view to winning the hearts and minds of deviants and doubters,

---

[6]Against Mandeville, Law, *Works*, vol. 2. On Mandeville, see Willey, *Eighteenth-Century Studies*.
[7]Law, *Works*, vol. 2, pp. 51–4.
[8]Law, *Works*, vol. 2.
[9]Law, *Works*, vol. 6.

and showing that salvation restores the true nature of humanity as it came from the hand of God at creation, a God-breathed soul.

High Church moralist

Two of Law's works, the *Serious Call* and his *Three Letters to the Bishop of Bangor* (Hoadly), illustrate in a little more detail the two aspects of his thought, the mystical and the polemical, and reveal him as the pre-eminent High Church moralist of his time. Law's *Serious Call to a Devout and Holy Life* (1728)[10] is marked by an incisive analysis of human motivation and our propensity for self-deception – it leaves no escape or subterfuge – and a fervent devotion that seeks to consecrate the whole of one's life to God and Christian service. Law is a typical thinker of the eighteenth century in the way that – even in this fervent treatise on total surrender of the life to Christ – he equates the reasonable and the natural: reason and nature, reason and religion, are constantly equated as what God requires. It is our religious duty to live by reason and nature. There is no tinge of the anti-rational here. But we live not only under the eye of God, but in God's very presence. Law's many characters and scenarios reflect the 'experimental', inductive, empirical method and to that extent his approach is characteristic of the age. Law stands in the Anglican tradition of devotional, ascetic, spirituality, but one that is not Puritan, but liturgical and sacramental. Jeremy Taylor is a precursor with his *Holy Living* and *Holy Dying* and *The Worthy Communicant*.[11] Law mediates that tradition to the Tractarians, for whom Taylor – author also of *The Liberty of Prophesying*, a plea for toleration and free rational debate[12] – would have been regarded as too liberal.

John Wesley, who maintained a profound regard for Law in spite of their bitter theological dispute, described the *Serious Call* as 'a treatise which will hardly be excelled, if it be equaled, in the English tongue, either for beauty of expression, or for justness and depth of thought'.[13] George Whitefield was also deeply impressed by it.

---

[10]Law, *Serious Call*.
[11]Jeremy Taylor, *Worthy Communicant*. The full title indicates a fusion of sacramental and ascetic theology, spiritual direction and devotional tone.
[12]Jeremy Taylor, *Liberty of Prophesying, Works*, vols. 7 and 8.
[13]Wesley, *Works*, vol. 4, p. 121 (Sermon 125).

Dr Johnson praised it as 'the finest piece of hortatory theology in any language' and confessed that his reading of it prompted him to serious spiritual reflection for the first time.[14] Gibbon, the sceptic, acknowledged its power (Law had been tutor to Gibbon's father). The chronicler of the crimes and follies of medieval Christendom commented that Law 'exposes, with equal severity and truth, the strange contradiction between the faith and practice of the Christian world'.[15] John Keble kept the *Serious Call* in a drawer for reverence's sake and would not have it casually talked about.

Law achieved fame by his brilliant attack on Benjamin Hoadly, the notorious, much promoted, latitudinarian Bishop of Bangor. Preaching on the text, 'My kingdom is not of this world,' Hoadly claimed that Christ left no visible authority in his Church with regard to spiritual matters, and he effectively negated the institutional means of grace and the succession of ordinations. Inge comments that Law's tract 'raised its author to the front rank of controversialists' (of whom, we might add, there was no dearth in the eighteenth-century Church of England!).[16] In his *Three Letters to the Bishop of Bangor* (1717–19), Law defended the visibility of the Church, its institutional structure and the authority of tradition and of oversight in the Church against Hoadly's spiritualizing of the text, 'My kingdom is not of this world.' As polemical satire, these letters rank with Pascal's *Lettres Provinciales*. In 1893 Charles Gore, the *enfant terrible* of the Anglo-Catholics, would edit a reprint of this famous but little-read work.[17] For the eighteenth-century High Churchmen (as later for the Tractarians), the authority of tradition and of conscience would work together against the critical reason of the *philosophes*. (But, as we shall see in the sequel to this volume, it is a remarkable feature of Gore's mind that it was precisely on grounds of *conscience* that he sometimes could not accept tradition.)

In later life, Law became increasingly anti-intellectual and anti-rational, in reaction to both rationalist deism and rationalist counter-attacks on deism. But he remains the pre-eminent High Church moralist and controversialist of the period. He lived in the golden

---

[14]Boswell, *Life of Johnson*, pp. 50, 440.
[15]Gibbon, *Autobiography*, pp. 17–18.
[16]Inge, *Studies*, p. 128.
[17]Law, *Defence of Church Principles*.

(or 'Augustan') age of English letters and literary controversy –
the era of Defoe, Swift, Addison, Pope, Butler, Dryden, Johnson,
Goldsmith and so on. But, as Alexander Whyte justly says, 'In sheer
intellectual strength Law is fully abreast of the very foremost of his
illustrious contemporaries, while in that fertilising touch which is
the true test of genius, Law simply stands alone.'[18] Law's writings –
not only the *Serious Call*, but also his *Christian Perfection* – deeply
influenced John Wesley, though Wesley eventually denounced Law's
doctrine.

John Wesley

Anglican theologian

Why do I include John Wesley (1703–91) as a figure of the Anglican
Enlightenment? I suspect that many Methodists in Britain, America
and the rest of the world are only dimly aware that John and Charles
Wesley, who together with George Whitefield (1714–70), were the
founders of the Methodist movement in the mid-eighteenth century,
were all their lives Anglican priests, clergymen of the Church of
England by law established. The fact is that, thanks to worldwide
Methodism, John Wesley is the best known, most famous Anglican
cleric of all time, and Charles Wesley (1707–88) is the second best
known and (with Thomas Cranmer through the Book of Common
Prayer, used by Anglicans and Methodists for centuries) the most
quoted, as his hymns continue to be sung, not only by Methodists,
but by Christians of all stripes around the world. Among the
great names of Anglicanism, the fame and reputation of the name
'Wesley' exceeds that of Cranmer and Hooker. The Church of
England, for one, has very properly included the Wesley brothers
in its liturgical commemorations: they are there not only because
they are ornaments of the Christian tradition in its broadest sense,
alongside many other saints and heroes of faith, but because they
are among the greatest, most gifted sons of the Church of England
and outstanding exponents of a particular strand of the Anglican
tradition of theology and spirituality.

---

[18]Whyte, *Thirteen Appreciations*, p. 199.

As Methodist historians readily acknowledge, John Wesley has been the prisoner of Methodist hero-worship and of the myths that grew up around him and which he certainly helped to create.[19] He has been taken out of his historical context, and seen as a teacher of timeless spiritual truths, as though he had been sent straight from heaven (his own rather messianic language about himself helped to create this image). One way of putting him back where he belongs historically is to reclaim his Anglican, Church of England identity. Another is to recognize his credentials as an intellectual of the British and Anglican Enlightenment.

Enlightenment intellectual

If many Methodists find it strange to think of John Wesley as an Anglican clergyman, who lived and died in the communion of the Church of England, they probably hardly conceive of him at all as an Enlightenment figure. But recent scholarship has reclaimed the Enlightenment background and context of the Wesley brothers. Both their thought and their actions are redolent of their 'enlightened' age.[20] To take a rather trivial but telling example, in their journals both John Wesley and Dr Johnson say the same thing about rugged landscape: 'horrid mountains'.[21]

Trained in Oxford Aristotelianism, John imbibed Locke's empirical epistemology with its stress on experience, the evidence of the senses and the role of reflection, and he reinforced this with the empirical philosophy of Peter Browne, though he also valued the Platonic stress on the intuition of spiritual truths. Outler comments that John was 'a trained logician and much more of a rationalist than the pietists among his followers have ever recognised'.[22] He is deeply implicated in the Newtonian worldview, though not without

---

[19]Heitzenrater, 'John and Charles Wesley'.
[20]Rack, 'Man of Reason and Religion?'; Jeremy Gregory, 'Long Eighteenth Century'. For the impact of the Enlightenment on Evangelicalism more widely see Bebbington, *Evangelicalism in Modern Britain*, ch. 2. For the broader context see Sykes, *Church and State in England*; Walsh, Haydon and Taylor (eds.), *The Church of England, c.1689-c.1833*; Gibson, *Church of England 1688-1832*.
[21]Rack, 'Man of Reason and Religion', p. 12. Johnson's comments in the Hebrides have been noted above.
[22]Albert Outler, 'Introduction', in id., ed., *Sermons I*, in Wesley, *Works*, vol. 1, p. 99.

some hesitations, but his God is personal, heart-warming and transforming. He quotes Newton on space as 'the sensorium of the Deity' in his sermon on 'The Imperfection of Human Knowledge' (itself a Butlerian theme).[23] As part of his huge publishing activity, John produced a *Survey of the Wisdom of God in Creation, OR, A Compendium of Natural Philosophy*, which by 1777 had grown to five volumes.[24] The 'experimental method' is also at work in the way that John collected and published accounts of religious experience from various sources: biographies, autobiographies, conversion narratives, deathbed accounts and letters – amassing evidence. For Wesley, the right experience is the touchstone of true Christianity. He commissioned the life-stories of his preachers and published them.[25] Charles' preoccupation in his poems/hymns with religious experience and emotion belongs with the Enlightenment focus on empiricism and sentiment.[26]

However, along with John's powerful reasoning faculty and empirical method was an admixture of belief in witches, strange arts, demon-possession, the miraculous and the occult, which jarred with the progressive, critical attitudes of his sophisticated contemporaries. Belief in special providences, that is to say, acts of divine intervention, in his own life and those of his followers were highlighted, as were spiritual deliverances from demonic power, and judgements on his and their enemies. Wesley revelled in accounts of poltergeists, spirits and apparitions.[27] Those who abandon belief in the reality of witchcraft, he comments in his journal, do so 'in direct opposition not only to the Bible but to the suffrage of the wisest and best of men in all ages and nations . . . giving up witchcraft is in effect giving up the Bible.'[28] Again, he records in his journal, 'I cannot give up to all the deists in Great Britain the existence of witchcraft, till I give up the credit of all history, sacred and profane.'[29] Johnson thought Wesley too quick to believe a Newcastle girl's

---

[23]Sermon 69, *Works*, vol. 2, p. 570.

[24]See further, Maddox, 'Wesley's Engagement with the Natural Sciences'.

[25]Rivers, *Reason, Grace and Sentiment*, vol. 1, pp. 220–2.

[26]Jeremy Gregory, 'Charles Wesley and the Eighteenth Century', in Newport and Campbell (eds.), *Charles Wesley*.

[27]Rack, 'Man of Reason and Religion', pp. 14–16.

[28]Wesley, *Works*, vol. 22, p. 135 (1768).

[29]Ibid., vol. 23, p. 17 (1776). Cf. Rack, *Reasonable Enthusiast*, pp. 348, 387–8, 431–6.

story of a speaking ghost, though Johnson by no means excluded the possibility that ghosts were real: 'this is a question', he replied to an incredulous comment about this incident, 'which, after five thousand years, is yet undecided; a question, whether in theology or philosophy, one of the most important that can come before the human understanding'.[30] In spite of his passion for self-improvement and edifying reading among Methodists, Wesley colluded with the anti-intellectual, philistine elements among his uneducated or semi-educated followers; he was not interested in helping them to think for themselves, but only to think as he himself thought: a case of *trahison des clercs*?[31]

Evangelist, spiritual director, organizer, strategist, entrepreneur, educator and publicist (including self-publicist) – this is how most people who know something of John Wesley probably think of him. But we should see him also as an intellectual, a trained scholar and a man interested in contemporary ideas.[32] Wesley was a theologian and deserves a place among the Anglican divines of the Enlightenment era. He was not unique in his time in choosing to expound his doctrinal theology in the form of the printed sermon. The fact that his sermons were well-crafted, solidly constructed, biblically dense and conceptually demanding discourses raises the question of what their relationship was to what he preached. As William Abraham points out, 'The cerebral nature of these printed sermons makes it hard to see how Wesley should have been such an effective and controversial preacher.' Drawing on Heitzenrater's work, Abraham concludes that, though Wesley enlivened the spoken word with homely illustrations and anecdotes, the continuity of substance between his preaching and his published sermons was considerable.[33]

John Wesley did not live in a sort of pious cocoon. He was the most travelled person of his age within Britain and Ireland. Though

---

[30]Boswell, *Life of Johnson*, p. 951.
[31]The words 'anti-intellectual' and 'philistine' are those of Plumb, *England in the Eighteenth Century*, p. 96, but I find myself obliged to endorse them.
[32]The reading of the young John Wesley is listed in V. H. H. Green, *Young Mr. Wesley*, Appendix 1.
[33]Abraham, 'Wesley as Preacher', in Maddox and Vickers (eds.), *Cambridge Companion to Wesley*, pp. 107–8. See also Gibson in Francis and Gibson (eds.), *Oxford Handbook of the British Sermon*, p. 22. See further Downey, *Eighteenth-Century Pulpit*, pp. 189–225.

he professed to disdain the society of the great, Wesley was a public figure who spoke or corresponded with many of the leading men and women of Enlightenment Britain. Dr Johnson regretted that Wesley was 'never at leisure' and could not spare more time to talk.[34]

Few individuals have made such an impact on their world and on posterity as John Wesley. In his moral power, stupendous energy, exceptional gifts, range of interests, extent of acquaintances and general influence for good on society and culture, Wesley invites comparison with the mighty Gladstone, High Churchman and theologian as well as four times Prime Minister, in the following century. Both Wesley and Gladstone wrestled with issues of religious faith as undergraduates of Pembroke College, Oxford, in their time. Wesley is like Gladstone too in his undeviating seriousness, lack of a sense of humour (not least about himself), abundance of vital spirits and insensitivity to the reactions of others.

John Wesley was profoundly catholic in his range of reading and knew his way around the Christian traditions of theology and spirituality, including Roman Catholic and Eastern Orthodox sources. His spirit was particularly shaped by Nonconformist Puritan and Anglican streams of spirituality, and he promoted them by his writing and editing, together with older Roman Catholic writers. He knew his Anglican divines from Cranmer and Hooker to Tillotson and Law. In developing his position (or positions!) on the doctrine of Christian Perfection, John acknowledges his debt, in chronological order, to Jeremy Taylor, Thomas à Kempis and William Law. His emphasis on 'heart religion' was drawn from the Puritan experiential divines of the previous century.

John was attracted to Law by his Puritan and High Church upbringing and by his reading of Taylor's *Holy Living* and *Holy Dying* and *The Imitation of Christ*. But Law and Wesley fell out: there was a clash of authority and a difference of theology. Law's *amour propre* was wounded; Wesley condemned Law's teaching as 'another gospel', lacking 'the essence of Christianity' and

---

[34]Boswell, *Life of Johnson*, p. 900. However, as late as 1777, Johnson strongly disparages Wesley's (and Whitefield's) self-promotion through their respective journals (ibid., p. 853). His own account of his tour of the Hebrides, which had been published just two years before, is objective, analytical and informative, not a means of promoting either himself or his cause.

(correctly) heavily dependent on the mystical writings of Jacob Boehme, which Wesley regarded as a farrago of nonsense, 'often flatly contrary to Scripture, to reason, and to itself', because it did not convey the notion of justification by faith, felt in the heart. John had taken Law's ethical, spiritually exacting form of Christianity with him to Georgia, where it had failed him (or he had failed it). It was Moravian teaching about free justification applied to the heart, the feelings, that delivered him.[35] The sweet taste of Christ's presence in the heart was the pledge of redemption. August Spangenburg asked the question, 'Does the Spirit of God bear witness with your Spirit?.' Peter Bohler challenged him, 'Have you the witness within yourself?.' John recalled that his father, Samuel, on his deathbed in 1735 said to him, 'Son, the inward witness . . . that is the proof, the strongest proof of Christianity.'[36] John's famous Aldersgate experience of 24 May 1738 was of the heart, the heart 'strangely warmed'. The experience of salvation was analogous to physical sensation.[37] This is a version of Christianity that has proved remarkably successful, but in its origin it both derives from Enlightenment empiricism and anticipates the Romantic preoccupation with personal feelings and the cultivation of individuality. Indeed, the lyrical fervour of Methodist hymnody helped to create the Romantic movement in England.[38]

In his Preface to his *Christian Library*, John claims: 'There is not in the world a more complete body of practical divinity, than is now extant in the English tongue, in the writings of the last and the present century,' and Wesley went on to claim that this was a judgement based not on prejudice in favour of our own country, but on 'solid, rational observation'.[39] Outler suggests that his 'baseline

---

[35]Wesley, *Plain Account of Christian Perfection*, pp. 5–6; id., *Works*, vol. 21, p. 279; J. Brazier Green, *Wesley and Law*, p. 131. Of Law's mentor and inspiration in his later years, Jacob Boehme, Wesley said, 'I have scarce met a greater friend to darkness' (ibid., p. 138).

[36]John Wesley, *Works*, ed. Thomas Jackson, 3rd edn, (London: John Mason, 1830), vol. 12, p. 98, accessed on line.

[37]Rivers, *Reason, Grace and Sentiment*, vol. 1, p. 237.

[38]Freeman, *Ecumenical Theology of the Heart*; Podmore, *Moravian Church in England*; Gill, *Romantic Movement and Methodism*. For the emotional dimension of Methodism, especially among women, see Mack, *Heart Religion*.

[39]Wesley, *Works*, ed John Emory (New York, 1831), vol 7, p. 524, accessed on line.

tradition' was the Erasmian tradition of Christian humanism, especially in its Anglican form in Cranmer and Hooker, though I feel that he has more than a touch of Luther, rather than Erasmus, in his careless arrogance with regard to established order, precedent, seemliness and loyalty to the institution.[40] But John's mind was shaped by wider, non-Anglican, non-British influences. We have noted the impact of Thomas à Kempis among many Catholic sources; Pascal's *Pensées* is another source. John's parents Samuel and Susannah Wesley were devotees of Pascal and introduced their children to his writings. John saw him as an exponent of lively, experiential faith, presumably because of his mystical experience of assurance in the night of fire (Pascal kept a record of it close to his heart) and included him in his *Christian Library* – though Pascal was too much of a fideist, an advocate of the risk of faith, fully to appeal to the coolly rational Wesley.[41]

John Wesley's Bible

The first thing, possibly, that strikes the modern reader of John Wesley is that what he says is a tissue of quotations and allusions from the English Bible, many of them taken out of context and used proverbially, so to speak. Wesley made a virtue of this feature of his language. Writing to John Newton, the converted slave-trader who became Vicar of Olney, the friend of William Cowper and a hymn writer in his own right ('How sweet the name of Jesus sounds'), Wesley explained, 'The Bible is my standard of language as well as sentiment. I endeavor not only to think but *to speak* as the oracles of God.'[42] It does indeed show how well Wesley knew the Bible, but as spoken or written discourse it seems unnatural, especially since he reverts to the 'thee', 'thou', and 'thy' forms of address, which were archaic even in 1611 when the King James Bible was published. But Wesley's biblical discourse was of a piece with his professed intention (in his sermons) to use 'plain words for plain people' and (in his *Notes on the New Testament*) to 'write chiefly for plain, unlettered men, who understand only their mother tongue,

[40]Outler in Wesley, *Works*, vol. 1, p. 56.
[41]Cf. Barker, *Strange Contrarieties*.
[42]Cited Wall, 'Wesley as biblical interpreter', in Maddox and Vickers (eds.), *Cambridge Companion to Wesley*, p. 114.

and yet reverence and love the Word of God, and have a desire to save their souls'.[43] The driving aim of Wesley's use of Scripture was pastoral and evangelistic and that purpose goes a long way to explaining the element of pragmatism in his interpretations and any lack of consistency in his doctrine of biblical authority.[44]

Wesley famously claimed to be a man of one book: *homo unius libri* – 'the Book of God' that shows the way to heaven.[45] While the Scriptures contain the perfection of truth, Wesley was in fact a man who read, wrote and edited many books. To any of his helpers who boasted that they read only the Bible, he retorted, 'You need preach no more.'[46]

Wesley began his comments on the Bible with the Old Testament, publishing three volumes on the Old Testament and one on the New in 1768 (he sent a set to Dr Johnson in 1775). Not until 1790 did Wesley publish his translation of the New Testament with his notes. He made a huge number of revisions to the text of the KJB (about 12,000), and though he was by no means shy of giving a personal interpretation in his exegesis, he drew on a community of Protestant scholarship, replicating especially the comments of the great Dissenting commentators Matthew Henry, Matthew Poole and Philip Doddridge, together with the Anglican John Heylyn and especially the Lutheran Johann Bengel whose Greek New Testament of 1734 was at the cutting edge of textual study at that time.[47] Although Wesley was curious about many things, he was not, it seems, open to ideas of biblical criticism that were emerging in his lifetime. In his *Notes upon the New Testament*, he states his intention of avoiding 'all curious and critical inquiries' and to 'decline going deep into many difficulties, lest I should leave the ordinary reader behind me'.[48] He assumes, for example, the primacy of Matthew's Gospel and the Petrine authorship of 2 Peter. He plays down the human element in Scripture, employing what amounts to a dictation theory of inspiration.[49] He is vituperative

---

[43]Wesley, *Works*, vol. 1, p. 104; id., *Explanatory Notes upon the New Testament*, p. 6 (Preface).
[44]Cf. Phillips, 'Methodism and the Bible', p. 224.
[45]Wesley, *Works*, vol. 1, p. 105. See also Maddox, 'Rule of Christian Faith'.
[46]Jones, *Wesley's Conception and Use of Scripture*, p. 35.
[47]Baker, 'John Wesley, Biblical Commentator'.
[48]Wesley, *Notes*, p. 7 (Preface).
[49]Jones, *Wesley's Conception and Use of Scripture*, pp. 18–19.

about David Hume's theories (casting doubt on miracles, etc.), but does not directly address the issues raised by Hume and various deists. Unlike Butler, he does not try to meet critics of divine revelation halfway in order to win them over.

Though in his version of the BCP for American Methodists, Wesley deleted the reference to the Apocrypha in Article 5 of the Thirty-nine Articles, he was not personally hidebound by Protestant scruples about the Apocrypha. In practice, he makes no distinction between the Hebrew Canon and the Apocryphal books, and is particularly drawn to the Book of Wisdom.

Wesley followed 'the Scripture principle' of the Reformers. 'The Scriptures are a complete rule of faith and practice; and they are clear in all, necessary points.'[50] He makes much of 'the analogy of faith', that is to say, seeking to understand a given text in the light of others that might (or we may think, might not) bear upon it. The analogy of faith stands for the general tenor of Scripture, the scheme of salvation.[51] The analogy of faith, as a hermeneutical method, is inherently circumscribed and is conducive to harmonization of discrepancies. Wesley insists on the factual inerrancy of Scripture in a way that anticipates the nineteenth-century rationalizations of Charles Hodge, Benjamin B. Warfield and others in the Reformed, Princeton ambit. 'Nay, if there be *any* mistakes in the Bible,' he protests, 'there may as well be a thousand. If there be one falsehood in that book, it [the Bible] did not come from the God of truth.'[52] That is not the spirit in which Luther, Calvin and Hooker, trained in Renaissance humanism, approached the Bible. In its demand for precision and quantifiable truth, in its either-or, black and white sort of judgement, Wesley's ultimatum is redolent of an Enlightenment obsession with instrumental, critical, empirical reason.

Reason and religion

Wesley made a public appeal to 'men of reason and religion'.[53] These were the majority of the educated, genteel population, either

---

[50]Cited ibid., p. 43.

[51]Ibid., pp. 45–9.

[52]Wesley, *Works*, vol. 23, p. 25.

[53]Ibid., vol. 11: *The Appeals to Men of Reason and Religion and Certain Related Open Letters*, ed. Gerald R. Cragg.

nominal professors of Christianity or deistically inclined unbelievers. Although Wesley deplored the existence of many 'practical atheists', that is those who lived their lives as though there were no God, he claimed to have met only two 'speculative atheists', that is those who held a doctrine that there is no God, in a lifetime of travel.[54] 'We join with you then', says Wesley to his critics, the critics of Methodism, 'in desiring a religion founded on reason, and every way agreeable thereto . . . to the essential nature of things.'[55] What can be more reasonable, he asks, than a religion that teaches us to love God and our neighbour? Jesus was the 'strongest reasoner' ever and St Paul the next strongest.[56] While all our ideas derive from sense experience, God can give us 'spiritual senses . . . a new class of senses . . . internal senses' in the soul to enable us to see spiritual truths.[57] But this insight is no less reasonable.

He is typical of his age in professing the paramount value of reason. Reason is a divine gift and the Holy Spirit works alongside and through our reason. Education and study can renovate the reasoning faculty, damaged by the Fall.[58] Usually Wesley connects reason and Scripture; sometimes reason and experience, but he regards both reason and experience as open to the Spirit. Rational religion is opposed to enthusiasm ('a species of religious madness'), bigotry (an excessive attachment to our own party, church or religion) and excess of zeal.[59] In Sermon 70, 'The Case of Reason Impartially Considered', Wesley outlines a middle way between those who 'despise and vilify reason', including enthusiasts who take 'the dreams of their own imagination to be revealed from God', and those who go to the opposite extreme and deify reason, regarding it as infallible. For Wesley, reason is functional; it has work to do, comprising apprehension, judgement and discourse. Its role is to interpret and explain Christian truth and to help to resolve

---

[54]Ibid., vol. 4, p. 171.
[55]Ibid., vol. 11, p. 55.
[56]Ibid., p. 56.
[57]Ibid.
[58]Rack, 'Man of Reason and Religion', pp. 11–12.
[59]Wesley, *Works*, vol. 2, Sermon 17, 'The Nature of Enthusiasm'; Sermon 18, 'A Caution Against Bigotry'; vol. 3, Sermon 92, 'On Zeal'; vol. 4, Sermon 119, 'Walking by Sight and Walking by Faith'; cf. vol. 11, p. 66 for another reference to 'the candle of the Lord'.

cases of conscience. It is, he says, quoting the favourite biblical text of the Cambridge Platonists, 'the candle of the Lord'. Reason is vital in both laying the foundation and erecting the superstructure of religious truth. He rebukes those who rant against the place of reason in religion.[60]

But the scope of reason for Wesley was strictly circumscribed; it was not allowed free rein. Where reason was made to stop, inner experience took over. One could say that heartfelt experience was superimposed on reasoning and overlaid it. It is also plausible to suggest that the emphasis on felt spiritual experience was a defence mechanism against the threats from rationalism and deism. The traditional 'external' evidences of Christianity – an infallible Bible, supported by miracles and prophecies – had received a battering and Wesley had sometimes felt its force. However, inward assurance was proof against the challenge. 'If then it were possible (which I conceive it is not),' he wrote to the formidably controversial clergyman Conyers Middleton in 1749, 'to shake the traditional evidence of Christianity, still he that has the internal evidence . . . would stand firm and unshaken.'[61]

There is an extraordinary outburst against Luther in Wesley's journal. It was the reading of Luther's preface to Romans that had been instrumental in Wesley's Aldersgate experience of assurance (or, as he tended to call it, conversion) on 24 May 1738. In 1778, Wesley translated a life of Luther from the German and published it in his *Arminian Magazine*.[62] But here he attacks Luther for 'mysticism', lack of regard for the Old Testament law, and hostility to reason. 'How does he (almost in the words of Tauler [fourteenth-century German Dominican spiritual writer]) decry *reason*, right or wrong, as an irreconcilable enemy to the gospel of Christ! Whereas, what is *reason* (the faculty so called) but the power of apprehending, judging, and discoursing? Which power is no more to be condemned in the gross, than seeing, hearing or feeling.'[63] For all Luther's extravagant language, this was a serious and culpable misunderstanding of his view of reason.

---

[60]Ibid., vol. 2, pp. 587–90.
[61]Cited Walsh, 'Origins of the Evangelical Revival', in Bennett and Walsh (eds.), *Essays in Modern English Church History*, p. 153.
[62]Wesley, *Works*, vol. 20, p. 285.
[63]Ibid., vol. 19, pp. 200–1.

Wesley does not include Locke in his condemnations of extreme rationalists, but mentions him with respect. He accepts the Lockean, empiricist doctrine that all knowledge is derived from sense-experience, quoting the Latin tag, *Nihil est in intellectu quod non fuit prius in sensu* (nothing is in the mind that was not first in the senses).[64]

Wesley strikes a Butlerian note in his Sermon 69 on 'The Imperfection of Human Knowledge', where he enumerates many areas where the workings of nature and providence are profoundly obscure ('impenetrable darkness'). It is what in the twentieth century came to be called the 'God of the gaps' argument. He adds, following Butler, 'if this be improved into an objection against revelation it is an objection that lies full as much against natural as revealed religion'.[65]

In his notable biography of John Wesley, Henry Rack labels him 'Reasonable Enthusiast', suggesting that Wesley was not innocent of the excessive fervour that he condemned in others. His ministry, Rack suggests, was 'rational in form but enthusiast in substance'.[66] Wesley attempted to rebut accusations of 'enthusiasm' (i.e. fanaticism, irrationalism and the cultivation of extreme emotional states), both serious and scurrilous, especially by Butler of Bristol (see below), Lavington of Exeter (the scurrilous version) and Gibson of London (serious but overstated). Wesley trounced Lavington and dealt effectively, though respectfully, with Gibson. But there is no smoke without fire and as we read Wesley's defence, there is a sense that he 'doth protest too much'.[67]

Tradition, law and conscience

As we have noted, Wesley draws extensively on the traditions of spirituality of the Church through the ages; tradition is a source of inspiration and enrichment. But it cannot really be said that Wesley was guided in his teaching and decisions by tradition. His early enthusiasm for the Fathers gave way to a more critical attitude.

---

[64]Ibid., vol. 4, p. 51; cf. p. 200.
[65]Ibid., vol. 2, p. 583.
[66]Rack, *Reasonable Enthusiast*, p. 388.
[67]Wesley, *Works*, vol. 11.

'Tradition' is a word that 'has only negative connotations for Wesley.'[68] Outler claims that continuity was important to Wesley,[69] but his breaches of church order, especially his persistent acts of ordination and his quite drastic revisions of the BCP for American Methodists (eliminating saints' days, apart from All Saints, for example) make this doubtful. He valued a spiritual continuity perhaps, especially one of a pattern of conversion, assurance and perfection, but not one of outward ordering. Tradition, especially of polity, was not a constraint to John as it was to Charles.

Like Johnson, Wesley had little time for the emerging historical science of his time. He is dismissive of an essay on taste by Montesquieu, the founder of 'philosophic history,' and the master of Hume, Gibbon and Burke.[70] He keeps up, on horseback, with the voluminous historical works of William Robertson, the eminent Presbyterian minister, but condemns him for not tracing the hand of Providence in his history of America, but speaking instead of 'chance' and 'fortune'. He reflects ruefully on the phenomenon of 'a Christian divine writing a history with so little of Christianity in it'; adding, 'he seems studiously to avoid saying anything which might imply that he believes the Bible'.[71] We have already noted Wesley's vituperative comments about Hume.

Conscience, however, is pivotal in his thought, though he argues for the eccentric notion that conscience is not truly 'natural', though found in all people, but is in each individual a supernatural gift of prevenient or 'preventing' grace. It is the witness of the Holy Spirit within and therefore cannot be a property of fallen humanity. Conscience is to be obeyed at all times, provided its promptings are checked against Scripture. A scrupulous conscience is pathological.[72]

Wesley has his own version of the threefold use of biblical law: to convict, to convert and to sustain – all within and following justification by faith – or, as he puts it, to kill, to revive and to keep

[68]Jones, *Wesley's Conception and Use of Scripture*, pp. 81–3, 63.

[69]Outler in Wesley, *Works*, vol. 1, p. 74.

[70]Wesley, *Works*, vol. 23, pp. 120–1. Wesley did Robertson a injustice; the providential framework is implicit in his history of America and explicit in his history of Charles V: see Smitten, 'William Robertson'.

[71]Ibid., pp. 213–14 (*Journal*, 1781).

[72]Ibid., vol. 3, pp. 482–8 (Sermon 105).

alive. In other words, Wesley has the third use of the law, to guide, to restrain and to direct the believer in their Christian life. In this respect, he stands with the post-Luther Protestant traditions, that is to say the Reformed, English Puritan and High Church Anglican traditions, and not with Luther himself.[73]

With Pope's epitaph for Newton, quoted above ('Nature and Nature's laws lay hid in night.' God said, 'Let Newton be! and all was light'),[74] we should compare Charles Wesley's Pentecost hymn 'Come, Holy Ghost, our hearts inspire':

Expand thy wings, celestial Dove,
brood o'er our nature's night;
on our disordered spirits move,
and let there now be light.

The Holy Spirit, not the Spirit's human instrument, is invoked in the beautiful image of the dove 'expanding' its wings in a sheltering, embracing, self-giving motion. Nature here is not the ordered, mechanical cosmic system of Isaac Newton, but fallen human nature in the state of chaos depicted in Genesis 1.2 ('And the earth was without form and void; and darkness was upon the face of the deep. And the Spirit of God moved upon the face of the waters,' KJB). It is light upon the human soul in all its hidden depths that the Spirit is asked to bestow. This is a truly evangelical enlightenment.

Joseph Butler

Joseph Butler (1692–1752) is one of the greatest and most seminal of Anglican theologians – second in stature and influence only to Richard Hooker. Butler stands supreme among the divines of the Anglican Enlightenment and helped to shape the Scottish Enlightenment too: Hume, Kames, Reid and Adam Smith all acknowledge a debt to Butler.[75] He shaped the mind of the Oxford Movement, especially Keble, Newman and Gladstone, more than

---

[73]Ibid., vol. 2, pp. 15–16 (see Sermons 34–6).
[74]Pope, *Poetical Works*, p. 371.
[75]Tennant, *Conscience, Consciousness and Ethics*, p. 5.

any other thinker.[76] 'The greatest name in the Anglican Church,' was Newman's tribute. Newman's thought, in his Roman Catholic as well as in his Anglican phase, owed much to Butler, though Newman came to renounce Butler's most distinctive doctrine, that of probability as the guide to life and truth. W. E. Gladstone applied his mighty intellect to the study of Butler and edited an edition of his works. Gladstone regarded Butler's argument in *The Analogy of Religion, Natural and Revealed to the Constitution and Course of Nature* as among the masterpieces of the human mind and as unfolding the entire revealed method of God's dealing with God's creatures.[77] The biblical scholar and Butler's later successor as Bishop of Durham, J. B. Lightfoot, regarded Butler as the greatest of the Bishops of Durham and the *Analogy* as the greatest work of English theology; he chose to preach on Butler at his own enthronement in 1879.[78] For Henry Phillpotts, who succeeded Butler in his Durham parish and later became a redoubtable Bishop of Exeter, Butler was 'the greatest of uninspired men,' that is the greatest outside the biblical canon.[79] The *Analogy* went through about a hundred editions in the nineteenth century, which is striking when we consider that its original occasion, the intellectual battle with deism was long over.[80] Butler has not only appealed to Anglicans: great figures within the British Dissenting

---

[76]So Church, 'Bishop Butler', in *Pascal and Other Sermons*, p. 25. See also generally Downey, *Eighteenth-Century Pulpit*, pp. 30–57.

[77]Gladstone, *Studies Subsidiary*, p. 9. For an account of the contemporary reception of Gladstone's advocacy of Butler, see Garnett, 'Butler and the *Zeitgeist*'. References to the *Analogy*, the *Dissertations* and the fifteen sermons from the Rolls Chapel are to Butler, *The Analogy of Religion, Natural and Revealed to the Constitution and Course of Nature, to which are added, Two Brief Dissertations: On Personal Identity, and on The Nature of Virtue; and Fifteen Sermons*. References to this edition of most of Butler's works are placed in my main text and show page; A = *Analogy*, with part and chapter; S = *Sermons*; D = *Dissertations*. References to the *Six Sermons*, the meeting with Wesley and the correspondence with Samuel Clarke are to W. E. Gladstone's edition of Butler's *Works* (1896). Gladstone's edition is flawed because he took it upon himself to restructure the paragraphing and to supply subheadings to make the argument clearer. I have not had convenient access to the edition edited by J. H. Bernard (1900).

[78]Lightfoot, 'Joseph Butler', in *Leaders of the Northern Church*, p. 161.

[79]Henson, 'Joseph Butler, 1692–1752', *Bishoprick Papers*, p. 146.

[80]For Butler's subsequent reputation and influence see Mossner, *Bishop Butler*, chs. VII and VIII.

tradition have also acknowledged a debt to him. Thomas Chalmers said that Butler made him a Christian. Alexander Whyte's tributes are fulsome. Yet who, apart perhaps from academic ethicists, reads Butler today?

The son of a Dissenting tradesman, Butler, became the confidant and protegé of Queen Caroline, the consort of King George II. Appointed to the wealthiest living in the Church of England, Stanhope, County Durham, which sat on a coal seam, Butler dutifully resided in his parish, before being appointed first as Bishop of Bristol, a poor, under-endowed see and then – from one extreme to the other – as Bishop of Durham, the grandest see in the Church after Canterbury and 'the very synonym of prelacy at its proudest,' as Hensley Henson, one of Butler's successors at Durham, called it.[81] But it mattered not to Butler whether he enjoyed wealth or endured poverty. When he had resources at his disposal, he combined munificent charity with personal austerity (and 'proud' is the last word one would use of Butler). We know little about his personal life; his writings are the best window into this rare soul. The second-generation Tractarian R. W. Church said of Butler that, like the elusive author of the *Imitation of Christ*, 'the man is lost in his mind and writings, and in those deep and solemn thoughts, the clear, calm utterance of which it was given him to unfold to us'.[82] One picture that has come down to us is of Bishop Butler riding on a small black pony around Durham and its environs – at top speed to escape the swarm of beggars who waited for him to emerge from his palace.

Butler came on the scene at a time when Christianity was being attacked both by sophisticated thinkers, including the more militant deists, and by vulgar scoffers, including fashionable hedonists. In his Charge to the Durham clergy, he lamented the decline of serious religion and the increasing numbers of Christianity's enemies and their growing boldness. Though, like Dr Johnson, given to melancholy, Butler insisted that a Christian should never despair.[83] Butler knew his limitations: it was said that he declined

---

[81]Ibid., p. 142.
[82]Church, 'Bishop Butler', p. 47.
[83]Joseph Butler, *Charge Delivered to the Clergy*, pp. 5–6. Butler's favourite themes of probability and the practical nature of religion recur in the *Charge*, pp. 9, 13. The *Charge* is also included in Butler, *Works*, vol. 2.

Canterbury on the grounds that it was too late to save a falling church. But through his writings he infused Anglican theology with fresh spiritual and moral power. Cometh the hour, cometh the man.[84]

Butler's quality of mind

Butler is generally recognized as the most thoughtful, reflective and discerning of English theologians and moralists, with an unrivalled power of awakening thoughtfulness in the reader. The sermons and the *Analogy* manifest identical moral and intellectual qualities; they are patently the work of a single mind, and a mind of the rarest quality. These writings, says Alexander Whyte, reveal 'the same profound thoughtfulness, the same deep seriousness, the same sober-mindedness, the same intellectual and moral humility, the same scrupulous truthfulness, the same fairness to opponents, the same immediate and unquestioning submission to the will of God, and the same subordination of everything to the sovereignty of conscience'.[85]

It is a measure of the esteem in which Butler was held that Hume tried (in vain) to obtain his advice on the manuscript of his first book, *A Treatise of Human Nature* (1739–40), removing the section on miracles so as not to offend the bishop. Butler would have endorsed Hume's contention, in what became his essay 'Of Miracles,' that 'a wise man . . . proportions his belief to the evidence' and his stress on probability, but would have taken offence at his snide conclusion that Christianity 'not only was at first attended with miracles, but even at this day cannot be believed by any reasonable person without one', so that a person who has faith is conscious of a miracle within himself 'which subverts all the principles of his understanding, and gives him a determination to believe what is most contrary to custom and experience.'[86] Hume's writings on religion engage with Butler's arguments and evince respect for them. (The common identification of the character Cleanthes in

---

[84]For further reflections on this theme, see Avis, *Identity of Anglicanism*, ch. XI, 'Anglicanism in Memory and Hope'.
[85]Whyte, *Thirteen Appreciations*, p. 255.
[86]Hume, *Essays*, pp. 520–1, 544.

Hume's *Dialogues Concerning Natural Religion* with Butler has been challenged.)[87]

Our concern is not to assess whether Butler's philosophical and theological arguments are valid – many others, noted in the references, have done that – but to seek to discern his method and the light that it sheds on questions of authority in theology. Our focus is, therefore, on the *Analogy* and on the sermons only in so far as they shed light on Butler's theological method and not for their theological or ethical theory itself.[88] It is worth noting R. W. Church's comment that 'There is as much to be learned from Bishop Butler's tone and manner as there is from the substance of his reasonings.' What appealed to Dean Church was Butler's readiness to understate his case (not to pressurize his auditors), to state things with care, not claiming too much, but only as much as he needed to secure his argument; the sense of 'strength in reserve'.[89] Penelhum has pointed to Butler's 'deep suspicion of quick theoretical victories'.[90] Unlike Dr Johnson, Butler was not interested in 'arguing for victory'[91]; his calling was not to debate theories, but to fashion Christ-like lives.

Butler's theological method

Gladstone's view, which I share, was that Butler's method was the most significant aspect of his work.[92] Butler's method in the *Analogy* is characteristic of his age, the 'experimental' method, empirical and inductive. Immediately prior to the *Analogy* George (soon to be Bishop), Berkeley had adopted the same empirical method in his hard-hitting work of apologetics *Alciphron* (1732), which was cast in the form of Platonic dialogues.[93] The object of this method, in Butler's hands, is not the physical cosmos that could be known by observation and experiment, but the human spirit. Butler shares

[87]Hume, *Dialogues Concerning Natural Religion*; Jeffner, *Butler and Hume*; Mossner, *Bishop Butler*.
[88]For an analysis of Butler's ethical theory see Broad, *Five Types*, ch. 3; and Cunliffe (ed.), *Butler's Moral and Religious Thought*, passim.
[89]Church, *Pascal and Other Sermons*, pp. 27, 30–1.
[90]Penelhum, *Butler*, p. 3.
[91]Boswell, *Life of Johnson*, pp. 421, 734, 1150.
[92]Gladstone, *Studies Subsidiary*, pp. 1–15.
[93]Berkeley, *Works*, vol. 3.

William Law's unnerving insight into the dimmer recesses of human nature with its many moral subterfuges. Butler distinguishes two possible methods: enquiry into 'the abstract relations of things', on the one hand, which he eschews, and starting from matters of fact, the 'nature of man' and the human constitution, on the other (p. 371, S), which he adopts. The scope of Butler's enquiry according to this chosen method includes beliefs (theism, deism), behaviours (benevolence), moral intuitions (conscience, reflection) and emotions (passions, sentiments). He elicits certain key insights from what he finds and draws consequences from them that have the potential to convert, to transform lives. Butler's method is conducive to a certain temper of mind and cast of thought that is ethical as much as intellectual. A modern successor in the See of Durham, Ian Ramsey, suggested that what Butler was driving at was twofold: 'a fuller discernment' and 'a total commitment'. Like Butler, Ian Ramsey had an apologetic intent – not as with Butler, in the face of deistic critics of credal Christianity, but vis-à-vis the logical positivist philosophy of language that excluded any transcendent reference. Ramsey too looked for analogies from 'ordinary' life, analogies that offered moments of discernment, flashes of insight, into something transcendent, the unseen, that teaches us that there is more to life than meets the eye.[94] The method of these two bishops of Durham is comparable, though the context is hugely different. Both have a limited aim: to prize open a space for a richer, more adequate view of the world, one that does justice to the deeper aspects of experience. They are saying, 'Consider that there may be more to consider.' But Butler touches the God-nerve with unerring aim.

Butler transcends his contemporary intellectual worldview and looks on it with critical detachment, especially morally. He notes ironically 'a wonderful frugality' in everything related to religion and 'extravagance in every thing else'.[95] Although Butler works out of the dominantly Scottish moral sense school of philosophy, which includes Hutcheson, Adam Smith and Adam Ferguson, he lifts the analysis of moral experience and of conscience to a new level. If Newton applies the experimental method to the natural world, Locke to human experience and Hume to our cognitive ability, Butler deploys it in an introspective analysis of our ethical

---

[94]Ramsey, *Religious Language*, ch. 1.
[95]Butler, *Charge Delivered to the Clergy*, p. 17.

nature and moral experience and extrapolates from that to theological truths. As Henson puts it, 'Butler's argument advances cautiously from the known to unknown, and rests at every point on the firm ground of experience. Reason and common sense are his pilot stars.'[96] Both Butler and Hume reject Hobbes' jaundiced assessment of human motivation that it is driven solely by fear and egotism. Butler finds 'benevolence' in the human heart (though he does not underestimate the power of self-love) and Hume speaks of 'sympathy', 'humanity,' and 'benevolence'.

Both Butler and Hume acknowledge what Hume calls 'the authority of experience'.[97] But while Hume is concerned to undermine easy confidence in drawing analogies from experience, Butler has no such scruples: his major work obviously presupposes the reliability of experience and of nature and the consistency of revelation with natural theology: they both have the 'same author and cause' (p. 75, A, Introduction). Butler's sermons as well as his major work are pervaded by arguments from analogy, the *Analogy of Religion* being a development and refinement of the method first essayed in the sermons. Butler and Hume found the expression 'the analogy of nature' (*naturae analogia*) in Newton.[98] But the measure of Butler's distance from Newton is his sense of the wonderful intimacy of the presence of God to the human spirit, especially in the conscience.

Butler does not offer knock-down logical proof (demonstrative reasoning), but frankly acknowledges that his arguments are cumulative (p. 72, A, Introduction). Cumulative, converging probabilities reveal an underlying pattern in the way that the world and human life are constituted, a pattern that is open to God's activity and particularly to divine revelation.

Reason in Butler

Mossner comments that the Age of Reason 'alternately created and destroyed its religion by the same rational means'.[99] Accordingly, Butler fights reason with reason: the defective, sometimes profane

---

[96]Henson, *Bishoprick Papers*, p. 153.
[97]Cited Jeffner, *Butler and Hume*, p. 42.
[98]Ibid., p. 60.
[99]Mossner, *Bishop Butler*, p. xiii.

reason of the deists with the holy, scriptural reason of orthodox theology. Butler's concept of reason shows affinities with Locke's theory of knowledge, but since it is not his purpose to adumbrate a cognitive theory for its own sake, he does not provide enough evidence for a comprehensive assessment of his debt to Locke's philosophy, though the concept of probability is one that they have in common.

Butler establishes common ground with the deists with regard to the scope of reason. He is clear that reason is 'the only faculty we have wherewith to judge concerning anything, even revelation itself' (p. 219, A). And he insists that 'reason can, and it ought to judge, not only of the meaning, but also of the morality and the evidence of revelation.' First, '[i]t is the province of reason to judge of the morality of the scripture . . . whether it contains things plainly contradictory to wisdom, justice, or goodness; to what the light of nature teaches us of God.' Secondly, '[r]eason is able to judge, and must, of the evidence of revelation, and of the objections urged against that evidence' (pp. 229–31, A). Daniel Whitby, a Latitudinarian, had already written (in 1714) of reason (albeit 'feeble reason') as 'the only faculty which God hath given you, whereby to judge of truth and falsehood, or of the sense of his revealed words' and Whichcote had said much the same.[100]

There is no polarization of revelation and reason in Butler; both are from God: 'all knowledge from reason is as really from God as revelation is'.[101] Butler's is a critical reason; its role is discriminatory, even judicial; its task is to assess the evidence. But it knows its limitations, it serves an overriding moral purpose, and it has the capacity to apprehend transcendent truth. Under the steadily advancing influence of Locke's empiricism, however, a more restricted, less elevated conception of reason began to prevail, one that was diffident about transcendental aspirations.

Butler has been accused of a lack of imagination; in fact, he constantly disparages 'imagination'. Bagehot alleged that Butler lacked the power to envisage the scenarios that he describes, that he wanted the power of delineation. According to Bagehot, the aesthetic dimension is absent, and the moral is total. Although he acknowledges that Butler holds that humans seek happiness in all things and that God desires happiness for his children, Bagehot

---

[100]Whitby, *Dissuasive from Enquiring*, pp. 6–7.
[101]Butler, *Works*, vol. 2, p. 285 (Sermon 1 of the *Six Sermons*).

insists that such happiness for Butler comes from doing right, not from pleasure in what is beautiful and that his religion is at root one of fear not one of enjoyment. 'No one could tell from his writings that the universe was beautiful.'[102] Gladstone and Whyte defend Butler against Bagehot here. It is true, admits Whyte, that Butler 'does not take time in his high argument to describe dramatically and dilate eloquently on the vast visions that pass before his heaven-soaring mind. His imagination does not come out in purple patches on his pages'. But again and again, Whyte suggests, Butler invites the reader to enter a new imaginative space: 'suppose, suppose, suppose'. Indeed, what Butler attacks as 'imagination' is not the imagination that we associate with Blake, Coleridge and other Romantics, but a self-indulgent, morally irresponsible fantasizing about life, a lack of truthfulness with regard to the nature of this world and an unwillingness to face reality, what Gladstone defined as errors of 'unbridled fancy and caprice; of unbalanced, ill-regulated judgement'.[103] R. W. Church has no hesitation in finding 'touches of imagination and feeling', which partly because they are rare, give us 'a momentary glimpse . . . into the depths of a great mind.'[104] Butler's thought is by no means as dry; granted, he is measured, cautious, restrained and cerebral; but there are explicit intimations of ideas and experiences that we tend to associate with Romanticism: feeling, sensibility, humanity, the heart and compassion. He often speaks of beauty and his God is a God of 'grace and beauty' (p. 527, S).[105]

In Butler's thought, the Christian revelation presupposes and builds on our natural knowledge of God. Christianity is, first, a 'republication' of 'natural or essential religion' for civilized humanity and gives it institutional embodiment; second, it brings a new dispensation of things hidden from human reason and adds a number of positive precepts to it: 'For though natural religion is the foundation and principal part of Christianity, it is not in any sense the whole of it' (p. 195, A). 'The Law of Moses then, and the Gospel of Christ, are authoritative publications of the religion of nature' (p. 197, A). Revelation must be consonant with natural religion. Any interpretation of a biblical text that clashes explicitly with natural

---

[102]Bagehot, 'Bishop Butler' (1854), in *Literary Studies*, vol. 3, pp. 127, 115.
[103]Whyte, *Thirteen Appreciations*, pp. 266–9; Gladstone, *Studies Subsidiary*, p. 93.
[104]Church, *Pascal and Other Sermons*, p. 41.
[105]Cf. Gladstone, *Studies Subsidiary*, p. 94.

religion cannot be correct. On the other hand, Scripture can teach matters that are unknown to natural religion (p. 210, A). Before we can even consider revealed doctrine, centred on redemption through Christ, 'we must presuppose that the world is under the proper moral government of God', that there is a religious basis to the world (p. 240, A).

Butler's argument is imbued with scriptural truth. He very rarely refers to Christian theologians. He exhibits no explicit debt to either the Anglican Reformers or the seventeenth-century divines. His handling of Scripture shows his characteristic reverence, humility and submission towards its divine author and a desire to inculcate those qualities in the reader. Like a divine of the old school, he *applies* the Scriptures to the heart, mind and conscience of his auditors as the Word of God to them. But though he speaks eloquently of the fact, the reality, of divine revelation, when it comes to giving an account of the content of revelation, Butler falters. He is not ashamed to confess that Scripture does not explain how Christ's sacrifice is redemptive (p. 252, A). And Butler seems almost oblivious of the pioneering developments in critical biblical study being made by Richard Bentley, Robert Lowth, Thomas Newton and John Heylyn.[106] The second, more doctrinal part of the *Analogy* lacks the fluency of the first part and is somewhat laboured in parts. As a philosophical and ethical apologist, Butler is in his element; as an expositor of the doctrinal substance of revelation, he struggles. Yet, as a recent symposium has convincingly argued, apologetics has integrity when it is imbued with the very heart of the Christian faith, rather than skirting around the edges of it, when it confesses the faith in an attractive and persuasive way, hooking on to the points either of trust or of anxiety in the prevailing culture.[107]

Butler and Wesley

Two of the most gifted churchmen of the century met and clashed on 16 and 18 August 1739.[108] Butler, Bishop of Bristol, was

---

[106]Tennant, *Conscience, Consciousness and Ethics*, p. 6.
[107]Davison (ed.), *Imaginative Apologetics*. See Avis, 'Apologetics and the Rebirth of the Imagination'.
[108]Butler, *Works*, vol. 2, pp. 434–7; Tennant, *Conscience, Consciousness and Ethics*, pp. 130–40; Rack, *Reasonable Enthusiast*, p. 209.

provoked by John Wesley's field preaching in his diocese, which at that time included Dorset. The exchange gave rise to Butler's most famous utterance: 'Sir, the pretending to extraordinary revelations and gifts of the Holy Ghost is a horrid thing, a very horrid thing,' which was elicited by George Whitefield's claim that there were promises yet to be fulfilled in him, which to Butler savoured of 'enthusiasm', the claim to experience direct divine inspiration. Locke had attacked 'enthusiasm' as 'rising from the conceits of a warmed or overweening brain' and persuading us that what we are inclined to do comes as a commission from heaven.[109] Johnson defined 'enthusiasm' in his *Dictionary* as 'A vain belief of private revelation; a vain confidence of divine favour or communication' – which is spot on in this case. Butler had read Whitefield's *Journals*, there had been an exchange of letters, and Butler made a donation to Whitefield's orphanage. Whitefield was a phenomenon that could not be ignored, 'the most controversial preacher of the eighteenth century, and perhaps the greatest extemporaneous orator in the history of the English church'.[110] Wesley rather disingenuously distanced himself from Whitefield's delusions of spiritual grandeur, though he himself was given to language reminiscent of the Christ of the Fourth Gospel, speaking about the work that he had come into the world to perform. Butler – reserved, introvert, cautious, deep – was the antithesis, in character, of Wesley and Whitefield. He was not an inspiring leader, as John Wesley was, or an excitable demagogue like Whitefield, but a profound thinker and a skilled physician of the soul. The chemistry between Butler and Wesley was impossible. Whyte takes Wesley's report of their meeting as 'absolutely conclusive as to Butler's utter lack of sympathy with apostolic and evangelical preaching'. The most serious complaint, according to Whyte, that has been lodged against Butler, is 'his extraordinary *deficiency in apostolical and evangelical truth*', evinced by his 'emasculated and meagre gospel'.[111] There is little point in denying Butler's limited appreciation of the Puritan approach to preaching, with its emphasis on bringing about

---

[109]Locke, *Essay Concerning Human Understanding*, pp. 288–96, at p. 290 (IV, xix, 6–7).
[110]Downey, *Eighteenth-Century Pulpit*, p. 155.
[111]Whyte, *Thirteen Appreciations*, pp. 278–80. Thomas Chalmers, notably, attacked Butler for this.

justification felt on the pulse, which was shared by Wesley and Whyte. Butler, however, was an evangelist in his own way and just as effective and influential as Wesley: he evangelized the minds of generations to come. The failure of mutual comprehension in this ill-fated interview has a tragic quality. Henson comments: 'The two best Christians of the age met only to part in anger.'[112]

Probability our guide

The first sentence of the *Analogy* is decisive for Butler's whole approach: 'Probable evidence is essentially distinguished from demonstrative by this, that it admits of degrees . . . from the highest moral certainty, to the very lowest presumption' (p. 72, A, Introduction). Butler's teaching on probability has been the most seminal of all his ideas. As a precocious schoolboy, Butler engaged the eminent (and heterodox) Dr Samuel Clarke in correspondence. He had, Butler confessed, since he was first able to reason, sought for demonstrative proof of divine truth, natural and revealed, but had found only 'very probable arguments'.[113]

Butler was not the first to develop a theology of probability. Bishop Wilkins has similar arguments and there are parallels with Tillotson – the 'wager'. Butler was familiar with Pascal's *Pensées*.[114]

Butler is paraphrasing Locke when in *The Analogy* he lays it down that 'probability is the very guide of life' and that the assurance it provides, though limited, is appropriate to 'the very condition of our being' in our earthly state of moral probation (pp. 73, 315, A). The sermons also stress 'the frailty of this mortal state we are passing through' (p. 442, S), and Butler often refers to 'such a world as this' (p. 507, S) and 'so imperfect a creature as man in this mortal state we are passing through' (p. 513, S). He is not concerned with probability in the logical, but in the moral sense, inseparably connected to his doctrine of probation: this life is a preparation and a testing for the life to come. Butler also derives the link between probability and analogy from Locke: it is analogy

---

[112]Henson, *Bishoprick Papers*, p. 148.
[113]The correspondence is included in Butler, *Works*, vol. 1, pp. 413–35; this quote p. 414.
[114]Barker, *Strange Contrarieties*.

that makes probability feasible. But he deploys probability in a way that owes more to Pascal than to Locke (though Butler's premises are not the same as Pascal's): if we are prudent, even a slight degree of probability demands that we act upon it; to ignore it is to deny 'the very condition of our being' (p. 274, A; p. 312, A; p. 315, A).[115] We should reflect that the perplexities that attend religious faith are part of our probation. Our testing in this mortal life includes the fact that we cannot be completely sure of truth and lack answers to all our questions. How do we respond to uncertainty? (p. 269, A). The notion of probation is integral to the religious outlook (p. 273, A). Butler's pervasive moral concern and his use of the doctrine of probation (this mortal life is a test and a preparation for the next) help to lift his work to a level well above the normal rational apologetics. And, as Scott Holland pointed out in 1908, Butler's idea of probability is not, as might appear, an attempt to settle upon the lowest common denominator in the argument with deism, but rather to find the highest common factor. It is not a negative argument but a positive one, for, to Butler's mind, probability is moral conviction, sufficient to act upon.[116]

The moral dimension

Leslie Stephen suggested that Butler's 'deep more earnestness' was his 'great claim upon our respect'.[117]

For Butler, conscience is supreme among the components of the human mind.[118] Butler speaks out of his own profound sense of moral obligation. He feels the claim of right and duty pressing upon him and understands it as the voice of God. Butler finds conscience a major theme of the Bible, which 'treats chiefly of our behaviour towards God and our own consciences'.[119] Stephen aptly refers to the 'deification' of conscience in Butler.[120]

---

[115]Penelhum, 'Butler and Human Ignorance', pp. 124–5; cf. id., *Butler*, ch. 4.
[116]Holland, *Optimism of Butler's 'Analogy'*.
[117]Stephen, *History of English Thought*, vol. 1, p. 235.
[118]Tennant, *Conscience, Consciousness and Ethics*, p. 218, claims that Butler's 'central thesis' in his ethics is that conscience begets consciousness, so that the human mind is compelled to 'interpret and negotiate everything ethically'.
[119]Butler, *Works*, vol. 2, p. 318 (Sermon 3 of the *Six Sermons*).
[120]Stephen, *History of English Thought*, vol. 1, p. 258.

Butler disdains the frivolity of the fashionable world and is disgusted by the superficiality and falseness of the lives he had known at court and in London. Preaching in the capital, he insists that slaves on the plantations and native peoples are children of God for whom Christ died and who should share in the ministrations of grace – though he does not directly condemn slavery.[121] In his *Charge* to the clergy of the Durham Diocese (1751), he laments the decay of religion.[122] Butler assimilates the reason to the conscience or moral sense and uses interchangeable language about them. Vicious passions darken the mental light, 'that *candle of the Lord within*, which is to direct our steps' and corrupt the conscience 'which is the guide of life' (p. 484, S). In Butler, though not in Hutcheson or Hume, the moral sense is intimately related to reason: it is not merely an emotional reflex. For Hume, the passions are dominant, but for Butler reason can rule them. The aim of the *Analogy* is to lead good, sincere theists and open-minded doubters to practise Christianity. Practice creates mental habit – here Butler draws on Aristotle and Aquinas – leading to the formation of character.

Butler's view of conscience is affected by the prevailing uniformitarianism of the age. The deliverances of conscience are the same for all people at all times. There is a 'universally acknowledged standard of virtue'. Butler defines this universal standard as justice, truthfulness and concern for the common good. But it seems to me that his theory could accommodate the idea that perceptions of justice and the common good vary from culture to culture: the peoples of Mexico before the Spanish conquest believed that daily human sacrifice was necessary for the common good and that the victims, captured from another tribe, were getting their just deserts – otherwise the sun might not rise tomorrow. It was an ethical imperative, though a hideously distorted one.[123]

For Butler, moral experience is the strongest evidence for God, bringing not only conviction but motivation. 'The proper motives to religion are the proper proofs of it from our moral nature, from the presages of conscience, and our natural apprehension of God

---

[121]Butler, *Works*, vol. 2, pp. 286–7 (Sermon 1 of the *Six Sermons*).
[122]Butler, *Charge Delivered to the Clergy*.
[123]Butler, *Dissertation 2*, '*On the Nature of Virtue*'. Cf. Hebblethwaite, 'Butler on Conscience and Virtue', pp. 199–200.

under the character of a righteous Governor and Judge; a nature and conscience and apprehension given us by him' and confirmed by reason (pp. 191–2, A).

Conscience wields authority: we cannot think of conscience without thinking of direction, judgement and supervision; to preside and govern are concepts internal to the notion of conscience. To follow the dictates of conscience is to follow the law of our nature; to flout conscience is to go against the law of our nature. When we consider what makes for human flourishing, it is clear that virtue is natural and vice unnatural. Conscience is there to be followed and to do so is to go with the grain of our nature, though sometimes our passions get the better of conscience (Preface and Sermon 2). Conscience, or the principle of reflection, is integral to our nature and constitution; without it we lack the organizing principle that is essential to a sense of identity.[124]

Respect for the consciences of Dissenters was Butler's motive for insisting that the establishment of the Church of England should be reasonable, defensible and on a basis of toleration. A religious establishment without toleration for those who cannot in conscience conform is 'a general tyranny; because it claims absolute authority over conscience'. This is how despotism, a wider tyranny, begins. The Roman Catholic Church fails to respect conscience because it enforces its decrees, where it can, with persecution, instead of 'reasonable conviction'.[125]

The moral element and the emphasis on the authority of conscience – the idea that the practice of a faithful Christian life validates the belief on which it is based – are found equally strongly in the High Churchmen and the Nonjurors, with whom, however, it is united not so much with reason but with tradition and the authority of the Church. 'You will not be able, by all the strength of reason,' declared Bishop Wilson of Sodor and Man (later much admired by the Tractarians) 'to subdue one lust, or support your mind under any great affliction.'[126] But we are reminded not to play off the High Churchmen against the rational theologians with whom they shared the spirit of the age, when we also read in Wilson's *Maxims*: 'The mysteries of Christ are above our reason;

---

[124]See Darwall, 'Conscience as Self-Authorizing'.
[125]Butler, *Works*, vol. 2, pp. 365–9 (Sermon 5 of the *Six Sermons*).
[126]Wilson, *Maxims of Piety*, p. 119.

but we believe them, because we have all the proofs necessary to convince any reasonable man that God has revealed them as certain truths.'[127]

Butler's realism

'How *real* he is,' said R. W. Church, pointing out how difficult that is to achieve.[128] Butler's realism is summed up in the phrase, repeated in various permutations, 'Everything is what it is, and not another thing' (p. 383, S, Preface). 'Things and actions are what they are, and the consequences of them will be what they will be: why then should we desire to be deceived?' (p. 452, S). 'Either there is a difference between right and wrong, or there is not: religion is true, or it is not' (p. 483, S 10, 'Upon Self-deceit'). Butler is watchful against self-deception, in himself and in the reader. He teaches us not to rush to judgement, to be willing to wait on truth, to learn and to exercise progressive discernment. Butler had dedicated himself from his youth to the pursuit of truth. His two great questions are: what is due to truth and what is the rule of life? (p. 370, S).

A notable aspect of Butler's clear-eyed truthfulness about what is the case is his realism about the human moral condition and intellectual limitations. Although he directly attacks Hobbes' cynicism about human motivation (S 5 and 6 'Upon Compassion', especially pp. 425–7, and S 11 and 12, 'Upon the Love of our Neighbour'), he is a realist about the role of 'cool self-love' in our makeup; it 'belongs to man as a reasonable creature reflecting upon his own interest or happiness' (p. 485, S). While he insists on the place of benevolence, his assessment of human nature is not rose-tinted. Acknowledging that 'nothing can be of consequence to mankind or any creature, but happiness' (pp. 508–9, S), Butler believes that happiness comes not by following the demands of self-love, but by fulfilling the requirements of virtue (e.g. S 2). He also makes capital out of the limitations of human knowledge, giving greater moral profundity to what Locke had already said. Whyte says of Butler's sermon 'On the Ignorance of Man': 'Nowhere else, in such short space, do Butler's immense depth of mind; his

---

[127]Ibid.
[128]Church, *Pascal and Other Sermons*, p. 28.

constitutional seriousness of mind, even to melancholy; his humility and his wisdom, all come out, and all at their best.'[129]

Butler's emphasis on the limitations of our condition, especially on our human ignorance of the wider purposes of the universe, relates to his notions of reason, probability, method and conscience. In Butler this approach does not point towards scepticism, but rather towards humility and receptivity (as it does in Locke, to whom his debt is clear). As Penelhum points out, Butler's emphasis on the cognitive limitations of our condition owes nothing directly (unlike Pascal's) to the sceptical tradition.[130] Butler makes explicit what is implied in Locke, that our ignorance is part of a providential dispensation, and it has a purpose in the plan of God, a purpose for our good. We are unfit to judge as to when and how God would reveal himself to humankind and what that revelation would or would not include. Acknowledging our ignorance, accepting probability and therefore the need for prudential action and behaviour are religious dispositions. In Newman's hands, Butler's basic approach became exaggerated and unbalanced, with sceptical and fideistic results, when he gave a blank cheque to papal authority in 1845 (later qualified). Mossner claimed that a 'general defect' of the *Analogy* is 'its unpremeditated though implicit skepticism': I would rather say, intellectual humility.[131]

Butler as apologist[132]

In the *Analogy*, Butler is addressing those who already believe in a Creator and in divine providence, but do not accept special revelation in Scripture and for whose faith Jesus Christ, human and divine, is not significant – the deists. He shares the foundation

---

[129]Whyte, *Thirteen Appreciations*, p. 252.

[130]Penelhum, 'Butler and Human Ignorance', p. 118.

[131]Mossner, *Bishop Butler*, p. 103. On the oft-repeated claim that William Pitt the Younger and James Mill suggested that Butler's method, with its stress on human ignorance and on probability, raised more problems than it solved, see Gladstone, *Studies Subsidiary*, pp. 30–3.

[132]In addition to Mossner and Jeffner, see David Brown, 'Butler and Deism', in Cunliffe (ed.), *Butler's Moral and Religious Thought*, and for the wider context Sykes, *Church and State in England*. For a survey of deistic literature and Butler's response see Stephen, *History of English Thought*, vol. 1.

tenet of the deists, the identification of reason and nature, while suggesting that our knowledge of what is natural will be enlarged in proportion to our greater knowledge of the works of God and of God's providence (p. 97, A). 'Nature' provides Butler with a basis for his use of analogy because it means what is 'similar, stated, or uniform' (p. 98, A).

Tennant suggests that, rather than attempting to crush the deists, Butler was sympathetic towards them and was attempting to build bridges and to create a consensus by showing that all human knowledge rests on probability.[133] Stephen suggests that the rational Protestant could meet the deist halfway.[134] It is true that Butler's approach is conciliatory, moderate and disarming, but he was not drawn to the remote, transcendent, uninvolved God of the deists. For him God is 'more intimately present to us than anything else can be' and our relationship with him is closer than with any creature (p. 384, S, Preface). We enjoy 'an habitual sense of God's presence with us' and this is to '*walk with God*' (p. 523, S, 'Upon the Love of God'). It is no doubt Butler's sense of the nearness of God that impels him to reach out persuasively to those whose beliefs preclude their sharing this assurance.

However, the superstructure of Butler's apologetic is barely relevant today: we could not use his specific arguments. As Basil Mitchell points out, vast cultural shifts separate us from him – the whole phenomenon of modernity, beginning with Romanticism.[135] Butler's operative distinction between natural and revealed knowledge of God, though it runs through the Christian tradition, has faded in modern thought. Apologetics today cannot presuppose belief in a Creator and providential governor of the world, as Butler was able to do (p. 76, A, Introduction). Our situation and starting point are other than Butler's.

However, Butler's overall approach, if not all his arguments, in the face of unbelief, retains its validity. First, Mitchell suggests that Butler's independence of mind, his refusal to accept uncritically certain assumptions in the prevailing culture, and his confidence in the resources of Christian theology to respond convincingly to its critics, are a model for theologians and apologists today.

---

[133]Tennant, *Conscience, Consciousness and Ethics*, pp. 3–4, 7, 15.
[134]Stephen, *History of English Thought*, vol. 1, p. 75.
[135]Mitchell, 'Butler as a Christian Apologist'.

Second, Butler's minimal aim is to show that religion is not 'a subject of ridicule'. He aims to get Christianity taken seriously. His words in the 'Advertisement' to the first edition of the *Analogy* are famous: 'It is come, I know not how, to be taken for granted, by many persons, that Christianity is not so much as a subject of inquiry; but that it is, now at length, discovered to be fictitious . . . a principal subject of mirth and ridicule . . . for its having so long interrupted the pleasures of the world' (p. 37). He crushes those who scoff and think themselves superior to 'the foolishness of God'. He is said to have silenced the deists: there were no replies to the *Analogy* in the eighteenth century. Like Hooker, Butler was definitive and unanswerable.

Third, while Butler's comprehensive assimilation of biblical revelation to natural religion is dangerous even as an apologetic tactic – no modern theologian, post-Kierkegaard, post-Barth, would adopt that gambit – he is surely right to insist that talk of the revelation and redemption in Jesus Christ makes no sense unless we have already established that there is a Creator and moral governor of the world. The *praeparatio euangelica* remains a vital dimension of apologetics.

Fourth, as C. D. Broad suggested, one of Butler's great merits – one that makes him stand out among philosophers and theologians as a tribe – was to have claimed no more than probability for his conclusions. His credibility is enhanced by persuasive arguments that are sufficient for Christian conversion without giving unnecessary intellectual hostages to fortune. Ian Ramsey, Basil Mitchell and Richard Swinburne are recent Anglican apologists (though the last became a Roman Catholic) who follow Butler's method in apologetics, the path of cumulative probability, asking: What does it all point to?

Fifth, Butler's method retains its independence of changes in our knowledge of the natural world and so has not been discredited by advances in scientific knowledge since his day. On the contrary, Butler has an affinity with modern philosophy of science which depends on perceiving analogies and eventuates in probable predictions.[136] It is an enormous strength in Butler to have devised an apologetic method that is independent of revolutions in the scientific worldview. He achieves this by being true to human

---

[136]Broad, 'Butler as a Theologian', in *Religion, Philosophy and Psychical Research.*

experience. As a young man, he had testified to Samuel Clarke that the pursuit of truth was the object of his life. We owe his continuing relevance to his virtues of intellectual honesty and realism. Not his cleverness but his goodness and his closeness to God are the source of his greatness. Let those, who think Butler too outdated to bother with, read his sermons on the love of God: they will find a very exceptional spiritual insight and passion.

Edmund Burke

Edmund Burke (1729–97), parliamentarian, statesman, philosopher, moralist, man of letters, was hailed by Macaulay, half a century after his death, as 'the greatest man since Milton'. Gladstone also reverenced Burke and at a critical time (the Irish Question, 1886) read him daily at his North Wales home, Hawarden, finding him 'sometimes almost divine'.[137] Burke was the only person of Dr Johnson's acquaintance of whom he stood in awe and who was a match for him in conversation. Johnson said of Burke, 'His stream of mind is perpetual.' Once, when Johnson was unwell and Burke was mentioned, Johnson rejoined, 'That fellow calls forth all my powers. Were I to see Burke now it would kill me.' Burke was one of the coffin-bearers at Johnson's funeral in Westminster Abbey in 1784.[138] Coleridge commented a good deal on Burke as a man and a writer and is lavish with his superlatives. He was not uncritical, but he recognized Burke's 'transcendant [sic] greatness'.[139]

Burke would not normally be considered an Anglican theologian. But he was certainly an Anglican thinker and a thinker about Anglican things. The heterodox Dissenting minister Joseph Priestley (1733–1804), his sworn foe, called him a 'lay divine',[140] and as such he belongs with Locke and Johnson before him and with Coleridge and Gladstone after. Burke's thought on reason, imagination, history, tradition and moral discernment is hugely significant in the development of Anglican theological method. He stands squarely

[137]Trevelyan, *Life and Letters of Macaulay*, vol. 2, p. 305; Morley, *Life of Gladstone*, vol. 2, p. 389.
[138]Boswell, *Life of Johnson*, pp. 696, 1394.
[139]Coleridge, *Collected Works, Table Talk*, vol. 2, p. 213 (8 April 1833).
[140]Aston, 'A "lay divine"', p. 186. Cf also Harris, 'Burke and Religion'.

in the tradition of Hooker and Butler. He was well versed in the writings of Hooker, the seventeenth-century Anglican divines, and – from the previous generation – Butler. He has Hooker's sense of the primacy of law in the universe – not as an abstract code of ethics, but as the deep rationality of the world as God created it. Like Hooker he believes that Church and state in England comprise a single, indivisible community, that a religious basis for the state is essential to its makeup, that the Christian Church properly takes a national form and that a nation is a moral community and has moral personality.[141] Burke follows the tradition of practical reason of Aristotle, Aquinas and Hooker in holding that prudence and equity should guide the application of theological, moral and political principles to particular circumstances.[142]

Burke and the Enlightenment

Burke is assuredly a man of the Enlightenment, though he wonderfully transcends it. He was a disciple of Locke, Hume and the Scottish 'common sense' school in his epistemology; of Butler and Adam Smith in his moral philosophy; and of Montesquieu in his social and historical thought. He was a companion of Sir Joshua Reynolds, Dr Johnson and Adam Smith in The Club. But Burke attacked the side of the Enlightenment associated with Voltaire, the Encyclopaedists, Rousseau and the French Revolutionaries, the side that was hostile to the biblical and Christian tradition. This stance does not set him against the Enlightenment. 'Liberal, conservative, and Marxist historiographies have all mistaken Burke's enlightened opposition to doctrinaire attacks on organized religion for a wholesale counter-enlightenment crusade. This confusion has been encouraged by a secular teleology anxious to reduce enlightenment to the criticism of religion. As a result, Burke's espousal of sceptical Whiggism and Protestant toleration is curiously reinterpreted as hostile to the very principles of enlightenment he was in fact defending.'[143] O'Brien observes: 'Burke's Enlightenment was ecumenical,' and this is true both culturally and theologically speaking, as we shall see.[144]

---

[141]See further, Avis, *Church, State and Establishment*, pp. 47–50.
[142]Canavan, *Political Reason*, p. ix.
[143]Bourke, 'Burke, Enlightenment and Romanticism', p. 3.
[144]O'Brien, *The Great Melody*, p. 609; cf. Pocock, *Barbarism and Religion*, vol. 1, p. 7.

Though thoroughly a man of the Enlightenment, who was personally acquainted with the *philosophes* through his Paris visit in 1773 and had observed Rousseau during the latter's time in England,[145] Burke is also a transitional figure on the road to the Romanticism and the philosophical idealism of the early nineteenth century in respect of his reshaping of reason, his rehabilitation of emotion, his revaluation of tradition and his empathetic historical imagination. Burke forged his principles not in the abstract, but in their application to epoch-making political, constitutional and social issues affecting nations, peoples and continents. His total immersion in these issues further deepened his sense of their complexity. Burke stands out in the 'age of reason' for holding together in tension reason and sentiment, judgement and passion, ratiocination and imagination – which strove against each other for mastery within his own breast.[146]

In his early work *On the Sublime and Beautiful* (1756), Burke explored extreme feelings in a way that Dr Johnson and Bishop Butler would have shrunk from. 'Whatever is fitted . . . to excite the ideas of pain and danger . . . whatever is . . . terrible . . . is the source of the *sublime* . . . the strongest emotion which the mind is capable of feeling.' In nature, the sublime generates 'astonishment, admiration, reverence and respect'. In Milton's description of Death personified in *Paradise Lost*, Book II, writes Burke, 'all is dark, uncertain, confused, terrible, and sublime to the last degree'.[147]

Against the legacy of Descartes, Hobbes and Locke concerning clear and distinct ideas as a criterion of truth, Burke argues in this work that ideas marked by clarity and distinctness are abstractions and are simply not informative. An eminently clear idea makes little impact on us; it barely affects the imagination and does little to fire the passions (note: imagination and passions are seen as salutary at this stage). The ideas of eternity and infinity are two of the greatest, most awesome of ideas, yet they tell us very little; when we use those words, we remain largely ignorant of what they

[145]Burke, *A Letter from Mr. Burke to a Member of the National Assembly in Answer to some Objections to his Book on French Affairs* (1791), in *Reflections*, pp. 262–8.
[146]Dwan, 'Burke and the Emotions'.
[147]Burke, *A Philosophical Enquiry into the Origin of our Ideas of the Sublime and Beautiful; with an Introductory Discourse concerning Taste*, in *Works*, vol. 1, pp. 32, 38–9.

stand for. But, insists Burke, poetic images, which are the ones that have the profoundest effect on us, are always obscure. 'A clear idea is another name for a little idea.' Terror, obscurity and power together inspire awe. Only the Scriptures are adequate to this theme. Whenever God is represented as appearing or speaking 'everything terrible in nature is called up to heighten the awe and solemnity of the divine presence'. However, Christianity has softened and humanized the idea of God and brought it 'somewhat nearer to us' by telling of the love of God. And what evokes love in us we call beautiful.[148]

Against abstract speculation

It was Burke's imaginative sympathy, his fellow-feeling for those oppressed by injustice – for Irish Roman Catholics under penal legislation, for the population of India suffering extortion by the corrupt East India Company, and the American settlers excessively taxed by a remote colonial government – as well as his pragmatic realism, that led him to reject the uniformitarian assumptions of the Enlightenment. Burke insists that 'Nothing universal can be rationally affirmed on any moral or any political subject.' Distancing himself from the intellectual model of mathematical logic stemming from Descartes and Hobbes and affirming the role of prudence and equity in judgements of human affairs, Burke continued:

> Pure metaphysical abstraction does not belong to these matters. The lines of morality are not like ideal lines of mathematicks. They are broad and deep as well as long. They admit of exceptions; they demand modifications. These exceptions and modifications are not made by the process of logick, but by the rules of prudence. Prudence is not only the first in rank of the virtues political and moral, but she is the director, the regulator, the standard of them all. Metaphysicks cannot live without definition, but prudence is cautious how she defines.[149]

---

[148]Ibid., pp. 39–40, 42, 47.
[149]Burke, *Appeal from the New to the Old Whigs*, in *Works*, vol. 1, p. 498. Frisch, 'Burke on Theory', stresses Burke's debt to Hume for the role of feeling, especially sympathy, in his thought; but this could equally well be due to Butler's *Sermons*, as well as to wider influences.

Burke recalled elsewhere that Aristotle had cautioned against 'this species of delusive geometrical accuracy in moral arguments, as the most fallacious of all sophistry'.[150] In his appeals on behalf of the American settlers, he made the same point: unlike propositions in geometry and metaphysics, which must be either true or false and cannot be anything in between, 'social and civil freedom, like all other things in common life, are variously mixed and modified, enjoyed in very different degrees, and shaped into an infinite diversity of forms, according to the temper and circumstances of every community'.[151] In his *Reflections on the Revolution in France*, he protested that it was impossible to reach a judgement on any aspect of social life 'stripped of every relation, in all the nakedness and solitude of metaphysical abstraction' (which is how he saw the platform of the Revolutionaries, derived from the *philosophes*). It is circumstances that give 'colour and discriminating effect' to every policy proposal.[152] The catalogue of disasters that the Revolution had produced were due to one fault – 'that of considering certain general maxims, without attending to circumstances, to times, to places, to conjunctures, and to actors'. If we do not pay attention to all these factors, 'the medicine of today becomes the poison of tomorrow'.[153]

Nevertheless, Burke acknowledged the role of theory. He was not a mere pragmatist and not a utilitarian, as some have charged. He is an exponent of *praxis*, prudent practice guided by sound theory. 'I do not vilify theory and speculation,' he insisted, 'no, because that would be to vilify reason itself. . . . Whenever I speak against theory, I mean always a weak, erroneous, fallacious, unfounded theory.'[154]

Burke is the philosopher of particularity, following Butler, and the historian of diversity, following Montesquieu. Burke, paraphrasing Montesquieu, understood that common humanity is 'infinitely modified by climate, geography, history, religion, nationality, and race, by institutions, customs, manners, and habits, by all the civil circumstances of times, places and occasions which cut across and

---

[150]Cited Stanlis, *Burke and the Natural Law*, p. 110.
[151]Burke, *Speeches and Letters*, p. 221.
[152]Burke, *Reflections*, p. 6.
[153]Ibid., p. 277.
[154]Cited Cobban, *Burke and the Revolt*, p. 76.

qualify, but do not impair the different means by which the Natural Law is best fulfilled'.[155] Humankind is essentially one, but receives a 'second nature' through the impress of circumstances. For Burke enduring moral principles are worked out in the flux of dynamic, diverse historical processes.[156]

History and tradition

Burke's thinking was infused with a sense of history. 'In the sweep of Burke's vivid historical imagination, the complex and varied phenomena of national life were transformed into the living effects of causes that had their roots deep in the history of the nation's past.'[157] History, nature and providence were different ways of speaking about the same given reality. 'Never, no never, did Nature say one thing and Wisdom another.'[158] Nature for Burke is neither the wretched state of mutual enmity postulated by Hobbes nor the primal paradise of the noble savage painted by Rousseau. The state of nature is one of ordered, hierarchical society. 'The state of civil society . . . is a state of nature; and much more truly so than a savage and incoherent mode of life. . . . Art is man's nature.'[159] For the *philosophes* 'nature' means what naked theory proposes, without regard for history, tradition, convention and prudent consideration of the consequences for future generations. But for Burke, 'nature' is what has come to be through a long process of development, adaptation and human usage. 'Nature,' says Burke in the *Reflections*, is 'wisdom without reflection, and above it.' He adds significantly, 'People will not look forward to posterity, who never look backward to their ancestors.'[160]

The study of history teaches not abstract truths but the virtue of prudence, not as a set of precedents but as a habit of moral and intellectual discernment. Burke's sense that history was 'the known march of the ordinary providence of God' was totally alien to the

---

[155]Ibid., pp. 87–8.
[156]Kilcup, 'Reason and the Basis of Morality in Burke'.
[157]Osborn, *Rousseau and Burke*, p. 107.
[158]Cited from Burke, *A Regicide Peace* by Kilcup, 'Burke's Historicism', p. 396.
[159]Burke, *Appeal, Works*, vol. 1, p. 525.
[160]Burke, *Reflections*, p. 31.

philosophes.[161] '[T]he awful Author of our being is the author of our place in the order of existence. . . .'[162] In contrast to the rather simplistic prescriptions of the *philosophes*, Burke held that 'The nature of man is intricate; the objects of society are of the greatest possible complexity.'[163] A society was a corporate, organic and evolving reality.[164] But Burke was at one with the *philosophes* in his humanitarian concern for suffering humanity.[165]

Lord Acton (1834–1902) described Burke as 'the most historically minded of English statesmen'. Acton acknowledged him as 'his master' and marvelled at 'the greatness and vastness of his mind'. But Acton also criticized him for seeking for what ought to be in what has been and is. (Incidentally, Acton added, 'Is not that essentially Anglican?'[166] and Stanlis also suggests, without explaining, that it was Burke's Anglicanism that gave him a concept of human nature in which reason, emotion and faith were held in synthesis.)[167] G. M. Young's view is harsher than Acton's. It was not historical empathy that gave Burke his love of things as they have come to be, asserts Young. 'That passion wells up from a deeper source, and the vehemence with which he gives it utterance, a vehemence sometimes verging on frenzy, is by itself a proof that prescription, order and stability were things necessary to his mind: change, and the fear of change, started somewhere in the depths of his being a horror, a blind horror, which set the mind rocking on its foundations.'[168] But Acton and Young seem to have misunderstood Burke at this point, and it is important to see why they did so in order to grasp Burke's view of tradition.

Young's critique involves a false antithesis: a profound conservatism about the present and a love of the past are not in opposition; they belong together and can feed each other. Burke reserved his horror for rampant abstract ideology, riding roughshod over human lives and bringing social and political chaos in its train. But in any

---

[161]Cf. Weston, 'Burke's View of History'.
[162]Burke, *Appeal*, *Works*, vol. 1, p. 522.
[163]Burke, *Reflections*, p. 59.
[164]Love, 'Burke's Idea of the Body Corporate'.
[165]O'Gorman, *Burke: His Political Philosophy*, p. 57.
[166]Deane, 'Lord Acton and Edmund Burke', at p. 330, citing the Cambridge MSS; Mathew, *Acton*, pp. 5, 86, 88, 99.
[167]Stanlis, *Burke and the Natural Law*, p. 182.
[168]G. M. Young, 'Burke', pp. 22–3; *Yesterday and Today*, pp. 88–9.

case, Burke was not opposed to change in principle: he supported American independence and stood up to King George III for it. He wanted the Roman Catholic Church in Ireland to become established by law and urged greater toleration for Protestant Dissenters too, without prejudice to the establishment of the Church of England, the Church of Ireland and the (Presbyterian) Church of Scotland, so that three different Christian confessions would be established in the United Kingdom of Britain and Ireland – a remarkably progressive way of dealing with the inequalities that are inseparable from the establishment of any church by law.[169] The *status quo* is not normative for Burke and is not static: every concatenation of circumstances is filled with dynamism. 'A state without the means of some change is without the means of its conservation.'[170] His conservatism was by no means absolute; he was a reformer, a moral reformer, by nature. 'Would to God,' he wrote, 'it were in our power to keep things *where they are*, in point of form; provided we are able to improve them in point of Substance.'[171] There are, said Burke, 'some fundamental points on which Nature never changes, but these are few and obvious, and belong rather to morals than to politics'. But in the political realm 'the human mind and political affairs are susceptible of infinite modifications, and of combinations wholly new and unlooked for'.[172] And again: 'We must all obey the great law of change. It is the most powerful law of nature, and the means perhaps of its conservation.'

However, Burke preferred that significant change should proceed 'by insensible degrees'![173] He is not eccentric in this stance: Montesquieu – enormously influential in eighteenth-century England and a model of scholarship, judgement and historical method for Burke – commented in his *Lettres persane* (1721) that sometimes it is necessary to change certain laws, but the case is exceptional and, when it arises, they should be touched only with a trembling hand.[174] Montesquieu is also a model for Burke in relation to the

---

[169]Dalston, 'A "lay divine"', pp. 197–8; cf. p. 189: 'I would have toleration a part of establishment, as a principle favorable to Christianity, and as a part of Christianity.'
[170]Burke, *Reflections*, pp. 19–20.
[171]Cited O'Gorman, *Burke: His Political Philosophy*, p. 57.
[172]Cited Kilcup, 'Burke's Historicism', p. 408.
[173]Cited Canavan, *Political Reason*, p. 170 (*à propos* Roman Catholic emancipation in Ireland – Burke's native country).
[174]Cited Courtney, *Montesquieu and Burke*, p. 9, from *Lettre* 129.

constitution: his discussion of the origins of the French constitution is handled not by reference to theories of rights or a social contract, but in the light of history.[175] Burke acknowledged Montesquieu as a kindred spirit, a thinker who had defended the same values as he had himself. This sense of fellowship was vindicated by the fact that Montesquieu, who contributed to the *Encyclopédie*, was attacked by fellow *philosophes* for the empirical and conservative nature of his thought and for his admiration of the British constitution with its constitutional monarchy. But by the time he came to write his *Reflections on the Revolution in France* Burke had moved on from Montesquieu's comparative historical method to a preoccupation with the moral interpretation of events.[176]

Cobban took a different view to Acton and Young: he said of Burke, together with Coleridge, Wordsworth and Southey, that 'a historical sense is the creative force in their revolt against the eighteenth century'.[177] And Butterfield stated that Burke 'exerted the presiding influence over the historical movement of the nineteenth century'.[178] Burke has been presented as an exponent of a reconstructed modern hermeneutics that relies not on formal rules but on historical and cultural empathy, insight and discernment – what Sir Joshua Reynolds called 'sagacity', 'prejudice' and 'habitual reason', and Burke ascribed to 'taste', that is to say practical reason, *phronesis*, sensing the logic of discrete circumstances in an imaginative judgement.[179] Thus too O'Brien has proposed Burke as an exponent of Vico's concept of *fantasia*, not fantasy but imaginative historical empathy and insight.[180]

Community and continuity

Burke's concept of tradition is applied to the nation and to the Church within it as continuous realities. Whether nation or Church is in question, Burke repudiated the idea that a community is merely an aggregate of individuals or that it can be understood simply

---

[175]Ibid., p. 25.
[176]Ibid., pp. 150–1.
[177]Cobban, *Burke and the Revolt*, p. 258.
[178]Butterfield, *Man on His Past*, p. 18; cf. 68.
[179]Weinsheimer, *Eighteenth-Century Hermeneutics*, ch. 7.
[180]O'Brien, *Great Melody*, esp. pp. xxxi, lx.

as it exists in the present. No, a community such as a church or nation is 'an idea of continuity, which extends in time as well as in numbers and in space'. The constitution and governance of such a community is made 'by the peculiar circumstances, occasions, tempers, dispositions, and moral, civil, and social *habitudes* of the people, which disclose themselves only in a long space of time'.[181] These apparently contingent factors are not accidental, but the outworking of divine providence. He could well say with Shakespeare, 'There's a divinity that shapes our ends, Rough-hew them how we will.'[182] A nation, Burke insists, is 'a moral essence, not a geographical arrangement'.[183]

Possibly Burke's most powerful statement of this theme, in which he approaches a mystical concept of community verging on the theological doctrine of the *sanctorum communio*, comes in his *Reflections on the Revolution in France*, where he is attacking the idea that society is held together by a 'social contract' à la Rousseau.[184] Society or the state is indeed a contract or partnership, Burke begins, but not a partnership or contract concerned only with trade which is subject to the whim of the contracting parties.

> It is to be looked on with other reverence; because it is not a partnership in things subservient only to the gross animal existence of a temporary and perishable nature. It is a partnership in all science; a partnership in all art; a partnership in every virtue, and in all perfection. As the ends of such a partnership cannot be obtained in many generations, it becomes a partnership not only between those who are living, but between those who are living, those who are dead, and those who are to be born.[185]

Burke is not finished yet; he goes on to invoke natural law, sustained by God's creative will:

> Each contract of each particular state is but a clause in the great primaeval contract of eternal society, linking the lower with

---

[181]Cited Parkin, *Moral Basis*, p. 59.
[182]Shakespeare, *Hamlet*, Act V, scene 2.
[183]Cited Parkin, *Moral Basis*, p. 62. See also Pocock, 'Burke and the Ancient Constitution'.
[184]Rousseau, *Social Contract*.
[185]Burke, *Reflections*, p. 93.

the higher natures, connecting the visible and invisible world, according to a fixed compact sanctioned by the inviolable oath which holds all physical and all moral natures, each in their appointed place.[186]

Those who wilfully rebel against this divinely sanctioned order 'are outlawed, cast forth, and exiled, from this world of reason, and order, and peace, and virtue, and fruitful penitence, into the antagonist [sic] world of madness, discord, vice, confusion, and unavailing sorrow'.[187]

There is a 'correspondence', for Burke, between the constitution of the world and the nature of human society. The mixed constitution of the United Kingdom of Great Britain and Ireland, with its organic character and its checks and balances, was true to nature. 'Our political system is placed in a just correspondence and symmetry with the order of the world [and] by preserving the method of nature in the conduct of the state . . . we are guided . . . by the spirit of philosophic analogy.'[188] Here Burke was perpetuating medieval ideas of order and hierarchy (related to the concept of 'the great chain of being')[189] and of analogy and symmetry within the cosmos, the commonwealth and the human individual and between them. Radical Romanticism (Blake, Shelley, Byron in England) would reject the hierarchical, ordered aspect, but retain the analogy and connection – a connection and analogy of creativity and development. The Tractarians, being Romantics but also political and social reactionaries, would struggle to retain the sort of synthesis and analogy represented by Burke. In Newman we find the values of order and obedience to authority existing in tension with a holistic sense of the development of the person and of ideas. In Coleridge we have yet another manifestation of the struggle between order and creativity and an attempt to resolve it in terms of differentiation within an organic identity, on the analogy of the Holy Trinity. But Romanticism, both radical and reactionary, remains to be explored in the sequel to this study.

To respect the embeddedness of the individual in the whole body is not to devalue the individual person or to ride roughshod

---

[186]Ibid., pp. 93–4.
[187]Ibid., p. 94.
[188]Cited Greenleaf, *Order, Empiricism and Politics*, pp. 260–1.
[189]Lovejoy, *Great Chain of Being*; Lewis, *Discarded Image*.

over their rights. On the contrary, it protects the person because, as the French Revolution showed, benevolence for humanity as an abstraction meant lack of sympathy for individuals and entailed the destruction of many persons. Abstract reason knows no limits; it is hungry, imperialistic, unrestrained, driven by passion and let loose in the realm of imagination ('passion' and 'imagination' now have adverse connotations). Burke speaks of the 'infinite void of the conjectural world'. Reason is safe when it works on the concrete, limited and definable, when it tackles real problems in the real world. The good to be achieved by political action will be concrete, practicable, complex, but always imperfectly realized. What needs to be done stands plainly before us and is determined by what is given in the mysterious providence of God. 'We have obligations to mankind at large which are not in consequence of any special voluntary pact [social contract].' These obligations arise from the relation of person to person, and the relation of a person to God, 'which relations are not matters of choice'. This principle belongs to the divine economy whereby moral obligations arise from given physical realities: 'Dark and inscrutable are the ways by which we come into the world. The instincts which give rise to this mysterious process of nature are not of our making. But out of physical causes, unknown to us, perhaps unknowable, arise moral duties, which as we are able perfectly to comprehend, we are bound indispensably to perform.'[190] Here and elsewhere we hear Burke the theologian speaking and his doctrine is wholly in keeping with the teaching and spirit of Butler.

Legitimation through use

A bias towards what has worked tolerably well in the past is healthy, because what exists already can be reformed; development is inevitable and welcome, while radical innovation on the basis of abstract, untested theories is uncertain and dangerous.[191] Moreover, to be guided by disembodied theory is humanly unreal: 'Man acts from adequate motives relative to his interest, and not on metaphysical speculations.'[192] Burke exercises a preferential option

---

[190]Burke, *Appeal, Works*, vol. 1, p. 523.
[191]Canavan, *Political Reason*, pp. 168–70, 174–5.
[192]Burke, *Speeches and Letters*, p. 131.

for what has stood the test of time, especially a nation's institutions, including the Church. 'Reverence to antiquity' is his watchword: it was such deference to antiquity that, in his view, characterized the English Reformation, the Restoration of the monarchy in 1660 and the constitutional Revolution of 1688.[193]

His doctrine of prescription, the concept of legitimation by use and time, fitted the English constitutional context ('our constitution is a prescriptive constitution; it is a constitution whose sole authority is, that it has existed time out of mind').[194] But this is not mere English traditionalism, informed by the English legal system's appeal to common or customary law and to precedent, as Pocock suggested, but a philosophical view of how we come to know the good and the true. Burke's doctrine of 'prescription' is, if not original to him, distinctive of his outlook. Prescription is not found unqualified in most expositions of natural law or in the various traditions of jurisprudence with which Burke would have been familiar. It is an aspect of his historical consciousness, married to his Hookerian sense that wisdom is the fruit of maturity and is embodied not in abstract theories but in moral communities, that is to say historic institutions: destroy the institution and the wisdom is lost.[195]

'Prejudice' reflects the individual's history of thinking, grounded in communion with the mind of a society over the generations, a steady trajectory of thought and feeling combined. 'The reason which inheres in just prejudice . . . is more deeply based and stable than the abstract reason of the head alone. It ensures a more accurate and steady moral perception than the naked reason.'[196] Burke said of the French revolutionaries, 'By what they call reasoning without prejudice, they leave not one stone upon another in the fabrick of human society. They subvert all the authority which they hold, as well as all that which they have destroyed.'[197] What has endured represents a conspiracy of mind with mind over a long period and is the product of the thoughts of many minds over time.[198] Thus it is not

---

[193]Burke, *Reflections*, pp. 20–32, 146, at p. 29.

[194]Cited Canavan, *Political Reason*, p. 120.

[195]Lucas, 'On Edmund Burke's Doctrine'; cf. Pocock, 'Origins of Study of the Past', at pp. 236–7.

[196]Cited Parkin, *Moral Basis*, p. 115.

[197]Burke, *Appeal*, *Works*, vol. 1, p. 525.

[198]Burke, *Reflections*, p. 165; Parkin, *Moral Basis*, p. 118.

lightly to be disregarded. Looking backward, Burke's case against the *philosophes* could be Hooker's against the Puritans. Looking forward, Burke's historical imagination and notion of prejudice point towards the hermeneutical revolution of the twentieth century and in particular Gadamer's hermeneutic of the two horizons in *Truth and Method*.[199]

The Anglican Enlightenment in perspective

I have to postpone an attempt at a theological assessment of the Enlightenment to a future volume. For the present, let me offer some very concise reflections:

1 The Enlightenment remains a highly contested notion. It is not self-evident what the Enlightenment includes and what it stands for. It does not stand in its own light. It is possible to shine different lights on the Enlightenment. Some writers and thinkers whom modern secular scholars and historians claim for their own cause were actually men who took religion seriously, and were either Christian or theistic. Of course, there were those who were neither and who set out to deconstruct the very core of Christian belief. But they were a small minority. The secularist interpretative framework for the Enlightenment, that takes the subversive anti-Christian minority as the authentic Enlightenment, is not to be trusted.

2 There was clearly an explicitly, confessedly Christian Enlightenment going on. In fact it was the main and mainstream Enlightenment in most of Europe. Overall, its Christian manifestation was the dominant expression of the Enlightenment. It manifested itself in all the major Christian traditions. Christian writers identified themselves with the ideology of Enlightenment; they used the same imagery of light and invoked reason, just as non-Christians and those on the edge of the Church did. The Enlightenment is not at all synonymous

---

[199]Gadamer, *Truth and Method*; Thiselton, *New Horizons*.

with a secular, anti-Christian stance, let alone with 'modern paganism', as Gay has claimed.

3 It follows that, as theologians working today, we should inhabit the Enlightenment as part of the inheritance of Christian theology. The Enlightenment is not an unfortunate aberration to be skirted around until we can pick up the high road of theology again with the great Romantic theologians: Herder, Schleiermacher and Coleridge – or, even more mistakenly, assuming that the true continuity is from Calvin straight to Barth with nothing much in between. There is a continuity of theological reflection and theological struggle that runs through the middle of the Enlightenment. It has its proper part in the making of modern Christian theology. Twenty-first-century theology should be at home in the Enlightenment.

4 This more generous perspective has the effect of broadening the scope of our theological heritage. The Christian theological tradition in the West includes radical, subversive thinkers. They are the gadflies, the grit in the oyster, the ones who ask the awkward questions and move us on in our thinking. I find a place in the theological tradition for the likes of Bacon, Montaigne, Charron, Descartes, Hobbes, Locke, Bayle and Vico – figures who are claimed by some as subversive pioneers of a secular worldview and a corrosive, sceptical rationality. The fact that some of them were driven by the sceptical tradition in Western philosophy does not put them outside the mainstream of Christian theology, as some non-theologians seem to assume – far from it. The apophatic component in Christian theology, that speaks of a God who is hidden from us, shrouded in the cloud of unknowing, sits well with an epistemology that stresses the limitations of our knowledge and that probability is the guide of life. Knowledge of the amazing diversity of the Christian tradition helps us to recognize such writers as these as committed religious, Christian thinkers – with whom we should engage.

5 Criticisms of aspects of Christianity by Enlightenment figures – or by more recent challengers – should be taken to heart. Enlightenment figures who looked somewhat askance at Christianity were often more anticlerical and antiecclesiastical than anti-Christian as such. Those elements

in the early Church that Gibbon objected to – fanaticism, credulity, masochism, lack of civic commitment – also make most modern western Christians acutely uncomfortable when they study the Christians of the first few centuries. The unsparing critics of Christianity as they know it are not necessarily enemies of the gospel; they may be friends in disguise. We may even be found to have 'entertained angels unawares' (Heb. 13.1 KJB). It should not be left to those outside the Church or on its margins to expose our failings and abuses. The heart of the matter is this: the critique of Christianity belongs within Christianity itself. Criticism of unacceptable aspects of historical and contemporary Christianity is an evangelical exercise and can be an ecclesial action, if it is intended to lead to the purification, reformation, and renewal of the Church. That is after all precisely what the sixteenth-century Reformers, with whom we began this narrative, set out to achieve. *Ecclesia reformata semper reformanda.*

I conclude by revisiting Mark Pattison's assessment of where the Anglican Enlightenment had led by the mid-nineteenth century. In the collection – notorious in its time – *Essays and Reviews* (1860), Pattison contributed a remarkable essay on 'Tendencies of Religious Thought in England, 1688–1750'. Pattison, once captivated by Tractarianism, but now sardonically detached from the Church (and soon to become rector of Lincoln College, Oxford), focused on the question of authority in theology. He concluded his essay with the wry observation: 'Whoever would take the religious literature of the present day [the mid-nineteenth century] as a whole and endeavor to make out clearly on what basis Revelation is supposed by it to rest, whether on Authority, on the Inward Light, on Reason, on self-evidencing Scripture, or on the combination of the four, or some of them, and in what proportions, would probably find that he had undertaken a perplexing but not altogether profitless inquiry.'[200] What were the reasons for this confused situation? Looking back on the period from the end of the seventeenth to the middle of the eighteenth centuries, Pattison identified three developments that had shaped his own times, the mid-nineteenth century: (1) the growth of toleration by means of the gradual adjustment of the relations

---

[200]Pattison, 'Tendencies', p. 329.

between Church and State in England; (2) the evangelical revival
('the great rekindling of the religious consciousness of the people'),
which produced the evangelical party within the Established Church
and the Methodist movement which was now outside it; and (3)
the growth and dominance of 'rationalism' in all religious thinking
('the supremacy of reason').[201]

It could be argued, though Pattison himself does not do this,
that toleration fosters adventurous thinking, in that it allows for
free enquiry and the open expression of ideas, while evangelical
fervour, with its emphasis on the emotions and on a few simple
beliefs, suppresses it. But this argument would be rather simplistic.
As we have seen, John Wesley claimed the rational high ground
and sensed no contradiction with heartfelt religion. William Law
combined the appeal to reason with the High Church tradition and
with a mystical bent. However, it was not creative and adventurous
rationality that Pattison had in mind. Reason may be arid and
formulaic. In the eighteenth century, reason was not opposed to
revelation; it was not incompatible with deep spiritual experience:
it ran through everything. As Pattison puts it: 'throughout all
discussions, underneath all controversies, and common to all
parties, lies the assumption of the supremacy of reason in matters
of religion . . . rationalism was not an anti-Christian sect outside
the Church making war against religion. It was a habit of thought
ruling all minds. . . . The title of Locke's treatise *The Reasonableness
of Christianity*, may be said to have been the solitary thesis of
Christian theology in England for great part of a century.'[202] The
rationalizing method took over almost the whole theological
enterprise. With few exceptions, Pattison alleged, religious writers
were obsessed with trying to 'prove' the truth of the Christian faith,
and in the second half of the eighteenth century this took the form
of marshalling 'evidences' in support of Christianity. Doctrinal
theology had ceased to exist. 'Every one [sic] who had had anything
to say on sacred subjects drilled it into an array of argument against
a supposed objector. Christianity appeared made for nothing else
but to be "proved"; what use to make of it when it was proved was
not much thought about. Reason was at first offered as the basis of
faith, but gradually became its substitute.'[203]

---

[201]Ibid., pp. 256–7.
[202]Ibid., pp. 257–8.
[203]Ibid., pp. 259–60.

Paley's *Evidences of Christianity* (1794) sits at the peak of this genre.[204] Coleridge's attack on Paley and his professed disdain for the argument from evidences – '*Evidences* of Christianity! I am weary of the Word. Make a man feel the *want* of it; rouse him, if you can, to the self-knowledge of his *need* of it; and you may safely trust to its own Evidence . . .'[205] – have put Paley's work under a cloud and inclined us to be patronizing about him. Yet his work is a strong example of its kind and not to be despised. Paley begins with Hume's challenge to the credibility of miracles: in Paley's words, 'it is contrary to experience that a miracle should be true, but not contrary to experience that testimony should be false'.[206] He majors on the evidences from miracles and the fulfilment of prophecy. His argument is largely historical, stressing the combined testimony of the New Testament writers, but precritical. He treats the Gospel-writers as 'historians' or as writers of 'memoirs' and believes that the discrepancies between the Gospels can be harmonized. In all these ways, Paley's apologetic was already behind the times; the argument had moved on. A defence of Christianity based on rational assent to evidence was not going to convince a generation beginning to imbibe the works of the Romantics. But my summary so far does not do full justice to Paley's approach. The weight of the evidence that he presents is not only historical but also moral and stands firmly in the tradition of Bishop Butler. Like Butler, Paley appeals to the argument from degrees of probability, stresses probation (the last words of his treatise are 'to try us') and points out that there is an antecedent likelihood that a divine revelation would contain aspects that seem strange to us and insists that difficulties over details do not discredit the substantive argument. The pattern of divine providence overseeing the vicissitudes of Christian history is 'analogous to most other provisions for happiness'.[207] His aim is to persuade the reader to focus on essentials. 'What is clear in Christianity, we shall find to be sufficient, and to be infinitely valuable; what is dubious, unnecessary to be decided, or of very subordinate importance.'[208] Paley's *Evidences* is an estimable work

---

[204]Paley, *Evidences*.
[205]Coleridge, *Collected Works, Aids to Reflection*, pp. 405–6 (Conclusion). Nevertheless, Coleridge professed huge admiration for Paley (ibid., p. 408).
[206]Paley, *Evidences*, p. 33.
[207]Ibid., p. 370.
[208]Ibid., p. 363.

of apologetic and not to be dismissed, even though in its own time it did not quite hit the nail on the head.

During the course of the eighteenth century, the concept of reason had degenerated, from the devout and reverent reason, infused with a sense of a corporate past, of Richard Hooker, or the intuitive, divine, contemplative reason of the Cambridge Platonists, later to be revived by Coleridge, to the common-sense, functional, natural reason of the rationalistic evidence-mongers. The imaginative, contemplative or speculative reason was a lost faculty. Pattison condemns the theology of the Hanoverian divines, as 'a theology which excludes on principle not only all that is poetical in life, but all that is sublime in religious speculation'.[209] According to Pattison, theology had sunk to its lowest level not because it was rational, but because it was mere 'common reason', an appeal to educated common sense, which governed theological discussion. In these terms, Pattison had set the scene for the passionate reaction against rationalism, the outburst of romantic feeling in theology, that produced both the Coleridgeans and the Tractarians in the first quarter of the nineteenth century.

By the time that Pattison wrote his essay on tendencies of religious thought – just as Darwin's *The Origin of Species* (1859) was being published – Anglican theological method, with reference to Scripture, tradition and reason and conscience, had become highly problematic. The authority of Scripture was being challenged by scientific discovery and biblical higher criticism, some examples of which were included in *Essays and Reviews*; historical research stemming from the later Enlightenment was emphasizing the diversity of cultures and traditions, including Christian ones; reason, in a strongly analytical, critical form, was eroding the foundations of traditional faith; the Christian conscience was pulling in a new direction. This was the enormous challenge to Anglican theology that such thinkers as Coleridge, Newman, Maurice, Gladstone, Westcott and Gore in the nineteenth century, and their successors from William Temple to Michael Ramsey in the twentieth, would take up, as we shall see in the sequel to the present study.

---

[209]Pattison, 'Tendencies', pp. 293; cf. 261.

BIBLIOGRAPHY OF
WORKS CITED

Abraham, William J., 'Wesley as Preacher', in Maddox and Vickers (eds.),
   Cambridge Companion to Wesley (Cambridge: Cambridge University
   Press, 2010).
Addison, Joseph, *Works*, ed. Richard Hurd (London: Bell, 1899), vol. 2
   [*Tatler* and *Spectator*].
—, *Miscellaneous Works of Joseph Addison*, ed. A. C. Guthkelch (London:
   Bell, 1914), vol. 2.
Agrippa, Cornelius, *The Vanity of Arts and Sciences* (London, 1676):
   http://archive.org/stream/vanityartsandsc00unkngoog#page/n33/
   mode/2up.
Alberigo, J., et al. (eds.), *Conciliorum Oecumenicorum Decreta* (Freiburg
   im Breisgau: Herder, 1962).
Allison, C. F., *The Rise of Moralism: The Proclamation of the Gospel
   from Hooker to Baxter* (London: SPCK, 1966).
Allison, Henry E., *Lessing and the Enlightenment* (Ann Arbor, MI:
   University of Michigan Press, 1966).
Althaus, Paul, *The Theology of Martin Luther*, trans. Robert C. Shultz
   (Philadelphia, PA: Fortress Press, 1966).
Andrewes, Lancelot, *Of Episcopacy: Three Epistles of Peter Moulin . . .
   Answered by Lancelot Andrews* [sic] (1647 [1618]).
—, *The Devotions of Bishop Andrewes* [2 vols in one], vol. 1 trans. from
   the Greek by John Henry Newman; intro. H. B. Swete; vol. 2 trans.
   from the Latin by John Mason Neale (London: SPCK; New York:
   Macmillan, 1920).
Aquinas, Thomas, *Summa Theologiae*, Latin/English Blackfriars edn
   (London: Eyre & Spottiswoode; New York: McGraw-Hill, 1964).
Arnold, Matthew, *Essays in Criticism, First Series*, ed. Sister Thomas
   Marion Hoctor SSJ (Chicago: University of Chicago Press, 1968
   [1863]).
Ashworth, E. J., 'Descartes' Theory of Clear and Distinct Ideas', in
   R. J. Butler (ed.), *Cartesian Studies* (Oxford: Blackwell, 1972).

Aston, Nigel, 'A "lay divine": Burke, Christianity and the Preservation of the British State 1790–1797', in id. (ed.), *Religious Change in Europe* (Oxford: Clarendon Press, 1997).

— (ed.), *Religious Change in Europe 1650–1914: Essays for John McManners* (Oxford: Clarendon Press, 1997).

—, 'Horne and Heterodoxy: Anglican Beliefs in the Late Enlightenment', *English Historical Review*, 108 (1993), pp. 895–919.

Atkinson, Nigel, *Richard Hooker and the Authority of Scripture, Tradition and Reason: Reformed Theologian of the Church of England* (Carlisle: Paternoster Press, 1997).

Aubrey, John, *Brief Lives* (Harmondsworth: Penguin, 1972).

Augustine, *Confessions*, trans. R. S. Pine-Coffin (Harmondsworth: Penguin, 1961) or trans. Henry Chadwick (Oxford: Oxford University Press, 1991).

Aulén, Gustaf, *Reformation and Catholicity*, trans. Eric H. Wahlstrom (Edinburgh and London: Oliver and Boyd, 1962).

Avis, Paul (P. D. L.), 'Moses and the Magistrate: A Study in the Rise of Protestant Legalism', *JEH*, 26.2 (1975), pp. 149–72.

—, *The Church in the Theology of the Reformers* (London: Marshall, Morgan & Scott, 1981; reprinted Eugene, OR: Wipf and Stock, 2002).

—, *Foundations of Modern Historical Thought: From Machiavelli to Vico* (London: Croom Helm, 1986).

—, *God and the Creative Imagination: Metaphor, Symbol and Myth in Religion and Theology* (London and New York: Routledge, 1999).

—, *Church, State and Establishment* (London: SPCK, 2001).

—, *Anglicanism and the Christian Church*, 2nd edn (London and New York: T&T Clark, 2002).

—, *A Ministry Shaped by Mission* (London and New York: T&T Clark, 2005).

—, *Beyond the Reformation? Authority, Primacy and Unity in the Conciliar Tradition* (London and New York: T&T Clark, 2006).

—, 'John Jewel: Anglicanism's Bane or Blessing?', *Ecclesiology* 4.3 (2008), pp. 345–55.

—, *The Identity of Anglicanism: Essentials of Anglican Identity* (London and New York: T&T Clark, 2008).

—, 'The Church and Ministry', in Whitford (ed.), *T&T Clark Companion to Reformation Theology* (London and New York: T&T Clark, 2012).

—, 'The Book of Common Prayer and Anglicanism', in Platten and Woods (eds.), *Comfortable Words* (London: SCM Press, 2012).

—, 'Apologetics and the Rebirth of the Imagination' (Editorial), *Ecclesiology* 9.3 (2013), pp. 301–9.

Awad, Najeeb George, 'The Influence of John Chrysostom's hermeneutics on John Calvin's exegetical approach to Paul's *Epistle to the Romans*', *SJT*, 63.4 (2010), pp. 414–36.

Ayris, P. and D. Selwyn (eds.), *Thomas Cranmer: Churchman and Scholar* (Woodbridge, Suffolk: Boydell Press, 1993).

Backus, Irena (ed.), *The Reception of the Church Fathers in the West: From the Carolingians to the Maurists*, vol. 2 (Leiden: Brill, 1997).

—, 'Ulrich Zwingli, Martin Bucer and the Church Fathers', in Backus (ed.), *Reception of the Church Fathers* (Leiden: Brill, 1997).

—, 'Calvin and the Church Fathers', in Selderhuis (ed.), *Calvin Handbook* (Grand Rapids, MI: Eerdmans, 2009).

Bacon, Francis, *Works*, ed. J. Spedding, R. L. Ellis and D. D. Heath (London: Longmans, 1861).

—, *Essays and Colours of Good and Evil*, ed. W. Aldis Wright (London: Macmillan, 1890).

—, *Philosophical Works*, ed. J. M. Robertson (London: Routledge, 1905).

—, *The Advancement of Learning* (London: Dent; New York: Dutton [Everyman], 1915).

—, *The Philosophy of Francis Bacon: An Essay on its Development from 1603 to 1609 with new translations of Fundamental Texts*, ed. Benjamin Farrington (Liverpool: Liverpool University Press, 1964).

Bagehot, Walter, *Literary Studies*, ed. R. H. Hutton (London: Longmans, Green & Co., 1898).

Bainton, Roland H., *Here I Stand: A Life of Martin Luther* (New York: Mentor Books; Nashville, TN: Abindon Press, 1950).

—, 'The Bible in the Reformation', in Greenslade (ed.), *Cambridge History of the Bible: The West from the Reformation to the Present Day* (London: Cambridge Univsersity Press, 1963).

Baker, Frank, 'John Wesley, Biblical Commentator', *Bulletin of the John Rylands Library*, 71 (1998), pp. 109–20.

Ballentine, Samuel E. and John Barton (eds.), *Language, Theology, and the Bible: Essays in Honour of James Barr* (Oxford: Clarendon Press, 1994).

Barker, John, *Strange Contrarieties: Pascal in England during the Age of Reason* (Montreal: McGill-Queen's University Press, 1975).

Barnard, Leslie W., 'The Use of the Patristic Tradition in the Late Seventeenth and Early Eighteenth Centuries', in Drewery and Bauckham (eds.), *Scripture, Tradition and Reason* (Edinburgh: T&T Clark, 1998).

Barth, Karl, *Church Dogmatics*, ed. G. W. Bromiley and T. F. Torrance (Edinburgh: T&T Clark, 1936–).

—, *The Theology of John Calvin*, trans. Geoffrey W. Bromiley (Grand Rapids, MI: Eerdmans, 1995).

Baur, J., *Gott, Recht und Weltliche Regiment im Werke Calvins* (Bonn: Bouvier, 1965).

Baxter, Richard, *Autobiography* [condensed from the *Reliquiae Baxterianae* (1696)], ed. J. M. Lloyd Thomas (London and Toronto: Dent; New York: Dutton (Everyman), 1931).

Bayle, Pierre, *Oeuvres diverses*, ed. Elisabeth Labrousse, vol. 3 (Hildesheim: G. Olms, 1964–82).

—, *Dictionnaire historique et critique*, ed. Alain Niderst (Paris: Éditions Sociales, 1974) (art. 'Spinoza').

—, *Historical and Critical Dictionary*, ed. and trans. Richard H. Popkin (Indianapolis: Bobs Merrill, 1965; reprinted Indianapolis: Hackett, 1991).

Bebbington, David W., *Evangelicalism in Modern Britain: A History from the 1730s to the 1980s* (London and New York: Routledge, 1989).

Becker, Carl, *The Heavenly City of the Eighteenth-Century Philosophers* (New Haven: Yale University Press, 1932).

Bedford, R. D., *The Defence of Truth: Herbert of Cherbury and the Seventeenth Century* (Manchester: Manchester University Press, 1979).

Bennett, G. V. and J. D. Walsh (eds.), *Essays in Modern English Church History in Memory of Norman Sykes* (London: A. & C. Black, 1966).

Bentley, Jerry H., *Humanists and Holy Writ: New Testament Scholarship in the Renaissance* (Princeton, NJ: Princeton University Press, 1983).

Berkeley, George, *Works*, ed. A. A. Luce and T. E. Jessop (London: Nelson, 1950).

Berlin, Isaiah, *Vico and Herder: Two Studies in the History of Ideas* (London: Hogarth Press, 1976).

—, *Against the Current: Essays in the History of Ideas* (Oxford: Oxford University Press, 1981 [1979]).

—, *The Crooked Timber of Humanity*, ed. Henry Hardy (London: Fontana, 1991).

—, *The Magus of the North: J. G. Hamann and the Origins of Modern Irrationalism* (London: John Murray, 1993).

Bernard, G. W., *The King's Reformation: Henry VIII and the Remaking of the English Church* (New Haven and London: Yale University Press, 2005).

Besterman, Theodore, 'Reason and Progress', *SVEC*, 24 (1963), pp. 27–41.

Biéler, André, *Calvin's Economic and Social Thought*, trans. James Greig (Geneva: World Alliance of Reformed Churches/World Council of Churches, 2005).

Black, J. B., *The Art of History: A Study of Four Great Historians of the Eighteenth Century* (London, 1926; reprinted New York: Russell and Russell, 1965).

Blake, William, *The Complete Poems*, ed. Alicia Ostriker (Harmondsworth: Penguin, 1977).

Bodin, Jean, *Method for the Easy Comprehension of History*, trans. B. Reynolds (New York: University of Columbia Press, 1945).

Bohatec, J., *Calvins Lehre von Staat und Kirche* (Breslau: Gierke, 1937).
Bonhoeffer, Dietrich, *Christology*, trans. John Bowden (London: Fontana, 1971).
Booty, John E., *John Jewel as Apologist of the Church of England* (London: SPCK, 1963).
— (ed.), *The Book of Common Prayer 1559: The Elizabethan Prayer Book* (Charlottesville, VA; Washington, DC: Virginia University Press/ Folger Shakespeare Library, 1976).
Bornkamm, Heinrich, *Luther and the Old Testament*, trans. W. Eric and Ruth C. Gritsch (Philadelphia, PA: Fortress Press, 1969).
Boswell, James, *Life of Johnson*, ed. R. W. Chapman (London: Oxford University Press, 1953).
Bourgault, Sophie and Robert Sparling (eds.), *A Companion to Enlightenment Historiography* (Leiden: Brill, 2013).
Bourke, Richard, 'Burke, Enlightenment and Romanticism', in David Dwan and Christopher Insole (eds.), *Cambridge Companion to Edmund Burke* (Cambridge: Cambridge University Press, 2012).
Bousma, William J., 'Renaissance and Reformation: An Essay in Their Affinities and Connections', in Oberman (ed.), *Luther and the Dawn of the Modern Era* (Leiden: Brill, 1974).
Braaten, Carl and Robert Jenson (eds.), *Union with Christ: The New Finnish Interpretation of Luther* (Grand Rapids, MI: Eerdmans, 1998).
Bray, Gerald (ed.), *Tudor Church Reform: The Henrician Canons of 1535 and the* Reformatio Legum Ecclesiasticarum (Woodbridge: The Boydell Press/Church of England Record Society, 2000).
Brinton, Crane, *Ideas and Men: The Story of Western Thought* (New York: Prentice Hall, 1950).
Broad, C. D., *Five Types of Ethical Theory* (London: Routledge & Kegan Paul, 1930).
—, *Religion, Philosophy and Psychical Research* (London: Routledge & Kegan Paul, 1953; New York: Humanities Press, 1969).
Brown, K. C. (ed.), *Hobbes Studies* (Oxford: Blackwell, 1965).
Brown, Stewart J. (ed.), *William Robertson and the Expansion of Empire* (Cambridge: Cambridge University Press, 1997).
—, and Timothy Tackett (eds.), *The Cambridge History of Christianity, Vol. VII, Enlightenment, Reawakening and Revolution 1660-1815* (Cambridge: Cambridge University Press, 2006).
Browne, Sir Thomas, *Browne's Religio Medici and Digby's Observations* (Oxford: Clarendon Press, 1909, corrected facsimile).
—, *Pseudodoxia Epidemica: Or Enquiries Into many Received Tenents And commonly presumed Truths*, ed. Robin Robbins (Oxford: Clarendon Press, 1981).
Broxap, H., *The Later Non-Jurors* (Cambridge: Cambridge University Press, 1924).

Brumfitt, J. H., 'History and Propaganda in Voltaire', *SVEC*, 24 (1963), pp. 271–87.

Brunner, Emil, *The Christian Doctrine of God (Dogmatics* I), trans. Olive Wyon (London: Lutterworth Press, 1949).

Brush, C. B., *Montaigne and Bayle: Variations on the Theme of Skepticism* (The Hague: Nijhof, 1966).

Brydon, Michael, *The Evolving Reputation of Richard Hooker: An Examination of Responses, 1600–1714* (Oxford: Oxford University Press, 2006).

Burckhardt, Jacob, *The Civilization of the Renaissance in Italy* (London: Phaidon, 1965).

Burnet, Gilbert, *History of the Reformation*, vol. 1 (Oxford, 1829).

—, Gilbert Bishop of Sarum, *An Exposition of the XXXIX Articles of the Church of England* (Oxford: Oxford University Press, 1845).

—, *A History of his own Times from the Restoration of King Charles the Second to the Treaty of Peace at Utrecht in the Reign of Queen Anne* (London: William S. Orr & Co., 1850 [1723, 1734]).

Burnett, Amy Nelson, ' "According to the Oldest Authorities": The Use of the Church Fathers in the Early Eucharistic Controversy', in Johnson, Anna Marie and John A. Maxfield (eds.), *The Reformation as Christianization: Essays on Scott Hendrix's Christianization Thesis* (Tübingen: Mohr Siebeck, 2012).

Burnett, Richard, 'John Calvin and the *Sensus Literalis*', *SJT*, 57.1 (2004), pp. 1–13.

Burke, Edmund, *The Works of the Right Hon. Edmund Burke*, vol. 1 (London: Holdsworth and Ball, 1834).

—, *Speeches and Letters on American Affairs* (London: Dent; New York: Dutton (Everyman), 1908).

—, *Reflections on the Revolution in France* (London: Dent; New York: Dutton (Everyman), 1910).

Burke, Peter, *The Renaissance Sense of the Past* (London: Arnold, 1969).

Burtt, Edwin A., *The Metaphysical Foundations of Modern Physical Science*, 2nd edn, (London: Routledge and Kegan Paul, 1949 [1932]).

Bury, J. B., *The Idea of Progress: An Inquiry into its Origin and Growth* (London: Macmillan, 1920).

Butler, Joseph, *A Charge Delivered to the Clergy at the Primary Visitation of the Diocese of Durham* (Durham, 1751).

—, *The Analogy of Religion, Natural and Revealed to the Constitution and Course of Nature, to which are added, Two Brief Dissertations: On Personal Identity, and on The Nature of Virtue; and Fifteen Sermons* (London: Bell, 1889).

—, *Works*, ed. W. E. Gladstone (Oxford: Clarendon Press, 1896).

Butler, R. J. (ed.), *Cartesian Studies* (Oxford: Blackwell, 1972).

Butterfield, Herbert, *The Origins of Modern Science 1300–1800* (London: Bell, 1949).

—, *Man on His Past* (Cambridge: Cambridge University Press, 1955).

Byrne, Peter, *Natural Religion and the Nature of Religion: The Legacy of Deism* (London and New York: Routledge, 1989).

Calvin, John, *Tracts and Treatises*, vol. 1, *On the Reformation of the Church*, trans. Henry Beveridge, notes and intro. T. F. Torrance (Grand Rapids, MI: Eerdmans, 1958).

—, *Calvin, Commentaries (LCC)*.

—, *Calvin's Commentaries*, ed. D. W. Torrance and T. F. Torrance (Edinburgh: The Saint Andrew Press, 1959–).

—, *Institutes of the Christian Religion*, trans. Henry Beveridge (London: James Clarke, 1962).

Cameron, Euan, 'Primitivism, Patristics and Polemics in Protestant Visions of Early Christianity', in Van Liere, Ditchfield and Louthan (eds.), *Sacred History* (Oxford: Oxford University Press, 2012).

Canavan, Francis P., *The Political Reason of Edmund Burke* (Durham, NC: Duke University Press, 1960).

Carrigan, Henry L. Jr, art. 'Bible', in Hillerbrand (ed.), *Encyclopedia of Protestantism*, vol. 1 (London and New York: Routledge, 2004).

Cassirer, Ernst, *The Philosophy of the Enlightenment* (Princeton: Princeton University Press, 1951).

—, *The Platonic Renaissance in England*, trans. James P. Pettegrove (Edinburgh: Nelson, 1953).

Cellini, Benvenuto, *Autobiography*, trans. George Bull (Harmondsworth: Penguin, 1956).

Chadwick, Owen, *From Bossuet to Newman: The Idea of Doctrinal Development* (Cambridge: Cambridge University Press, 1957).

—, *The Early Reformation on the Continent* (Oxford: Oxford University Press, 2001).

Champion, J. A. I., *The Pillars of Priestcraft Shaken: The Church of England and its Enemies 1660–1730* (Cambridge: Cambridge University Press, 1992).

—, (Justin), *Republican Learning: John Toland and the Crisis of Christian Culture, 1696–1722* (Manchester: Manchester University Press, 2003).

Chapman, Mark, *Anglican Theology* (London and New York: T&T Clark, 2012).

Charron, Jean Daniel, *The 'Wisdom' of Pierre Charron* (Chapel Hill, NC: University of North Carolina, 1960).

Charron, Pierre, *Les Trois Veritez* (Bordeaux, 1595).

—, *Of Wisdom* (London, 1651).

Childs, Brevard, 'Biblical Scholarship in the Seventeenth Century: A Study in Ecumenics', in Ballentine and Barton (eds.), *Language, Theology, and the Bible* (Oxford: Clarendon Press, 1994).

Chillingworth, William, *The Religion of Protestants a Safe Way to Salvation* (London: Bohn, 1846).

Chung-Kim, Esther, 'Use of the Fathers in the Eucharistic Debates between John Calvin and Joachim Westfall', *Reformation*, 14 (2009), pp. 101–25.

Church, R. W., (ed.), *Book I Of the Laws of Ecclesiastical Polity*, 2nd edn (Oxford: Clarendon Press, 1876).

—, *Pascal and Other Sermons* (London: Macmillan, 1895).

Clarendon, Earl of, *Miscellaneous Works* (London, 1751).

Clark, J. C. D., *Samuel Johnson: Literature, Religion, and English Cultural Politics from the Restoration to Romanticism* (Cambridge: Cambridge University Press, 1994).

—, *English Society, 1660–1832: Religion, Ideology and Politics during the Ancien Regime*, 2nd edn (Cambridge: Cambridge University Press, 2000).

Clark, Stuart, 'Bacon's *Henry VII*: A Case Study in the Science of Man', *History and Theory*, 13 (1974), pp. 97–118.

Clifford, James L., *Young Samuel Johnson* (London: Heinemann, 1955).

Cobban, Alfred, *Edmund Burke and the Revolt against the Eighteenth Century: A Study of the Social Thinking of Burke, Wordsworth, Coleridge and Southey* (London: Allen and Unwin, 1929 [2nd edn, 1960]).

—, 'The Enlightenment', in *New Cambridge Modern History*, vol. 7, *The Old Regime* (Cambridge: Cambridge University Press, 1957).

Cole, Graham, '"Who can refute a sneer?" Paley on Gibbon', *Tyndale Bulletin*, 49.1 (1998), pp. 57–70.

Coleridge, Samuel Taylor, *Collected Works*, ed. Kathleen Coburn (Princeton: Princeton University Press; London: Routledge, 1976–).

Colie, Rosalie L., 'Spinoza in England 1665–1730', *Proceedings of the American Philosophical Society*, 107.3 (1963), pp. 183–219.

Collins, Jeffrey R., *The Allegiance of Thomas Hobbes* (Oxford: Oxford University Press, 2005).

Common Worship (London: Church House Publishing, 2000).

Condren, Conal, 'The Creation of Richard Hooker's Public Authority: Rhetoric, Reputation and Reassessment', *Journal of Religious History*, 21 (1997), pp. 35–59.

Congar, Yves M.-J., *Tradition and Traditions* (London: Burns and Oates, 1966).

Cooke, Paul D., *Hobbes and Christianity: Reassessing the Bible in Leviathan* (Lanham, ML: Rowman and Littlefield, 1996).

Costelloe, Timothy M., '"In every civilized community": Hume on belief and the demise of religion', *International Journal for Philosophy of Religion*, 55 (2004), pp. 171–85.

Courtney, C. P., *Montesquieu and Burke* (Oxford: Blackwell, 1963).

Covell, William, *A Just and Temperate Defence of the Five Books of Ecclesiastical Polity written by Richard Hooker*, ed. and intro. John A. Taylor (Lewiston: Edwin Mellen Press, 1998, based on the 1830 edition of B. Hanbury).

Cragg, G. R., *From Puritanism to the Age of Reason: A Study of Changes in Religious Thought within the Church of England 1660 to 1700* (Cambridge: Cambridge University Press, 1966).

Crane, R. S., 'Anglican Apologetics and the Idea of Progress', *Modern Philology*, 31 (1934), pp. 273–306, 349–82.

Cranston, Maurice, *John Locke, A Biography* (London: Longmans, Green and Co., 1957).

Cranz, F. E., *An Essay on the Development of Luther's Thought on Justice, Law and Society* (Harvard, CT: Harvard University Press, 1959).

Croce, Bernadetto, *History: Its Theory and Practice*, trans. Douglas Ainslie (New York: Russell, 1960).

Crocker, Lester, 'The Enlightenment: What and Who?', in J. Yolton and L. E. Brown (eds.), *Studies in Eighteenth-Century Culture*, vol. 17 (Michigan: Colleagues Press: American Society for Eighteenth-Century Studies; Woodbridge: Boydell and Brewer, 1998).

Cross, Claire, *The Royal Supremacy in the Elizabethan Church* (London: Allen and Unwin, 1969).

Cummings, Brian (ed.), *The Book of Common Prayer: The Texts of 1549, 1559, and 1662* (Oxford: Oxford University Press, 2011).

Cunliffe, Christopher (ed.), *Joseph Butler's Moral and Religious Thought* (Oxford: Clarendon Press, 1992).

Daillé, Jean, *Traicté de l'employ des Saincts Peres* (Geneva, 1632; ET, *A Treatise concerning the Right Use of the Fathers*, London, 1651).

Daniell, David, *William Tyndale: A Biography* (New Haven and London: Yale University Press, 1994).

Darwall, Stephen, 'Conscience as Self-Authorizing in Butler's Ethics', in Cunliffe (ed.), *Butler's Moral and Religious Thought* (Oxford: Clarendon Press, 1992).

D'Assonville, Victor E., 'Exegesis and *Doctrina*', in Selenhuis (ed.), *Calvin Handbook* (Grand Rapids, MI: Eerdmans, 2009), p. 380.

Daston, Lorraine, 'Probability and Evidence', in Garter and Ayers (eds.), *Cambridge History of Seventeenth-Century Philosophy*, vol. 2.

Davies, H. S. and G. Watson (eds.), *The English Mind* (Cambridge: Cambridge University Press, 1964).

Davison, Andrew (ed.), *Imaginative Apologetics: Theology, Philosophy and the Catholic Tradition* (London: SCM Press, 2011).

Deane, S. F., 'Lord Acton and Edmund Burke', *JHI*, 33.2 (1972), pp. 325–35.

D'Entrèves, A. P., *The Medieval Contribution to Political Thought: Aquinas, Marsilius, Hooker* (New York: Humanities Press, 1959).

Denzinger H., and A. Schönmetzer S. J. (eds.), *Enchiridion Symbolorum; Definitionum et Declarationum de Rebus Fidei et Morum* (Freiburg im Breisgau: Herder, 1963).

de Pauley, William Cecil, *The Candle of the Lord: Studies in the Cambridge Platonists* (London: SPCK, 1937, reprinted Freeport, NY: Books for Libraries Press, 1970).

Descartes, René, *Discourse on Method* and the *Meditations*, trans. F. E. Sutcliffe (Harmondsworth: Penguin, 1968).

Devolvé, Jean, *Religion, Critique et Philosophie Positive chez Pierre Bayle* (New York: Burt Franklin, 1971; reprint of edition, Paris: Alcan, 1906).

Dewar, Lindsay, *An Outline of Anglican Moral Theology* (London: Mowbray, 1968).

Dickens, A. G. and John M. Tonkin with the assistance of Kenneth Powell, *The Reformation in Historical Thought* (Oxford: Blackwell, 1985).

Diderot, Denis, *The Nun*, trans. Leonard Tancock (Harmondsworth: Penguin, 1974).

Dixon, R. W., *History of the Church of England from the Abolition of the Roman Jurisdiction* (London: Routledge, 1878).

Donagan, Alan, 'Spinoza's Theology', in Garrett (ed.), *Cambridge Companion to Spinoza* (Cambridge: Cambridge University Press, 1996).

Dost, Timothy P., *Renaissance Humanism in Support of the Gospel in Luther's Early Correspondence: Taking all things captive* (Farnham, Surrey and Burlington, VT: Ashgate, 2001).

Douglas, Brian, *A Companion to Anglican Eucharistic Theology*, vol. 1, *The Reformation to the 19th Century*; vol. 2, *The 20th Century to the Present* (Leiden: Brill, 2012).

Dowling, Maria, 'Cranmer as Humanist Reformer', in Ayris and Selwyn (eds.), *Thomas Cranmer* (Woodbridge, Suffolk, UK: The Boydell Press, 1993).

Downey, James, *The Eighteenth-Century Pulpit: A Study of the Sermons of Butler, Berkeley, Secker, Sterne, Whitefield and Wesley* (Oxford: Oxford University Press, 1969).

Drewery, Benjamin and Richard J. Bauckham (eds.), *Scripture, Tradition and Reason: A Study in the Criteria of Christian Doctrine; Essays in Honour of Richard P. C. Hanson* (Edinburgh: T&T Clark, 1988).

Dudley, Martin, *The Collect in Anglican Liturgy: Texts and Sources 1549–1989* (Alcuin Club Collection No. 72, Collegeville, Minnesota: Liturgical Press, 1994).

Duffy, Eamon, *The Stripping of the Altars: Traditional Religion in England 1400–1580* (New Haven and London: Yale University Press, 1992).

—, *The Voices of Morebath* (New Haven: Yale, 2001).

Dugmore, C. W., *The Mass and the English Reformers* (London: Macmillan, 1958).

Dwan, David, 'Edmund Burke and the Emotions', *JHI*, 72.4 (2011),
     pp. 571–93.
Dwan, David and Christopher Insole (eds.), *The Cambridge Companion
     to Edmund Burke* (Cambridge: Cambridge University Press, 2012).
Ebeling, Gerhard, *Word and Faith*, trans. James W. Leitch (London: SCM
     Press, 1963).
—, *The Word of God and Tradition*, trans. S. H. Hooke (London: Collins,
     1968).
—, *Luther: An Introduction to his Thought*, trans. R. A. Wilson (London:
     Collins; Philadelphia: Fortress Press, 1970).
Eccleshall, R., 'Richard Hooker and the Peculiarities of the English: The
     Reception of the *Ecclesiastical Polity* in the Seventeenth and Eighteenth
     Centuries', *History of Political Thought*, 2 (1981), pp. 63–117.
Edsall, H. S., 'The Idea of History and Progress in Fontenelle and
     Voltaire', *Yale Romanic Studies*, 18 (1941), pp. 163–84.
Eells, H., *The Attitude of Martin Bucer toward the Bigamy of Philip of
     Hesse* (New Haven: Yale University Press, 1924).
Ehrensperger, Kathy and R. Ward Holder (eds.), *Reformation Readings of
     Romans* (London and New York: T&T Clark, 2008).
Elert, W., *The Christian Ethos*, trans. Carl J. Schindler (Philadelphia, PA:
     Fortress Press, 1957).
Eliot, T. S., *For Lancelot Andrewes: Essays on Style and Order* (London:
     Faber & Gwyer, 1928).
Elton, G. R., *The Tudor Constitution: Documents and Commentary*
     (Cambridge: Cambridge University Press, 1972).
Erasmus of Rotterdam, *Enchiridion Militis Christiani (The Manual of the
     Christian Knight)* (London: Wynkyn de Worde, 1533 [1513]; reprinted
     London: Methuen, 1905).
—, *In Praise of Folly* and *Letter to Martin Dorp*, *1515*, trans. Betty
     Radice (Harmondsworth: Penguin, 1971).
Essays and Reviews, 9th edn (London: Longman, Green, Longman, and
     Roberts, 1861).
Evans, G. R., *The Language and Logic of the Bible: The Earlier Middle
     Ages* (Cambridge: Cambridge University Press, 1984).
—, *The Language and Logic of the Bible: The Road to Reformation*
     (Cambridge: Cambridge University Press, 1985).
—. *Problems of Authority in the Reformation Debates* (Cambridge:
     Cambridge University Press, 1992).
Every, G., *The High Church Party, 1688–1718* (London: SPCK, 1956).
Faulkner, J. A., 'Luther and the Bigamous Marriage of Philip of Hesse',
     American Journal of Theology, 17 (1913), pp. 206–31.
Ferguson, Arthur B., 'The Historical Perspective of Richard Hooker:
     A Renaissance Paradox', *Journal of Medieval and Renaissance Studies*,
     3 (1973), pp. 17–49.

—, *Clio Unbound: Perception of the Social and Cultural Past in Renaissance England* (Durham, NC: Duke University Press, 1979).

Feyerabend, Paul, *Against Method: Outline of an Anarchistic Theory of Knowledge* (London: NLB, 1975).

Field, Richard, *Of the Church, Five Books* (Cambridge: Cambridge University Press for the Ecclesiastical History Society, 1847–).

Flannery, Austin. OP (ed.), *Vatican Council II: The Conciliar and Post Conciliar Documents*, New Revised Edition (Northport, NY: Costello; Dublin: Dominican Publications, 1992).

Flint, Robert, *History of the Philosophy of History*, vol. 1: *Historical Philosophy in France [etc]* (Edinburgh: Blackwood, 1893).

Forbes, Duncan, '"Scientific Whiggism": Adam Smith and John Millar', *Cambridge Journal*, 7 (1954), pp. 643–70.

Ford, Alan, *James Ussher: Theology, History, and Politics in Early-Modern Ireland and England* (Oxford: Oxford University Press, 2007).

Foster, Stephen Paul, *Melancholy Duty: The Hume-Gibbon Attack on Christianity* (Dordrecht: Kluwer, 2010).

Fraenkel, Peter, *Testimonia Patrum: The Function of the Patristic Argument in the Theology of Philip Melanchthon* (Geneva: Librairie E. Droz, 1961).

France, Peter, *Diderot* (Oxford: Oxford University Press, 1983).

Francis, Keith A. and William Gibson (eds.), *The Oxford Handbook of the British Sermon 1689–1901* (Oxford: Oxford University Press, 2012).

Frankel, Charles, *The Faith of Reason: The Idea of Progress in the French Enlightenment* (New York: King's Crown Press, 1948).

Franklin, J. H., *Jean Bodin and the Sixteenth-century Revolution in the Methodology of Law and History* (New York: Columbia University Press, 1963).

Freeman, Arthur J., *An Ecumenical Theology of the Heart: The Theology of Count Nicholas Ludwig von Zinzendorf* (Bethlehem, PA: Moravian Church in America, 1998).

Frere, W. H. and W. P. M. Kennedy (eds.), *Visitation Articles and Injunctions* (London: Longmans, Green & Co., 1910).

Frisch, Morton J., 'Burke on Theory', *Cambridge Journal*, 7.5 (1954), pp. 292–7.

Furbank, P. N., *Diderot* (London: Minerva, 1993).

Furet, François, 'Civilization and Barbarism in Gibbon's History', *Daedalus*, 105.3 (1976), pp. 209–16.

Fussner, F. Smith, *The Historical Revolution: English Historical Writing and Thought, 1580–1640* (New York: Columbia University Press; London: Routledge and Kegan Paul, 1962).

Gadamer, Hans-Georg, *Truth and Method*, 2nd edn (London: Sheed and Ward, 1979).

Garber, Daniel and Michael Ayers (eds.), *The Cambridge History of Seventeenth-Century Philosophy*, vol. 2 (Cambridge: Cambridge University Press, 2008).

Gargett, Graham, 'Voltaire and Protestantism', *SVEC*, 188 (1980).

Garnett, Jane, 'Bishop Butler and the *Zeitgeist*: Butler and the Development of Christian Moral Philosophy in Victorian Britain', in Cunliffe (ed.), *Butler's Moral and Religious Thought* (Oxford: Clarendon Press, 1992).

Garrard, Graeme, *Rousseau's Counter-Enlightenment: A Republican Critique of the Philosophes* (New York: State University of New York, 2003).

Garrett, Don (ed.), *The Cambridge Companion to Spinoza* (Cambridge: Cambridge University Press, 1996).

Gaskin, J. C. A., *Hume's Philosophy of Religion,* 2nd edn (Basingstoke: Macmillan, 1988).

—, 'Hume on Religion', in Norton (ed.), *Cambridge Companion to Hume* (Cambridge: Cambridge University Press, 1993).

Gay, Peter, *The Party of Humanity: Studies in the French Enlightenment* (London: Wiedenfeld & Nicolson, 1964).

—, *The Enlightenment: An Interpretation, I, The Rise of Modern Paganism* (London: Weidenfeld and Nicolson, 1966); *II, The Science of Freedom* (London: Weidenfeld and Nicolson, 1970).

—, 'Why was the Enlightenment?', in id. (ed.), *Eighteenth-Century Studies* (Hanover, NH: University Press of New England, 1972).

— (ed.), *Eighteenth-Century Studies presented to Arthur M. Wilson* (Hanover, NH: University Press of New England, 1972).

—, *Style in History* (London: Cape, 1975).

Geach, Peter, 'The Religion of Thomas Hobbes', *Religious Studies*, 17 (1981), pp. 549–58.

George, C. H. and K. George, *The Protestant Mind of the English Reformation 1570–1640* (Princeton, NJ: Princeton University Press, 1961).

Gerrish, Brian A., *Grace and Reason: A Study in the Theology of Luther* (Oxford: Clarendon Press, 1962).

—, *The Old Protestantism and the New: Essays on the Reformation Heritage* (Edinburgh: T&T Clark, 1982).

Gert, B. (ed.), *Hobbes: Man and Citizen:* De Homine *and* De Cive (Hassocks, Sussex: Harvester Press, 1972).

Gibbon, Edward, *Autobiography* (London: Dent; New York: Dutton (Everyman), 1911).

—, *The Decline and Fall of the Roman Empire*, abridged with an introduction by D. M. Low (Harmondsworth: Penguin, 1963).

Gibbon, *The Decline and Fall of the Roman Empire and other Selections from the Writings of Edward Gibbon*, ed. H. R. Trevor-Roper (New York: Washington Square Press, 1963; London: New English Library, 1966).

Gibbs, Lee W., 'Richard Hooker's *Via Media* Doctrine of Scripture and Tradition', *HTR*, 95.2 (2000), pp. 227–35.

Gibson, William, *The Church of England 1688–1832: Unity and Accord* (London and New York: Routledge, 2001).

—, Peter Forsaith and Martin Wellings (eds.), *The Ashgate Research Companion to World Methodism* (Farnham; Burlington, VT: Ashgate, 2013).

Gilbert, Felix, *Machiavelli and Guicciardini* (Princeton: Princeton University Press, 1965).

Gill, Frederick C., *The Romantic Movement and Methodism* (London: Epworth Press, 1937).

Gilley, Sheridan, 'Christianity and Enlightenment: An Historical Survey', *History of European Ideas*, 1.2 (1981), pp. 103–21.

Gilmore, Myron P., 'Italian Reactions to Erasmian Humanism', in Oberman and Brady (eds.), *Itinerium Italicum* (Leiden: E. J. Brill, 1975).

Ginsberg, Robert, 'David Hume versus the Enlightenment', *SVEC,* 88 (1972), pp. 599–650.

Gladstone, William Ewart, *Studies Subsidiary to the Works of Bishop Butler* (Oxford: Clarendon Press, 1896).

Glendinning, Victoria, *Jonathan Swift* (London: Hutchinson, 1998).

Glover, Willis B., 'God and Thomas Hobbes', in Brown (ed.), *Hobbes Studies* (Oxford: Blackwell, 1965).

Gooch, G. P., *Political Thought in England from Bacon to Halifax* (London: Williams and Norgate, 1914).

—, *Catherine the Great and Other Studies* (London: Longmans, Green, 1954).

Gossman, Lionel, *Medievalism and the Ideologies of the Enlightenment* (Baltimore, ML: Johns Hopkins Press, 1968).

Grafton, Anthony, 'Church History in Early Modern Europe: Tradition and Innovation', in Van Liere, Ditchfield and Louthan (eds.), *Sacred History* (Oxford: Oxford University Press, 2012).

Green, F. C., *Rousseau and the Idea of Progress* (Oxford: Oxford University Press, 1950; reprinted Norwood Editions, 1978).

Green, J. Brazier, *John Wesley and William Law* (London: Epworth Press, 1945).

Green, Louis, *Chronicle into History* (Cambridge: Cambridge University Press, 1972).

Green, V. H. H., *The Young Mr. Wesley* (London: Epworth Press [Wyvern Books], 1963 [Edward Arnold, 1961]).

Greenleaf, W. H., *Order, Empiricism and Politics: The Traditions of English Political Thought, 1500–1700* (Oxford: Oxford University Press, 1964).

Greenslade, S. L., *The English Reformers and the Fathers of the Church* (Oxford: Clarendon Press, 1960).

— (ed.), *The Cambridge History of the Bible: The West from the Reformation to the Present Day* (Cambridge: Cambridge University Press, 1963).

Greer, Rowan A., *Anglican Approaches to Scripture: From the Reformation to the Present* (New York: Crossroad, 2006).

Gregory, Jeremy, 'Charles Wesley and the Eighteenth Century', in Newport and Campbell (eds.), *Charles Wesley* (Peterborough: Epworth Press, 2007).

—, 'Long Eighteenth Century', in Maddox and Vickers (eds.), *Cambridge Companion to John Wesley* (Cambridge: Cambridge University Press, 2010).

Gregory, Tullio, 'Pierre Charron's "Scandalous Book"', in Hunter and Wootton (eds.), *Atheism from the Reformation to the Enlightenment* (Oxford: Oxford University Press, 1992).

Grierson, Herbert and J. C. Smith, *A Critical History of English Poetry* (Harmondsworth: Penguin, 1962 [1944]).

Griffiss, James E., *The Anglican Vision* (Cambridge, MA: Cowley Publications, 1997).

Grislis, Egil, 'The Assurance of Faith According to Richard Hooker', in McGrade (ed.), *Hooker and the Construction of Christian Community* (Tempe: Medieval & Renaissance Texts & Studies, 1997).

Grosshans, Hans-Peter, 'Luther on Faith and Reason', in Helmer (ed.), *Global Luther* (Minneapolis, MN: Fortress Press, 2009).

Guibbory, A., 'Francis Bacon's View of History: The Cycles of Error and the Progress of Truth', *Journal of English and German Philology*, 74 (1975), pp. 336–50.

Ha, Polly and Patrick Collinson (eds.), *The Reception of the Continental Reformation in Britain* (Oxford: Oxford University Press for the British Academy, 2010).

Haakonssen, Knud (ed.), *Enlightenment and Religion: Rational Dissent in Eighteenth-Century Britain* (Cambridge: Cambridge University Press, 1996).

Hacking, Ian, *The Emergence of Probability: A Philosophical Study of Early Ideas about Probability, Induction, and Statistical Inference* (Cambridge: Cambridge University Press, 1975).

Hales, John, *Golden Remains* (London, 1688).

—, *A Tract Concerning Schism and Schismatics* (London, 1700).

—, *Works* (Glasgow, 1765).

Hall, Basil, *Humanists and Protestants 1500–1900* (Edinburgh: T&T Clark, 1990).

—, 'The Geneva Version of the English Bible', in Stephens (ed.), *The Bible, the Reformation and the Church* (Sheffield: Sheffield Academic, 1995).

Hampshire, Stuart, *Spinoza* (Harmondsworth: Penguin, 1951).

Hampton, Stephen, *Anti-Arminians: The Anglican Reformed Tradition from Charles II to George I* (Oxford: Oxford University Press, 2008).

Harris, Ian, 'Burke and Religion', in Dwan and Insole (eds.), *Cambridge Companion to Edmund Burke* (Cambridge: Cambridge University Press, 2012).

Harrison, Peter, *'Religion' and the Religions in the English Enlightenment* (Cambridge: Cambridge University Press, 1990).

Harrison, W. H., 'Prudence and Custom: Revisiting Hooker on Authority', *ATR*, 84.4 (2002), pp. 897–913.

Hartle, Ann, 'Montaigne and Skepticism', in Langer (ed.), *Cambridge Companion to Montaigne* (Cambridge: Cambridge University Press, 2005).

Haskins, C. H., *The Renaissance of the Twelfth Century* (Cambridge: Cambridge University Press, 1927).

Haugaard, W. P., *Elizabeth and the English Reformation* (Cambridge: Cambridge University Press, 1968).

—, 'Renaissance Patristic Scholarship and Theology in Sixteenth-Century England', *The Sixteenth Century Journal*, 10.3 (1979), pp. 37–60.

Hauser, Alan J. and Duane F. Watson (eds.), *A History of Biblical Interpretation*, vol. 2: *The Medieval through the Reformation Periods* (Grand Rapids, MI: Eerdmans, 2009).

Hazard, Paul, *The European Mind 1680–1715*, trans. J. Lewis May (Harmondsworth: Penguin, 1964 [1953]).

Headley, John M., *Luther's View of Church History* (New Haven and London: Yale University Press, 1963).

Hebblethwaite, Brian, 'Butler on Conscience and Virtue', in Cunliffe (ed.), *Butler's Moral and Religious Thought* (Oxford: Clarendon Press, 1992).

Heilbroner, Robert L., 'The Paradox of Progress: Decline and Decay in *The Wealth of Nations*', *JHI*, 34 (1973), pp. 243–62.

Heitzenrater, Richard P., 'John and Charles Wesley: Life, Ministry and Legacy', in Yrigoyen (ed.), *T&T Clark Companion to Methodism* (London: T&T Clark International, 2010).

Helm, Paul, *John Calvin's Ideas* (Oxford: Oxford University Press, 2004).

Helmer, Christine (ed.), *The Global Luther: A Theologian for Modern Times* (Minneapolis, MN: Fortress Press, 2009).

Hendrix, Scott H., *Recultivating the Vineyard: The Reformation Agendas of Christianization* (Louisville and London: Westminster John Knox Press, 2004).

Henson, Herbert Hensley, *Bishoprick Papers* (London: Oxford University Press, 1946).

Herbert of Cherbury, *The Life of Lord Herbert of Cherbury, written by Himself and continued until his Death* (London: Cassell, 1893).

—, *De Veritate*, trans. Meyrick H. Carré (Bristol: University of Bristol Press, J. W. Arrowsmith, 1937; facsimile reprint: Thoemmes Continuum, 1999).

Heyd, Michael, 'A Disguised Atheist or a Sincere Christian? The Enigma of Pierre Bayle', *Bibliothèque d'Humanisme et Renaissance*, 39.1 (1977), pp. 157–66.

Hill, W. Speed (ed.), *Studies in Richard Hooker: Essays Preliminary to an Edition of his Works* (Cleveland and London: The Press of Case Western Reserve University, 1972).

Hillerbrand, Hans J. (ed.), *The Encyclopedia of Protestantism* (London and New York: Routledge, 2004).

Hobbes, Thomas, *English Works*, ed. W. Molesworth (London, 1843).

—, *Leviathan*, ed. and intro. C. B. Macpherson (Harmondsworth: Penguin, 1968).

—, *De Homine* and *De Cive*, in Gert, B. (ed.), *Hobbes: Man and Citizen* (Indianapolis: Hackett, 1991).

Hogan, Linda, *Confronting the Truth:Conscience in the Catholic Tradition* (Mahwah, NJ: Paulist Press, 2000).

Holder, R. Ward, 'Revelation and Scripture', in Whitford (ed.), *T&T Clark Companion to Reformation Theology* (London and New York: T&T Clark, 2012).

Holland, Henry Scott, *The Optimism of Butler's 'Analogy'* (Oxford: Clarendon Press, 1908).

Hooker, Richard, *The Folger Library Edition of the Works of Richard Hooker*, ed. W. Speed Hill, 7 vols (vols. 1–5, Cambridge, MA and London: The Belknap Press of Harvard University Press, 1977–90; vol. 6, Binghampton, NY: Medieval and Renaissance Texts & Studies, 1993; vol. 7, Tempe, AZ: Medieval and Renaissance Texts and Studies, 1998).

Horowitz, Maryanne Cline, 'Pierre Charron's View of the Source of Wisdom', *Journal of the History of Philosophy* 9.4 (1971), pp. 443–57.

Hulliung, Mark, *The Autocritique of Enlightenment: Rousseau and the Philosophes* (Cambridge, MA: Harvard University Press, 1994).

Hulme, P. and L. Jordanova (eds.), *The Enlightenment and its Shadows* (London and New York: Routledge, 1990).

Hume, David, *Essays, Moral, Political and Literary* (*The World's Classics*, London: Grant Richards, 1903).

—, *Dialogues Concerning Natural Religion*, ed. Martin Bell (Harmondsworth: Penguin, 1990 [1779]).

—, *A Dissertation on the Passions; The Natural History of Religion*, ed. Tom L. Beauchamp (Oxford: Clarendon Press, 2007).

Hunt, Arnold, *The Art of Hearing: English Preachers and Their Audiences, 1590–1640* (Cambridge: Cambridge University Press, 2010).

Hunter, Michael and David Wootton (eds.), *Atheism from the Reformation to the Enlightenment* (Oxford: Oxford University Press, 1992).

Inge, W. R., *Studies of English Mystics* (London: John Murray, 1907).

Israel, Jonathan, *Radical Enlightenment: Philosophy and the Making of Modernity* (Oxford: Oxford University Press, 2001).

—, *Enlightenment Contested: Philosophy, Modernity, and the Emancipation of Man 1670–1752* (Oxford: Oxford University Press, 2006).

Jacob, Margaret C., *The Radical Enlightenment: Pantheists, Freemasons and Republicans* (London: George Allen and Unwin, 1981).

James, D. G., *The Life of Reason: Hobbes, Locke, Bolingbroke* (London: Longmans, 1949).

Jeffner, Anders, *Butler and Hume on Religion: A Comparative Analysis* (Stockholm: Diakonistyrelsens Bokförlag, 1966).

Jenkins, Gary W., *John Jewel and the English Church: The Dilemmas of an Erastian Reformer* (Aldershot, Hants and Burlington VT: Ashgate, 2006).

Jesseph, Douglas M., 'Hobbes's Atheism', *Midwest Studies in Philosophy*, 26 (2002), pp. 140–66.

Jewel, John, *An Apology of the Church of England*, ed. J. E. Booty (Ithaca, NY: Cornell University Press for The Folger Shakespeare Library, 1963).

Johnson, Anna Marie and John A. Maxfield (eds.), *The Reformation as Christianization: Essays on Scott Hendrix's Christianization Thesis* (Tübingen: Mohr Siebeck, 2012).

Johnson, Paul, 'Hobbes' Anglican Doctrine of Salvation', in Ross, et al. (eds.), *Hobbes in his Time* (Minneapolis, MN: University of Minnesota Press, 1974).

Johnson, Samuel, *Journey to the Western Islands of Scotland* and James Boswell, *Journal of a Tour to the Hebrides with Samuel Johnson LL.D.*, ed. R. W. Chapman (London: Oxford University Press, 1924).

—, *Lives of the English Poets* (London: Dent; New York: Dutton [Everyman], 1925).

—, *Selected Writings*, ed. Patrick Cruttwell (Harmondsworth: Penguin, 1968).

—, *The History of Rasselas, Prince of Abissinia*, ed. Paul Goring (Harmondsworth: Penguin, 2007).

Jones, Scott J., *John Wesley's Conception and Use of Scripture* (Nashville, TN: Kingswood Books [Abingdon Press], 1995).

Joyce, A. J., *Richard Hooker and Anglican Moral Theology* (Oxford: Oxford University Press, 2012).

Kant, Immanuel, *Critique of Pure Reason*, trans. J. M. D. Meiklejohn, intro. A. D. Lindsay (London: Dent; New York: Dutton (Everyman), 1934).

—, *Kant's Political Writings*, trans. H. B. Nisbett and H. Reiss (Cambridge: Cambridge University Press, 1970)

Kaye, Bruce, 'Authority and the Interpretation of Scripture in Hooker's *Of the Laws of Ecclesiastical Polity*', *Journal of Religious History*, 21.1 (1997), pp. 80–109.

Kaye, Françoise, *Charron et Montaigne: Du Plagiat à l'Originalité* (Ottawa: University of Ottawa, 1982).

Keeling, S. V., *Descartes*, 2nd edn (Oxford: Oxford University Press, 1968).

Kelly, J. N. D., *Early Christian Doctrines*, 3rd edn (London: Adam and Charles Black, 1965).

Kendall, R. T., *Calvin and English Calvinism to 1649* (Oxford: Oxford University Press, 1979).

Kilcup, Rodney W., 'Burke's Historicism', *Journal of Modern History*, 49 (1972), pp. 394–410.

—, 'Reason and the Basis of Morality in Burke', *Journal of Historical Philosophy*, 17.3 (1979), pp. 271–84.

Killeen, Kevin, *Biblical Scholarship, Science and Politics in Early Modern England: Thomas Browne and the Thorny Place of Knowledge* (Farnham; Burlington, VT: Ashgate, 2009).

Kirby, W. J. Torrance, *Richard Hooker's Doctrine of the Royal Supremacy* (Leiden: Brill, 1990).

— (ed.), *Richard Hooker and the English Reformation* (Dordrecht: Kluwer, 2003).

— (ed.), *A Companion to Richard Hooker*, Foreword by Rowan Williams (Leiden and Boston: Brill, 2008).

Kirk, Kenneth, *Some Principles of Moral Theology and their Application* (London: Longmans, 1920).

—, *Ignorance, Faith and Conformity* (London: Longmans, Green and Co., 1925).

Kisch, Guido, *Melanchthons Rechts-und-Soziallehre* (Berlin: Walter de Gruyer & Co., 1967).

Knox, S. J., *Walter Travers: Paragon of Elizabethan Puritanism* (London: Methuen, 1962).

Kolb, Robert, *Martin Luther: Confessor of the Faith* (Oxford: Oxford University Press, 2009).

Koyré, Alexandre, *Newtonian Studies* (London: Chapman Hall, 1965).

Kristeller, Paul Oskar, *Renaissance Thought and its Sources*, ed. Michael Mooney (New York: Columbia University Press, 1979).

Kroll, Richard, Richard Ashcraft and Perez Zagoria (eds.), *Philosophy, Science and Religion in England 1640–1700* (Cambridge: Cambridge University Press, 1992).

Krutch, Joseph Wood, *Samuel Johnson* (New York and Burlingame: Harcourt, Brace and World, 1963).

Labrousse, Elisabeth, 'La mèthode critique chez Pierre Bayle et l'Histoire', *Revue internationale de philosophie*, 11 (1957), pp. 450–65.

—, *Pierre Bayle*, vol. 2, *Heterodoxie et Rigorisme* (The Hague: Nijhoff, 1964).

—, *Bayle* (Oxford: Oxford University Press, 1983).

Lake, Peter, *Moderate Puritans and the Elizabethan Church* (Cambridge: Cambridge University Press, 1982).

—, 'Lancelot Andrewes and the Myth of Anglicanism', in Lake and Questier (eds.), *Conformity and Orthodoxy in the English Church, c. 1560–1660* (Woodbridge: The Boydell Press, 2000).

Lake, Peter and Michael Questier (eds.), *Conformity and Orthodoxy in the English Church, c. 1560–1660* (Woodbridge: Boydell Press, 2000).

—, 'Business as Usual? The Immediate Reception of Hooker's *Ecclesiastical Polity*', *JEH*, 52 (2001), pp. 456–86.

Lane, Anthony N. S., *John Calvin: Student of the Church Fathers* (Grand Rapids, MI: Baker Books, 1999).

—, '*Sola Scriptura*: Making Sense of a Post-Reformation Slogan', in Satterthwaite and Wright (eds.), *A Pathway unto the Holy Scripture* (Grand Rapids, MI: Wm. B. Eerdmans Publishing Company, 1994).

Langer, Ullrich (ed.), *The Cambridge Companion to Montaigne* (Cambridge: Cambridge University Press, 2005).

Larmore, Charles, 'Scepticism', in Garber and Ayers (eds.), *Cambridge History of Seventeenth-Century Philosophy*, vol. 2 (Cambridge: Cambridge University Press, 2003).

Law, William, *Works* (London: Richardson, 1761; reprinted Brockenhurst: Moreton, 1892).

—, *William Law's Defence of Church Principles: Three Letters to the Bishop of Bangor*, ed. J. O. Nash and Charles Gore (London: Griffith Farran, 1893).

—, *A Serious Call to a Devout and Holy Life* (London: Dent; New York: Dutton (Everyman), 1906).

Lehner, Ulrich, L. and Michael Printy (eds.), *A Companion to the Catholic Enlightenment in Europe* (Leiden: Brill, 2013).

Léonard, E. G., *A History of Protestantism*, ed. H. H. Rowley, trans. Joyce M. H. Reid (London: Thomas Nelson, 1965), vol. 1: *The Reformation*.

Levin, Harry, *The Myth of the Golden Age in the Renaissance* (Bloomington: Indiana University Press, 1969).

Levy, Frank J., *Tudor Historical Thought* (San Marino, CA: Huntington Library, 1967).

Lewis, C. S., *The Discarded Image. An Introduction to Medieval and Renaissance Literature* (Cambridge: Cambridge University Press, 1964).

Lightfoot, J. B., *Leaders of the Northern Church: Sermons Preached in the Diocese of Durham* (London: Macmillan, 1890).

Lindsay, J. O. (ed.), *The New Cambridge Modern History*, vol. 7, *The Old Regime, 1713–63* (Cambridge: Cambridge University Press, 1957).

Littell, Franklin H., *The Anabaptist View of the Church: A Study in the Origins of Sectarian Protestantism*, 2nd edn (Boston, MA: Starr King Press, 1958).

Livingston, Donald W. and James T. King (eds.), *Hume: A Re-evaluation* (New York: Fordham University Press, 1976).

Lloyd, C. (ed.), *Formularies of Faith Put forth by Authority during the Reign of Henry VIII* (Oxford: Oxford University Press, 1825).

Locke, John, *A Letter Concerning Toleration*, *Works*, vol. 6 (London: Johnson, 1801a).

—, *The Reasonableness of Christianity*, *Works*, vol. 7 (London: Johnson, 1801b).

—, *The Conduct of the Understanding* (Oxford: Oxford University Press, 1901).

—, *An Essay Concerning Human Understanding* (London: Dent; New York: Dutton (Everyman), 1961).

—, *Two Treatises of Government: A Critical Edition with an Introduction and Apparatus Criticus*, ed. and intro. Peter Laslett (Cambridge: Cambridge University Press, 1960; Mentor Book, New York and Toronto: The New American Library; London: The New English Library, 1965).

Lohse, Bernhard, 'Conscience and Authority in Luther', in Oberman (ed.), *Luther and the Dawn of the Modern Era* (Leiden: Brill, 1974).

Lossky, Nicholas, *Lancelot Andrewes, the Preacher (1555–1626): The Origins of the Mystical Theology of the Church of England*, trans. Andrew Louth, intro. Michael Ramsey (Oxford: Clarendon Press, 1991).

Love, Walter D., 'Edmund Burke's Idea of the Body Corporate: A Study in Imagery', *Review of Politics*, 27 (1965), pp. 184–97.

Lovejoy, A. O., *The Great Chain of Being* (Cambridge, MA: Harvard University Press, 1953 [1936]).

Lucas, Paul, 'On Edmund Burke's Doctrine of Prescription, Or, An Appeal from the New to the Old Lawyers', *Historical Journal*, 11.1 (1968), pp. 35–63.

Luther, Martin, *D. Martin Luthers Werke* (Weimar: Weimarer Ausgabe, 1883–).

—, *The Bondage of the Will*, trans. J. I. Packer and O. R. Johnston (London: James Clarke, 1957).

—, *Luther and Erasmus on Freewill*, ed. E. G. Rupp (*LCC*).

—, *Martinus Lutherus contra Henricum Regem Angliæ*, Martin Luther against Henry King of England, trans. E. S. Buchanan (New York: Charles A. Swift, 1928): http://anglicanhistory.org/lutherania/against_henry.html.

McAdoo, H. R., *The Structure of Caroline Moral Theology* (London: Longmans, Green and Co., 1949).

—, *The Spirit of Anglicanism: A Survey of Anglican Theological Method in the Seventeenth Century* (London: A&C Black, 1975).

—, *The Eucharistic Theology of Jeremy Taylor* (Norwich: Canterbury Press, 1988).

McCloy, Shelby T., *Gibbon's Antagonism to Christianity* (London: Williams & Norgate, 1933).

—, *The Humanitarian Movement in Eighteenth-Century France* (Kentucky: Kentucky University Press, 1964).

McConica, J. K., *English Humanists and Reformation Politics under Henry VIII and Edward VI* (Oxford: Clarendon Press, 1965).

MacCulloch, Diarmaid, *Thomas Cranmer: A Life* (New Haven and London: Yale University Press, 1996).

—, *Tudor Church Militant* (London: Allen Lane, 1999).

—, 'Richard Hooker's Reputation', in Kirby (ed.), *Companion to Richard Hooker* (Leiden: Brill, 2008).

McCulloch, Peter, 'Absent Presence: Lancelot Andrewes and 1662', in Platten and Woods (eds.), *Comfortable Words* (London: SCM Press, 2012).

Macfarlane, Robert, *Mountains of the Mind: A History of a Fascination* (London: Granta Books, 2003).

McGrade, A. S. (ed.), *Richard Hooker and the Construction of Christian Community* (Tempe, AZ: Renaissance Texts and Studies, 1997).

McGrath, Alister, *The Intellectual Origins of the European Reformation* (Oxford: Blackwell, 1987).

MacIntyre, Alasdair, *After Virtue,* 2nd edn (London: Duckworth, 1985).

McKim, Donald K. (ed.), *Calvin and the Bible* (Cambridge: Cambridge University Press, 2006).

McLachlan, Herbert John, *Socinianism in Seventeenth-Century England* (London: Oxford University Press, 1951).

McLelland, Joseph C., *The Visible Words of God: A Study in the Theology of Peter Martyr 1500–1562* (Edinburgh and London: Oliver and Boyd, 1957).

McManners, John, 'Enlightenment: Secular and Christian', in id. (ed.), *Oxford Illustrated History* (Oxford: Oxford University Press, 1990).

— (ed.), *The Oxford Illustrated History of Christianity* (Oxford: Oxford University Press, 1990).

Mack, Phyllis, *Heart Religion in the British Enlightenment: Gender and Emotion in Early Methodism* (Cambridge: Cambridge University Press, 2008).

Maddox, Randy L., 'Wesley's Engagement with the Natural Sciences', in id. and Vickers (eds.), *Cambridge Companion to Wesley* (Cambridge: Cambridge University Press, 2010).

Maddox, Randy L. and Jason E. Vickers (eds.), *The Cambridge Companion to John Wesley* (Cambridge: Cambridge University Press, 2010).

—, 'The Rule of Christian Faith, Practice and Hope: John Wesley and the Bible', *Epworth Review*, 38.2 (2011), pp. 6–37.

Malebranche, Nicolas, *Oeuvres Completes*, vol. 2 (Paris: Librairie J. Vrin, 1963).

Maltby, Judith, '"Extravagancies and Impertinencies": Set Forms, Conceived and Extempore Prayer in Revolutionary England', in Mears and Ryrie (eds.), *Worship and the Parish Church* (Farnham, Surrey and Burlington, VT: Ashgate, 2013).

Mannermaa, Tuomo, *Christ Present in Faith: Luther's View of Justification* (Minneapolis: Fortress Press, 2005).

Manuel, Frank, 'From Equality to Organicism', *JHI*, 17.1 (1956), pp. 54–69.

—, *The Eighteenth Century Confronts the Gods* (Cambridge, MA: Harvard University Press, 1959).

—, *The Prophets of Paris* (Cambridge, MA: Harvard University Press, 1962).

—, *Isaac Newton, Historian* (Cambridge, MA: Belknap Press of Harvard University Press, 1963).

—, *The Religion of Isaac Newton* (Oxford: Clarendon Press, 1974).

Maritain, Jacques, *Three Reformers* (London: Sheed and Ward, 1928).

Marshall, John, 'Locke and Latitudinarianism', in Kroll, Ashcraft and Zagoria (eds.), *Philosophy, Science and Religion* (Cambridge: Cambridge University Press, 1992).

—, *John Locke: Resistance, Religion and Responsibility* (Cambridge: Cambridge University Press, 1994).

Marshall, John S., *Hooker and the Anglican Tradition* (London: A&C Black, 1963).

Martin, Jessica, *Walton's Lives: Conformist Commemorations and the Rise of Biography* (Oxford: Oxford University Press, 2000).

Martinich, A. P., *The Two Gods of Leviathan: Thomas Hobbes on Religion and Politics* (Cambridge: Cambridge University Press, 1992).

Marsak, Leonard M., *Bernard de Fontenelle: The Idea of Science in the French Enlightenment* (Philadelphia, PA: Transactions of the American Philosophical Society, 1959).

Mathew, David, *Acton: The Formative Years* (London: Eyre and Spottiswoode, 1946).

Mears, Natalie and Alec Ryrie (eds.), *Worship and the Parish Church in Early Modern Britain* (Farnham, Surrey and Burlington, VT: Ashgate, 2013).

Meinecke, Friedrich, *Historism: The Rise of a New Historical Outlook* (London: Routledge and Kegan Paul, 1972).

Melanchthon, Phillipp, *Melanchton and Bucer* (*LCC*).

Middleton, Arthur, *Fathers and Anglicans: The Limits of Orthodoxy* (Leominster: Gracewing, 2001).

Milton, John, *The English Poems of John Milton*, ed. H. C. Beeching (London: Oxford University Press (The World's Classics), 1918).

Mintz, Samuel I., *The Hunting of Leviathan: Seventeenth Century Reactions to the Materialism and Moral Philosophy of Thomas Hobbes* (Cambridge: Cambridge University Press, 1962).

Mitchell, Basil, 'Butler as a Christian Apologist', in Cunliffe (ed.), *Butler's Moral and Religious Thought* (Oxford: Clarendon Press, 1992).

Momigliano, Arnaldo, *Studies in Historiography* (London: Weidenfeld & Nicolson, 1966).

—, *Essays in Ancient and Modern History* (Oxford: Blackwell, 1977).

Montaigne, Michel de, *Journal de Voyage en Italie par la Suisse et l'Allemande en 1580–81*, ed. Charles Dédéyan (Paris: Société les Belles Lettres, 1946).

—, *The Complete Essays*, trans. M. A. Screech (Harmondsworth: Penguin, 1991).

Montesquieu, Charles de Secondat, Baron de, *The Spirit of Laws*, trans. Thomas Nugent (1752), revised J. V. Prichard (London: Bell, 1914).

More, Paul Elmer and Frank Leslie Cross (eds.), *Anglicanism: The Thought and Practice of the Church of England, Illustrated from the Literature of the Seventeenth Century* (London: SPCK, 1935).

Morley, John, *The Life of William Ewart Gladstone* (London: Edward Lloyd, 1908).

Morris, Colin, *The Discovery of the Individual 1050–1200* (Toronto: University of Toronto Press; London: SPCK, 1972).

Morrissey, Mary, *Politics and the Paul's Cross Sermons 1558–1642* (Oxford: Oxford University Press, 2011).

Mortimer, Sarah, *Reason and Religion in the English Revolution: The Challenge of Socinianism* (Cambridge: Cambridge University Press, 2010).

Mossner, E. C., *Bishop Butler and the Age of Reason* (Bristol: Thoemmes, 1990 [1936]).

Muirhead, John H., *The Platonic Tradition in Anglo-Saxon Philosophy* (London: George Allen & Unwin, 1931).

Muller, Richard A., *The Unaccommodated Calvin: Studies in the Foundation of a Theological Tradition* (Oxford: Oxford University Press, 2000).

—, *After Calvin: Studies in the Development of a Theological Tradition* (New York and Oxford: Oxford University Press, 2003).

Munz, Peter, *The Place of Hooker in the History of Thought* (London: Routledge and Kegan Paul, 1952; reprinted New York: Greenwood Press, 1970).

Nathan, George J., 'The Existence and Nature of God in Hume's Theism', in Livingston and King (eds.), *Hume: A Re-evaluation* (New York: Fordham University Press, 1976).

Neelands, David, 'Hooker on Scripture, Reason and "Tradition"', in McGrade (ed.), *Hooker and the Construction of Christian Community* (Tempe, AZ: Renaissance Texts and Studies, 1997).

Newman, John Henry, *An Essay on the Development of Christian Doctrine*, ed. J. M. Cameron (Harmondsworth: Penguin, 1974).
—, *The Via Media of the Anglican Church*, ed., intro, and notes H. D. Weidner (Oxford: Clarendon Press, 1990).
Newport, Kenneth G. C. and Ted A. Campbell (eds.), *Charles Wesley: Life, Literature and Legacy* (Peterborough: Epworth Press, 2007).
Newton, Isaac, *Newton's Philosophy of Nature: Selections from his Writings*, ed. H. S. Thayer (New York: Hafner; London: Collier Macmillan, 1953).
Nichols, Bridget (ed.), *The Collect in the Churches of the Reformation* (London: SCM Press, 2010).
Nicholson, Marjorie, *Newton Demands the Muse* (Princeton: Princeton University Press, 1946).
Niesel, Wilhelm, *The Theology of John Calvin*, trans. Harold Knight (London: Lutterworth Press, 1956).
Nietzsche, Friedrich, *Twilight of the Idols* and *The Antichrist*, trans. R. J. Hollingdale (Harmondsworth: Penguin, 1968).
Norton, David Fate (ed.), *The Cambridge Companion to Hume* (Cambridge: Cambridge University Press, 1993).
Novarr, David, *The Making of Walton's Lives* (Ithaca, NY: Cornell University Press, 1958).
Null, Ashley, *Thomas Cranmer's Doctrine of Repentance* (Oxford: Oxford University Press, 2000).
Oakeshott, Michael, *Hobbes on Civil Association* (Oxford: Blackwell, 1975).
Oberman, Heiko A., *The Harvest of Medieval Theology: Gabriel Biel and Late Medieval Nominalism* (Cambridge, MA: Harvard University Press, 1963).
— (ed.), *Luther and the Dawn of the Modern Era* (Leiden: Brill, 1974).
Oberman, Heiko A. and Thomas A. Brady Jnr (eds.), *Itinerium Italicum: The Profile of the Italian Renaissance in the Mirror of its European Tranformations* (Leiden: Brill, 1975).
—, *The Dawn of the Reformation* (Edinburgh: T&T Clark, 1986).
O'Brien, Conor Cruise, *The Great Melody: A Thematic Biography and Commented Anthology of Edmund Burke* (London: Minerva, 1993).
O'Day, Rosemary, *The Debate on the English Reformation* (London and New York: Methuen, 1986).
O'Donovan, Oliver, *On the Thirty-nine Articles: Conversations with Tudor Christianity*, 2nd edn (London: SCM Press, 2011).
O'Gorman, Frank, *Edmund Burke: His Political Philosophy* (London: Allen and Unwin, 1973).
Ollard, Richard, *Clarendon and his Friends* (New York: Atheneum, 1988).
O'Malley, John, *Trent: What Happened at the Council?* (Cambridge, MA: Belknap Press of Harvard University Press, 2013).

O'Neil, Onora, 'Enlightenment as Autonomy: Kant's Vindication of Reason', in Hulme and Jordanova (eds.), *Enlightenment and its Shadows* (London and New York: Routledge, 1990).

Opitz, Peter, 'Scripture', in Selderhuis (ed.), *Calvin Handbook* (Grand Rapids, MI: Eerdmans, 2009).

—, 'The Exegetical and Hermeneutical Work of John Oecolampadius, Huldrych Zwingli and John Calvin', in Saebø (ed.), *Hebrew Bible/Old Testament* (Göttingen: Vandenhoeck & Ruprecht, 2013).

Osborn, Annie Marion, *Rousseau and Burke: A Study of the Idea of Liberty in Eighteenth-Century Political Thought* (Oxford: Oxford University Press, 1940).

Overhoff, Jürgen, 'The Theology of Thomas Hobbes's *Leviathan*', *JEH*, 51.3 (2000), pp. 527–55.

Overton, J. H., *The Nonjurors* (London: Smith, Elder, 1902; reprinted Kessinger Publishing, 2010).

Oxford Dictionary of National Biography, from the Earliest Times to the Year 2000, ed. H. C. G. Matthew and Brian Harrison (Oxford: Oxford University Press, 2004).

Pacchi, Arrigo, 'Hobbes and the Problem of God', in Rogers and Ryan (eds.), *Perspectives on Thomas Hobbes* (Oxford: Clarendon Press, 1988).

Pagliaro, H. E. (ed.), *Irrationalism in the Eighteenth Century* (Cleveland, OH: Case Western Reserve University Press, 1972 [*Studies in Eighteenth-Century Culture*, vol. 2]).

Paley, William, *The Principles of Moral and Political Philosophy*, in *The Works Of William Paley, D.D.*, vol. 1 (London, 1825).

—, *A View of the Evidences of Christianity*, ed. Canon Birks (London: Religious Tract Society, n. d.).

Pannenberg, Wolfhart, *Systematic Theology*, vol. 3, trans. Geoffrey Bromiley (Grand Rapids: Eerdmans, 1997).

Parker, T. H. L., *Calvin's Old Testament Commentaries* (Edinburgh: T&T Clark, 1986).

—, *Calvin's New Testament Commentaries*, 2nd edn (Louisville, KY: Westminster/John Knox Press, 1993).

Parker, T. M., Review of Dugmore, *Mass*, in *JTS*, NS 12 (1961), pp. 132–46.

Parkin, Charles, *The Moral Basis of Burke's Political Thought* (Cambridge: Cambridge University Press, 1956).

Pascal, Blaise, *Pensées*, trans. A. J. Krailsheimer (Harmondsworth: Penguin, 1966).

—, *The Provincial Letters*, trans. A. J. Krailsheimer (Harmondsworth: Penguin, 1967).

Patey, Douglas Lane, *Probability and Literary Form: Philosophic Theory and Literary Practice in the Augustan Age* (Cambridge: Cambridge University Press, 1984).

Patrick, Simon, *A Brief Account of the New Sect of Latitudinarians: Together with Some Reflections upon the New Philosophy. By S. P. of Cambridge. In Answer to a Letter from his Friend at Oxford* (London, 1669).

—, *A Sermon Preached before the King* (London, 1678).

—, *A Discourse about Tradition* (London, 1683).

Patrides, C. A. (ed. and intro.), *The Cambridge Platonists* (London: Edward Arnold, 1969).

Pattison, Mark, 'Tendencies of Religious Thought in England, 1688–1750', in *Essays and Reviews*, 9th edn (London: Longman, Green, Longman, and Roberts, 1861).

Paulus, N., *Hexenwahn und Hexenprozess* (Freiburg im Breisgau: Herder, 1910).

Pearson, A. F. Scott, *Thomas Cartwright and Elizabethan Puritanism* (Cambridge: Cambridge University Press, 1925).

—, *Church and State: Political Aspects of Sixteenth Century Puritanism* (Cambridge: Cambridge University Press, 1928).

Pelikan, Jaroslav, *Luther the Expositor: Introduction to the Reformer's Exegetical Writings*, companion volume to LW (St Louis, Missouri: Concordia, 1959).

—, *Obedient Rebels: Catholic Substance and Protestant Principle in Luther's Reformation* (London: SCM Press, 1964).

—, *Spirit Versus Structure: Luther and the Institutions of the Church* (London: Collins, 1968).

Penelhum, Terence, *Butler* (London: Routledge, 1985).

—, 'Butler and Human Ignorance', in Cunliffe (ed.), *Butler's Moral and Religious Thought* (Oxford: Clarendon Press, 1992).

Perrott, M. E. C., 'Richard Hooker and the Problem of Authority in the Elizabethan Church', *JEH*, 49.1 (1998), pp. 29–60.

Peters, Richard, *Hobbes* (Harmondsworth: Penguin, 1956).

Petrarch, Francesco, *Petrarch's Secret: Or, The Soul's Conflict with Passion: Three Dialogues between himself and S. Augustine*, trans. William H. Draper (London: Chatto & Windus, 1911).

Phillips, Peter, 'Methodism and the Bible', in Gibson, Forsaith and Wellings (eds.), *Ashgate Research Companion to World Methodism* (Farnham; Burlington, VT: Ashgate, 2013).

Pico della Mirandola, *On the Dignity of Man*, trans. Charles Glenn Wallis; intro. Paul J. W. Miller (New York: Macmillan Publishing Company; London: Collier Macmillan, 1985).

Pitkin, Barbara, 'John Calvin and the Interpretation of the Bible', in Hauser and Watson (eds.), *History of Biblical Interpretation*, vol. 2 (Grand Rapids, MI: Eerdmans, 2009).

Platten, Stephen and Christopher Woods (eds.), *Comfortable Words: Polity, Piety and the Book of Common Prayer* (London: SCM Press, 2012).

Plumb, J. H., *England in the Eighteenth Century* (Harmondsworth: Penguin, 1950).

Pocock, J. G. A., 'Burke and the Ancient Constitution: A Problem in the History of Ideas', *Historical Journal*, 3.2 (1960), pp. 125–43.

—, 'The Origins of Study of the Past', *Comparative Studies in Society and History*, 4 (1961–62), pp. 209–46.

—, *Politics, Language and Time: Essays on Political Thought and History* (New York: Atheneum, 1971; London: Methuen, 1972).

—, *The Machiavellian Moment: Florentine Political Thought and the Atlantic Republican Tradition* (Princeton: Princeton University Press, 1975).

—, *Barbarism and Religion* (Cambridge: Cambridge University Press, 1999–).

Podmore Colin, *The Moravian Church in England 1728–1760* (Oxford: Clarendon Press, 1998).

Polanyi, Michael, *Personal Knowledge* (London: Routledge, 1958).

—, *The Tacit Dimension* (London: Routledge, 1967).

Pope, Alexander, *Poetical Works* (London: Frederick Warne, n.d.).

Popkin, Richard H., *The History of Scepticism from Erasmus to Descartes* (Assen: Van Gorcum, 1960).

—, 'Spinoza and Biblical Scholarship', in Garrett, (ed.), *Cambridge Companion to Spinoza* (Cambridge: Cambridge University Press, 1996).

Popper, Karl R., *The Logic of Scientific Discovery* (London: Hutchinson, 1959).

—, *Conjectures and Refutations: The Growth of Scientific Knowledge*, 3rd edn (London: Routledge and Kegan Paul, 1969).

Porter, H. C., *Reformation and Reaction in Tudor Cambridge* (Cambridge: Cambridge University Press, 1958).

—, 'Hooker, the Tudor Constitution, and the *Via Media*', in Hill (ed.), *Studies in Richard Hooker* (Cleveland and London: The Press of Case Western Reserve University, 1972).

Porter, Roy, 'The Enlightenment in England', in Porter and Teich (eds.), *The Enlightenment in National Context* (Cambridge: Cambridge University Press, 1981).

Porter, Roy and M. Teich (eds.), *The Enlightenment in National Context* (Cambridge: Cambridge University Press, 1981).

Powicke, Frederick J., *The Cambridge Platonists: A Study* (London and Toronto: Dent, 1926).

Quantin, Jean-Louis, 'The Fathers in Seventeenth Century Anglican Theology', in Backus (ed.), *Reception of the Church Fathers* (Leiden: Brill, 1997).

—, *The Church of England and Christian Antiquity: The Construction of a Confessional Identity in the 17th Century* (Oxford: Oxford University Press, 2009).

Quinones, Ricardo J., *The Renaissance Discovery of Time* (Cambridge, MA: Harvard University Press, 1972).

Quinton, Anthony, *Francis Bacon* (Oxford: Oxford University Press, 1980).

Rack, Henry, *Reasonable Enthusiast: John Wesley and the Rise of Methodism* (London: Epworth Press, 1989).

—, 'A Man of Reason and Religion? John Wesley and the Enlightenment', *Wesley and Methodist Studies*, 1 (2009), pp. 2–17.

Rahner, Karl, *Theological Investigations*, vol. 14 (London: Darton, Longman & Todd, 1976).

Ramsey, Ian, *Religious Language: An Empirical Placing of Theological Phrases* (London: SCM; New York: Macmillan, 1957).

Rasmussen, Barry G., 'The Priority of God's Gracious Action in Richard Hooker's Hermeneutic', in Kirby (ed.), *Richard Hooker and the English Reformation* (Dordrecht: Kluwer, 2003).

Redwood, John, *Reason, Ridicule and Religion: The Age of Enlightenment in England 1660–1750* (London: Thames and Hudson, 1976).

Reill, P. H., *The German Enlightenment and the Rise of Historicism* (Berkeley, CA: University of California Press, 1975).

Reventlow, Henning Graf, *The Authority of the Bible and the Rise of the Modern World* (London: SCM Press, 1984).

Richardson, C. C., *Zwingli and Cranmer on the Eucharist* (Evanston, IL: Seabury Western Theological Seminary, 1949).

Righter, A., 'Francis Bacon', in Davies and Watson (eds.), *The English Mind* (Cambridge: Cambridge University Press, 1964).

Rivers, Isobel, *Reason, Grace and Sentiment: A Study of the Language of Religion and Ethics in England, 1660–1780*; vol. 1, *Whichcote to Wesley;* vol. 2, *Shaftesbury to Hume* (Cambridge: Cambridge University Press, 1991, 2000).

Robertson, John, 'Hugh Trevor-Roper, Intellectual History and "The Religious Origins of the Enlightenment"', *English Historical Review*, 124 (December 2009), pp. 1389–421.

Rodger, P. C. and L. Vischer (eds.), *The Fourth World Conference on Faith and Order, Montreal 1963* (London: SCM Press, 1964).

Rogers, G. A. J. and Alan Ryan (eds.), *Perspectives on Thomas Hobbes* (Oxford: Clarendon Press, 1988).

Rome, Beatrice K., *The Philosophy of Malebranche* (Chicago: Chicago University Press, 1963).

Roseblatt, Helena, 'The Christian Enlightenment', in Brown and Tackett (eds.), *Cambridge History of Christianity, Vol. VII* (Cambridge: Cambridge University Press, 2006), ch. 15.

Rosenthal, Jerome, 'Voltaire's Philosophy of History', *JHI*, 16.2 (1955), pp. 151–78.

Ross, Ralph, Herbert W. Schneider, Theodore Waldman (eds.), *Thomas Hobbes in his Time* (Minneapolis, MN: University of Minnesota Press, 1974).

Rossi, Paulo L., *Francis Bacon: From Magic to Science* (London: Routledge, 1968).

Rousseau, Jean-Jacques, *Confessions*, trans. J. M. Cohen (Harmondsworth: Penguin, 1953).

—, *The Social Contract*, trans. Maurice Cranston (Harmondsworth: Penguin, 1968).

—, *Reveries of the Solitary Walker*, trans. Peter France (Harmondsworth: Penguin, 1979).

Rubanowice, R. J., 'Ernst Troeltsch's History of the Philosophy of History', *Journal of the History of Philosophy* 14 (1976), pp. 79–95.

Sabine, George H., 'Hume's Contribution to the Historical Method', *The Philosophical Review*, 15 (1906), pp. 17–38.

Saebø, Magne (ed.), *Hebrew Bible/Old Testament: The History of its Interpretation*, vol. 2: *From the Renaissance to the Enlightenment* (Göttingen: Vandenhoeck & Ruprecht, 2008).

Satterthwaite, P. E. and D. F. Wright (eds.), *A Pathway unto the Holy Scripture* (Grand Rapids: Eerdmans, 1994).

Scarisbrick, J. J., *Henry VIII* (Harmondsworth: Penguin, 1971).

Schargo, N. N., *History in the Encyclopédie* (New York: Columbia University Press, 1947).

Schlereth, Thomas J., *The Cosmopolitan Ideal in Enlightenment Thought* (Notre Dame, IN: University of Notre Dame Press, 1977).

Schmidt, James (ed.), *What is Enlightenment? Eighteenth-Century Answers and Twentieth-Century Questions* (Berkeley, CA: University of California Press, 1996).

Schneider, Herbert W., 'The Piety of Hobbes', in Ross, et al. (eds.), *Hobbes in his Time* (Minneapolis, MN: University of Minnesota Press, 1974).

Scholder, Klaus, *The Birth of Modern Critical Theology: Origins and Problems of Biblical Criticism in the Seventeenth Century* (London: SCM Press; Philadelphia: PA: Trinity Press International, 1990).

Schouls, P. A., *The Imposition of Method: A Study of Descartes and Locke* (Oxford: Clarendon, 1980).

—, *Descartes and the Enlightenment* (Toronto: McGill-Queens University Press; Edinburgh: Edinburgh University Press, 1989).

Schreiner, Susan, *Are You Alone Wise? The Quest for Certainty in the Early Modern Era* (Oxford: Oxford University Press, 2011).

Schulze, Manfred, 'Martin Luther and the Church Fathers', in Backus (ed.), *Reception of the Church Fathers* (Leiden: Brill, 1997).

Selderhuis, Herman J. (ed.), *The Calvin Handbook* (Grand Rapids, MI: Eerdmans, 2009).

—, *A Companion to Reformed Orthodoxy* (Leiden: Brill, 2013).

Sell, Alan P. F., *John Locke and the Eighteenth-Century Divines* (Cardiff: University of Wales Press, 1997).

Sermons or Homilies Appointed to be Read in Churches in the Time of Queen Elizabeth of Famous Memory, 4th edn (Oxford; Clarendon Press, 1816).

Shapiro, Barbara J., *Probability and Certainty in Seventeenth-Century England: A Study of the Relationship between Natural Science, Religion, History, Law, and Literature* (Princeton: Princeton University Press, 1983).

Sick, H., *Melanchthon als Ausleger des Alten Testaments* (Tübingen: Beiträge zur Geschichte der biblischen Hermeneutik, no. 2, 1959).

Sisman, Adam, *Boswell's Presumptous Task: Writing the Life of Dr Johnson* (London: Penguin, 2001).

Simuṭ, Corneliu C., *Richard Hooker and his Early Doctrine of Justification* (Aldershot, Hants, and Burlington, VT: Ashgate, 2005).

Sisson, C. J., *The Judicious Marriage of Mr Hooker and the Birth of The Laws of Ecclesiastical Polity* (Cambridge: Cambridge University Press, 1940).

Skinner, Quentin, *Reason and Rhetoric in the Philosophy of Hobbes* (Cambridge: Cambridge University Press, 1996).

Smalley, Beryl, *Historians in the Middle Ages* (London: Thames and Hudson, 1974).

—, *The Study of the Bible in the Middle Ages,* 3rd edn (Oxford: Blackwell, 1983).

Smith, David Dillon, 'Gibbon in Church', *JEH*, 35.3 (1984), pp. 450–63.

Smitten, Jeffrey, 'William Robertson: The Minister as Historian', in Bourgault and Sparling (eds.), *Companion to Enlightenment Historiography* (Leiden: Brill, 2013), ch. 3.

Soman, Alfred, 'Pierre Charron: A Revaluation', *Bibliothèque d'Humanisme et Renaissance*, 32.1 (1970), pp. 57–79.

Sorell, Tom (ed.), *The Cambridge Companion to Hobbes* (Cambridge: Cambridge University Press, 1996).

Sorkin, David, *The Religious Enlightenment: Protestants, Jews and Catholics from London to Vienna* (Princeton, NJ: Princeton University Press, 2008).

Southern, Richard W., *Medieval Humanism and Other Studies* (Oxford: Blackwell, 1970).

—, *History and Historians: Selected Papers of R. W. Southern*, ed. Richard J. Bartlett (Oxford: Blackwell, 2004).

Southgate, W. M., *John Jewel and the Problem of Doctrinal Authority* (Cambridge, MA: Harvard University Press, 1962).

Spadafora, David, *The Idea of Progress in Eighteenth-Century Britain* (New Haven and London: Yale University Press, 1990).

Spinoza, Benedict de, *Ethics and On the Improvement of the Understanding*, ed. James Gutmann (New York: Hafner, 1949).

—, *The Chief Works*, trans. and intro. R. H. M. Elwes (New York: Dover Publications, 1951), vol. 1, *Political Treatise* and *Theologico-Political Treatise*.

Spitz, L. W., Lewis Spitz, 'The Significance of Leibniz for Historiography', *JHI*, 13 (1952), pp. 333–48.

—, 'Luther's Ecclesiology and his Concept of the Prince as Notbischof', *CH*, 22 (1953), pp. 113–41.

Spragens, Thomas A., *The Politics of Motion: The World of Thomas Hobbes* (London: Croom Helm, 1973).

Springborg, Patricia, 'Hobbes on Religion', in Sorell (ed.), *Cambridge Companion to Hobbes* (Cambridge: Cambridge University Press, 1996).

Spurr, John, 'Latitudinarianism and the Restoration Church', *The Historical Journal*, 31 (1988), pp. 61–82.

—, '"A special kindness for dead bishops": The Church, History, and Testimony in Seventeenth-Century Protestantism', *Huntington Library Quarterly*, 68.1–2 (2005), pp. 313–34.

Stanlis, Peter, *Edmund Burke and the Natural Law* (Ann Arbor: University of Michigan Press, 1958).

Steinmetz, David C., *Misericordia dei: The Theology of Johannes von Staupitz in its Late Medieval Setting* (Leiden: Brill, 1968).

—, *Luther in Context*, 2nd edn (Grand Rapids, MI: Baker, 2002).

—, *Calvin in Context*, 2nd edn (Oxford: Oxford University Press, 2010).

Stephens, W. P., *The Theology of Huldrych Zwingli* (Oxford: Clarendon Press, 1986).

— (ed.), *The Bible, the Reformation and the Church: Essays in Honour of James Atkinson* (Sheffield: Sheffield Academic Press [*JSNT Supplement Series*, 105], 1995).

Stern, Frizt (ed.), *The Varieties of History*, 2nd edn (London: Macmillan, 1970).

Strauss, Leo, *The Political Philosophy of Hobbes* (Chicago: University of Chicago Press, 1952 [Oxford: Oxford University Press, 1936]).

—, 'The Spirit of Hobbes's Political Philosophy', in Brown (ed.), *Hobbes Studies* (Oxford: Blackwell, 1965).

Strehle, Stephen, *The Catholic Roots of the Protestant Gospel: Encounter between the Middle Ages and the Reformation* (Leiden: Brill, 1995).

Stephen, Leslie, *History of English Thought in the Eighteenth Century* (New York: Harcourt, Brace and World; London: Rupert Hart-Davis, 1962, from 3rd edn, 1902).

—, *Swift* (London: Macmillan 1908).

Streuver, Nancy L., *The Language of History in the Renaissance: Rhetoric and Historical Consciousness in Florentine Humanism* (Princeton, NJ: Princeton University Press, 1970).

Stromberg, Roland N., 'History in the Eighteenth Century', *JHI*, 12 (1951), pp. 295–301.

—, *Religious Liberalism in Eighteenth-Century England* (Oxford: Oxford University Press, 1954).

Sutherland, Stewart R., 'God and Religion in *Leviathan*', *JTS*, NS 25 (1974), pp. 373–80.

Swift, Jonathan, *Gulliver's Travels*, intro. Michael Foot (Harmondsworth: Penguin, 1967).

—, *An Argument to Prove that the Abolishing of Christianity in England May, as Things Now Stand Today, be Attended with Some Inconveniences, and Perhaps not Produce Those Many Good Effects Proposed Thereby* (1708): http://ebooks.adelaide.edu.au/s/swift/jonathan/s97ab/.

Sykes, Norman, *Church and State in England in the Eighteenth Century* (Cambridge: Cambridge University Press, 1934).

—, *Man as Churchman* (Cambridge: Cambridge University Press, 1960).

Tait, Edwin W., 'The Law and Its Works in Martin Bucer's 1536 Romans Commentary', in Ehrensperger and Holder (eds.), *Reformation Readings of Romans* (London and New York: T&T Clark, 2008).

Tappert, Theodore G. (ed.), *The Book of Concord: The Confessions of the Evangelical Lutheran Church* (Philadelphia, PA: Fortress Press, 1959).

Tavard, George H., *Holy Writ or Holy Church: The Crisis of the Protestant Reformation* (London: Burns and Oates, 1959).

Taylor, A. E., 'The Ethical Doctrine of Hobbes', *Philosophy*, 13 (1938), pp. 406–24; reprinted in Brown (ed.), *Hobbes Studies*.

Taylor, Jeremy, *Works*, ed. R. Heber (London, 1839).

—, Jeremy Taylor, *The Worthy Communicant: A Discourse of the Nature, Effects and Blessings consequent to the Worthy Receiving of The Lord's Supper; And of all the Duties required in order to a Worthy Preparation. Together with the Cases of Conscience occurring in the Duty of him that Ministers, and of him that Communicates. As also Devotions fitted to every part of the Ministration* (London: William Pickering, 1853).

—, *The Rule and Exercises of Holy Living* and *The Rule and Exercises of Holy Dying*, one vol. edn (London: Rivingtons, 1880).

Tennant, Bob, *Conscience, Consciousness and Ethics: Joseph Butler's Philosophy and Ministry* (Woodbridge: Boydell, 2011).

The Catholicity of Protestantism: Being a report presented to His Grace the Archbishop of Canterbury by a group of Free Churchmen, ed. R. Newton Flew and Rupert E. Davies, with a Foreword by The Archbishop of Canterbury [Geoffrey Fisher] (London: Lutterworth Press, 1950).

The Eucharist: Sacrament of Unity (London: Church House Publishing, 2001).

The First and Second Prayer Books of King Edward the Sixth (London: Dent (Everyman), 1910).

Thiselton, Anthony C., *New Horizons in Hermeneutics* (London: HarperCollins, 1992).

Thompson, W. D. J. Cargill, 'The Philosopher of the "Politic Society": Richard Hooker as a Political Thinker', in Hill (ed.), *Studies in Richard Hooker* (Cleveland and London: The Press of Case Western Reserve University, 1972).

Thompson, James, *The Seasons and the Castle of Indolence*, ed. James Sambrook (Oxford: Clarendon Press, 1972).

Thompson, Mark D., 'Biblical Interpretation in the Works of Martin Luther', in Hauser and Watson (eds.), *A History of Biblical Interpretation*, vol. 2: *The Medieval through the Reformation Periods* (Grand Rapids, MI: Eerdmans, 2009).

Thorndike, Herbert, *An Epilogue to the Tragedy of the Church of England, being a Necessary Consideration and brief Resolution of the Chief Controversies in Religion that divide the Western Church: Occasioned by the present Calamity of the Church of England: in three Books: I The Principles of Christian Truth; II The Covenant of Grace; III The Lawes of the Church* (LACT [1659]).

Tillyard, E. M. W., *The Elizabethan World Picture* (Harmondsworth: Penguin, 1963 [1943]).

Tindal, Matthew, *Christianity as Old as the Creation*; facsimile of 1730 edition; ed. Günter Gawlick (Stuttgart-Bad Cannstatt: Friedrich Frommann Verlag, 1967).

Toland, John, *Christianity Not Mysterious* (facsimile of 1696 edition, Stuttgart-Bad Cannstatt: Friedrich Frommann Verlag, 1964).

Torrance, T. F., 'Scientific Hermeneutics according to St Thomas Aquinas', *JTS*, NS, 13 (1962), pp. 259–89.

—, *Theology in Reconstruction* (London: SCM Press, 1965).

—, *The Hermeneutics of John Calvin* (Edinburgh: Scottish Academic Press, 1988).

Tracts for the Times by Members of the University of Oxford, new edn (London: Rivington; Oxford: Parker, 1839).

Trevelyan, George Otto, *The Life and Letters of Lord Macaulay*, 2 vols in 1 (Oxford: Oxford University Press, 1978 [1876]).

Trevor-Roper, H. R., 'The Historical Philosophy of the Enlightenment', *SVEC*, 22 (1963), pp. 1667–87 (also in *History and the Enlightenment*).

—, *Religion, the Reformation and Social Change* (London: Macmillan, 1967).

—, *Renaissance Essays* (London: Secker & Warburg, 1985; Fontana, 1986).

—, *Catholics, Anglicans and Puritans* (London: Secker and Warburg, 1987).

—, *History and the Enlightenment* (New Haven and London: Yale University Press, 2010).

Trueman, Carl R., *Luther's Legacy: Salvation and the English Reformers 1525–1556* (Oxford: Clarendon Press, 1994).

Trueman, Carl R. and R. S. Clark (eds.), 'Pathway to Reformation: William Tyndale and the Importance of the Scriptures', in Satterthwaite and Wright (eds.), *Pathway unto the Holy Scripture* (Grand Rapids: Eerdmans, 1994).

—, *Protestant Scholasticism: Essays in Reassessment* (Carlisle: Paternoster, 1999).

Tuck, Richard, 'Hobbes and Descartes', in Rogers and Ryan (eds.), *Perspectives on Thomas Hobbes* (Oxford: Clarendon Press, 1988).

—, 'The "Christian Atheism" of Thomas Hobbes', in Hunter and Wootton (eds.), *Atheism from the Reformation to the Enlightenment* (Oxford: Oxford University Press, 1992).

Tulloch, John, *Rational Theology and Christian Philosophy in England in the Seventeenth Century*, vol. 1, *Liberal Churchmen*; vol. 2, *The Cambridge Platonists* (Edinburgh and London: Blackwood, 1874; reprinted Hildesheim: Georg Olms Verlagsbuchhandlung, 1966).

Turnbull, Paul, 'The Supposed Infidelity of Edward Gibbon', *The Historical Journal*, 25.1 (1982), pp. 23–42.

Tyacke, Nicholas (ed.), *England's Long Reformation 1500–1800* (London: University College London Press, 1998; London and New York: Routledge, 2012).

Ullmann, Walter, *Medieval Papalism: The Political Theories of the Medieval Canonists* (London: Methuen, 1949).

—, *The Growth of Papal Government in the Middle Ages*, 2nd edn (London: Methuen, 1962).

—, *The Individual and Society in the Middle Ages* (London: Methuen, 1967).

—, *Medieval Foundations of Renaissance Humanism* (New York: Cornell University Press; London: Elek, 1977).

van den Belt, Henk, *The Authority of Scripture in Reformed Theology* (Leiden: Brill, 2008).

Van Liere, Katherine, Simon Ditchfield and Howard Louthan (eds.), *Sacred History: Uses of the Christian Past in the Renaissance World* (Oxford: Oxford University Press, 2012).

van Oort, Johannes, 'John Calvin and the Church Fathers', in Backus (ed.), *Reception of the Church Fathers* (Leiden: Brill, 1997).

Verkamp, Bernard J., *The Indifferent Mean: Adiaphorism in the English Reformation to 1554* (Athens, Ohio: Ohio University Press; Detroit, Michigan: Wayne State University Press, 1977).

Vickers, Brian, 'Public and Private Rhetoric in Hooker's *Lawes*', in McGrade (ed.), *Hooker and the Construction of Christian Community* (Tempe: Medieval & Renaissance Texts & Studies, 1997).

Vico, G. B., *Autobiography*, trans. M. H. Fisch and T. G. Bergin (Ithaca, NY: Cornell University Press, 1944).

—, *The New Science of Giambattista Vico*, trans. T. G. Bergin and M. H. Fisch (Ithaca, NY: Cornell University Press, 1948, 1970).

Vidler, Alec, *Christ's Strange Work* (London: SCM Press, 1963 [1944]).

Voak, Nigel, *Richard Hooker and Reformed Theology: A Study of Reason, Will and Grace* (Oxford: Oxford University Press, 2003).

—, 'Richard Hooker and the Principle of *Sola Scriptura*', *JTS*, NS, 59.1 (2008), pp. 96–139.

Voltaire, *Candide*, trans. John Butt (Harmondsworth: Penguin, 1947).

—, *La Philosophie de l'histoire*, ed. J. H. Brumfitt (*SVEC*, 28, 1963).

—, *Lettres Philosophiques* (Paris: Garnier Flammarion, 1964).

—, *Letters on England*, trans. Leonard Tancock (Harmondsworth: Penguin, 1980).

Vyverberg, Henry, *Historical Pessimism in the French Enlightenment* (Cambridge, MA: Harvard University Press, 1958).

Wade, Ira O., *The Intellectual Development of Voltaire* (Princeton: Princeton University Press, 1969).

—, *The Intellectual Origins of the French Enlightenment* (Princeton: Princeton University Press, 1971).

—, *The Structure and Form of the French Enlightenment*, vol. 1 (Princeton: Princeton University Press, 1977).

Wainwright, Geoffrey, *Doxology: The Praise of God in Worship, Doctrine and Life; A Systematic Theology* (London: Epworth Press, 1980).

Waligore, Joseph, 'The Piety of the English Deists: Their Personal Relationship with an Active God', *Intellectual History Review*, 22 (2012), pp. 181–97.

Wall, Robert W., 'Wesley as biblical interpreter', in Maddox and Vickers (eds.), *Cambridge Companion to Wesley* (Cambridge: Cambridge University Press, 2010).

Walsh, John, (J. D.), 'Origins of the Evangelical Revival', in Bennett and Walsh (eds.), *Essays in Modern English Church History* (London: A. & C. Black, 1966).

Walsh, John, (J. D.), Colin Haydon and Stephen Taylor (eds.), *The Church of England, c.1689-c.1833: From Toleration to Tractarianism* (Cambridge: Cambridge University Press, 1993).

Walton, Izaak, *Lives* (Oxford: Oxford University Press, 1966).

Warfield, B. B., *The Westminster Assembly and its Work* (New York: Oxford University Press, 1931).

Warncke, Wayne, 'Samuel Johnson on Swift: The Life of Swift and Johnson's Predecessors in Swiftian Biography', *Journal of British Studies*, 7.2 (1968), pp. 56–64.

Warrender, Howard, *The Political Philosophy of Hobbes: His Theory of Obligation* (Oxford: Clarendon Press, 1955; reprinted 2000).

Watkins, J. W. N., *Hobbes' System of Ideas* (London: Hutchinson, 1965).

Watson, G., 'Joseph Butler', in Davies and Watson (eds.), *The English Mind* (Cambridge: Cambridge University Press, 1964).

Weinsheimer, Joel C., *Eighteenth-Century Hermeneutics: Philosophy of Interpretation in England from Locke to Burke* (New Haven and London: Yale University Press, 1993).

Wendel, François, *Calvin: The Origins and Development of his Religious Thought*, trans. Philip Mairet (London: Collins, 1963).

Wengert, Timothy, 'Biblical Interpretation in the Works of Philip Melanchthon', in Hauser and Watson (eds.), *History of Biblical Interpretation*, vol. 2: *The Medieval through the Reformation Periods*.

Wertz, S. K., 'Hume, History and Human Nature', *JHI*, 36.3 (1975), pp. 481–96.

Wesley, John, *A Plain Account of Christian Perfection* (London: Epworth Press, 1952).

—, *The Works of John Wesley*, ed. Frank Baker (Nashville: Abingdon Press, 1984).

—, *Explanatory Notes upon the New Testament* (London: Charles H. Kelly, n.d.).

Westfall, Richard S., 'The Changing World of the Newtonian Industry', *JHI*, 37.1 (1976), pp. 175–84.

—, *Never at Rest: A Biography of Isaac Newton* (Cambridge: Cambridge University Press, 1980).

[Westminster] Confession of Faith, the Larger and Shorter Catechisms, etc. (Free Presbyterian Church of Scotland, 1970).

Weston, John C., Jnr, 'Edmund Burke's View of History', *Review of Politics*, 23 (1961), pp. 203–20.

Whichcote, Benjamin, *Whichcote's Aphorisms*, ed. W. R. Inge (London: Elkins, Mathews & Marrot, n.d.).

Whitby, Daniel, *Dissuasive from Enquiring into the Doctrine of the Trinity,* 5th edn (London, 1714).

Whitford, David M. (ed.), *T&T Clark Companion to Reformation Theology* (London and New York: T&T Clark, 2012).

Whitney, Lois, *Primitivism and the Idea of Progress* (Baltimore: Johns Hopkins Press, 1934).

Whyte, Alexander, *Thirteen Appreciations* (Edinburgh and London: Oliphant, Anderson and Ferrier, 1913).

Wilcox, D. J., *The Development of Florentine Humanist Historiography in the Fifteenth Century* (Cambridge, MA: Harvard University Press, 1969).

Wiles, Maurice, 'Newton and the Bible', in Ballentine and Barton (eds.), *Language, Theology and the Bible* (Oxford: Clarendon Press, 1994).

Willey, Basil, *The Seventeenth Century Background* (Harmondsworth: Penguin, 1962 [1934]).

—, *The Eighteenth-Century Background* (Harmondsworth: Penguin, 1962 [1940]).

—, *The English Moralists* (London: Chatto & Windus, 1964).

Williams, George Hunston, *The Radical Reformation* (London: Weidenfeld and Nicolson, 1962; 3rd edn, Kirksville, MO: Sixteenth Century Publishers, 1992).

Williams, Glanmor, *Reformation Views of Church History* (Richmond, VA: John Knox Press; London: Lutterworth Press, 1970).

Williams, Rowan, 'Hooker: Philosopher, Anglican, Contemporary', in McGrade (ed.), Hooker and the *Construction of Christian Community* (Tempe, AZ: Renaissance Texts and Studies, 1997).

—, 'Hooker the Theologian', *JAS*, 1.1 (2003), pp. 104–16 and, pp. 369–83.

—, *Anglican Identities* (London: Darton, Longman & Todd, 2004).

Wilson, Thomas, *Maxims of Piety and of Christianity*, ed. Frederick Relton (London: Macmillan, 1898).

Witte, John, *Law and Protestantism: The Legal Teachings of the Lutheran Reformation* (Cambridge: Cambridge University Press, 2002).

Wittgenstein, Ludwig, *Philosophical Investigations*, trans. G. E. M. Anscombe (Oxford: Blackwell, 1968).

Wooding, Lucy, *Rethinking Catholicism in Reformation England* (Oxford: Clarendon Press, 2000).

Wordsworth, William, *Poetical Works* (London: Oxford University Press, 1920).

Wormald, B. H. G., *Clarendon: Politics, Historiography and Religion* (Cambridge: Cambridge University Press, 1951).

Wright, D. F. (ed.), *Martin Bucer: Reforming Church and Community* (Cambridge: Cambridge University Press, 1994).

Yandell, Keith E., 'Hume on Religious Belief', in Livingston and King (eds.), *Hume: A Re-evaluation* (New York: Fordham University Press, 1976).

Young, B. W., *Religion and Enlightenment in Eighteenth-Century England: Theological Debate from Locke to Burke* (Oxford: Clarendon Press, 1998a).

—, '"Scepticism in Excess": Gibbon and Eighteenth-century Christianity', *The Historical Journal*, 41.1 (1998b), pp. 179–99.

Young, G. M., 'Burke', *Proceedings of the British Academy* (1943), pp. 19–36.

—, *Yesterday and Today: Collected Essays and Addresses* (London: Rupert Hart-Davis, 1948).

Yrigoyen, Charles Jr (ed.), *T&T Clark Companion to Methodism* (London and New York: T&T Clark, 2010).

Zachman, Randall C., *The Assurance of Faith: Conscience in the Theology of Martin Luther and John Calvin* (Minneapolis, MN: Fortress Press, 1993).

Zeeveld, W. G., *Foundations of Tudor Policy* (Cambridge, MA: Harvard University Press, 1948).

Zilsel, E., 'The Genesis of the Concept of Scientific Progress', *JHI*, 6 (1945), pp. 325–49.

Zwingli, Ulrich, *Of the Clarity and Certainty of the Word of God*, in *Zwingli and Bullinger*, trans. G. W. Bromiley (*LCC*).

INDEX OF NAMES